This book comes with access to more content online.

Quiz yourself, study with flashcards, and score high on test day!

Register your book or ebook at **www.dummies.com/go/getaccess.**

Select your product, and then follow the prompts to validate your purchase.

You'll receive an email with your PIN and instructions.

SIE Exam 2027/2028

5th Edition

by Steven M. Rice

SIE Exam 2027/2028 For Dummies®, 5th Edition

Published by: **John Wiley & Sons, Inc.,** 111 River Street, Hoboken, NJ 07030-5774, www.wiley.com

For general information on our other products and services, please contact our Customer Care Department within the U.S. at 877-762-2974, outside the U.S. at 317-572-3993, or fax 317-572-4002. For technical support, please visit https://hub.wiley.com/community/support/dummies.

Wiley publishes in a variety of print and electronic formats and by print-on-demand. Some material included with standard print versions of this book may not be included in e-books or in print-on-demand. If this book refers to media that is not included in the version you purchased, you may download this material at http://booksupport.wiley.com. For more information about Wiley products, visit www.wiley.com.

Library of Congress Control Number: 2026939333

ISBN 978-1-394-42170-1 (pbk); ISBN 978-1-394-42172-5 (ebk); ISBN 978-1-394-42171-8 (ebk)

SKY10154638_042026

Contents at a Glance

Table of Contents

Introduction

So, you want to be a securities industry professional such as a stockbroker? The good news is that a career in the securities field can be extremely lucrative and rewarding. The not-so-good news is that anyone who plans to become a stockbroker and sell securities in any of the 50 states must first pass the Securities Industry Essentials (SIE) exam as well as one of the required top-off exams. (Yes, you need to pass both the SIE exam and the respective top-off exam(s) to earn the license(s) you want.) Even the SIE exam alone is quite a challenge for most people. To pass the SIE, you have to commit time and effort.

I passed all my securities exams the first time with very high scores, but they all required weeks of study and sacrifice. Those who aren't totally prepared on exam day are in for an unpleasant wake-up call. As a test-prep instructor and tutor, I always had a few students in every class who enrolled after they already failed one of their exams. Most of them initially expected the same easy ride that they'd experienced in high school or college. Not only were they wrong, but they also had to pay a significant amount of money to reregister for the exam and wait another 30 days — a rule of the Financial Industry Regulatory Authority (FINRA) — before they could retake the exam.

Back to the good news again. You're obviously interested in doing well, so you probably won't be one of those people. This book can help you pass the SIE exam and achieve your goal.

About This Book

This book should be all you need to pass the exam, although I certainly encourage you to view other materials and take whatever exams you can get your hands on. But as a word of caution, if you're reviewing and taking tests from other books, please make sure that they're on target. I've seen more than a couple of books presenting information that is definitely not included in the SIE outline.

I cover the topics that appear on the test, offer formulas as needed, provide definitions, and go over the information you need to know. I also include lots of tips and a few memory tricks. But the real benefit of this book is finding out how to study and think through problems as well as you possibly can. That's why I help you choose a study program, explain how to handle specific question types, warn you about common mistakes, connect concepts, and show you how to pull questions apart and get to the bottom of what's being asked. Then you get to apply this knowledge in two full-length practice tests so you get a taste of the SIE exam experience.

This is a reference book, and most sections are self-contained. In other words, you can read a section and understand it without looking over the text that comes before it. When some background information is helpful, I give cross-references to related topics. Therefore, you can pretty much jump in and out whenever you find topics you like (and when you find those you don't). And like all good tour guides, I also point you to some other sites of interest — topics you can explore further on your own. If you're short on time (as you probably are) and aren't ready for a break just yet, you can skip the sidebars, those little gray boxes that contain interesting but nonessential information.

Foolish Assumptions

While writing this book, I made a few assumptions about you and why you picked up this book. For starters, I assume that you're looking for a no-nonsense study guide to supplement your textbook or prep course — one that provides expert insider advice along with a ton of example questions and some sample exams. Look no further! Whether you're preparing to take the test for the first time, retaking the test after a less-than-stellar performance, or looking for a refresher before you recertify, this is the book for you!

Icons Used in This Book

To make this book easier to read and use, I include some icons to help you find and fathom key ideas and information.

This icon highlights example SIE test questions (which I follow with helpful answer explanations).

This icon is attached to shortcuts and insider advice about studying for and passing the SIE exam.

This icon points to information that's especially important to remember to do well on the test.

This icon warns you away from actions that can harm your work and drop your score.

Beyond the Book

In addition to the material in this book, this product comes with access to some really useful online material. For additional tips and tricks, check out this book's free Cheat Sheet by going to www.dummies.com and typing "Securities Industry Essentials Exam For Dummies cheat sheet" in the search box.

You can also get access to four full-length online practice tests and hundreds of flash cards. To gain access to the online practice, all you have to do is register. Just follow these simple steps:

1. **Go to www.dummies.com/go/getaccess.**
2. **Create a new account or log in to an existing account.**

   If you create a new account you'll receive an email confirmation. Click through to finish creating a new account.

   Note: If you do not receive a confirmation email after creating your account, please check your spam folder before contacting us through our Technical Support website at http://support.wiley.com or by phone at 877-762-2974.

3. **After you've logged into your new or existing account, select Dummies under the Select the Brand for Your Product header.**
4. **Select your title from the drop-down list. Choose "SIE Exam 2027/2028 For Dummies."**
5. **Answer a validation question about the product and then click Redeem.**

REMEMBER

You must choose the correct title and edition from the drop-down list. Select the option that says, "SIE Exam 2027/2028 For Dummies."

Now you're ready to go! You can come back to the practice material as often as you want — simply log on with the username and password you created during your initial login.

Your registration is good for one year from the day you redeem your product.

Where to Go from Here

Although you can read this book from start to finish, you can certainly work your way through it in more creative ways. Where you start is up to you, but please, please don't start with the practice final exams! Give yourself a good grounding in the content here and then use the practice final exams to evaluate your understanding and show you where to focus your studies.

You can flip to the topics you think you understand fairly well to boost your confidence or skip directly to whatever's giving you trouble; let the index and the table of contents be your guides. If you have a good understanding of how to take the SIE exam, from how it's structured to how to tackle questions, you can go directly to the chapters in Parts 2 and 3, which address types of securities. If you're feeling shaky on the legal aspects, check out the FINRA rules and regulations in Part 4. Everyone, however, can probably benefit from Part 1's test-taking basics and info on study plans.

Wherever you go, feel free to take detours to your textbooks, flash cards, FINRA websites, and any other resources for more information. Just remember to come back so you don't miss anything here!

1

Getting Things Rolling: Starting Your SIE Journey

IN THIS PART . . .

Review the computerized exam format and the procedures for registering to take the SIE exam.

Select the right study course and materials to prepare yourself for exam day.

Understand how to organize your study time efficiently and effectively — even when your time is limited.

Examine test-taking tips to maximize your chances of selecting the correct answer choices.

Discover what to expect on test day (because the only surprises that day should involve the triumphant return of your social life).

IN THIS CHAPTER

» Introducing the SIE

» Taking a look at companion tests

» Registering to take the exam

» Uncovering topics tested on the SIE exam

» Mastering the computerized exam format

Chapter 1

Introducing the SIE (Securities Industry Essentials) Exam

Congratulations on your interest in becoming a financial professional! But before you can lose yourself in the energy of the office, the eager voices of your clients, and the warm glow of success, you have to face the SIE as well as one of the top-off (qualification) exams such as the Series 7 or Series 6. In this chapter, I give you an overview of the SIE exam, including its purpose, structure, format, scoring, and some helpful tips to guide you through the registration procedure.

This book's first four chapters go over things like what the exam is, how to study for it, how to take the test, and so on. If you feel that you have a handle on those things, feel free to jump to Chapter 5 to get right into the meat and potatoes of what you need to learn.

What Is the SIE Exam, Anyway?

Initially, the information in the SIE (Securities Industry Essentials) exam was included in books that covered the Series 6, Series 7, Series 22, and so on. The Financial Industry Regulatory Authority (FINRA) had the idea to strip similar information from these exams and create the SIE exam. What I've found is that besides stripping the information from these other exams, unfortunately for you and other exam-takers, FINRA added a lot more information. What this means is that you'll have to study a lot of information to answer 75 randomized questions.

The SIE is an introductory-level exam designed to test your basic knowledge of the securities industry and is open to anyone age 18 or older. Fortunately, association with a securities firm isn't required; individuals may take the SIE exam before or after being hired by a firm. You need to know certain terminology used in the securities industry, different securities products, how the market is structured, how the market functions, different regulatory agencies and their purposes, as well as regulated and prohibited practices.

Because *unsponsored* individuals (people not sponsored by a financial firm) are allowed to take the exam, you can take a step toward becoming a securities professional prior to being hired. (Although you can take the SIE exam and one of the corequisite exams in any order, for most people it certainly makes sense to take the SIE first.)

The purpose of the SIE and corequisite exams is to protect the investing public by ensuring that the individuals who sell or give information about securities have mastered the skills and general knowledge that competent practicing representatives need to have.

The SIE exam itself is a computer-based exam given by Prometric (`www.prometric.com/finra`), the testing company chosen by FINRA to provide and oversee their exams. You can take your exam at a Prometric test center throughout the United States or online at your desired location. (See the "So you want to take the test online" sidebar later in this chapter.) The 75-question exam, administered by FINRA, is 105 minutes in duration. A score of 70 percent or better will get you a passing grade and put a big smile on your face. After you pass the SIE, the results remain valid for four years from the date you pass. The passing rate for those taking the SIE exam for the first time is around 74 percent. If you include those who have taken the exam more than once, it's closer to 82 percent.

The sections later in this chapter explain the setup of the SIE exam and give a rundown of how to register for the exam. If you have other questions, visit `www.finra.org/registration-exams-ce/qualification-exams/securities-industry-essentials-exam`. If you have any questions, you can chat or schedule a call through their website.

Profiling the SIE Exam-Taker

The SIE exam is for people who want to become investment company reps, general securities reps, direct participation program (DPP) reps, securities traders, investment banking reps, private securities offerings reps, research analysts, or operations professionals.

When the SIE exam was first proposed, the idea was to strip the information that was similar in all the exams that had come before (Series 6, Series 7, Series 22, and so) and put it in one place, thus making it easier for people to add licenses to their résumés. So, to become a securities professional, you need to pass the SIE exam, one of the exams listed in the next section, and typically the North American Securities Administrators Association (NASAA) Series 63 or 66 exam. The Series 63 and Series 66 exams can also be taken without sponsorship, but individuals typically wait until they've passed one of the corequisite exams, such as the Series 7, before tackling one of these.

REMEMBER

People who have a long and sordid history of embezzlement, forgery, and fraud are generally disqualified and precluded from taking the exam. Candidates must disclose any criminal records, and the FINRA reviews applications on a case-by-case basis.

One's Not Enough: Tackling the Corequisite (Top-Off) Exams

The SIE exam is just your starting point. To become an industry professional, you have to take one of the top-off exams and, in most cases, the Series 63 or Series 66 state exam as well. As far as which top-off exam(s) you'll have to take, the answer depends on the job you want and/or are hired to do. After you pass the SIE exam, the financial institution that hires you will tell you which exams you need to take and will help you schedule them.

REMEMBER

In addition to taking the SIE exam and one of the top-off or corequisite exams listed in the following sections, you'll likely have to take either the NASAA Series 63 exam or the NASAA Series 66 exam. These exams go into *state* securities laws as opposed to federal securities laws, which are the focus of exams like the SIE. The difference between the Series 63 and Series 66 is that the Series 66 allows holders to become investment advisers as well. Your employer will let you know which exam to take. More and more broker-dealers want their agents to take the Series 66. Don't worry too much; neither of these exams are the beasts that some of the other listed exams are.

Series 6: Investment Company and Variable Products Representative Exam (IR)

Series 6 is the license required by most banks and insurance companies. This license allows the holder to sell products such as mutual funds, variable annuities, and variable life insurance (along with having an insurance license). To see the complete outline of what's covered, go to `www.finra.org/sites/default/files/Series_6_Content_Outline.pdf`.

Series 7: General Securities Representative Exam (GS)

Series 7 is the license exam that most people take. This license is required by most broker-dealers. The Series 7 allows you to sell equity securities, mutual funds, bonds, direct participation programs, options, and so on. To see the complete outline of what's covered, go to `www.finra.org/sites/default/files/Series_7_Content_Outline.pdf`.

TIP

As a side note, if you're taking the Series 7 exam after taking the SIE, I've also written *Series 7 Exam 2026-2027 For Dummies,* (John Wiley & Sons, Inc.), which is laid out in the same logical way as this book for ease of studying.

Series 22: DPP Representative (DR)

If you're planning to focus your career on selling direct participation programs (DPPs), the Series 22 exam is the one for you. This license allows you to solicit and sell limited partnership interest in DPPs such as real estate, oil and gas, and equipment leasing. To see the complete outline of what's covered, go to `www.finra.org/sites/default/files/Series_22_Content_Outline.pdf`.

Series 57: Securities Trader (TD)

The Series 57 license allows holders to execute trades in securities. Typically, a Series 57–licensed person works in the trading department, executing trades for individuals or firms. To see the complete outline of what's covered, go to www.finra.org/sites/default/files/Series_57_Content_Outline.pdf.

Series 79: Investment Banking Representative (IB)

The Series 79 Investment Banking Representative exam allows holders to work in the investment banking realm. As such, the holders' functions may include advising or facilitating equity or debt securities offerings through public offerings, private placements, and mergers and acquisitions. To see the complete outline of what's covered, go to www.finra.org/sites/default/files/Series_79_Content_Outline.pdf.

Series 82: Private Securities Offerings Representative (PR)

If you're planning to sell securities privately as opposed to publicly, Series 82 is the exam you'll need to pass. This exam tests you on the knowledge needed to perform functions of a private securities offerings rep, including the solicitation and sale of Regulation D private placement securities as part of a primary offering. To see the complete outline of what's covered, go to www.finra.org/sites/default/files/Series_82_Content_Outline.pdf.

Series 7 + Series 86 + Series 87: Research Analyst (RS)

If you love taking exams, this is the one for you. You have to pass not only the SIE exam, but also the Series 7, Series 86, Series 87, and either the Series 63 or Series 66. Yikes! If you want to be a research analyst, however, this route is the one you'll need to follow. A research analyst is required to prepare written and/or electronic communications that show an analysis of company securities and industry sectors. To see the complete outline of what's covered, go to www.finra.org/sites/default/files/Series_7_Content_Outline.pdf and www.finra.org/sites/default/files/Series_86-87_Content_Outline.pdf.

Series 99: Operations Professional (OS)

People who have a Series 99 license have proved that they have the knowledge needed to perform the critical functions of an operations professional. As such, their functions include client onboarding (welcoming new clients, addressing client concerns, making sure clients understand the services available to them, and so on), receipt and delivery of securities and funds, account transfers, reinvestment and disbursement of funds, and so on. To see the complete outline of what's covered, go to www.finra.org/sites/default/files/Series_99_Content_Outline.pdf.

Signing Up

One of the things I really like about the SIE exam is that you don't need to be sponsored to take it (most of the other securities exams require sponsorship by a brokerage firm, bank, insurance company, and so on), which means that you can take the exam on your own prior to being hired. This strategy allows you to get a leg up on the competition and shows your future employer that you're not fooling around.

Filling out an application to enroll

The easiest way to enroll to take the SIE is to go to `www.finra.org/registration-exams-ce/qualification-exams/securities-industry-essentials-exam`. Scroll down to the Enrollment Options section; and follow the instructions for individuals, which include creating an account, enrolling for the SIE, and paying for the exam (by credit card or Automated Clearing House [ACH] transfer).

It's a date! Scheduling your exam

After you've completed the online application and received your enrollment notification, you can schedule an appointment to take the exam by contacting the Prometric testing center. Locate the test center nearest you by calling (800) 578-6273 during business hours or by visiting `www.prometric.com/exams/1finra`, where you can make an appointment to take the exam at a Prometric test center or online (remotely).

At the present time, online testing is several years old. See the sidebar "So you want to take the test online" at the end of this chapter for information on taking the exam online.

Like enrollment in other securities exams, your SIE exam enrollment is valid for 120 days; you have to take the exam within this time frame. When scheduling your exam appointment, be ready to provide the following information:

- Your name and Social Security number and/or FINRA number
- The name of the securities exam you're registering to take
- Your desired test date, which must be chosen from available test dates

You may not be able to schedule an appointment immediately; it depends on how busy Prometrics is. Even if you're taking the exam online, you still need to have someone available to monitor the test while you're taking it. Prometric will confirm your appointment on the phone or via email.

TIP

I highly suggest putting pressure on yourself and scheduling the exam a little sooner than you think you'll be ready to take it; you can always move the test date back. (You'll be charged if you cancel within ten business days of your test date.) You know yourself best, but I think that most students study better when they have a target test date.

You have a choice of where to take the exam. If you travel often, you may want to schedule your exam at a location far away (maybe even in a different state) to get the test date you want. If you're having trouble scheduling the date and/or location of your choice, remember that you can take it online (at home or work, at a family member's house, and so on). See the sidebar "So you want to take the test online" later in this chapter.

TEST-CENTER AMENITIES

The test centers are required to comply with FINRA site guidelines, but some of the older centers may not have the amenities that the newer ones do (such as lockers and earplugs). To protect yourself from a variety of unpleasant, unexpected site surprises on exam day, the FINRA website (www.finra.org) offers general information, including test-center security guidelines (including candidate ID requirements, personal items allowed, and provided aids), test-center rules of conduct, and so on. For more specific questions, such as whether a cafeteria, vending machines, or lockers are on site, ask the center's administrator when you schedule your test date.

After you have your test date set, you may find that you're ready sooner or later than your scheduled appointment. The exam-center administrators are usually pretty accommodating about changing appointments and/or locations as long as you call before noon at least two business days before your test date, but a fee may be involved.

TIP

You can get an extension from the 120-day enrollment only if you call within ten days of your enrollment expiration and if no earlier test dates are available.

Planning for special accommodations

If you require special accommodations when taking your securities exam, you can't schedule your exam online. You have to contact the FINRA Special Conditions Team at (800) 999-6647 or fill out the special-accommodations form at www.finra.org/sites/default/files/SA-Eligibility-Questionairre.pdf. Read on for info on how the test administrators can accommodate you if you have a disability or if English isn't your first language.

WARNING

Depending on your testing center, you may have to receive authorization to bring medical devices and supplies — such as insulin pumps, eyedrops, and inhalers — into the testing room. If you need authorization, call your local Prometric testing center, and a staff member will be able to guide you on the approval process.

Americans with Disabilities Act (ADA) candidates

If you're disabled or learning-impaired, FINRA provides testing modifications and aids in compliance with the provisions of the Americans with Disabilities Act (ADA). To qualify for ADA provisions, your disabilities have to permanently limit a major life activity, such as learning, speech, hearing, or vision.

To apply for special accommodations, you need to submit documentation from your physician or licensed healthcare professional to the FINRA, requesting the special arrangements. Additionally, you have to submit the FINRA Special Accommodations Eligibility Questionnaire and Special Accommodations Verification Request Form for all special arrangement requests. You can find links to these forms at www.finra.org/industry/special-accommodations.

You may request the accommodations you want. Possible aids include:

- Extra time
- A written exam (pencil and paper)
- A reader, writer, or recorder
- A sign-language interpreter

» A large-print exam booklet

» Wheelchair-accessible locations

FINRA reserves the right to make final decisions about accommodations on a case-by-case basis.

English as a Second Language (ESL) candidates

If English is your second language, you can request additional time to take the exam when you schedule your SIE test date. If FINRA approves, you receive a little extra time to complete the exam. In general, FINRA gives an extra 30 minutes for exams shorter than 2 hours and an extra hour for exams longer than 2 hours.

To qualify for extra time because English is your second language, fill out the form at `www.finra.org/sites/default/files/LEP-request-form.pdf`.

Just in case: Canceling as an option

If something comes up or if you feel that you're just not ready, you can cancel your appointment to take the SIE exam without penalty if you do so at least ten business days before the exam date. If a holiday falls within the cancellation period, you have to cancel an additional business day earlier. If you're scheduled to take the exam on a Wednesday, for example, you have to cancel on Tuesday two weeks before your exam date. If a holiday falls between those dates, you have to cancel on Monday two weeks before your exam date. For more information, visit `www.finra.org/industry/reschedule-or-cancel-your-appointment`.

WARNING

If you cancel after the prescribed deadline, don't show up to take the exam, or show up too late to take the exam, you'll be charged a cancellation fee equal to the cost of the exam fee you paid. I'm sure that the old "I forgot" excuse has been tried, but I've never heard of it being effective.

Taking a Peek at the Tested Topics

As a practical exam, the SIE requires you to master vocabulary, handle customer accounts, understand the rules and regulations that govern the securities industry, and, yes, work with some math formulas (although very few). For ease of use, this book focuses on the information you need to pass the SIE exam. Here's an overview of what to expect:

» The underwriting process — how new securities come to market (Chapter 5)

» Common and preferred stock (Chapter 6)

» Corporate bonds and U.S. government securities (Chapter 7)

» Securities issued by local governments (municipal bonds) (Chapter 8)

» Investment companies, including mutual and closed-end funds (Chapter 9)

» DPPs (limited partnerships) (Chapter 10)

» Options (Chapter 11)

» Customer accounts (Chapter 12)

» Analyzing the benefits and risks associated with investments; making appropriate recommendations to customers (Chapter 13)

- Following how new securities are brought to the market and how existing securities are traded in the market (Chapter 14)
- Risk considerations and income tax implications that stock market investors face (Chapter 15)
- Rules and regulations governing the purchase and sale of securities and the registered representative's responsibility for maintaining accurate records (Chapter 16)

FINRA has released a list of the distribution of questions on the SIE exam. See Table 1-1 for the number of questions devoted to each topic as applied to a registered rep's performance.

TABLE 1-1 Distribution of SIE Exam Questions

Topic	Number of Questions	Percentage of Exam
Knowledge of capital markets	12	16
Understanding products and their risks	33	44
Understanding trading, customer accounts, and prohibited activities	23	31
Overview of regulatory framework	7	9
Total	*75*	*100*

Pretty much each of these topics falls under multiple areas of study. To correctly answer questions that address the topic of handling customer accounts, for example, you have to know enough about different types of stocks, bonds, and so on to guide your customers, including which investments are most beneficial to retirees and which work best for investors who are just entering the workforce.

Although Table 1-1 shows the outline of the exam, this book (and most other study materials) breaks the chapters down by similar content to make your life easier and keep you from having to jump back and forth.

Understanding the Exam Format and Other Exam Details

To make sure that you don't walk into the testing center, take one look at the computer screen, go into shock, and start drooling on the keyboard, I use the next few sections to cover some of the testing details for the SIE exam.

Reviewing the exam basics

The SIE exam is a computerized, closed-book (in other words, no book) exam that lasts 1 hour and 45 minutes. The exam consists of 80 multiple-choice questions, although only 75 of them count toward your score (see the next section).

TIP

Certainly, you can take bathroom breaks at any time, but the clock continues to tick away, so you may want to reconsider drinking a mega-jumbo iced latte the morning of your test.

For information on the types of questions to expect, see Chapter 3. Flip to Chapter 4 for an overview of how your exam day may progress.

Practicing on five additional trial questions

To ensure that new questions to be introduced in future exams meet acceptable standards before inclusion, you answer five additional, unidentified questions that don't count toward your score. In other words, you get 80 questions to answer, but only 75 are scored.

Note: Don't waste your time trying to figure out which questions are experimental; you likely won't know for sure. FINRA may use these as regular questions on future exams in order to move the passing rate up or down.

Mastering the computerized format and features

Although you don't need any computer experience to do well on the exam, you don't want your first encounter with a computerized exam to be on the date of the SIE exam. Being familiar with the way the questions and answer choices appear on the screen is essential. FINRA has been nice enough to provide a tutorial for taking its qualification exams, such as the SIE, at the following link: `www.finra.org/sites/default/files/external_apps/proctor_tutorial.swf.html`.

In addition, a friendly exam-center employee will give you an introductory lesson to familiarize you with operating the computer before the exam session begins. Although candidates receive different exam questions and some may get slightly easier tests than others, FINRA realizes that and will adjust scores (which you won't know about) to make sure that each candidate has an equal chance to pass the exam.

The following list describes some important computer exam features:

- Scroll bars for moving the questions on the screen.
- A time-remaining clock to help you track how much time you have left during each part. (If the clock is driving you batty, you can hide it with a click of the mouse.)
- A confirmation box that requires you to approve your answer choice before the computer proceeds to the next question.
- An indication of which question you're currently on.
- A choice of answering the questions by doing one of the following:
  - Holding down the Ctrl and Alt keys and typing the letter for the correct answer on the keyboard.
  - Using the mouse to click the correct answer.
- The capability to change your answers or mark questions that you're unsure of for later review, which allows you to go back and answer them at any time during that particular part. The Mark for Review button appears at the bottom of the screen when you select an answer. Also, a Previous button allows you to go to the previous question if you want to change an answer.
- Both Calculator and Notepad buttons are available in the top-left corner of the screen for you to use if necessary to help you answer the questions. Whatever you type in the notepad will be available the whole time you're taking the test.

» If, during the test, you forget how any of the test features works, you can always click the Help button in the top-left corner for instructions.

» When you complete the exam, you can click the Exit Exam button in the top-left corner. At that point, you can review questions or continue exiting the exam.

You can review your questions at any time during the test by clicking the Review Questions button on the bottom of the screen. At that point, you see a highlighted list of all the questions that you've answered as well as their question numbers; the question numbers marked for review have a green flag next to them. Just click the number to review questions you want to see again. You can remove a Marked for Review flag by clicking the Mark for Review button again. Click the Return to Test button at the top of the screen to get out of the review section.

TIP

Although you can review and change all your answers at the end of your test, I suggest that you refrain from going through all the questions again. Your brain is going to feel like it went through a blender by the time you finish the exam. Review only your *marked* questions and — this is important — change the answers only if you're 100 percent sure that you made a mistake. As an instructor, I've graded too many practice exams to count, and I know that people change a right answer to a wrong one five times more often than they change a wrong one to a right one.

Viewing exhibits

Some of the questions may require you to look at an exhibit such as an income statement or balance sheet to answer a question. Back when I took the exam, each candidate was given an exhibit book, and the question told you which exhibit you needed to look at in the book. Now the exhibits are right on the screen next to the questions, and the questions tell you to refer to the exhibit to extract the information you need. If a question requires more than one exhibit, thumbnails of the exhibits appear on the right. Just click each one to open it.

Instant gratification: Receiving and evaluating your score

Remember having to wait weeks for a standardized test score, hovering somewhere between eagerness and dread? Those days are gone. At the end of the SIE exam, the system calculates your score and lets you know whether you passed or failed; the results are displayed for you right there on the computer screen. Although the wait for your grade to pop up may feel like an eternity, it really takes only a few seconds to determine whether you're going to dance out of the testing center or walk out with a frown on your face. When you sign out, the test-center administrator will tackle you (well, approach you) and give you a printed exam report showing whether you passed or failed.

Each question on the SIE exam is worth an average of 11/3 points (some are worth more and some are worth less, depending on FINRA's feeling about how difficult a question is), and candidates need a score of 70 or better to achieve a passing grade. This percentage translates to 53 questions out of 75 that you have to answer correctly. The scores are always rounded down, so a grade of 69.33 is scored as 69 on the SIE.

Many moons ago, back when you actually got to see your grade, the passing grade was 70 (and the exam took up to 6 hours and was 250 questions long [260 with the experimental questions]). One of the other students in my class got a 69.6, which was rounded down to a 69, and he had FINRA review his exam to try to get him the extra point. Needless to say, FINRA ruled against him, and he had to take the exam again.

TESTING INFO FROM FINRA

The FINRA website (`www.finra.org`) is certainly worth checking out. It contains all the nitty-gritty details about the SIE and related exams. Use this website for the following:

- **FINRA Current Uniform Registration Forms for Electronic Filing in WEB CRD:** This page includes the registration forms and a link to the Uniform Forms Reference Guide, with contact numbers and other explanatory information for filers.
- **FINRA Test Center Rules of Conduct:** Just in case you're unable to distinguish the test center from that third-period algebra class you had back in high school, FINRA gives you the rules and regulations for taking the SIE. (Don't hide a list of equations under the brim of your baseball cap; don't roam the halls during your restroom break; and don't pass notes, no matter how bored you are.)
- **FINRA Registration and Exam Requirements:** This section gives you a comprehensive list of the categories of securities representatives and the exam requirements.
- **FINRA Appointments and Enrollment:** Here, you find FINRA tips for scheduling appointments to take securities exams, info about obtaining extensions, and the exam-cancellation policy.
- **FINRA Registration Exam Fee Schedule:** Check out this page to see the fees for registering for different securities exams.

You passed! Now what?

After you pass the SIE, FINRA will provide confirmation that you passed. At that point, if you haven't done so already, you can find a broker–dealer, bank, insurance company, or the like that wants you. After you're hired, your employer will let you know which other exams you have to take and will schedule them accordingly.

When you've passed your other exams and have become a licensed representative, you'll need to fulfill FINRA's yearly continuing-education requirements. All participants must complete their exams by December 31st of each year. You will be required to take a computer-based exam covering regulatory elements such as compliance, regulatory, ethical, and sales-practices standards at a Prometric exam center or online. In addition, a brokerage firm element requires broker–dealers to keep their registered representatives updated on job and product-related topics.

So you need a do-over: Retaking the exam

I'm sorry to end this chapter on a negative note, but the SIE is a relatively difficult exam, and some people need a do-over.

If you fail the SIE, you'll have to request a new test date and pay to retake the test. You should reapply immediately, though you have to schedule the new test date for at least 30 days after the day you failed. (That's 30 days of prime studying time!) If you fail the exam three times, you're required to wait 180 days before you can retake it.

Use the time between exams to understand what went wrong and fix it. Here are some of the reasons why people fail their securities exams and some of the steps you can take to be successful next time:

- **Lack of preparation:** You have to follow, and stick to, a well-constructed plan of study. You have your diagnostic printout after you take the exam; use it to focus on the areas of study where you fell short!

Prep courses can help you identify and focus on the most commonly tested topics and provide valuable tips for mastering difficult math problems. Also consider tutoring sessions tailored to accommodate your busy schedule and pinpoint the areas of study where you need the most help.

- **Nerves:** Some people are very nervous test-takers, and they need to go through the process to get comfortable in unfamiliar situations. Next time around, they'll know what to expect and will pass with flying colors.

REMEMBER

The people who are most nervous about taking the exam tend to be the ones who haven't prepared properly. Make sure that you're passing practice exams on a consistent basis with grades in at least the high 70s before you attempt to take the real exam.

- **Insufficient practice exams:** You need to take enough practice exams before you take the real test. I think that getting used to the question formats and figuring out how to work through them is as important as learning the material to begin with.

Check out Chapter 2 for info on setting up a study schedule and making the most of your practice exams.

WARNING

SO YOU WANT TO TAKE THE TEST ONLINE

Due to COVID-19 way back in 2020, many of the Prometric test-center locations closed, which meant that candidates weren't able to take their exams. FINRA and Prometric worked on setting things up so that you can take their exams online. Although the testing-center locations have reopened, the online testing option is still available. Obviously, you need some things (and need to know some things) before making an appointment to take the test at your location. I suggest that you review the complete list at www.prometric.com/sites/default/files/2020-04/PrometricProUserGuide_3.1_1.pdf.

This site lists requirements for your computer (speakers, microphone, movable camera, and so on) and operating system. It also provides downloading instructions and explanations of ID requirements, and it explains that an either AI and/or an agent (who works for Prometrics) will be monitoring you through video chat. It is up to that agent to make sure that your testing area meets their requirements, you have the proper ID, and that you're not cheating during the test.

If an individual is caught cheating, they face severe consequences, including permanently barring the candidate from taking any FINRA qualifying exams.

IN THIS CHAPTER

» Investing in a prep course versus studying on your own

» Finding time to study and using study strategies

» Staying focused and building test-taking skills

» Evaluating your readiness

Chapter 2
Getting Prepared to Take the SIE Exam

When you're preparing for the SIE exam, a good cup of java and an all-nighter just aren't gonna cut it. Neither will a frantic one-week study session like the ones that used to work miracles when you were taking high school or college finals. Although it has only 75 questions (80 if you're counting the experimental questions), the SIE is not to be taken lightly, so you need to train for it both mentally and physically.

In this chapter, I discuss your options for studying to take the SIE exam. I also help you organize your study time efficiently and effectively — even when your preparation time is limited.

Courses and Training Materials: Determining the Best Way to Study

When deciding how to go about studying for the SIE exam, your first mission is to identify the training mode that best suits your needs. Although live courses used to be widely available, they're pretty much nonexistent now. Most stockbroker training schools have closed their brick and mortar locations and have opted to sell books, teach live, online courses, and/or provide on-demand courses. Which type of study option you choose will depend on your comfort level and/or financial position. I've designed this book to give you everything you need to pass the SIE exam the first time. However, if you're more comfortable having an instructor-led online course, that is always an option.

Select prep material to study on your own

If you're the type of person who can follow a committed study schedule on your own every day, you may be able to pass the SIE exam without a prep course. Many types of study aids, like the book you're reading right now, are available to help you prepare.

REMEMBER

No matter what your learning style is, I'm a firm believer in using a textbook as a primary training aid. You can use online courses, online testing programs (available with this book), apps, and flash cards (available online with the purchase of this book) as supplements to your textbook, but you should definitely give your textbook the starring role. By virtue of its portability and ease of use (you don't have to turn a book on or plug it in, or access the Internet, and it can never, ever run out of batteries), the textbook for most people is simply the most efficient and effective choice.

Besides this book, my favorite textbook these days is Empire Stockbroker Training Institute's *SIE Course Textbook* by yours truly (`empirestockbroker.com`). The textbook focuses on the relevant exam topics, is easy to read and understand, and includes plenty of practice questions and detailed explanations. A lot of the better SIE course textbooks are available online rather than in bookstores. (Unfortunately, from what I've seen, some of the SIE textbooks, even from some of the more reputable companies, have a lot of information that isn't in the FINRA SIE outline.) In addition to this book and a textbook, consider investing in one or more of the following popular study aids:

- **Online testing:** I'm all for online testing. Certainly, the more exams you take, the better. If the practice exam simulates the real test, it's even more valuable. With this study aid, you have access 24 hours a day, 7 days a week, and can pace yourself to take the exams at your leisure. Fortunately, this book gives you access to four online tests (three new and one that is the same as the first practice final in this book). If you need more, select an online program that's able to offer hundreds of questions, along with answers and explanations (`empirestockbroker.com`, for example, always has the most current simulated exams).

  TIP

  As an additional option, recording your own notes — especially on topics you're having trouble with — is a wise use of your time. Putting the info in your own words, saying ideas out loud, and listening to the recordings can really help reinforce the concepts.

- **Flash cards:** For those who already have a grasp of the subject matter, flash cards are good because you can tuck 'em in your pocket and look at 'em anytime you want. As a matter of fact, this edition now contains flash cards that you can view online. Although I've made it easier for you, you might be better off making cards yourself that focus on the areas that are most problematic for you.
- **Apps:** As of the time of this writing, about a half dozen or so SIE exam prep apps are available. You can check out the reviews and screenshots to determine if study apps might be a good addition for you. I'm definitely in favor of your using whatever you can to make your studying easier. I suggest that if you're considering purchasing one of these apps, focus on ones with the biggest banks of test questions. After studying from this book, the best thing you can do is tackle more practice questions.

TAKING A COURSE ONLINE

As mentioned, it's pretty much impossible to take a class in bricks-and-mortar buildings anymore. For people who want to take a course but have scheduling constraints or lack a vehicle for commuting, instructor-led virtual classrooms may be an option. Students interact through online chats, email, message boards, and/or phone conferences. Live/online classes may be scheduled at specific times, or you may work on your own time at your own pace. Before purchasing an online course, find out whether you can monitor one for an hour or so to see whether it meets your needs.

Note: Some so-called online courses consist solely of a packet of study materials without any outside instruction. Make sure that the course you sign up for has the features you want.

Making the Most of Your Study Time

Unless you're a direct descendent of Albert Einstein, you probably need to allow yourself as much time as possible to prepare for the SIE. Even though the exam is only 75 questions, the amount of material you have to study in order to be prepared to answer those 75 questions out of the universe of possible questions is quite extensive.

TIP

Get your affairs in order. Go to the dentist to get that sore tooth filled, pay your bills, get your doctor visits out of the way, visit your friends and relatives, finish any critical home-improvement projects — basically, clear the decks as best you can so that you can concentrate on your studies. The following sections can help you establish a study plan.

Block out some time to study

You have to use your time efficiently, and to accomplish this task, you need to grab every spare moment and channel it into study time. If you're taking an online SIE prep course, your instructor(s) should provide information to help you set up a study schedule for before, during, and after you complete the course.

If you're in charge of carving out your study time, plan on putting in the time. You know yourself best, but some books recommend 20 hours of studying, and others recommend 100 to 150 hours. I think that most students who don't have some sort of background in securities would find it difficult, if not impossible, to pass with only 20 hours of studying. If you were a great student, 40 to 50 hours of studying might be achievable, but a majority of students are going to need 100 hours or more of study.

TIP

A good gauge for you is how well you do on practice exams the first time you take them. For advice on how to study well, see "Exploring Study Strategies" later in this chapter for details on setting up a schedule.

Especially for those of you who continue to work at a full-time job, now may be the time to have a heart-to-heart with your boss to negotiate some extra study time. After all, you need to work this schedule out only for the next few weeks. Can you take vacation time? Will your boss allow you flex time (letting you work two hours later each day for four days and have the fifth day off)? Can you arrange a quiet place at work to study during breaks and lunchtime?

For those of you who have family obligations, finding time to study may be especially difficult. Ideally, your spouse or other family members can take over some of the time-consuming things you do on a daily basis to help provide you much-needed study time.

TIP

Try to set aside a consistent time to study on a daily basis. If possible, schedule your study time around your internal clock. If you're the type who needs a brass band to wake up and get your mind functioning first thing in the morning, but you're wide awake and ready to go at midnight, you may be better off with a study schedule that begins later in the day and lasts into the night. By contrast, if you're leaping out of bed like a jack-in-the-box at the crack of dawn but are dead on your feet by 10 p.m. (that's me . . . lol), a morning study schedule would be more favorable. Ideally, it would be wise to schedule your exam during the time of day when you're at your best.

REMEMBER

You never know when extra time to study will present itself, so carry your textbooks, some flash cards, or an SIE app with you whenever you leave home. You can read or drill yourself whenever you find some spare time — on the train, waiting in line, and even during trips to the restroom.

It's a plan: Get into a study routine

Establishing and sticking to a study routine is essential. Many people find the SIE exam to be difficult because they have to absorb so much material in a relatively short time. Furthermore, most of the information on the test is easy to forget because it's not info you use every day. Therefore, you have to reinforce your knowledge on a daily basis by reviewing and revisiting the old information while learning new material. You'll continue to follow this routine over and over and over again.

Getting yourself organized so you can cover all the topics you'll be tested on is crucial.

TIP

If you're trying to study on your own, get yourself a course textbook and divide the pages by the number of days you have available for studying. Be sure to allow yourself a decent amount of extra time for practice exams. Review each chapter and complete each chapter exam until you have a firm grasp on a majority of the information. Take notes, highlight, and review the material you're having problems with until you feel comfortable with the concepts. Initially, you'll spend most of your time on new material; after that, you'll spend your time reviewing and taking chapter quizzes.

During the last several days or so leading up to the exam, take as many practice exams as possible. Remember to review each exam thoroughly before moving onto the next one. For more helpful tips, check out "Exploring Study Strategies" later in this chapter.

Give it a rest: Take short breaks

If you find yourself reading the same words over and over and wondering what the heck you just read, it's probably time to take a break. Taking short (five- to ten-minute) breaks can help you process and absorb information without confusing new ideas with the old.

SETTING UP SHOP: FINDING AN IDEAL PLACE TO STUDY

When you're learning new material, set yourself up in a place where you have as few distractions as possible: the local library, a separate room, or even the bathtub. One of my students used to retreat to his car in the driveway after dinner while his wife put their young kids to bed.

The exam room, with its small cubicles, places you in proximity with other people who are taking the exam at the same time. If mouse clicks, taps on the keyboard, the scratch of pencil on paper, and the frustrated sighs of less-prepared test-takers are likely to distract you, you may want to use earplugs, which are available at most exam centers. If you don't want to use earplugs, you can prepare for the worst by subjecting yourself to a somewhat-noisy study environment somewhere along the line. (When I was taking one of my securities exams before earplugs were permitted, a construction crew was working in the next room. Luckily, I'd studied in noisy settings before; otherwise, the sound of screw guns and workmen talking would have driven me to distraction!) Go to a coffee shop (or any populated establishment) during lunch hour or turn on a fan or a radio to familiarize yourself with background noise while you're taking your practice exams. Obviously, if you're taking the exam at home, you have more control of your environment.

REMEMBER

When you reach your saturation point and really start zoning out, you can practice a bit of productive procrastination. Walk the dog, take a shower, do some sit-ups and/or push-ups, grab a meal or a snack, or do anything else that lets you move around or take care of the little things that have to get done. A little human contact can go a long way too, provided that you have the discipline to hit the books again.

Sometimes, taking a break from one study method can be as good as taking a break from studying altogether. Use multiple types of study material (textbooks, class notes, flash cards, and so on). If you get sick of looking at a textbook, try reviewing your notes, flipping through or creating some flash cards, or taking some online practice exams. You can even have your significant other ask you some questions from the book.

Another idea is "chunking," in which you can spend 45-60 minutes studying, stop and do something else for a while, then go back to studying again. Repeat the process a few times a day, and you'll get a decent amount of study time in.

Stay focused from day to day

Passing the SIE exam is a rite of passage. It's your ticket to wealth, fame, and fortune (or at least a decent job). If you put time and effort into studying for the SIE, you'll be rewarded. If not, you'll have to relive the nightmare over and over until you reach your objective. To reap your reward as quickly as possible, make a resolution: Until you pass the SIE, commit to limiting your social life and devoting most of your waking hours to studying for the exam. Repeat after me: "This is my life for now."

If you find that you really need to take a mental health day off at some point, make sure that you don't separate yourself from your textbooks for more than one day. Jump right back into the SIE fire the next day.

WARNING

I suggest that under no circumstances (except in the case of a family emergency) should you take more than a day a week off from studying. Some of my students who were doing quite well came back to take another prep class because their test dates were too far off, and they'd put the books down for a while. The next thing they knew, they'd forgotten half of what they'd learned. Fortunately, the information comes back more quickly the second time around.

TIP

To keep focused on your studies without forgetting about otherwise-important life activities, prepare a file folder labeled "To do after I pass the SIE." If anything comes up while you're studying, instead of interrupting your study time or stressing about things that need to be done, write down the task or event on a piece of paper, place it in your to-do file, and put it out of your mind.

Devote time to practice tests

Certainly, when you're going over new material, you should spend most of your time learning the information and taking chapter quizzes. When you feel that you have a good handle on the material, you should start taking full practice exams to see where you stand. (This book includes some questions throughout Parts 2–4, followed by two 75-question practice exams with answers and explanations in Part 5.) In addition, with this book, you'll have access to online practice exams. The last several days to a week or so before the exam should be almost entirely devoted to taking practice exams and reviewing them.

After you move into the practice-test phase, continue to use your textbook not only to reference material you don't understand, but also to ensure that you don't forget what you've learned. Too many people rely solely on the tests and forget to read their textbook now and then. Figure on rereading up to two chapters per day. After taking a practice exam, *always* review it completely before you move on to the next one. And don't listen to the people who say you have to take three or four practice exams a day; you're better off taking one or two exams per day and spending twice as long reviewing it as you spent taking it. This method helps ensure that you know the subject matter and that you won't make the same mistakes twice.

Practice exams can help you gauge whether you're ready for the real SIE. See "Knowing When You're Ready" at the end of this chapter for details.

TIP

If you run out of exams to take, it's better to purchase more or see whether someone else in your firm has a different book with tests you can borrow than to take the same exams over and over.

Avoid study groups

Unless your study group includes an SIE instructor, I recommend that you avoid a study group like the plague. The problem with study groups is that everyone wants to study the information that they're having problems with, and chances are that not everyone is struggling with the same thing. Also, if everyone *is* having the same problem, who can help you? I strongly feel that your time is better spent studying on your own.

TIP

If you really feel that you'd benefit from studying with someone else, try to arrange a tutoring session with an SIE instructor.

Stay in shape

Ignoring the importance of physical fitness when you prepare to take the SIE exam is a big mistake. The exam itself (and the prep time you put into your study schedule) is not only mentally exhausting, but physically demanding as well. You have to be able to stay alert and concentrate on difficult questions for 1 hour and 45 minutes. In the weeks leading up to the test, any exercise you can do to keep yourself physically fit, including cardio such as jogging or bike riding, can help. A workout also gives you a great reason to take a study break. (The treadmill is a great place to study your notes or listen to your SIE recordings, if you're so inclined.)

Exploring Study Strategies

The more ways you work with a piece of information, the better able you'll be to recall it. Here are some study strategies to supplement your routine of reading your textbook and taking practice exams:

- **Aim to understand concepts and relationships, not just formulas and definitions.** Having a good grasp of how ideas are related can provide a safety net when rote memory fails; you may be able to make educated guesses, re-create formulas, or come up with something to jog your memory. When you see an equation, try to figure out where the numbers come from and what the formula really tells you.
- **Create an outline of your notes or write flash cards.** Using your own words, try to put the more-difficult areas of study into an outline or on flash cards. The whole process of condensing large mountains of information into your own abbreviated outline helps you process and absorb difficult concepts.

- **Mark up your textbook.** You don't have to return your textbook to the library, so use the margins to rephrase ideas, draw diagrams, repeat formulas or equations, and highlight unfamiliar words.
- **Record yourself reading your notes and play back the tape at night while you're falling sleep or when you're driving.** Although the play-it-at-night technique has been known to give some people nightmares, this temporary condition usually clears up after the exam. I've also heard some people proclaim that nighttime playback is "as soothing as melatonin." (If it prevents you from falling asleep, turn off the recording and opt for getting some rest.)

  Note: While you're sleeping, your brain may process ideas that you learned during your waking hours, but you generally have to be paying attention to remember something new. The main benefit comes from making the initial recording and letting study material be the last thing you hear before you fall asleep.
- **Use sticky notes to flag difficult topics or concepts.** As you study, put a sticky note on a section or page in the book where you need more work. After you've filled your book(s) with stickies, concentrate your study on those difficult areas (where the stickies are). When you feel that you have a good grasp of this information, remove the notes from the book. As you learn more and more, you'll whittle down the number of pages with stickies until you've removed them all from the textbook.

Building Concrete Exam-Taking Abilities

To be successful on the SIE exam, developing your test-taking skills is just as important as mastering the concepts that form the basis of the questions. The best way to develop test-taking skills is to take practice tests, such as the ones in this book. Following are some tips that can also help you polish your skills.

Read the question carefully

Don't be fooled. Exam creators love to trip you up by making you jump ahead and answer the question — incorrectly — before you read the entire problem. Often, one of the last words in the *call* (specific inquiry) of the question is worded in the negative, such as "all of the following are true *except*," "which of the following is the *least* likely to," and so on. When they're reviewing the answers to a practice test, these questions cause some students to groan or slap themselves in the head when they realize their mistake. Don't worry — this common reaction usually goes away when you start getting better at taking exams.

Look for phrases that lead to the topic tested

Try to identify the specific category that the question is testing you on. If you study for the number of hours that I recommend (refer to "Block out some time to study" earlier in this chapter), you'll most likely cover the material that the question references at some point, and you'll be able to identify the topic that the question applies to. After you know the topic, your brain can retrieve the information you need from its mental file cabinet, making it easier for you to focus on the applicable rule, equation, or concept so that you can answer the question correctly.

Work with what you have

If possible, work with the facts — and only the facts — in the question. Too often, students add their own interpretation to the question and turn a straightforward problem into a mess. Use the facts that are given, dump the garbage information that isn't necessary to answer the question, and don't make the question more difficult or assume that there's more to it than meets the eye.

Adding irrelevant information to a question seems to be a very common practice for students. My standard answer is "Did it say that in the question?" The response is usually no. Don't make your life more difficult by adding your own speculations to the question; just answer the question that's given you.

Don't obsess; mark for review

If you experience brain freeze while taking the exam, don't panic or waste valuable time on one question. Eliminate any answer(s) you know must be wrong (if any), take your best guess, and *mark the question for review* so you can easily return to it later. The question may even resolve itself. Another question might trigger your memory as you continue to take the exam, and the correct answer to the earlier question may become clear.

Keep track of time

Time yourself so that you're always aware of how much time you have left to complete the exam. One way to do so is to figure out which question you need to be up to at the end of each 15 minutes; use that figure as a benchmark to keep track of your progress. You have 1 hour and 45 minutes to complete the exam. You have to answer 80 questions (5 of which don't count toward your score). So, you have roughly 1.31 minutes (or 1 minute and 18.8 seconds) to answer each question.

Translating these numbers to quarter-hour benchmarks gives you the results shown in the following mini-table:

Time	Number of Questions Completed
15 minutes	11
30 minutes	23
45 minutes	34
1 hour	46
1 hour and 15 minutes	57
1 hour and 30 minutes	69
1 hour and 45 minutes	80

TIP

If you find yourself pressed for time when taking practice exams, memorize these benchmarks, write them on your scrap paper (or dry-erase board) as soon as the exam administrators allow you to begin, and keep referring to your watch or the clock on the computer screen to track your progress in relation to the benchmark. If you find yourself falling behind, pick up your pace. If you're really falling behind, mark the lengthier, more difficult questions for review, and spend your time answering the easier questions. Why waste 2 minutes on one long question for 11/3 points when you could answer two shorter questions in that time and earn twice as many points?

Most students don't have a problem finishing the SIE exam on time. If you easily and consistently finish 75-question SIE practice exams in less than 1 3/4 hours, you should be okay on the real SIE exam.

TIP

When you're taking the SIE exam at the test center, if you find yourself obsessing about the clock on the computer to the point that you can't concentrate on the question in front of you, hide it by clicking the bottom-left corner of the computer screen.

Master the process of elimination

The SIE exam is a standardized exam. This format makes it similar to other practical exams of this type: The best way to find the correct answer, if not obvious off the bat, may be to eliminate the incorrect answers one at a time. I help you develop this crucial skill as you tackle the topic-specific questions throughout this book.

Maintain your concentration

To maintain your concentration, read the *stem* of the question (the last sentence before the answer choices) first to keep yourself focused on what the question is asking. Next, read the entire problem (including the stem) to get a grip on the facts you have to consider in order to select the correct answer. Then you can anticipate the correct answer and read all the answer choices to see whether your anticipated answer is there. If you don't see your answer, and none of the other choices seems to fit, reread the stem to see whether you missed an important fact. Check out Chapter 3 for detailed test-taking tips.

TIP

You can also take care to keep yourself physically alert. The last 15 minutes or so is usually the most difficult. I recommend eating a small protein bar before starting the test to help keep your levels of energy and concentration high. Forget high-sugar/high-carb foods; leave them for after the exam. These foods boost your sugar level temporarily, but when the level drops, your energy and concentration levels sink like a lead balloon.

Low energy levels can lead to sloppy mistakes. If you feel yourself fading, do whatever it takes to stay alert and focused: Get up and get a drink of water, splash some water on your face, stretch, or dig your fingernails into your palms.

Think carefully before changing your answers

In general, if you select an answer and can't really explain why, maybe it was just a *gut* answer. You're much more likely to change to a wrong answer than to the right one, so change your answer only if

- You didn't read the question correctly the first time and missed a major point that changes the answer choice (because you didn't see the word *except* at the end of the question, for example).
- You're absolutely sure that you made a mistake.

Use the scrap paper wisely

In addition to clicking the Notes button in the top-left corner of the computer screen, if you're taking the test at a testing location, you receive a few pages of letter-size scrap paper (or a dry-erase board), all of which will be collected — so restrain yourself from writing any obscenities about the exam or its creators. Here are some more productive ways to use this valuable resource:

- **Mark dubious questions for review.** You have to answer each question before you can go to the next, so if you're not sure of the correct answer, eliminate the wrong answers, take your best guess, and mark the question for review later. On your scrap paper, write down the numbers of any questions you want to check before the end of the session.
- **Eliminate wrong answers.** You can't write on the computer screen, so for each question, you may find it helpful to write *A, B, C,* and *D* on your scrap paper (in a column) as they appear on the screen and eliminate answers directly on your paper.
- **Do a brain dump.** After the exam begins and before your brain gets cluttered with SIE exam questions, use your scrap paper or dry-erase board to jot down the topic matters that tend to give you problems so that you can refresh your memory during the exam.

  TIP

  When doing a brain dump, write down only the things that you're really having problems with — you know, the ones that you still feel the need to study the morning of the test. Don't worry about cataloguing things you already know and feel comfortable with, because doing that is a waste of your time (and paper). Those items should come to the surface of your brain as soon as you need them.
- **Time yourself.** Write down your 15-minute benchmarks (prepared for you in "Keep track of time" earlier in this chapter) on your scrap paper and check periodically to make sure you're staying on track.

Knowing When You're Ready

Although you only need to score a 70 on the real exam, your goal is to consistently score 80 to 85 percent (or better) on the sample tests you take to ensure that you're ready.

REMEMBER

To determine your readiness, consider your scores on the practice exams the *first time* you take them. In other words, don't convince yourself that you're ready if you score 85 percent on an exam that you've already taken three times. If you take a practice exam more than once, you may just be remembering the answers. I'm not against taking the same exams more than once, but don't use exams you've taken before to gauge how prepared you are.

IN THIS CHAPTER

» Exploring the composition of SIE exam questions

» Analyzing the purpose and intent of a question

» Identifying the correct answer

» Mastering the process of elimination

Chapter 3 Examining and Mastering Questions

The good news is that a vast majority of the questions on the SIE are straightforward (open-stem or closed-stem). You have the possibility of getting Roman numeral choices (see "Roman hell: Complex multiple-choice questions," later in this chapter), but it will be a handful at the very most. However, you still need to have good test-taking skills to use to your advantage.

In this chapter, I introduce you to the types of questions to expect on the SIE exam, and I show you how to analyze the facts in the questions and identify what the examiners are *really* testing you on. I also show you how to use the process of elimination to find the right answer and, if all else fails, how to logically guess the best answer.

TIP

FINRA understands that not all SIE exams are created equal. As such, some SIE exams are somewhat more difficult than others. In order to give every candidate an equal chance to pass the exam, they are graded on a sliding scale.

Familiarizing Yourself with Question Formats

Even though you'll only be answering 75 questions (80, if you're including the 5 that don't count), those 75 questions are pulled from a truly massive pool of questions that could be asked. The SIE exam is a challenging test that poses questions in many ways and shouldn't be taken lightly. You'll have to deal with open- and closed-ended sentences, and killers like *except* and *not.* In this section, I show you how the examiners phrase the questions and how they can trip you up if you aren't careful.

Working with the straight shooters: The straightforward questions

Straightforward question types include a group of sentences with the facts followed by a question or incomplete sentence. Then you get four answer choices, one of which correctly answers the question or completes the idea. A majority of the questions will be of this type.

Closed-stem questions

You'll find more closed-stem questions than any other question type on the SIE and corequisite exams, so you'd better get a handle on answering these babies for sure. Fortunately, closed-stem questions are fairly run-of-the-mill. They begin with one or more sentences containing information and end with a question (and, appropriately enough, a question mark). The question mark is what makes closed-stem questions different from open-stem questions, which I discuss in the next section. Your answer choices, lettered (A) through (D), may be complete or incomplete sentences. Here's a basic closed-stem question:

EXAMPLE

Mr. Bearishnikoff is a conservative investor. Which of the following investments would you recommend to him?

(A) Buying uncovered call options

(B) Buying long-term income adjustment bonds

(C) Buying common stock of an aggressive growth company

(D) Buying Treasury notes

The right answer is (D). The first sentence tells you that Mr. Bearishnikoff is a conservative investor. This detail is all the information you need to answer the question correctly, because you know that conservative investors aren't looking to take a lot of investment risks. U.S. government securities such as Treasury notes (T-notes) are considered to be the safest of all securities; they're backed by the fact that the government can always print more money to pay off the securities that it issues. As you'll find out as you proceed further along in this book, buying uncovered call options, income adjustment bonds, and buying stock of aggressive growth companies are all considered risky investments.

TIP

Sometimes, the phrasing of the answer choices can help you immediately cut down the number of feasible answer choices. Mr. Bearishnikoff probably would balk at investing in an aggressive growth company, for example; it certainly doesn't sound stable or safe. Check out the section titled "Picking up clues when you're virtually clueless: The process of elimination," later in this chapter, for details on raising your odds of answering questions correctly.

By the way, the *you* in the question refers to you on your good days, when you're considerate and rational and have had a sufficient amount of sleep. Mr. Bearishnikoff probably wouldn't appreciate any rogue-elephant investing, even if you think he should be more daring. The question also assumes normal market conditions, so don't recommend a different investment because you think the government is going to collapse and T-notes are going to take a dive. Just accept the conditions the problem presents to you.

TIP

Be careful to focus only on the information you need to answer the question. The securities-exam creators have an annoying tendency to include extra details in the question (such as the maturity date, coupon rate, investor's age, and so on) — details that you may not need. See "Focus on key information," later in this chapter, for some tips on zeroing in on the necessary info.

Open-stem questions

An open-stem question poses the problem as an incomplete sentence, and your mission, should you choose to accept it, is to complete the sentence with the correct answer. The following example shows how you can finish other people's thoughts skillfully:

EXAMPLE

The maturity date on a monthly option is

(A) on a date chosen by the board of directors

(B) the Saturday after the third Friday of the expiration month

(C) the third Friday of the expiration month

(D) the third Saturday of the expiration month

The answer you want is (C). *Options* give the purchaser the right to buy or sell securities at a fixed price within a specific time frame. (See Chapter 11.) Options are considered to be *derivatives* (securities that derive their value from another security) because they're linked to an underlying security. Standard "monthly" options mature on the third Friday of the expiration month.

The preceding example is quite easy. Anyone who has been studying for the SIE or Series 7 exam should know the answer. But what makes securities exams so difficult is the fact that the exams are loaded with so many date-oriented details. You have to memorize the initial maturities of all the different securities, and unfortunately (believe me, I feel your pain), you also have to remember a truckload of time frames. (Accounts are frozen for 90 days; new securities can't be purchased on margin for 30 days; an options account agreement must be returned within 15 days after the account is approved; and so on.)

TIP

Date-oriented details are excellent material to include in your flash cards. See Chapter 2 for more study suggestions.

Encountering quirky questions with qualifiers

To answer questions with qualifiers, you have to find the best answer to the question. The qualifier keeps all answer choices from being correct because only one answer rises above the rest.

Working with extremes: Most, least, best

Recognizing the qualifier in the question stem and reading every single answer choice carefully are very important. Check out the following example:

EXAMPLE

Which of the following companies would be **most** affected by interest rate fluctuations?

(A) SKNK Perfume Corp.

(B) Bulb Utility Co.

(C) Crapco Vitamin Supplements, Inc.

(D) LQD Water Bottling Co.

The answer is (B). Although all companies may be somewhat affected by interest-rate fluctuations, the question uses the word *most.* If interest rates increase, companies have to issue bonds with higher coupon (interest) rates. This higher rate in turn greatly affects the companies' bottom lines. Therefore, you're looking for a company that issues a lot of bonds. Utility companies are most affected by interest-rate fluctuations because they're *highly leveraged* (issue a lot of bonds).

Making exceptions: Except or not

When a question includes the word *except* or *not*, you're looking for the answer that's the exception to the rule stated in the stem of the question. In other words, the correct answer is always the one that doesn't meet the question's stated conditions. The question can be open (as it is in the next example) or closed.

WARNING

Right off the bat, look for *except* or *not* in the stem of every question on the SIE exam. Many students who really know their material accidentally pick the wrong answer on a few questions because they carelessly miss the *except* or *not*.

Take a look at the following exception problem:

EXAMPLE

A stockholder owns 800 shares of WHY common stock. WHY stockholders were given cumulative voting rights. If there are three vacancies on the board of directors, stockholders can cast any of the following votes **except**

(A) 800 for one candidate

(B) 800 for each candidate

(C) 2,400 for one candidate

(D) 900 for each candidate

The answer you're looking for is (D). Cumulative voting rights give smaller stockholders (not height-wise, but in terms of the number of shares they own) an easier chance to gain representation on the board of directors, because a stockholder may combine their total voting rights and vote the cumulative total in any way they want. Here, the stockholder has a total of 2,400 votes to cast (800 shares × 3 vacancies = 2,400 votes).

In this example, you may be tempted to select (A), (B), or (C), any of which would be correct if you were asked for the number of votes this stockholder *could* cast. The stockholder could use only 800 shares to vote for candidate (A), for example; they don't have to use all 2,400 votes. (B) is another possible voting arrangement, because nobody said the stockholder has to use all their votes for one candidate. (C) is an option because the stockholder has a total 2,400 votes to cast. In this question, however, you're looking for the number of votes the stockholder *can't* cast, because the word *except* in the question stem requires you to find a false answer. Therefore, (D) is the correct answer because to cast 900 votes for each candidate, the stockholder would need a total of 2,700 votes (900 × 3).

REMEMBER

If you're one of the unlucky people who gets an "all of the following are false except" question, you have to find the *true* answer. Don't forget that two negatives in a sentence make a positive statement. You may want to try rephrasing the question so that you know whether you're looking for a true or false answer.

Roman hell: Complex multiple-choice questions

As I state in the beginning of the chapter, by far, most of the questions on the exam are straightforward, but you'll likely see a few questions featuring Roman numeral options on the exam. Usually, you'll get standard A, B, C, D questions without the Roman numerals. However, in a lot of the corequisite exams, you'll get your fair share of Roman numeral questions. So, don't go too crazy at this point. However, I will give you a brief rundown on how to handle them for the off chance that you get some and for future reference.

Imposing order: Ranking questions

To answer a ranking question, you have to choose the answer that places the information in the correct order — first to last, last to first, highest to lowest, lowest to highest, and so on. Check out the following example:

EXAMPLE

In which order, from first to last, are the following actions taken when opening a new options account?

I. Send the customer an ODD.

II. Have the ROP approve the account.

III. Execute the transaction.

IV. Have the customer send in an OAA.

(A) I, II, III, IV

(B) II, I, IV, III

(C) III, I, II, IV

(D) I, III, II, IV

The correct answer is (A). Wasn't it nice of me to arrange all the answers in order for you? Because option transactions are so risky, the customer has to receive an options risk disclosure document (ODD) before opening the account. Statement I has to come first, so you can immediately eliminate (B) and (C), giving you a 50 percent chance of answering correctly. After the client receives the ODD, the registered options principal (ROP) needs to approve the account before any transactions can be executed; II has to come before III, so you can finish the problem here; the answer is (A). Last but not least, the customer signs and returns an options account agreement (OAA) within 15 days after the account is approved by the ROP.

Taking two at a time

The Roman-numeral format also appears on FINRA exams with questions that offer two answer choices as the correct response. In these types of questions, you choose the responses that best answer the question.

EXAMPLE

Which two of the following are the minimum financial requirements for an individual investor to be considered accredited?

I. An individual with a net worth of $500,000

II. An individual with a net worth of $1,000,000

III. An individual who earned $200,000 per year in the most recent two years and has a reasonable expectation of reaching that same level in the current year

IV. An individual who earned $300,000 per year in the most recent three years and has a reasonable expectation of reaching that same level in the current year

(A) I and III

(B) I and IV

(C) II and III

(D) II and IV

The correct answer is (C). Statements I and II both deal with net worth; III and IV deal with earnings. Therefore, you're dealing with two questions in one; to be accredited, the answer to at least one of these two questions must be satisfactory:

- What is the individual's minimum net worth?
- What is the individual's minimum income?

The definition of accredited investor has expanded greatly over the last several years, but related to this question, to be considered an *accredited* (sophisticated) investor, the minimum requirement is a net worth of $1 million and/or a yearly income of $200,000 in the most recent two years, with a reasonable expectation of reaching that same level in the current year. If the word *minimum* hadn't been used in the question, IV would also be correct.

A little mystery: Dealing with an unknown number of correct statements

In the preceding section, the question states that only two responses can be correct. The following question may have one, three, or four correct answers. You can recognize this type of question simply by glancing at your answer choices. To make the problem more difficult (don't hate me, now), I add an *except* because I'm feeling really good about you, and I just know you're up to it.

EXAMPLE

All of the following are true about open-end funds except

I. They issue common stock.

II. They issue preferred stock.

III. They issue debt securities.

IV. Shares can be purchased in the market.

(A) I only

(B) II only

(C) II, III, and IV only

(D) I, II, III, and IV

The correct answer is (C).

Open-end funds are mutual funds. Mutual funds are constantly issuing new shares (thus, the open-end name). Because mutual funds issue only common stock and can be purchased only directly from the issuer, the only true answer is I. But because we're looking for the exception(s), answers II, III, and IV are the correct ones. (Chapter 9 covers the information you need to know about open- and closed-end funds.) Had the example asked which is true regarding closed-end funds, the answer would have been (D).

Looking at exhibits: Diagram questions

The SIE exam isn't likely to give you more than a few of exhibit questions, if any. But even if you don't get an exhibit question on the SIE exam, you can use the following information to help on one of the companion exams you're going to have to take. Exhibit questions may include newspaper clippings, options prices, bond prices, trading patterns, income statements, balance sheets, and so on. Of the exhibit questions you get, some require you to find the correct information; others require a little calculating. I wouldn't be too concerned about them if I were you, because most of them are quite easy.

Take a look at the following problem:

GHI Corporation Balance Sheet at 12-31-XX
(In Thousands)

Assets		**Liabilities**	
Cash and cash equivalents	$8,000	Accounts payable	$1,000
Receivables (net)	$1,000	Wages payable	$800
Inventory	$3,000	Taxes payable	$700
Total current assets	**$12,000**	Interest payable	$500
		Total current liabilities	$3,000
Notes receivable due after one year	$1,000	Long-term debt 8%	$4,000
		Total liabilities	**$7,000**
Property, plant, and equipment (net)	$4,000		
Goodwill	$1,000	**Stockholder's Equity**	
Total long-term assets	**$6,000**	Preferred stock $100 par 9%	$2,000
		Common stock $1 par	$2,000
		Paid-in capital	$4,000
		Retained earnings	$3,000
		Total stockholder's equity	**$11,000**
Total assets	**$18,000**	**Total liabilities and stockholder's equity**	**$18,000**

EXAMPLE

The total amount of long-term liabilities of GHI Corporation based on its balance sheet are

(A) $1,000

(B) $1,000,000

(C) $4,000

(D) $4,000,000

The answer you're looking for is (D). Although tackling an exhibit question may seem intimidating, some of them may be as straightforward as this one. So, in this case, you'll find the liabilities on the right-hand side of the balance sheet. The long-term liabilities (long-term debt) in this case are $4,000,000. The reason that the answer is $4,000,000 instead of $4,000 is because the numbers listed in this balance sheet need to be multiplied by 1,000. When looking at the top of the balance sheet, you'll see "in thousands," which tells you all numbers in the balance sheet need to be multiplied by 1,000.

WARNING

When you answer exhibit questions, take care not to miss labels such as "in thousands" in headings or scales on a graph that would change your answer. Almost nothing is worse than missing a question you know because you carelessly overlooked something that was right in front of you.

Conquering the Questions: Tips and Tricks

In Chapter 2, I give you general exam proficiency tips. In this section, I show you how to improve your analysis of topic-specific SIE questions. I also provide more sample exam questions to further demonstrate the art of choosing the correct answer.

Focus on key information

The SIE and corequisite exam questions can be particularly difficult if you rush through the exam and miss details that change the meaning of the question.

TIP

When you start taking practice exams, read the question to determine what's being asked; then go back to the beginning of the problem to identify the key facts, and underline and/or highlight them. Marking the questions may seem to be time-consuming when you begin to study, but if you get into the habit of picking out key words in each question, zeroing in on the important information should be second nature by the time you take the test. You can't underline items on the computer screen at the testing center, of course; the test-center administrators would get upset if you wrote on the screen. Instead, if you find yourself getting distracted by useless information, use the scrap paper or dry-erase board to write down the information you do need.

This example zeroes in on the essential information:

EXAMPLE

A 55-year-old investor purchases a 6 percent DEF convertible mortgage bond at 90 with 10 years until maturity. If the bond is currently trading at 97, what is the current yield?

(A) 5.72%

(B) 6.00%

(C) 6.19%

(D) 6.67%

The correct answer is (C). When you're determining the current yield of a bond, all you need are the market price of the bond and the coupon (interest) rate. (See Chapter 7.) The fact that the investor is 55 years old or that the bond is a convertible mortgage bond that was purchased at $900 (90 percent of $1,000 par) with 10 years until maturity means nothing in terms of determining the answer. Underline or highlight what you do need (6 percent, 97, current yield) so you don't get distracted.

To determine the current yield, divide the annual interest by the market price. The annual interest is $60 (6 percent of $1,000 par), and the market price is $970 (97 percent of $1,000 par):

$$\text{current yield} = \frac{\text{annual interest}}{\text{market price}} = \frac{\$60}{\$970} = 6.19\%$$

TIP

To avoid confusion when faced with a math problem (but there aren't many on the SIE), read the stem of the question to determine what's being asked. Before you consider the rest of the question, jot down the formula you need to calculate your answer.

Answer me this: Pick the correct answer

The SIE exam is a practical multiple-choice exam. The correct answer has to be one of the choices. This setup means that you don't have to *provide* the correct answer; you just have to *recognize* it when you see it.

Picking up clues when you're virtually clueless: The process of elimination

When you don't straight-out know an answer, your approach can definitely make the difference between passing and failing the exam. Your best strategy may be eliminating the wrong answers. In theory, you should be able to eliminate, one by one, three incorrect answers for each question.

Even if you can't eliminate three incorrect answers, you'll certainly be able to eliminate one or two answers that are definitely wrong. Don't try to guess the right answer until you've axed as many wrong answers as you can. Obviously, if you can get the choices down to two potential answers, you have a 50-50 chance of answering correctly.

REMEMBER

For an answer choice to be correct, every aspect has to be correct, and the selection has to specifically answer the question that's asked. As a rule of thumb on the SIE exam, a more precise answer is correct more often than a less precise answer, and a longer answer usually (but not always) prevails over a short answer.

If a response is potentially correct, write *T* for *true* next to the answer in your practice exam, and if a response is wrong, eliminate it by writing *F* for *false* next to the answer. If you do this step correctly, you should end up with three Fs and one T, with T indicating the correct answer. Or if the question is looking for an answer that doesn't fit the conditions of the question, you should end up with three Ts and one F. (Refer to "Making exceptions: Except or not" earlier in this chapter for more info on this scenario.) On the actual test, you can write the letters A through D on your scrap paper or dry-erase board and then mark the answer choices appropriately.

TIP

Always look to eliminate any wrong answers you can. Pay attention to the wording and get rid of choices that simply sound wrong or that make statements that are too broad or absolute. If you're still undecided, use your scrap paper or dry-erase board to write down the question number and the answer choices that remain. Take your best guess and mark the answer for review. When you review, look at your scrap paper or dry-erase board to zero in on potential answers. Change your answer only if you're sure that you made a mistake.

Stop opposing me: Dealing with opposite answers

If you see two opposing answer choices, only one can be right. Traditionally, in practical exams like the SIE, when you see two answer choices that are complete opposites, the exam creators are trying to test your knowledge of the correct rule, procedure, or law, so one of those opposing choices is most likely the correct answer. Take a look at the following example:

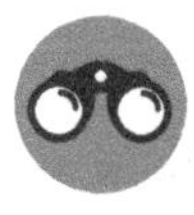
EXAMPLE

Which of the following is true of UGMA accounts?

(A) There can be only one minor and one custodian per account.

(B) There can be more than one minor and one custodian per account.

(C) Securities can be purchased only on margin.

(D) They must be set up for children who have reached the age of majority.

The answer you want is (A). Notice that (A) and (B) oppose each other. If you have two opposing answers, in almost all cases, one of them is the right answer. Therefore, you can ignore (C) and (D), which gives you a 50 percent chance of getting the answer right. Uniform Gifts to Minors Act (UGMA) accounts are set up for minors who are too young to have their own accounts. Each account is limited to one minor and one custodian. (See Chapter 12 for details on custodial accounts.)

Facing Roman numerals: Not as hard as you think

As stated previously, most of the questions on the exam will be straightforward, without Roman numerals. However, feel free to peruse if you'd like on the off chance you get a few. Besides, it'll come in handy when taking corequisite exams.

Complex (two-tiered) multiple-choice questions with both Roman numerals and letters can be really frustrating, because they usually signal that the test-taker (you) needs more than one correct answer. Well, today's your lucky day, because I show you a shortcut that can help you blow these questions right out of the water.

Traditionally, the first tier of these types of questions gives you several statements preceded by Roman numerals; the second tier (preceded by letters) provides you choices about which of those statements are correct. Fifteen combinations of I, II, III, and IV are possible (16 if you count "none of the above," which is almost never correct), but each problem can list only four of them in the answer choices. Because of the limited answer choices, you may not have to evaluate every statement; certain combinations of Roman numerals may be logically impossible.

TIP

Read the question carefully and then mark *T* for *true* or *F* for *false* next to the Roman numerals to indicate whether they're correct answers to the question. If a Roman-numeral statement is correct, circle that number in the choices that follow the letters in the second tier. If the Roman-numeral statement is false, all the letter answers that include that numeral must also be false, and you can cross them out. If you're really lucky, three of the Roman numerals can be eliminated right away, leaving you with one answer choice.

Look over this Roman-numeral question:

EXAMPLE

Which of the following is true of The 5% Markup Policy?

I. It covers commissions charged to customers when executing trades on an agency basis.

II. It covers markups on stock sold to customers from inventory.

III. It covers markdowns on stock purchased from customers for inventory.

IV. Riskless and simultaneous transactions are covered.

(A) I and IV only

(B) IV only

(C) II and III only

(D) I, II, III, and IV

The correct answer is (D). The 5% Markup Policy applies to nonexempt securities sold to or purchased from customers. This situation is one in which you should look at the Roman-numeral statements and pick out those that you know answer the question. If you know that statement I is right (which it is), put a *T* (for *true*) next to it. Next, look at (A), (B), (C), and (D), and eliminate (B) and (C), because neither one includes the Roman numeral I. Because both answers that remain, (A) and (D), include the Roman numerals I and IV, you don't even have to bother reading statement IV; it's in both remaining answers, so you know that it has to be true. Write *T* next to the Roman numeral IV. If you know that either statement II or III is correct (both are), the answer has to be (D), because it's the only one that lists all the correct choices.

GETTING DOWN WITH NUMBERS: ELIMINATING SOME MATH

The process of elimination can get you out of some messy calculations. When dealing with math, look at the answer choices before you begin working out the problem. You may be able to get the answer without doing any calculations at all. If you have a forward stock split, for example, you know that the number of shares has to increase and that the price of the stock has to decrease. (See Chapter 6.) If three of the answers fail to meet these conditions, you have your answer right off the bat. Or, if you have a bond with a coupon rate of 20%, it is likely to be a wrong answer because most bonds have a coupon rate in the 3% to 12% range. You can start out by eliminating unreasonable answers.

Don't make the same mistake twice

TIP

When you're studying for the SIE exam, the practice exams can help you pinpoint your weaker areas of knowledge. The questions you answer incorrectly can be your best learning tools if you thoroughly review the explanations for each wrong answer. You may be tempted to jump from one practice exam to the next without taking adequate time to review your wrong answers. Don't do it! If you put the effort into finding out *why* your choices are wrong when you're practicing, you're less likely to repeat the same mistake on the SIE exam, when it really counts.

IN THIS CHAPTER

» Getting ready the day before

» Arriving at the test center and checking in

» Experiencing the exam

» Viewing your exam results

Chapter 4
Surviving Test Day

You've done your homework, taken practice exams, and completed your self-study and/or online course, and now the day of reckoning is upon you. You're ready to exchange the gazillion hours of study and hard work for your SIE license. The last hurdle awaits you at the test center.

In this chapter, I give you a snapshot of the SIE exam experience so you know the procedure before, during, and after you take the exam and can hit the ground running.

Note: This chapter relates mostly to people who are taking the exam at a testing center. In mid-2020, during the COVID-19 pandemic, the Financial Industry Regulatory Authority (FINRA) and Prometrics added an option that enables you to take the test online. Even though we're quite a few years from the start of the pandemic, taking the test online remains an alternative. If you're interested in taking the test online, please see the end of Chapter 1 for more information.

Composing Yourself the Day Before

On the day before the exam, review the information that you're still having problems with until noon; then call it a day. Get away from the books; go out to dinner (maybe skip the spicy foods and alcohol) or go to a movie. Rest your mind. If you've put the required time and effort into studying up to now, you'll benefit more from a good night's rest than from anything you can learn in the final hours the night before your exam. Taking the evening off can help prevent brain fatigue and make honing into exam mode easier tomorrow, when it counts most.

REMEMBER

Before you go to sleep, gather the items you need to take with you to the exam. If you prepare yourself the night before, you'll be more relaxed on exam day. Here are some activities to complete the night before the exam to finalize your preparations for the big day:

» Make sure that you have the proper government-issued ID bearing your name, signature, and a recent photo. The name on your ID must match the name on the Web CRD registration form. An expired ID won't be accepted. Official (primary) identification can be in the form of a valid passport, a driver's license, or a military ID card. A current (unexpired) state ID is acceptable in lieu of a driver's license, as long as it includes the person's full name as it appears on the Web CRD registration form, an expiration date, your signature, and a current photograph.

If you use a military ID that doesn't have a signature, you need to bring a secondary form of ID with a signature. Your secondary ID can be a valid credit card, a bank automatic teller machine (ATM) card, a library card, a U.S. Social Security card, an employee ID/work badge, or a school ID.

- Pack earplugs (if they're allowed; ask when you schedule your exam).
- Put a snack with the rest of your stuff.
- Bring study materials — including the topics and/or math formulas you're having trouble with — for a final review before you enter the test center.
- Have your watch ready to make sure that you're on time.
- Lay out your clothes. (Dress in layers in case the test center feels like either your refrigerator or your oven.)
- Review the directions to the exam site. Make sure that you have a charged cellphone and the test-center number in case you get lost.
- Also, if your test is early in the morning, don't forget to set one, maybe two, alarms to avoid oversleeping.

Additionally, you have to bring at least one finger with you, preferably yours, so that the exam administrators can take a fingerprint (though you probably have that packed already).

REMEMBER

You can't bring study material, textbooks, briefcases, purses, electronic devices, cellphones, notes of any kind, or your really smart friend with you into the testing room. In addition, they may inspect your glasses, ask you to turn your pockets inside out, and so on. Calculators, pencils, and scrap paper or a dry-erase board will be provided for you at the exam center, and the exam administrators will collect the calculators, pencils, and all scrap paper (used and unused) and dry-erase boards at the end of each session.

DOING TEST RUNS IN THE FINAL WEEKS

Getting too little sleep (you'll be a nervous wreck) or too much sleep (you'll be in a stupor) the night before the exam can be a disaster. For the week before the exam (if possible), follow the routine you'll be following on the day of your exam. Set your alarm at the same time you'll wake up on exam day, take a complete practice exam for the 1 hour and 45-minute interval at the same time as you'll be taking the real exam, and so on.

Also, the day of the exam is not the time to find out that a big construction project is underway on the exact route you're taking to get to the test center, the traffic is backed up for miles, and you'll be at least an hour late. The last thing you need to worry about on exam day is getting to the test center late and having to reschedule your exam.

To avoid this disaster, do a test run sometime before the test date. Travel the route you'll take at the same time (and, if possible, on the same day of the week) as your exam date to get a preview of what you can expect. You may even be able to check your local newspaper or state government website for details on upcoming construction or repairs that may affect roadways and public transportation. Having an alternative route established in advance is also a good idea in case your route of choice isn't the best option on exam day. Certainly, using a GPS can help you avoid any slowdowns along the way as well.

Making the Most of the Morning

Now the big day is here. Certainly, you don't have to dress up for the pictures that the SIE administrator takes, but you should at least do what you need to do to feel awake, alive, and good about yourself (do some push-ups, take a quick walk, take a shower, shave, whatever).

Be sure to eat at least a light breakfast. You may feel that you're too nervous to eat, but if you're hungry when you take the exam, you won't be able to concentrate. And if you overeat, you'll be wasting valuable energy (and blood flow!) digesting the meal — energy that your brain needs to sustain you. To avoid an energy crash, I suggest a protein bar, fruit, and/or veggies rather than sugar or carbs.

Grab everything you packed up the night before (see the preceding section) and head out the door.

TIP

If you're feeling extremely well prepared, leave your home in time to arrive at the test center at least 30 minutes before your scheduled exam so that you have time to check in. However, if you still have some info that's not committed to memory, I recommend that you arrive at the test center 1 1/2 hours before the exam so you have 1 hour to review the topics and/or math formulas that give you the most trouble and a half hour to check in.

Arriving on the Scene When Taking the Exam at a Physical Location

The SIE exam and other securities exams are administered by Prometric, and you can contact the center for additional information. In this section, I cover the steps you need to take upon arrival at the exam center.

TIP

In Chapter 1, I discuss the availability of special accommodations if you're disabled or learning-impaired or if English is your second language. If you require special accommodations, contact the FINRA Special Conditions Team at (800) 999-6647 for information about registration and for instructions about arriving at the exam center.

Take advantage of one last chance to cram

The information you review just before the exam will be on the surface of your mind. When you arrive at the exam center (or even during your commute, if you take public transportation), do some last-minute cramming. Review the topics and/or math formulas you're having trouble with.

Each SIE exam center is set up differently; you may find areas in the building where you can study, or you may have to study in your car, on a bench, or at a nearby coffee shop. When you're ready to enter the exam center (30 minutes before the exam), you can leave your books in your vehicle if the exam center doesn't have lockers (see "Get seated" later in this chapter).

Sign in

To enter the exam center, you have to show the administrators valid ID. (Refer to "Composing Yourself the Day Before" to see what constitutes a valid ID.) When you're inside the test center, you have to sign in and then get photographed and fingerprinted. In addition, before you begin the exam, you have to read a form called the Rules of Conduct and agree to the terms. A preview of the Rules of Conduct is available on the FINRA website (`www.finra.org/registration-exams-ce/qualification-exams/exam-day/msrb-qual-exam-rules-conduct`).

Get seated

Basically, the only things you may bring into the testing room are your own sweet self and possibly a set of earplugs. You can store all other personal property in a locker at the exam center. (All new testing sites are supposed to have lockers, but some older sites may have been grandfathered without them. You can ask when you make your appointment.) For a list of the (mostly) medical items you can bring into the exam room, including which ones need inspection or preauthorization, please call your testing center.

Some exam centers have cafeterias and/or vending machines with snacks and drinks, but you can't even bring chewing gum into the exam room. I don't know why — maybe because of the noise or maybe so the exam staff doesn't have to scrape gum wads off computer screens.

The exam administrators escort you to the exam room. In the testing room, you receive scrap paper (or a dry-erase board), a pencil, and a basic calculator. You'll have to return the paper, pencil, and calculator to the administrators at the end of the session. (Yes, even the unused scrap paper.) You can't bring anything else into the cubicle where you take the exam.

TIP

You can watch a video provided by Prometrics to see what a test center looks like and review some of their safety procedures. Go to `www.prometric.com/on-exam-day`.

Tackling the SIE

Take a deep breath, crack your knuckles, and get ready to make things count; this SIE exam is the genuine article. The exam is 1 hour and 45 minutes in duration, and you're graded on a total of 75 questions. The test designers have even prepared a bonus for you: To ensure that any new questions to be introduced in future exams meet acceptable standards, you also answer five additional, unidentified questions that don't count toward your score. Lucky you! This means that you answer 80 questions, but only 75 really count toward your score.

REMEMBER

Most test centers offer the inspirational creature comforts of a typical office cube farm setup: You take your SIE in — yes — a cubicle (approximately 4 feet wide) with a computer and a small desk area. You may leave your cubicle for restroom breaks at any time, if necessary. The clock continues to run, however, so try to limit your intake of fluids before each session.

Just before you begin your exam, a member of the test-center staff will walk you through how to use the computerized system. Don't worry. You don't need any computer experience to understand the way the computer operates; it's easy. If you do have any tech problems during the test, you can click a Help button or summon the exam administrators.

As the test begins, you're ready to put all those test-taking skills to use. (Check out Chapter 2 for a rundown of those skills.) Right off the bat, write down everything you think you're likely to forget. Keep track of time. Mark questions for review. Concentrate on the facts in question and look for key words that can give you clues. Use your amazing powers of elimination to identify wrong answer choices. Work your magic with specific question types. (See Chapter 3.) You've done your homework, so be confident.

STAYING RELAXED, FOCUSED, AND CONSCIOUS

Here are some ways to keep stress at bay and make sure that you're giving the test the attention it deserves:

- If you feel tense, take a few slow, deep breaths, and give yourself a mini-massage.
- If you find yourself growing tired, stretch, sit up straight, or go to the restroom just for a chance to walk around.
- Give your eyes a rest from the computer screen by looking away from the computer every so often.

  Avoid looking at someone else's computer screen; it's not only frowned upon, but also will get you ejected.
- If you have trouble focusing, write down significant details from the question. If you're stuck on a multipart question, break the question into segments. Try drawing diagrams. If you're still having trouble, choose a tentative answer and mark the question for review.
- Don't lose track of your mission; now is not the time to let up. Visualize success and hang in there!

Before your session ends, double-check the questions you marked for review. Don't change any answers unless you're certain that your initial answer is wrong.

If you've completed your review of the questions you've marked for review, you can do a review of all of your questions if you want and have time. This is a time to make sure you didn't make any careless errors, such as missing an *except* or *not*, and change your answers if necessary. If you're looking at a question the second time and are 50/50 whether your first answer is correct or it's another answer, leave it alone. You'll do more harm than good by second-guessing.

Revealing Your Results

You've completed many hours of studying. You've deprived yourself of weekend parties and long afternoons of leisure. Your social life has been almost nonexistent, and if you're the type who becomes unpleasant in a stressful state of being, you may have alienated the people who used to hang out with you.

After surviving 1 hour and 45 minutes of mental abuse from taking the SIE exam, you're ready to click the button that reveals your score and can change your life.

The time may seem much longer, but in reality, you have to wait only a little while to find out if you passed or failed. *Passed* or *failed* will appear on the computer screen. If your grade is 70 or better, which means you got 53 or more questions of the actual test questions correct, you pass the exam. (Please remember that you're a professional now and refrain from doing a victory dance in the middle of the test center.) If your score is less than 70, you don't pass the exam, and your grade will be shown on the computer screen, which will let you know how much work you need to do. Don't call your friends and tell them that you've decided to become an astronaut or firefighter instead. You can retake the test, so you may still have a future on Wall Street. See Chapter 1 for what to do next.

Regardless of whether you pass or fail the exam, you receive a printout of your grade and the breakdown of your performance on the SIE exam topics — which, unfortunately, is pretty vague. Employers receive a copy of the results in the mail, or if they're tied into the FINRA computer system, they can get results online.

2

Starting at Square One: Basic Security Investments

IN THIS PART . . .

Get familiar with basic securities — stocks and bonds, including municipal securities — that form the foundation of an investor's portfolio.

Review the registration procedure that securities go through before they can be sold to the public and find out which securities are exempt from registration.

Distinguish common stock from preferred stock, corporate bonds from U.S. bonds, and municipal bonds from general obligation bonds.

IN THIS CHAPTER

» Understanding the specifics of registering securities

» Knowing the types of offerings

» Spotting exempt securities

» Testing what you know

Chapter 5
Securities Underwriting: The Process and the Team Players

All issuers of securities need a starting point, just as all securities need a birth date (just not the kind that's celebrated with funny-looking hats and a cake). Most securities go through a registration procedure before the public can buy them. The SIE exam tests your ability to recognize the players and institutions involved in the registration process.

In this chapter, I cover topics related to bringing new issues (securities) to market. You find out about key players, types of securities offerings, kinds of securities that don't need to be registered, and other details about the underwriting process, where firms prepare to raise money from investors for issuers. At the end of the chapter, you get a chance to see how much you've learned by taking a quick exam.

Bringing New Issues to the Market

A lot of things need to happen before securities hit the market. Unless exempt (see later in this chapter) not only do the securities have to be registered with the SEC, but the issuer also has to find a broker–dealer (like your firm) to sell the securities to the public. The SIE exam tests your ability to answer questions about this process.

Starting out: What the issuer does

For an entity to become a corporation, the corporate founders must file a document called a *corporate charter* (bylaws) in the home state of their business. Included in the corporate charter are the names of the founders, the type of business they're running or planning to run, the location of business, the number of shares (authorized shares) that can be issued, and so on. If a corporation wants to sell securities to the public, it has to register with states and the U.S. Securities and Exchange Commission (SEC). Read on for info on how the registration process works.

THE SECURITIES ACTS

Registration helps ensure that securities issued to the public adhere to certain regulations (though anti-fraud rules also apply to exempt securities). The following acts are designed to protect investors from unscrupulous issuers, firms, and salespeople. (See Chapter 16 for details on other rules and regulations.)

Securities Act of 1933: This act (also called the Truth in Securities Act, the Paper Act, the Full Disclosure Act, the Prospectus Act, and the New Issues Act) regulates new issues of corporate securities. An issuer of corporate securities must provide full and fair disclosure about itself and the offering. Included in this act are rules to prevent fraud and deception.

Securities Exchange Act of 1934: The Act of 1934, which established the SEC, was enacted to protect investors by regulating the over-the-counter (OTC) market and exchanges, such as the New York Stock Exchange (NYSE). (Chapter 14 tells you more about markets.) In addition, the Act of 1934 regulates

- The extension of credit in margin accounts (see Chapter 12)
- Transactions by insiders
- Customer accounts
- Trading activities

Trust Indenture Act: This act was originally known as the Trust Indenture Act of 1939 and prohibits bond issues valued at more than $50 million from being offered to investors without an indenture. A *trust indenture* is a written agreement that protects investors by disclosing the particulars of the issue (coupon rate, maturity date, any collateral backing the bond, and so on). As part of the Trust Indenture Act, all companies must hire a trustee who's responsible for protecting the rights of bondholders.

Registering securities with the SEC

For securities not exempt from registration (see "Exempt securities" later in this chapter), when a company wants to go public (sell stock to public investors), it has to file a registration statement and a prospectus (see "Getting the lowdown on the issue and issuer: The prospectus" later in this chapter) with the SEC.

The *registration statement* includes

- The issuer's name, address, and description of its business
- The company's articles of incorporation (unless previously supplied)
- The names and addresses of the underwriter(s) and all commissions or discounts they will receive from the sale, either directly or indirectly
- The price at which the security will be offered to the public
- The names and addresses of all the company's control personnel, such as officers, directors, and anyone who owns more than 10 percent of the corporation's securities (and how much they hold of the corporation's securities)
- The estimated net proceeds of the sale from the security to be issued and what the proceeds will be used for, including property (initially), or other businesses to be purchased (if any)
- The company's *capitalization* (all financing-related debt and equity)
- Complete financial statements, including balance sheets and income statements

- Any legal proceedings against the corporation that may affect it
- Any net proceeds derived from any security sold by the issuer in the previous two years, along with the underwriter's particulars
- The names and addresses of the attorneys who have vouched for the legality of the issue and a copy of their opinion(s) on the legality of the issue
- Any agreements or indentures that might affect the securities being offered

The preceding information regarding the registration statement is known as *Schedule A*, and it typically applies to corporations issuing new securities. A *Schedule B* applies to foreign government issues. The information required when a local government issues securities (typically municipal bonds) is — as you can imagine — geared to what a local government would have to supply in its registration statement. Most of the information required is very similar; in fact, you can substitute *municipality* for *company* or *corporation* for most of the items required. You need to know the name of the borrowing government or subdivision, what it's raising the money for, the amount of funded (long-term) debt and the amount of unfunded (short-term) debt there will be after the new security is issued, whether the issuer has defaulted on debt in the past 20 years, the names of all people involved (in other words, attorneys, underwriters, and so on), commission to be paid to the underwriters, copies of the agreements made with the underwriters, a legal opinion made by the attorney with regard to the legality and possible tax-free nature of the issue, and so on.

Because the registration process to sell securities is a somewhat daunting and costly process for issuers, they may register more securities than they may need to sell now. *Shelf registration* (SEC Rule 415) allows issuers to sell securities that were previously registered with the SEC without additional permission. Shelf registration gives issuers up to three years (depending on their status) to sell previously registered shares.

Awaiting approval: The cooling-off period

After the issuer files a registration statement (the filing date) with the SEC, a 20-day cooling-off period begins. (The 20-day cooling-off period is not required for a well-known seasoned issuer, also referred to as a *WKSI*.) During the 20-day (and sometimes longer) period, the good old SEC reviews the registration statement. At the end of the cooling-off period, the issue will (ideally) be cleared for sale to the public (the effective date of registration). In the event that the registration statement must be amended or additional information is needed, the SEC issues a deficiency letter and halts the registration process until it receives the required information. If the SEC finds that the registration statement is misleading because the issuer included untrue statements of material fact or omitted a material fact, it issues a *stop order (deficiency letter)* which suspends the effectiveness of the registration statement. At this point, the issuer is required to amend the registration statement and answer any questions posed by the commission to continue the registration process.

Neither the SEC nor any self-regulatory organization approves an issue. The SEC only clears the issue for sale. Also, the SEC is not responsible for making sure that the information included on the registration statement is complete, true, or accurate. As a matter of fact, it's unlawful to represent that the SEC approved of an issue or issuer (known as the No Approval Clause).

During the cooling-off period, the underwriter(s) can obtain indications of interest from investors who may want to purchase the issue. Agents scramble to get indications of interest from prospective purchasers of the securities. Although the underwriter(s) may keep records of indications of interest, they *may not* accept any money in advance of the public offering.

REMEMBER

Indications of interest aren't binding on customers or underwriters. Customers always have the prerogative to change their minds, and underwriters may not have enough shares available to meet every prospective buyer's needs.

A *tombstone advertisement* — a newspaper ad that's shaped like . . . well, a tombstone (typically, rectangular with black borders) — is an announcement (but not an offer) of a new security for sale. It's the only advertisement allowed during the cooling-off period. These ads aren't required and don't have to be filed with the SEC. Tombstone ads contain a simple statement of facts about the new issue (the name of the issuer, type of security, number of shares or bonds available, underwriter's name, and so on). In addition, tombstone ads often provide investors information about how to obtain a prospectus. Tombstone ads may or may not include the price of the security being offered. Tombstone ads are the only form of advertisement allowed prior to the effective date, although they may appear after the effective date. They must contain a disclaimer stating that the advertisement isn't an offer to sell or a solicitation of an offer for any of these securities; this offer is made only through a prospectus.

Underwriters and selling group members use the *preliminary prospectus* to obtain indications of interest from prospective customers. The preliminary prospectus must be made available to all customers who are interested in the new issue during the cooling-off period. I talk more about what that prospectus has to include in "Getting the lowdown on the issue and issuer: The prospectus" a little later in this chapter.

Holding the required due-diligence meeting

Toward the end of the cooling-off period, the lead underwriter holds a due-diligence meeting. This meeting is required by law. During this meeting, the underwriter provides information about the issue and what the issuer will use the proceeds of the sale for. This meeting is designed to provide such information to syndicate members (syndicate group or syndicate desk), selling group, brokers, analysts, institutions, and so on and allows them to ask questions.

REMEMBER

The last time syndicate members can back out of an underwriting agreement is toward the end of the cooling-off period (around the time of the due-diligence meeting). You can assume that if syndicate members are backing out, the reason is most likely negative market conditions.

Registering with the states: Blue skies

All *blue-sky laws* — state laws that apply to securities offerings and sales — say that to sell a security to a customer, the broker–dealer (brokerage firm), the registered representative, and the security must be registered in the customer's home state. The issuer is responsible for registering the security not only with the U.S. Securities and Exchange Commission (SEC), but also with the administrator in each state in which the securities are to be sold. Although the laws usually are quite similar, all states have their own securities laws, which are overseen by state securities regulators.

Here are the methods of state security registration:

- **Notification (registration by filing):** Notification is the simplest form of registration for established companies. Companies that previously sold securities in a state can renew their previous application.
- **Coordination:** This method involves registering with the SEC and states at the same time. The SEC helps companies meet the blue-sky laws by notifying all states in which the securities are to be sold. This type of registration is typically used for initial public offerings (IPOs).

- **Qualification:** Companies use this registration method for securities that are exempt from federal (SEC) registration but require registration with the state through the State Administrator.

Roll call: Introducing the team players

The following list explains who's involved in the securities registration and selling process. Registered reps can work for any of these firms:

- **Investment banking firm:** An *investment banking firm* is an institution (a broker–dealer) that's in the business of helping issuers raise money. You can think of investment bankers as being the brains of the operation, because they help issuers raise money by providing advice for mergers, acquisitions, reorganizations, as well as selling securities. Because they help the issuer decide what securities to issue, how much to issue, the suggested selling price, and so on, they usually underwrite the issue and become the managing underwriter in the offering of new securities.
- **Underwriter:** An *underwriter* is a broker–dealer who helps the issuer bring new securities to the public. They take the financial risk and, therefore, receive an extra fee for taking that risk. Underwriters purchase the securities from the issuer and sell them to the public for a nice profit. (Yay!)
- **Syndicate (syndicate group or syndicate desk):** When an issue is too large for one firm to handle, the syndicate manager (managing underwriter) forms a *syndicate* to help sell the securities and relieve some of the financial burden on the managing underwriter. Each syndicate member is responsible for selling a portion of the securities to the public.
- **Managing (lead) underwriter:** The *managing underwriter* (syndicate manager) is the firm that's responsible for putting together a syndicate and dealing directly with the issuer. The managing underwriter receives financial compensation (buckets-o-bucks) for every share sold.
- **Selling group:** In the event that the syndicate members need more help selling the securities, they can recruit selling group members. These members are brokerage firms that aren't part of the syndicate. Selling group members help distribute shares to the public but don't make a financial commitment (that is, don't purchase shares from the issuer) and, therefore, receive less money per share when selling shares to the public.

Although corporations could use a bidding process to pick the underwriter for new issues, they typically choose the underwriter directly. This type of offering is called a *negotiated offering.* Because municipal general obligation (GO) bonds are backed by the taxes of the people in the community, the issuers are most likely to choose a *competitive offering* (bidding process) to ensure that they're getting the best deal (highest bond price and/or lowest coupon payment) for taxpayers. (This topic is covered in more detail in Chapter 8.)

Signing an agreement among underwriters

When an issuer hires an underwriter (dealer) to sell its securities to the public, the parties must sign an agreement among underwriters, which is also known as an *underwriting agreement* or *syndicate agreement.* The underwriting agreement outlines, among other things, the method of distribution (firm commitment, best efforts, or standby; more on these options in the upcoming paragraphs).

The underwriting agreement is a contract between the issuer of the securities and the managing or lead underwriter. It must be agreed on and signed before any securities can be sold to the public. Now, for SIE purposes, you don't need to know all the details about the underwriting agreement, but you should have a basic understanding of the types of underwritings: firm commitment and best efforts.

Committing to the deal: Firm-commitment underwriting

In a firm-commitment underwriting, the lead underwriter and syndicate members (other underwriters who may be helping in the sale of the securities) agree to purchase all the securities that remain unsold after the offering. In this case, the underwriter assumes all the financial risk.

Another type of firm commitment offering is a standby. A standby underwriter signs an agreement with the issuer to purchase any stock not purchased by the public if and when an issuer has a rights offering. (See Chapter 6 for more on that topic.)

Taking your best shot: Best-efforts underwriting

In a best-efforts underwriting, the underwriter agrees to make its best effort to sell all the securities to the public. If, however, the underwriter can't sell all the securities to the public, the issuer has the right to cancel the offering or take back some of the unsold securities, depending on the type of best-efforts offering:

- **All-or-none (AON):** If the offering is set up as an AON agreement, all the securities must be sold by the deadline; otherwise, the deal is canceled, and the money must be returned to the investors.
- **Mini-max:** A mini-max offering is one in which a specified minimum number of securities must be sold in order for the deal not to be cancelled. If that minimum threshold is reached, more securities may be sold up to the maximum amount is reached. The issuer will take back any securities that remain unsold.

You should be aware that if securities are sold on a best-efforts basis, purchasers and potential purchasers must be made aware that the offering could be canceled. Purchasers' money is held in an escrow account until the terms are met or the deal is canceled. When the specified number of securities is sold, the underwriter releases the securities to the purchasers. If the underwriter doesn't sell enough of the securities by the deadline, the purchasers get their money back.

According to FINRA, "A member, in the conduct of its business, shall observe high standards of commercial honor and just and equitable principles of trade." So regardless of whether the securities offered during an IPO are sold on a firm commitment or best-efforts underwriting, it must be a *bona fide offering* of the securities at the public offering price. Firms can't hold back securities for themselves, associates, immediate family members, industry insiders, portfolio managers, and so on.

Getting the lowdown on the issue and issuer: The prospectus

The issuer prepares a preliminary prospectus (sometimes with the help of the underwriter) that's sent in with the registration statement. The preliminary prospectus must be available for potential purchasers when the issue is in registration (during the cooling-off period) with the SEC. The preliminary prospectus is abbreviated, but it contains all the essential facts about the issuer and issue except the final public offering price (POP) and the *effective date* (the date when the issue will first be sold). (A broker–dealer *may not* accept payment for a new issue until the registration becomes effective.)

A preliminary prospectus is sometimes called a *red herring*, not because it smells fishy (or is totally misleading and irrelevant), but because a statement in red letters on the cover of the preliminary prospectus declares that it's not the final version and that some items may change in the meantime. The statement is often in the margin and elsewhere.

The *final prospectus*, which is prepared toward the end of the cooling-off period, is a legal document that the issuer prepares, containing material information about the issuer and new issue of securities. The final prospectus has to be available to all potential purchasers of the issue. It includes

- The final offering price
- The underwriters' *spread* (the profit the underwriters make per share)
- The *delivery date* (when the securities will be available)

Note: Because all mutual (open-end) funds, which I cover in Chapter 9, issue new securities constantly, they must always have a prospectus available. In addition, many mutual funds provide a *statement of additional information* (SAI), which provides more detailed information about the fund's operation that may be useful to some investors. A statement of additional information is also known as Part B of a fund's registration statement.

Counting the securities along the way

When a company issues securities that are traded in the market, someone has to be responsible for keeping track of the owners of the securities and someone has to make sure that the number of securities in the market isn't greater than it's supposed to be. These jobs are assigned to a registrar and a transfer agent:

- **Registrar:** The *registrar* is an independent financial institution that works along with a company's transfer agent to maintain a record of stock and bond owners. The main function of a registrar is to make sure that the outstanding shares don't exceed the amount of stock the issuer authorizes under its corporate charter or bylaws (rules the company lives by).
- **Transfer agent:** The *transfer agent* is a person or institution that maintains records of a corporation's stock and bond owners (much like a registrar) but also cancels and issues certificates as well as distributes dividends.

TIP

An easy way to keep these folks straight is to remember that a registrar is responsible for counting things, and a transfer agent is responsible for transferring or sending things.

Getting Up to Speed on the Types of Securities Offerings

Table 5-1 deals with the types of offerings that you (as a megabroker) should be familiar with. The offerings that follow usually require the services of an underwriter or underwriting syndicate to sell the securities to the public.

For unlisted IPOs (IPOs of non-NMS securities — securities that are not listed on an exchange or Nasdaq, in other words), a final prospectus needs to be available to all purchasers for 90 days after the effective date.

TABLE 5-1 Types of Securities Offerings

Type	Description	Who Benefits
Initial public offering (IPO)	The first time an issuer sells stock to the public to raise capital; issuers usually hold back some stock for future primary offerings.	The bulk of the moolah raised goes to the issuer, and the rest goes to the underwriters.
Primary offering	An offering of new securities from a new issuer or an issuer that has previously issued securities; a company can have an initial public offering and several primary offerings if it wants to.	The proceeds of sale go to the issuer and underwriters.
Secondary offering	A sale of a large block of outstanding (stockholder-owned) securities or previously outstanding securities (Treasury stock, or stock the issuer has repurchased). Typically, one or more major stockholders of a corporation make the secondary offerings; new investors are essentially buying used, so the number of shares outstanding doesn't change.	The proceeds don't go to the issuer (except with Treasury stock); they go to the big shots who sell the securities.
Split (combined) offering	A combination of a primary and secondary offerings, with both new and outstanding securities.	A portion of the proceeds goes to the issuer, and a portion goes to the selling stockholders.

For IPOs of NMS securities (securities listed on an exchange or Nasdaq), a final prospectus must be available for 25 days after the effective date.

In the event that a member is acting as a dealer or has some other financial interest in recommending a security other than the commission received from the buyer, that fact must be disclosed in writing to the client at or before the completion of the transaction. So, in that regard, all buyers must be notified in writing if your firm is involved in a primary or secondary distribution of securities.

Reviewing Exemptions

Certain securities are exempt from registration because of the type of security or the type of transaction involved. You may find that those securities which are exempt because of who's issuing them are a bit easier to recognize. You'll probably have to spend a little more time on the securities that are exempt from registration because of the type of transaction.

Exempt securities

Certain securities are exempt from the registration requirements under the Securities Act of 1933. These securities come from issuers that either have a high level of creditworthiness, or it's the case that another government regulatory agency has some sort of jurisdiction over the issuer of the securities. These types of securities include

- Securities issued by the U.S. government (Treasury bills, Treasury notes, Treasury bonds, and so on) or federal agencies
- Municipal securities (local government bonds and notes)
- Securities issued by banks, savings institutions, and credit unions
- Public utility stocks or bonds

- Securities issued by religious, educational, or not-for-profit organizations
- Notes, bills of exchange, bankers' acceptances, and commercial paper (unsecured corporate debt securities with an initial maturity of 270 days or less)
- Insurance policies and fixed annuities

Fixed annuities are not securities and are exempt from SEC registration because the issuing insurance company guarantees the payout. Variable annuities require registration, however, because the payout varies depending on the performance of the securities held in the separate account. For more info on annuities and other packaged securities, see Chapter 9.

Exempt transactions

Some securities that corporations offer may be exempt from the full registration requirements of the Securities Act of 1933 due to the nature of the sale. The following list shows these exemptions:

- **Intrastate offerings (Rule 147):** An *intrastate offering* includes the *80% rule*. In order for a company to be eligible for the exemption, *at least 80%* of the corporation's *assets* must be in the state OR at least *80%* of *the company's revenues* must be generated from *in-state business* OR at least 80% of *money raised* from the offering must be used in the state of the offering. In addition, at least 50% of the company's employees must work in the state of the offering. The securities still require registration at the state level and 100% of the purchasers must be within the state.

  Rule 147A allows offers of securities to residents outside the state as long as sales are made to in-state residents only. In addition, the issuing company may be registered out of the state as long as it "principal place of business" is in the state.

  WARNING

  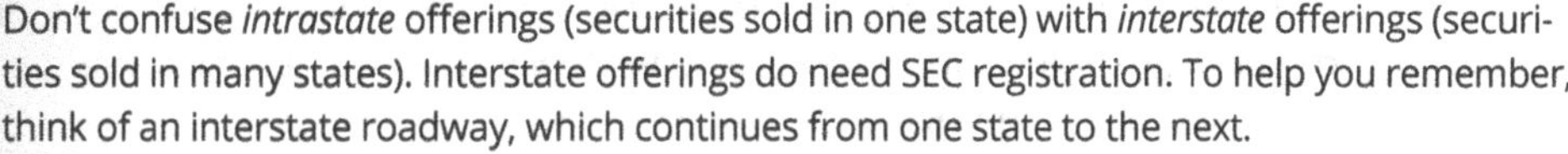

  Don't confuse *intrastate* offerings (securities sold in one state) with *interstate* offerings (securities sold in many states). Interstate offerings do need SEC registration. To help you remember, think of an interstate roadway, which continues from one state to the next.

- **Regulation A (Reg A, Regulation A+, or Reg A+) offerings:** An offering of securities worth $20 million or less (Tier 1) or $75 million or less (Tier 2) within a 12-month period is Regulation A+. Although this company may seem to be large to you, it's relatively small in market terms. Regulation A+ offerings are exempt from full registration requirements, but the issuer still has to file a simplified registration or abbreviated registration statement. In addition, the issuer also has to file an *offering circular* and provide it to potential investors. An offering circular is similar to a prospectus but not quite as extensive.

- **Regulation D (Reg D) offerings:** Also known as a *private placement* (private securities offering), a Regulation D offering is an offering to no more than 35 unaccredited (nonaccredited) investors per year. Companies that issue securities through private placement are allowed to raise an unlimited amount of money but are limited in terms of the number of unaccredited investors. Sales of Reg D securities are subject to the sales limitations set forth under Rule 144. All unaccredited investors must meet specific suitability requirements.

  Persons who do not match any of the items on the following list are considered unaccredited. The list of who or what is considered to be an *accredited investor* was expanded to include the following:

  - Financial institutions (banks, insurance companies, pension funds, and so on)

- Insiders of the private placement issuer (officers, directors, and/or owners of 10 percent or more of the outstanding shares, as well as their immediate family members)
- Investors with a net worth of at least $1 million, excluding primary residence
- Investors who have had a net income of at least $200,000 ($300,000 joint) for the previous two years and are expected to meet the requirement during the current year and going forward
- Corporations, partnerships, or organizations with a net worth of at least $5 million
- Reps who are registered and in good standing with the SEC, FINRA, and/or at least one state who have passed the Series 7, Series 65, Series 66, and/or Series 82 exam
- Knowledgeable employees of private funds (hedge funds, private equity funds, and so on) who have the ability to raise money privately
- Rural business investment companies (investment companies that raise money to invest in small rural businesses)
- Limited liability companies (LLC) with more than $5 million in assets
- Family offices with at least $5 million in assets under management

» **Rule 144:** This rule covers the sale of restricted stock (such as stock sold through private placement), unregistered, and control securities (stock owned by control persons [affiliates], which includes directors, officers, or other people who own 10 percent or more of the issuer's voting stock). According to Rule 144, sellers of these securities must wait at least six months before selling the fully paid securities to the public. Additionally, the most an investor can sell at one time is 1 percent of the outstanding shares or the average weekly trading volume for the previous four weeks, whichever is greater. (Note: The volume restrictions apply to affiliates only.)

» **Rule 144A:** This rule allows unregistered domestic and foreign securities to be sold to *Qualified Institutional Buyers* (QIBs) in the United States without a holding period. QIBs include insurance companies, registered investment companies, registered investment advisers, pension plans, corporations, partnerships, and so on.

To see if you are getting the hang of this, take a look at the following example, which deals with Rule 144.

EXAMPLE

John Bullini is a control person who purchased shares of restricted stock and wants to sell under Rule 144. John has paid fully for the shares and has held them for more than one year. There are 1.5 million shares outstanding. Form 144 is filed on Monday, May 28, and the weekly trading volume for the restricted stock is as follows:

Week Ending	Trading Volume
May 25	16,000 shares
May 18	15,000 shares
May 11	17,000 shares
May 4	15,000 shares
April 27	18,000 shares

What is the maximum number of shares John can sell with this filing?

(A) 15,000

(B) 15,750

(C) 16,200

(D) 16,250

The right answer is (B). The test writers often try to trick you on the SIE exam by giving you at least one week more than you need to answer the question. Because John has held the restricted stock for more than a year, John can sell 1 percent of the outstanding shares or the average weekly trading volume for the previous four weeks, whichever is greater:

$$1\% \times 1{,}500{,}000 \text{ shares outstanding} = 15{,}000 \text{ shares}$$

$$\frac{16{,}000 + 15{,}000 + 17{,}000 + 15{,}000}{4 \text{ weeks}} = \frac{63{,}000}{4 \text{ weeks}} = 15{,}750 \text{ shares}$$

WARNING

In this case, the previous four weeks are the top four in the list, but be careful, the examiners are just as likely to use the bottom four to give the table a different look.

Figure out 1 percent of the outstanding shares by multiplying the outstanding shares by 1 percent. (Easy, right?) In this case, you come up with an answer of 15,000 shares. The other possible answer is the average weekly trading volume for the previous four weeks. Add the trading volume for the previous four weeks (the top four in the chart) and divide by 4 to get an answer of 15,750 shares. Because you're looking for the greater number, the answer is (B).

Testing Your Knowledge

This chapter covers what you need to know about underwriting securities (at least as far as the SIE exam goes). When you're ready, use this section to attack some questions. Read carefully so that you don't make any careless mistakes and be sure to check your answers and understanding later in this section.

Practice questions

1. Which of the following agreements specify that any unsold securities are retained by the underwriters?

   (A) Firm commitment

   (B) All-or-none

   (C) Firm commitment, all-or-none, or mini-max

   (D) All-or-none, best efforts, or mini-max

2. Which of the following are exempt transactions?

   (A) Private placements and intrastate offerings

   (B) Private placements, securities issued by the U.S. government, and commercial paper

   (C) Securities issued by the U.S. government and commercial paper

   (D) Private placements, securities issued by the U.S. government, intrastate offerings, and commercial paper

3. The trading volume for BBB Corporation for the previous five weeks is as follows:

March 31: 50,000 shares

March 24: 38,000 shares

March 17: 44,000 shares

March 10: 40,000 shares

March 3: 42,000 shares

BBB Corporation is listed on an exchange and has 4.2 million shares outstanding. What is the maximum number of shares an insider can sell under Rule 144 on April 4 of the following year?

(A) 41,000

(B) 42,000

(C) 43,000

(D) 44,000

4. Bullbear Broker–Dealer is managing an IPO that won't be on the NYSE, Nasdaq, or any exchange. How long after the effective date must Bullbear provide a final prospectus to all purchasers of the security?

(A) 25 days

(B) 40 days

(C) 45 days

(D) 90 days

5. A preliminary prospectus would include which of the following?

I. An SEC disclaimer

II. The names of the officers of the issuing corporation

III. The public offering price

IV. An explanation of what the funds raised by the offering would be used for

(A) I and IV

(B) I, II, and IV

(C) II, III, and IV

(D) I, II, III, and IV

6. Which federal law regulates the initial sale of stock to the public?

(A) Securities Act of 1933

(B) Securities Exchange Act of 1934

(C) Trust Indenture Act

(D) All of the above

7. Which of the following may be included in a tombstone advertisement?

(A) The number of securities to be sold

(B) The issuer's name

(C) All underwriters' names

(D) All of the above

8. The post-filing cooling-off period usually lasts about

(A) 20 days

(B) 30 days

(C) 45 days

(D) 90 days

9. At what point is a broker–dealer allowed to accept payment for a new issue?

(A) After the customer has received the red herring

(B) Once the registration is effective

(C) During the cooling-off period

(D) As soon as the registration statement has been filed

10. All of the following securities are exempt from registration under the Securities Act of 1933 **except**

(A) Treasury bonds

(B) General obligation bonds

(C) Eurodollar bonds

(D) ADRs

Answers and explanations

1. **A.** In a firm-commitment underwriting, all securities left unsold are retained by the underwriters. All-or-none and mini-max are actually best-efforts underwritings.

2. **D.** This one is tricky, because all the transactions are exempt. Regulation D private placements and intrastate offerings are exempt based on the type of transactions. But securities issued by the U.S. government and commercial paper are exempt based on the type of security.

3. **C.** Because the holding period has been met, the maximum number of shares that can be sold by an insider under Rule 144 is 1 percent of the outstanding shares or the average trading volume for the previous four weeks, whichever is greater. Check out the math:

$$1\% \times 4{,}200{,}000 = 42{,}000 \text{ shares}$$

$$\frac{50{,}000 + 38{,}000 + 44{,}000 + 40{,}000}{4 \text{ weeks}} = \frac{172{,}000 \text{ shares}}{4 \text{ weeks}} = 43{,}000 \text{ shares}$$

   In this case, the previous four weeks were the top ones on the list, but be careful; they're just as likely to be the bottom four. In this case, the answer is 43,000 shares because it's larger than 42,000.

4. **D.** For IPOs, a final prospectus must be available to all purchasers for 90 days after the effective date.

5. **B.** All the choices would be in the preliminary prospectus (red herring) except the final offering price. The offering price at this point hasn't been determined. The offering price, the underwriting spread, and the delivery date would be included in the final prospectus.

6. **A.** The Securities Act of 1933 (Truth in Securities Act, Paper Act, Full Disclosure Act, Prospectus Act, or New Issues Act) regulates new issues of corporate stocks and bonds. Included in the act are rules to prevent fraud and deception, as well as rules about the issuer's providing information about itself and the securities being offered.

7. **D.** Tombstone advertisements may include the name of the issuer, the type of security being offered, the offering price (or approximate offering price), the names of the underwriters, and the number of securities being offered.

8. **A.** The cooling-off period is when an issuer files a registration statement with the SEC. During this time, the SEC reviews the registration statement to see whether it needs to be amended or additional information is needed. It typically takes 20 days for the SEC to review the registration statement. This period is sometimes referred to as the *20-day cooling-off period.*

9. **B.** After the registration is effective (the effective date), the broker–dealer is allowed to accept payments for the new issue.

10. **D.** U.S. Treasury securities (Treasury bonds, Treasury notes, Treasury bills, TIPS, and so on), municipal bonds (general obligation bonds, revenue bonds, and so on), and Eurodollar bonds are exempt from SEC registration. U.S. Treasury securities are backed by the federal government, and municipal bonds are backed by a state or local government. Eurodollar bonds are dollar-denominated bonds issued in Europe, and, therefore, must register in the country of issue. ADRs (American Depositary Receipts) are receipts for foreign securities traded in the United States and, therefore, must be registered in the United States.

IN THIS CHAPTER

» Understanding the types of equity securities

» Comparing common stock with preferred stock

» Calculating certain values for stock questions

» Testing yourself

Chapter 6

Equity Securities: Corporate Ownership

Equity securities — such as common and preferred stock — represent ownership interest in the issuing corporation. All publicly held corporations issue common stock to investors. Investors love these securities because they've historically outperformed most other investments, so an average (or outstanding, in your case) stockbroker typically sells more of these types of securities than any other kind.

The SIE exam tests your ability to recognize the types of equity securities and some other basic information. Although you may find that the SIE doesn't test you heavily on the info provided here, this chapter forms a strong foundation for many other chapters in the book, as well as a good base for other securities exams you may be taking after this one. For argument's sake, I think you'll find it difficult (if not impossible) to understand what an option or mutual fund is if you don't know what a stock is. Needless to say, even though this chapter is small, don't ignore it; if you do, it may come back to bite you.

At the end of this chapter, you can find some equity security questions to reinforce what is covered in this chapter. This section is where you get to shine.

Starting with the Basics: Common Stock

Corporations issue common stock (as well as other securities, such as bonds) to raise business capital (money). As an equity security, common stock represents ownership of the issuing corporation. If a corporation issues 1 million shares of stock, each share represents one-millionth ownership of the issuing corporation. The market value of a common stock is based on the worth (or perceived worth) of the company — how many shares are outstanding, supply and demand, and so on.

Stockholders have a *right of inspection*. This means that they have the right to inspect some books and records of the issuer. These include a list of stockholders and the minutes of the stockholders' meetings. This information is typically available through an audited annual report.

Stockholders have *limited liability*. Stockholders' liability is limited to the amount invested. In other words, if a corporation that you invested in goes belly up (Chapter 11 bankruptcy), you lose only what you invested; nobody will come knocking on your door for additional bucks. If a corporation happens to go bankrupt, however, it must distribute any remaining assets in the following way (also known as the *order of liquidation*):

1. Unpaid workers
2. The Internal Revenue Service (IRS)
3. Secured creditors

   Secured creditors have issued loans that are secured with collateral, bonds, and so on.
4. General creditors

   General creditors have issued unsecured loans, which aren't secured with collateral (bank loans, accounts payable, debentures, and so on).
5. Subordinated debentures

   Subordinated debentures are junior unsecured bonds; holders of subordinated debentures are the last creditors to be paid in the event of corporate bankruptcy.
6. Preferred stockholders
7. Common stockholders

REMEMBER

Common and preferred stockholders get paid after the creditors (if there's any money left). Common stockholders have what are known as *residual rights*, which means that they're the last to get paid in the event of corporate bankruptcy. Bonds and preferred stock are considered to be *senior securities* in relationship to common stock.

Understanding a shareholder's voting rights

One of the most basic rights that most common stockholders receive is voting rights, although certain corporations will issue *nonvoting common stock* in rare circumstances, sometimes to protect their board of directors. But nonvoting stock is not as attractive to investors who like to have some control of who's running the company. Most preferred stock, however, is nonvoting. (See "Getting Preferential Treatment: Preferred Stock" later in the chapter.)

When investors have voting rights, every so often a corporation may have those investors vote to change members of the board of directors. Although investors may be able to vote on other issues, such as stock splits (see "Splitting common stock" later in this chapter), the SIE focuses on voting to change board members.

Because having all stockholders attend the annual corporate meeting to vote would be difficult, stockholders usually vote by *proxy* — absentee ballot, in other words. (See "Proxies: Voting by mail" later in this chapter.)

Statutory (regular) voting

Statutory, or regular, voting is the most common type of voting that corporations offer their shareholders. This type of voting is quite straightforward. Investors receive one vote for every share they own, multiplied by the number of positions to be filled on the board of directors (or issues to be decided). But investors have to *split the votes evenly* for each item on the ballot.

For example, if an investor who decides to vote owns 500 shares and there are four positions that need to be filled on the board of directors, the investor has a total 2,000 votes (500 × 4 candidates), which the investor must split evenly among all open positions (500 each). The investor votes yes or no for each candidate.

Cumulative voting

Cumulative voting is a little different from statutory voting. Although the investor still gets the same number of overall votes as in statutory voting, the stockholder can vote the shares in any way they see fit. Cumulative voting gives smaller shareholders (in terms of shares) an easier way to gain representation on the board of directors.

If an investor owns 1,000 shares, and three positions on the board of directors are open, the investor has a total of 3,000 votes (1,000 shares × 3 candidates), which the investor can use to vote for any candidate(s) in any way they see fit.

REMEMBER

Cumulative voting doesn't give an investor more voting power — just more voting flexibility. The only way to get more voting power is to buy more shares.

Try your hand at the following cumulative voting question.

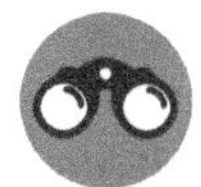
EXAMPLE

Under cumulative-voting rules, an owner of 1,000 shares of DEF common stock who is voting for four members on the DEF board of directors could cast:

(A) 1,000 votes for each of the four candidates

(B) 3,500 votes for one candidate and split the remaining votes over the other three positions

(C) 4,000 votes for one candidate

(D) All of the above

The answer you're looking for is (D). Cumulative voting allows investors to split their votes in any way. In this case, an owner of 1,000 shares of DEF common stock voting for four members on the board of directors would have a total 4,000 votes (1,000 shares × 4 board positions). So (A), (B), and (C) are all possibilities. Under statutory voting, the only way the investor could vote is (A).

Proxies: Voting by mail

Regardless of whether a corporation offers statutory or cumulative voting, when a corporation requires a vote on certain issues — such as splitting its stock, voting for members on the board of directors, and so on — shareholders (because they're owners) are allowed to vote unless the corporation issued nonvoting stock (Class B shares). Certainly, the more shares you own, the more voting power you have.

Now, suppose that you live in New York City, and the vote is taking place in Los Angeles. What do you do? Well, short of taking a trip across the country, you can vote by proxy (basically, an absentee ballot). The issuer will send you a proxy, which describes the issue(s) to be voted on. You can check the box describing how you want to vote and mail the proxy back. By doing that, you're authorizing (giving limited power of attorney to) another person to vote according to your wishes. A *transfer agent* is responsible for sending out proxies.

A *proxy fight* or *proxy battle* is an unfriendly event that occurs when a group of stockholders of a corporation decide to vote together to gain control of the corporation. This situation usually happens when the stockholders aren't happy with the way the corporation is being run. Typically, they're trying to replace members of the board of directors or people in management positions.

Categorizing shares corporations can sell

All publicly held corporations have a certain quantity of shares that they can sell based on their corporate charter. These shares are broken into a few categories, depending on whether the issuer or investors hold the shares:

- **Authorized shares:** *Authorized shares* are the number of shares of stock that a corporation can issue. The issuer's bylaws or *corporate charter* (a document filed with the state that identifies the names of the founders of the corporation, the company's objectives, and so on) states the number of shares the company is authorized to sell. The issuer usually holds back a large percentage of the authorized stock, which it can sell later as needed through a primary offering. (See Chapter 5 for details on offerings.) In the event that the issuer wishes to sell more shares than were previously authorized, the issuer's corporate charter would have to be updated, which would require a vote by stockholders.
- **Issued shares:** *Issued shares* are the portion of authorized shares that the issuer has actually sold to the public to raise money, including shares owned by founding shareholders. Logically, the portion of authorized shares that hasn't been issued to the public is called *unissued shares.* Unissued shares do not carry the rights and privileges of issued shares. Under SEC Rule 415, shares may be kept unissued for up to three years (shelf registration). (See Chapter 5 for more on this topic.)
- **Outstanding shares:** Outstanding shares are the number of shares that are in investors' hands. This quantity may or may not be the same number as the issued shares. At times, an issuer may decide to repurchase its stock in the market for numerous reasons, including to help increase the demand (and the price) of the stock trading in the market or to avoid a *hostile takeover* (when another company is trying to gain control of the issuer). Stock that the issuer repurchases from the outstanding shares is called *Treasury stock.* Only the issuer can own Treasury stock; stock owned by the CEO or founders is considered part of the outstanding stock.

  The standard formula for outstanding shares is

  $$\text{outstanding} = \text{issued} - \text{Treasury}$$

Here's a quick question about calculating outstanding shares. See how you do:

EXAMPLE

DEF Corp. has 20,000,000 shares of authorized stock. DEF has issued 15,000,000 shares and has since repurchased 1,500,000 shares. How many shares are outstanding?

(A) 13,500,000

(B) 15,000,000

(C) 16,500,000

(D) 20,000,000

The answer you're looking for is (A). Using the numbers given, you see that the corporation has 20,000,000 shares of authorized stock but has issued only 15,000,000. Since that time, the corporation has repurchased 1,500,000 shares (Treasury stock), so the number of outstanding shares is 13,500,000. Here's the equation:

$$\text{outstanding} = \text{issued} - \text{Treasury}$$
$$\text{outstanding} = 15{,}000{,}000 - 1{,}500{,}000 = 13{,}500{,}000$$

Establishing the par value of common stock

Par value (nominal or original value) for common stock is more or less a bookkeeping value for the issuer. Although issuers may set the par value at $1 (or 1 cent, $5, $10, or whatever), the market price is usually much more. A common stock's par value *has no relationship* to the market price of the stock. Although much rarer, some companies even issue stock with no par value. Par value for common stock isn't as important to investors as it is to bondholders and preferred stockholders (see "Considering characteristics of preferred stock" later in this chapter).

REMEMBER

The amount over par value that an issuer receives for selling stock is called *additional paid-in capital, paid-in surplus,* or *capital in excess of par.*

The *stated par value* is printed on the stock certificate; it may change as the result of corporate actions such as a stock split (see "Splitting common stock" later in this chapter). If an issuer issues *no par value stock* (stock issued without a stated par value), the stock has a stated value that the corporation uses for bookkeeping purposes. A lack of par value doesn't affect investors.

Considering corporate actions

Besides just attempting to build their business, corporations may take other actions that affect the price of their securities. They can split their stock (see the next section, "Splitting common stock"); reverse-split their stock (see the section "Reverse stock splits"); or engage in buybacks, tender offers, exchange offers, rights offerings (see the later section "Rights: Buying new shares at a discount"), mergers, or acquisitions.

Here are some of the corporate actions:

- **Buybacks:** A buyback happens when a cash-rich corporation repurchases some of its own shares in the market, turning them into Treasury stock. Buybacks typically increase the market value of the underlying security. After a successful buyback, fewer shares are outstanding.
- **Tender offers:** A tender offer occurs when a corporation, person, or group attempts to gain control (make a *takeover bid*) of a corporation (the *target corporation*). A tender offer is typically announced in financial publications, and the offer will be at a premium to the market value of the securities. Tender offers are good for a specified period and specified minimum number of holders of shares (in other words, holders of more than 50 percent of the outstanding shares of the target corporation) must agree; otherwise, the offer is canceled. Tender offers increase the market price of the securities being targeted.
- **Exchange offers:** Sometimes, a corporation decides to exchange some of its securities for other ones. A corporation may offer its bondholders the right to exchange certain debt securities for stock to reduce the corporation's debt. Or a corporation may offer to exchange 4 percent bonds due to mature in 2 years with 5 percent bonds due to mature in 20 years, thus extending the amount of time the corporation has to pay back its debt.
- **Mergers:** Two existing corporations may decide to merge their two companies, often to gain market share, expand one corporation's reach, or possibly to expand into new segments. Mergers typically have a positive impact on investors.
- **Acquisitions:** Compared with a merger, in which two corporations work together to make one big corporation, an acquisition happens when a larger corporation takes control of a smaller one or a portion of another corporation. For one corporation to acquire another, it must obtain majority ownership of the target corporation.

TIP

As you can imagine, in the event of a corporate action such as a stock split, a merger, an acquisition, and so on, investors of the securities must be notified. For public companies listed on an exchange such as the New York Stock Exchange (NYSE), the exchanges handle notification of clients and make the information available online. If the securities trade over the counter (OTC), the Financial Industry Regulatory Authority (FINRA) is responsible for handling the announcement.

Splitting common stock

You may ask "Why would a company split its stock?" Obviously in addition to showing investors that their company is growing, it also makes the market price of the security more attractive. The normal unit of trading is 100 shares of stock *(a round lot)*, and if the share price of a security gets too high, the number of investors who can purchase it becomes limited. If Microsoft had never split its stock (which it has done nine times, all 2-for-1 or 3-for-2, the last time being in 2003), a round lot would cost investors over $12 million. Know a lot of investors who could afford that?

Alternatively, companies may use a *reverse-split*, consolidating shares to raise the price of the stock and perhaps keep the price of their stock from dropping too low and possibly face being delisted. The next couple of sections take you through splits so that you know them forward and backward.

REMEMBER

Stockholders can vote on stock splits. (Refer to "Understanding a shareholder's voting rights," earlier in the chapter, for info on types of voting.) Be aware that after a stock split, investors may have more or fewer votes, but they still hold the same percentage of votes. When a company splits its stock, the number of authorized shares needs to be changed on the *corporate charter* (refer to "Categorizing shares corporations can sell" earlier in this chapter).

Forward stock splits

During a *forward stock split*, or simply a *split*, the number of shares increases, and the price decreases without affecting the total market value of the outstanding shares. After a company forward-splits its stock, investors receive additional shares, but the market price (and par value) per share drops. A forward split may be *even* (2-for-1, 3-for-1, 4-for-1, and so on) or *uneven* (3-for-2, 5-for-3, 5-for-2, and so on). You'll find that whether the forward split is even or uneven, the same formula works. Check out the following equations, in which *A* represents the first number and *B* represents the second number.

Use the following calculations to figure out an investor's position after an *A*-for-*B* split:

$$\text{shares after a split} = \text{shares} \times \frac{A}{B} \qquad \text{price after a split} = \text{stock price} \times \frac{B}{A}$$

The following question tests your ability to answer a forward-stock-split question.

EXAMPLE

Bob Billingham owns 1,200 shares of DEF common stock at a current market price of $90 per share. If DEF splits its stock 3-for-1, what would Bob's position be after the split?

(A) 400 shares at $270 per share

(B) 400 shares at $90 per share

(C) 3,600 shares at $33.33 per share

(D) 3,600 shares at $30 per share

The answer you're looking for is (D). A forward stock split, like a 3-for-1, increases the number of shares and decreases the price of the stock, so you can immediately cross off (A) and (B). Choice (C) doesn't work because the price of the stock would have to be 1/3 of $90, which is $30, not $33.33. Now check your work:

$$1{,}200 \text{ shares} \times \frac{3}{1} = 3{,}600 \text{ shares} \qquad \$90 \times \frac{1}{3} = \$30$$

TIP

A good way to double-check your work is to make sure that the overall value of the investment doesn't change after the split. Using the example, Bob had $108,000 worth of DEF (1,200 shares × $90) before the split, and after the split, Bob has $108,000 worth of DEF (3,600 shares × $30).

Reverse stock splits

A reverse stock split has the opposite effect on a security from a forward split. In a reverse-split, the market price of the security increases, and the number of shares decreases. As with forward stock splits, the overall market value of the securities doesn't change. A company may reverse-split its stock if the market price gets too low, which may make potential investors think that the company has a problem.

In the event of a reverse-split, investors usually have to send their old shares to the transfer agent to receive the new shares. If a company were executing a 1-for-3 reverse-split, investors would receive one new share for every three they sent in.

TIP

You can use the same formula to determine an investor's position after a reverse-split that you use for forward splits.

The following question tests your ability to answer a reverse-stock-split question.

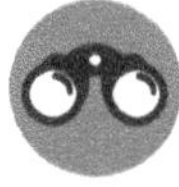

EXAMPLE

Betty Billings owns 3,600 shares of GHI common stock at a current market price of $2 per share. If GHI reverse-splits its stock 1-for-5, what would Betty's position be after the split?

(A) 600 shares at $10 per share

(B) 720 shares at $10 per share

(C) 18,000 shares at 40 cents per share

(D) 18,000 shares at $10 per share

The correct answer is (B). In a reverse-split, the number of shares has to decrease and the price has to increase, so you can immediately eliminate (C) and (D). Choice (A) doesn't work because the investor would end up with too few shares. Check your work:

$$3{,}600 \text{ shares} \times \frac{1}{5} = 720 \text{ shares} \qquad \$2 \times \frac{5}{1} = \$10$$

Sharing corporate profits through dividends

If a corporation is profitable (and the board of directors is in a good mood), the board of directors may decide to issue a stock dividend to investors. If and when the corporation declares a dividend, each shareholder is entitled to a *pro rata* share of dividends, meaning that every shareholder receives an equal proportion for each share that they own. The SIE exam expects you to know the forms of dividends an investor can receive and how the dividends affect both the market price of the stock and an investor's position. Although the investor can receive dividends in cash, stock, or *property forms* (stock of a subsidiary company or sample products made by the issuer), I focus on cash and stock dividends because those scenarios are more common.

REMEMBER

Investors can't vote on dividends; instead, the board of directors decides dividend payouts. You can imagine that if this decision were left in the investors' hands, they'd vote for dividends weekly! For more info on voting, refer to "Understanding a shareholder's voting rights" earlier in this chapter. Even profitable companies may not pay a cash dividend because they may want to reinvest profits back in the company.

Cash dividends

Cash dividends are a way for a corporation to share its profits with shareholders. When an investor receives cash dividends, the payout is a taxable event. Corporations aren't required to pay dividends, but dividends provide a good incentive for investors to hold onto stock that isn't experiencing much growth. Although cash dividends are nice, the market price of the stock falls on the *ex-dividend date* (the first day the stock trades without a dividend) to reflect the dividend to be paid on the payment date announced:

$$\text{stock price} - \text{dividend} = \text{price on ex} - \text{dividend date}$$

Try your hand at answering a cash-dividend question.

EXAMPLE

The closing price for ABC stock is $49.50 on the day before the ex-dividend date. If ABC previously announced a dividend of 75 cents, what will the next day's opening price be?

(A) $48.25

(B) $48.75

(C) $49.50

(D) $50.25

The correct answer is (B). Check your work:

$$\$49.50 - \$0.75 = \$48.75$$

The math's as simple as that. Because now stocks are trading in pennies instead of eighths, as they used to, calculating the price on the ex-dividend date is a snap.

Stock dividends

Stock dividends are just like forward stock splits in that the investor receives more shares of stock (refer to "Splitting common stock" earlier in this chapter), but the corporation offers a percentage dividend (5 percent, 10 percent, and so on) instead of splitting the stock 2-for-1, 3-for-1, or whatever. Unlike cash dividends, stock dividends aren't taxable to the stockholder because the investor's overall value of investment doesn't change.

The primary reason for a company to give investors a stock dividend is to make the market price more attractive to investors (if the market price gets too high, it limits the number of investors who can purchase the stock), thus adding *liquidity* (ease of trading) to the stock.

The following question tests your expertise in answering stock-dividend questions.

EXAMPLE

An investor owns 400 shares of OXX common stock at $33 per share. OXX previously declared a 10 percent stock dividend. Assuming that there's no change in the market price of OXX before the dividend, what is the investor's position after the dividend?

(A) 400 shares at $30

(B) 440 shares at $33

(C) 400 shares at $36.30

(D) 440 shares at $30

The answer you want is (D). In this case, you can find the answer without doing any math. Because the number of shares increases, the price of the stock has to decrease. Therefore, the only answer that works is (D). I can't guarantee that you'll get a question for which you don't have to do the math, but don't rule it out; scan the answer choices before pulling out your calculator.

Anyway, here's how the numbers work. You have to remember that the investor's overall value of investment doesn't change. The investor gets a 10 percent stock dividend, so they receive 10 percent more shares. Now the investor has 440 shares of OXX (400 shares + 40 shares [10 percent of 400]). Next, you need to determine their overall value of investment:

$$400 \text{ shares} \times \$33 = \$13{,}200$$

Because the overall value of investment doesn't change, the investor needs to have $13,200 worth of OXX after the dividend:

$$\frac{\$13{,}200}{440 \text{ shares}} = \$30 \text{ per share}$$

Their position after the split is 440 shares at $30 per share.

REMEMBER

When you or one of your clients own securities subject to corporate actions such as splits, stock dividends, mergers, and so on, the securities are going to change. In some cases, such as forward stock splits and stock dividends, you or your client will receive more shares at a lower cost basis, and the cost basis of the shares held will be lowered accordingly. The adjustment to the cost basis is important for tax purposes when determining the amount of capital gains or losses.

For argument's sake, suppose that you purchased 1,000 shares of UPPP Corporation at $40 per share. In this case, you have stock with a cost basis of $40,000 (1,000 shares at $40 per share). If the stock splits 2-for-1, you have two shares for every one purchased. The corporation isn't just giving you another $40,000 worth of stock; it cut the price in half to adjust for the split. As the market price gets cut in half, so does the cost basis per share. In the example, now you have 2,000 shares with a cost basis of $20 per share ($40,000 cost basis) even if the market value is $55,000. In the event of a split, the issuer would adjust your shares to reflect a lower par value. In the event of an exchange offer, merger, or acquisition, the security that you're holding would likely change. In this case (assuming that you physically held the security), the issuer would be responsible for mailing the new security. Whether the securities are physically held, which is becoming increasingly rare, or in book-entry form, the issuer must update its books for any changes.

Getting Preferential Treatment: Preferred Stock

Equity securities represent shares of ownership in a company, and debt securities represent . . . well, debt. (See Chapters 7 and 8 for info on debt securities.) Although preferred stock (sometimes called *preferreds*) has some characteristics of both equity and debt securities, preferred stock is an equity security because it represents ownership of the issuing corporation the same way that common stock does.

Considering characteristics of preferred stock

One advantage of purchasing preferred stock instead of common stock is that preferred shareholders receive money back (if any is left) before common stockholders do if the issuer declares bankruptcy. However, the main difference between preferred stock and common stock has to do with dividends. Issuers of common stock typically pay a cash dividend only if the company is in a position to share corporate profits based on a vote by the board of directors. By contrast, issuers of preferred stock typically pay consistent cash dividends. Depending on the corporation's financial condition, they may reduce or stop the dividend payments. Preferred stock generally has a par value of $100 per share (although it could be $50, $25, and so on) and tends to trade in the market much closer to its par value than common stock does.

Because preferred stocks receive (or are supposed to receive) a consistent dividend, they're somewhat like debt securities receiving interest. Because of that similarity, like debt securities (bonds), many preferred stocks are rated by rating agencies such as Moody's, Standard & Poor's, and Fitch. (For more on rating agencies, see Chapter 7.)

Some of the drawbacks of investing in preferred stock instead of common stock are the lack of voting rights, the sometimes-higher cost per share, and lack of growth. You can assume for SIE exam purposes that preferred stockholders don't receive voting rights unless they fail to receive their expected dividends. (A few other exceptions exist, but you don't need to worry about them now.) Also, because most preferred stock pays consistent dividends, the market price will increase or decrease depending on prevailing interest rates similar to debt securities.

REMEMBER

If the issuer can't make a payment because earnings are low, and if the preferred stock is *cumulative* (see "Getting familiar with types of preferred stock," the next section in this chapter), owners are still owed the missing dividend payment(s). The dividend (sharing of profits) that preferred stockholders receive is based on par value. Thus, although par value may be nothing more than a bookkeeping value when you're dealing with common stock, par value is definitely important to preferred stockholders.

To calculate the annual dividend, multiply the percentage of the dividend by the par value. If a customer owns a preferred stock that pays a 6 percent dividend, and the par value is $100, set up the following equation:

$$6\%\ \text{preferred stock} \times \$100\ \text{par} = \$6\ \text{per year in dividends}$$

If the issuer were to pay this dividend quarterly (once every three months), an investor would receive $1.50 ($6/4) every three months for each share owned.

REMEMBER

When working on a dividend question on preferred stock, you need to look for the par value in the problem. Par value normally is $100, but it could be $25, $50, and so on.

Getting familiar with types of preferred stock

You need to be aware of several types of preferred stock for the Series 7. This section gives you a brief explanation of the types. Some preferred stock may be a combination of types, as in cumulative convertible preferred stock. Here are the distinctions between noncumulative and cumulative preferred stock:

- **Noncumulative (straight) preferred:** This type of preferred stock is rare. The main feature of preferred stock is that investors typically receive a consistent cash dividend. In the event that the issuer doesn't pay the dividend, the company usually still owes it to investors. This isn't the case for noncumulative preferred stock. If the preferred stock is noncumulative, and the issuer fails to pay a dividend, the issuer doesn't owe it to investors. An investor may choose noncumulative preferred stock over common stock because the company is still supposed to pay a consistent cash dividend and, in the event of corporate bankruptcy, preferred stockholders still get paid before common stockholders. Because noncumulative preferred stock is riskier for investors, they're typically offered a higher dividend.

» **Cumulative preferred:** Cumulative preferred stock is more common. If an investor owns cumulative preferred stock and doesn't receive an expected dividend, the issuer is in arrears and still owes that dividend. Before paying a common dividend, the issuer first has to make up all delinquent payments to cumulative preferred stockholders, then other preferred shareholders. As such, cumulative preferred stock is a safer investment than noncumulative preferred stock.

REMEMBER

Because preferred stock is senior to common stock, if the issuer misses a dividend payment to preferred stockholders, the issuer can't make a dividend payment to its common stockholders until the preferred dividend payments resume.

The following question tests your understanding of cumulative preferred stock.

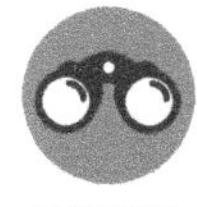
EXAMPLE

An ABC investor owns 8 percent cumulative preferred stock ($100 par). In the first year, ABC paid $6 in dividends; in the second year, it paid $4 in dividends. If a common dividend is declared the following year, how much must the preferred shareholders receive?

(A) $6

(B) $8

(C) $12

(D) $14

The right answer is (D). Because ABC is cumulative preferred stock, issuers have to catch up preferred stockholders on all outstanding dividends before common shareholders receive a dividend. In this example, the investor is supposed to receive $8 per year in dividends ($8 \times \$100\,\text{par}$). In the first year, the issuer shorted the investor $2; in the second year, $4. The investor hasn't yet received payment for the following year, so they are owed $8. Add up these debts:

$$(\$8 - \$6) + (\$8 - \$4) + \$8 = \$2 + \$4 + \$8 = \$14$$

All preferred stock has to be either cumulative or noncumulative. Both types may have other features, including the capability to turn into other kinds of stock, offerings of extra dividends, and other VIP treatment. I run through some of these traits in the list that follows:

» **Convertible preferred:** Convertible preferred stock allows investors to exchange their preferred stock for common stock of the same company at any time. Because the issuers are providing investors another way to make money, investors usually receive a lower dividend payment than with nonconvertible preferred stock.

The *conversion price* is the dollar price at which a convertible preferred stock par value can be exchanged for a share of common stock. When the convertible preferred stock is first issued, the conversion price is specified, based on the preferred's par value. The *conversion ratio* tells you the number of shares of common stock that an investor receives for converting one share of preferred stock.

You can use the following conversion ratio formula for convertible preferred stock and also for convertible bonds (see Chapter 7 for info on convertible bonds):

$$\text{conversion ratio} = \frac{\text{par value}}{\text{conversion price}}$$

REMEMBER

The conversion ratio helps you determine a *parity price* at which the convertible preferred stock and common stock would be trading equally. Suppose that you have a convertible preferred stock that's exchangeable for four shares of common stock. If the convertible preferred stock is trading at $100, and the common stock is trading at $25, they're on parity because four shares of stock at $25 equal $100. If there's a disparity in the exchange values, however, converting may be profitable. If the convertible preferred stock is trading at $100, and the common stock is trading at $28, the common stock is trading above parity; converting would be profitable because investors are exchanging $100 worth of securities for $112 worth of securities ($28 × 4). Convertible preferred stock typically trades very close to the parity price.

- **Callable preferred:** Callable preferred stock allows the issuer to buy back the preferred stock at any time after a defined date at the price (the *call price*) on the certificate. This stock is a little riskier for investors because they don't have control of how long they can hold the stock, so corporations usually pay a higher dividend on callable preferred stock than on regular preferred stock. A call feature may be added to other types of preferred stock such as callable convertible preferred.
- **Participating preferred:** Although rarely issued, participating preferred stock allows the investors to receive common dividends in addition to the usual preferred dividends up to a certain amount. Most preferred stock is non-participating, meaning that they don't receive common dividends, only preferred dividends.
- **Prior (senior) preferred:** Your run-of-the-mill preferred stockholders receive compensation before common stockholders in the event of corporate bankruptcy. Senior preferred stockholders, however, receive compensation even before other preferred stockholders. Because of the extra safety factor, senior preferred stock pays a slightly lower dividend than other preferred stock from the same issuer.
- **Adjustable (variable- or floating-rate) preferred:** Holders of adjustable preferred stock receive a dividend that's reset every three months to match movements in the prevailing interest rates. Because the dividend adjusts to changing interest rates (usually based off of a certain benchmark such as the T-bill rate), the stock price remains more stable.

Securities with a Twist

Some securities fall outside the boundaries of the more normal common and preferred stock, but I still include them in this equities chapter because they involve ownership in a company or the opportunity to get it. This section gives you an overview of those special securities.

Opening national borders: ADRs

American Depositary Receipts (ADRs) are receipts for foreign securities traded in the United States. ADRs are negotiable certificates (they can be sold or transferred to another party, in other words) that represent a specific number of shares (usually, one to ten) of a foreign stock. In many cases, ADR investors don't have voting privileges because the shares are held by the bank. In some cases, ADR holders may be able to give voting instructions to the bank, who can vote on their behalf. U.S. banks issue these stock certificates; therefore, investors receive dividends in U.S. dollars. The certificates are held in a foreign branch of a U.S. bank (the custodian bank). To exchange their ADRs for the actual shares, investors return the ADRs to the bank that's holding the shares.

In addition to the risks associated with stock ownership in general, ADR owners are subject to *currency risk* (the risk that the value of the security may decline because the value of the currency of the issuing corporation may fall in relation to the U.S. dollar) as well as *political risk*, which may be higher than U.S. securities. For information on how the strength of the dollar affects the relative prices of goods in the international market, flip to Chapter 13.

Rights: Buying new shares at a discount

Corporations offer special privileges known as *rights* (subscription or preemptive) to their common stockholders. To maintain stockholders' proportionate ownership of the corporation, rights allow existing stockholders to purchase new shares of the corporation at a fixed *discounted price* directly from the issuer, before the shares are offered to the public. Stockholders receive one right for each share they own. The rights are short-term — usually, 16 to 30 days, but in some cases may go up to 60. The rights are marketable, and stockholders may sell them to other investors. If existing stockholders don't purchase all the shares, the issuer offers any unsold shares to a *standby underwriter* — a broker-dealer that purchases any shares that weren't sold in the rights offering and resells them to other investors.

TIP

For the SIE exam, you can assume that common stockholders automatically receive rights.

Warrants: The right to buy shares of stock at a fixed price

Warrants are certificates that entitle the holder to buy a specific amount of stock at a fixed price and are usually issued along with a new bond, preferred stock, or other securities offering. Warrant holders have no voting rights and receive no dividends. Bundled bonds and warrants or bundled stock and warrants are called *units*. Unlike rights, warrants are long-term and sometimes perpetual (without an expiration date). Warrants are *sweeteners* because they're something that the issuer throws into the new offering to make the deal more appealing, but they can also be sold separately just like any other marketable security. As you can imagine, when warrants are issued, the warrant's *exercise price* (the price at which the investor can utilize the warrant to buy the stock) is set well above the underlying stock's market price.

Suppose that QRS warrants give investors the right to buy QRS common stock at $20 per share when QRS common stock is trading at $12. Certainly, exercising their warrants to purchase QRS stock at $20 wouldn't make sense for investors when they can buy QRS stock in the market at $12. If QRS rises above $20 per share, however, holders of warrants can exercise their warrants and purchase the stock from the issuer at $20 per share.

TIP

On the SIE exam, both rights and warrants may be referred to as *derivative securities* because their value is derived from the value of an underlying security (common stock of the issuer).

Testing Your Knowledge

Now that you've learned what you need to know about equity securities (at least as far as the SIE exam goes), it's time to attack some questions. Read carefully so that you don't make any careless mistakes.

Practice questions

1. Common stockholders have the right to vote for which of the following?

   (A) Stock splits and cash dividends

   (B) Stock splits and the board of directors

   (C) Cash dividends and the board of directors

   (D) Stock splits, cash dividends, and the board of directors

2. DIMM Corporation has just declared bankruptcy. Remaining assets would be distributed in which way (from first to last)?

   (A) IRS, unpaid workers, general creditors, preferred stockholders, secured creditors, subordinated debenture holders, and common stockholders

   (B) Common stockholders, general creditors, preferred stockholders, subordinated debenture holders, secured creditors, IRS, and unpaid workers

   (C) Unpaid workers, IRS, secured creditors, general creditors, subordinated debenture holders, preferred stockholders, and common stockholders

   (D) IRS, unpaid workers, secured creditors, subordinated debenture holders, general creditors, preferred stockholders, and common stockholders

3. Ayla K. owns 2,000 shares of JKL common stock. JKL has four vacancies on the board of directors. If the voting is cumulative, Ayla may vote in any of the following ways **except**

   (A) 2,000 votes for each of the four candidate positions

   (B) 4,000 votes each for two candidate positions

   (C) 5,000 votes for one candidate position and 3,000 votes for another candidate position

   (D) 3,000 votes for each of three candidate positions

4. The par value of a common stock is

   (A) in direct relation to the market value

   (B) used only for bookkeeping purposes

   (C) always set at $1 unless the stock is issued as no par value

   (D) the basis for which cash dividends are paid

5. Tender offers typically ______________ the price of the outstanding shares of a corporation.

   (A) increase

   (B) decrease

   (C) don't affect

   (D) increase or decrease

6. Which of the following are true regarding ADRs?

   I. They're receipts for foreign securities in U.S. markets.

   II. Dividends are paid in the foreign currency.

   III. They're negotiable.

   (A) I and III

   (B) I and II

   (C) II and III

   (D) I, II, and III

7. Declan Hudson owns 1,200 shares of ABCD Corporation common stock. ABCD announces a 1-for-2 reverse-split. If the price of ABCD closed at $10 the day before the split, what would Declan's position be after the split?

(A) 2,400 shares at $20

(B) 2,400 shares at $5

(C) 600 shares at $5

(D) 600 shares at $20

8. An investor purchased 200 shares of DDD common stock at $41 per share. DDD previously announced a 5 percent stock dividend payable to shareholders of record. On the date before the ex-dividend date, DDD closed at $44 per share. What would the investor's position be on the ex-dividend date?

(A) 200 shares at $39.05 per share

(B) 200 shares at $41.90 per share

(C) 210 shares at $39.05 per share

(D) 210 shares at $41.90 per share

9. WXY Corporation common stock closed at $45 on the business day before the ex-dividend date. If WXY previously announced a 77-cent dividend, at what price will the stock open the next trading day?

(A) 44.22

(B) 44.23

(C) 45.00

(D) 45.77

10. A corporation has issued 6 percent $100 par cumulative preferred stock. It paid $4 in dividends the first year and $3 in dividends the second year. If the corporation wants to declare a dividend for common shareholders the following year, how much must it pay per share to its cumulative preferred stockholders?

(A) $5

(B) $6

(C) $11

(D) $14

11. Which of the following preferred stocks would most likely pay the highest dividend if issued by the same corporation?

(A) Callable preferred

(B) Convertible preferred

(C) Prior preferred

(D) Can't be determined

12. Rights are automatically received by

(A) convertible preferred stockholders

(B) senior preferred stockholders

(C) common stockholders

(D) both (A) and (B)

13. Which of the following is/are true of warrants?

(A) They're long-term.

(B) They're considered to be sweeteners.

(C) They're marketable.

(D) All of the above.

14. STU Corporation would like to offer its existing shareholders the privilege to purchase additional shares at a fixed price. Which of the following securities would STU issue?

(A) Convertible preferred stock

(B) Call

(C) Rights

(D) Futures

15. Under statutory voting, an individual stockholder may vote for each vacancy on the board of directors equal to

(A) the number of vacancies on the board of directors

(B) the number of shares owned multiplied by the number of vacancies on the board of directors

(C) the number of shares owned by the stockholders

(D) any of the above

16. When a corporation splits is its stock,

(A) the price of their common stock increases

(B) the price of their common stock decreases

(C) each shareholder's proportionate ownership increases

(D) each shareholder's proportionate ownership decreases

17. In June, JKL Corporation announced a 20 percent stock dividend for its common shareholders. Ayla K. holds 2,000 shares of JKL common stock at $40 per share. After payment of the dividend, what would Ayla's new price per share be and how many shares would she be holding?

(A) 1,600 shares at $48.00

(B) 2,000 shares at $32.00

(C) 2,400 shares at $32.00

(D) 2,400 shares at $40.00

18. If a corporation were to go bankrupt, which of the following entities would have the highest claim on the assets in a Chapter 11 proceeding?

(A) Preferred shareholders

(B) Common shareholders

(C) Secured debt holders

(D) Unsecured debt holders

Answers and explanations

1. **B.** Of the choices given, common stockholders have the right to vote for stock splits and for members of the board of directors. Common stockholders can't vote for cash or stock dividends.

2. **C.** In the event that a corporation declares bankruptcy, the corporate assets are distributed in the following way: unpaid workers, IRS, secured creditors, general creditors, subordinated debenture holders, preferred stockholders, and finally (if there's anything left) common stockholders.

3. **D.** Because the voting is cumulative, Ayla has the right to vote as she sees fit. Ayla has 2,000 shares and is voting on 4 positions on the board of directors, so she has a total 8,000 votes (2,000 shares × 4 positions), which she can use in any way. The reason that (D) doesn't work is that it would require Ayla to have 9,000 votes (3,000 votes × 3 positions).

4. **B.** The issuer uses the par value of a common stock for bookkeeping purposes. Par value has no relationship with the market value; it has no relationship with dividends paid (if any); and even though it's often set at $1, it doesn't have to be.

5. **A.** Tender offers occur when a corporation, person, or group attempts to take control of a particular corporation, attempting to buy enough shares in the market to gain control. To purchase enough shares, the corporation, person, or group offers a premium over the current market price to sellers who are willing to sell a large number of securities. Because the offer is at a premium, tender offers drive up the price of the outstanding securities.

6. **A.** ADRs are receipts for foreign securities traded in the United States. ADRs are negotiable (can be sold or transferred to another party). Investors receive dividends in U.S. dollars, not the foreign currency. Because ADRs are receipts, investors don't receive the actual certificates.

7. **D.** Because ABCD is doing a reverse-split, Declan would have fewer shares after the split, and the price of the stock would increase. This transaction is a 1-for-2 reverse-split, so to determine the shares, you have to multiply them by 1 divided by 2. To get the price, you have to multiply it by 2 divided by 1. Check out the following equation:

$$\text{Shares after the split} = 1{,}200 \text{ shares} \times \frac{1}{2} = 600 \text{ shares}$$

$$\text{Price after the split} = \$10 \times \frac{2}{1} = \$20$$

8. **D.** You can cross out two answers to this question without doing the math. The investor received a stock dividend, so the number of shares had to increase. Therefore, (A) and (B) are out. Next, ignore the purchase price; you have to look at the overall value of the investment on the day before the ex-dividend date (the first day the stock trades without a dividend). In this case, the investor had 200 shares at $44 per share. Check out the math:

$$200 \text{ shares} \times \$44 = \$8{,}800$$

You can see that the investor had an overall value of investment on the day before the ex-dividend date of $8,800. That doesn't change due to the dividend. So, on the ex-dividend date, the investor still had $8,800 worth of stock. Now, however, the investor has 210 shares (200 shares + 10 shares [5% of 200]). By dividing the $8,800 shares by 210 shares, you'll get a price of $41.90 per share:

$$\frac{\$8{,}800}{210\text{ shares}} = \$41.90\text{ per share}$$

9. **B.** On the ex-dividend date, the stock would be reduced by the amount of the dividend. This question is fairly easy, but check out the math:

$$\begin{aligned}&\text{Stock price} - \text{dividend} = \text{price on the ex} - \text{dividend date}\\&\$45 - \$0.77 = \$44.23\end{aligned}$$

10. **C.** Because the stock is cumulative preferred stock, the corporation must make up any missed dividends to its cumulative preferred stockholders before paying a dividend to its common stockholders. In the first year, the corporation shorted its preferred stockholders $2 per share; it was supposed to pay $6 ($100 par × 6%) but paid only $4. In the second year, the corporation paid shareholders only $3, so they were shorted $3. So far, so good. But the key to this question is that the corporation wants to pay a common dividend the following year, so you have to add the $6 in dividends for that year also. Here's how it looks:

$$(\$6 - \$4) + (\$6 - \$3) + \$6 = \$11$$

11. **A.** Of the choices listed, callable preferred would most likely pay the highest dividend. Remember that more risk equals more reward. In other words, people who purchase callable preferred can't necessarily hold the stock as long as they want because after a predetermined date, the stock can be called by the issuer. Because the shares can be called, the issuer has to pay a higher dividend to entice investors to buy. Investors can convert convertible preferred stock to common stock of the issuing corporation at any time, so because that option is safer and gives investors more flexibility, the issuer would pay a lower dividend. Prior or senior preferred adds another layer of safety for investors; if the corporation were to go bankrupt, holders would get paid before other preferred stockholders. Accordingly, they receive a lower dividend.

12. **C.** Rights allow shareholders to purchase new shares issued by a corporation at a discount. Rights are short-term (typically, 30–45 days) and are available only to common stockholders.

13. **D.** Warrants allow shareholders to purchase shares of a corporation at a fixed price and are typically bundled with a stock or bond offering to sweeten the deal. Warrants are long-term and sometimes perpetual (never-ending). Because they can be traded separately, they're marketable securities.

14. **C.** If a corporation would like to offer its existing shareholders the right to purchase additional shares at a fixed price, they would have a rights offering. When there is a rights offering, existing shareholders have the right — but not the obligation — to purchase the new shares at a fixed price, which is at a discount from the market price at the time of the offering. Rights offerings typically only last from a couple of weeks up to 30 days. Any shares not purchased during the rights offering would be placed with a standby underwriter to sell.

15. **C.** Under statutory (regular) voting rules, individual stockholders may vote up to the amount of shares they own for each open position on the board of directors.

16. **B.** When a corporation splits its stock (2-for-1, 3-for-1, 3-for-2, and so on), the price of the stock decreases, and the amount of shares each shareholder has increases. This means that after the split, each shareholder will own more shares at a lower price and still keep their proportionate ownership the same.

17. **C.** In this case, you didn't even have to do the math. They're giving Ayla a 20 percent stock dividend, so she will have more shares. This eliminates answers (A) and (B). If they're increasing the amount of shares, the price has to decrease. The only answer that works is (C). To double-check your work, Ayla had $80,000 worth of stock before the split (2,000 shares × $40), so after the split, she should still have $80,000 worth of stock (2,400 shares × $32).

18. **C.** In a Chapter 11 proceeding, debt holders have a higher claim on the corporation's assets than shareholders. And, secured debt holders (debt secured with collateral), would have a higher claim on the assets than unsecured debt holders.

IN THIS CHAPTER

» Understanding the specifics of bonds

» Examining securities issued by the U.S. government

» Looking at short-term bonds

» Practicing with some sample questions

Chapter 7 Debt Securities: Corporate and U.S. Government Loans

Instead of giving up a portion of their company (via stock sales), corporations can borrow money from investors by selling bonds. Local governments (through municipal bonds; see Chapter 8) and the U.S. government also issue bonds. For SIE exam purposes, most bonds from the same issuer are considered to be safer than stocks.

Bondholders aren't owners of a company, as stockholders are; they're creditors. Bondholders who purchased bonds in the primary market are lenders of money to an institution for a fixed period and receive interest for doing so. This arrangement allows the institution to borrow money on its terms (with its chosen maturity date, scheduled interest payments, interest rate, and so on), which it can't do when borrowing from a lending institution.

The SIE exam tests you on your ability to understand the types of bonds issued, the terminology used, and (yes) some math. This chapter has you covered on topics relating to corporate and U.S. government debt securities. At the end of this chapter, I've added a quick chapter quiz to help you get a feel for questions you might see on the real SIE exam.

Diving Into Bond Terms, Types, and Traits

Before you delve deeper into bonds, make sure that you have a good handle on the basics. Understanding bond basics is a building block that can make all the rest of the bond stuff easier. In this section, I first review basic bond terminology and then move on to some bond characteristics.

Covering bond terminology

The SIE exam designers expect you to know general bond terminology. (And I give it to you here; that's why I get paid the big bucks!) If you've already studied another textbook or taken a course, this section serves as a review. This stuff is basic, but the SIE exam does test it:

- **Maturity date:** All issued bonds have a stated maturity (for example, 20 years, 30 years, and so on). The *maturity date* is the date bondholders get paid back for the loans they made. At maturity, bondholders receive par value (see the next item) plus any interest due. Because not as many investors are looking to tie up their money for a long period, short-term bonds are typically more liquid (actively traded) than long-term bonds.
- **Par value:** *Par value* is the face value or denomination of the bond. Although par value isn't significant to common stockholders (whose issuers use it solely for bookkeeping purposes), it's important to bondholders. Although U.S. Treasury securities trade in smaller denominations, you can assume that the par value for each bond is $1,000 unless otherwise stated in the question.

  REMEMBER

  Bond prices are quoted as a percentage of par value, most often without the percent sign. A bond trading at 100 is trading at 100 percent of $1,000 par. Regardless of whether investors purchase a bond for $850 (85), $1,000 (100), or $1,050 (105), they'll receive par value plus any interest due at the maturity date of the bond, usually with semiannual interest payments along the way. Corporate bonds are usually quoted in increments of 1/8 percent (1/8% = 0.00125 or $1.25), so a corporate bond quoted at 993/8 (99.375 percent) would be trading at $993.75.

  If you see something like "the last transaction in ABC 7.50s 2035 was at 101", this means that ABC bonds with a coupon rate of 7.50 and an expiration of 2035 last traded at $1,010 (101% of 1,000 par). This means that the bonds traded at a premium (over par value).
- **Coupon rate:** Investors aren't lending money to issuers for nothing, of course; they receive interest for providing loans to the issuer. The *coupon rate* on the bond tells them how much annual interest they'll receive. Although bonds are no longer issued with physical coupons, some bonds previously required investors to detach dated coupons (bearer bonds and partially registered bonds) from their bonds and turn them in to receive their interest payments. Bonds with a set or fixed coupon rate are considered *fixed-income securities*.

  The coupon rate is expressed as a percentage of par value. A bond with a coupon rate of 6 percent, for example, would pay annual interest of $60 (6% × $1,000 par value). You can assume that bonds pay interest semiannually (twice a year) unless otherwise stated. So, in this example, an investor would receive $30 every six months for each bond owned.

  REMEMBER

  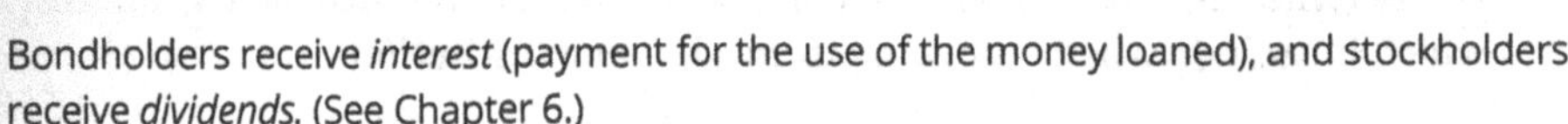

  Bondholders receive *interest* (payment for the use of the money loaned), and stockholders receive *dividends*. (See Chapter 6.)
- **The bond indenture:** The *indenture* (also known as *deed of trust* or *resolution*) is the legal agreement between the issuer and its *trustee* and is printed on or attached to the bond certificate. All indentures contain basic terms:
  - The maturity date
  - The par value
  - The coupon rate (interest rate) and interest payment dates
  - Any collateral securing the bond (See "Comparing secured and unsecured bonds" later in this chapter.)
  - Any callable or convertible features (Check out "Contrasting callable and putable (put) bonds" and "Popping the top on convertible bonds" later in this chapter.)

A *trustee* is a legal entity hired to protect bondholder's rights. It ensures that the bond issuer meets all the terms and conditions associated with the borrowing. Essentially, the trustee tries to make sure that the issuer does the right thing.

The following question tests your knowledge of bond interest.

EXAMPLE

Melissa R. purchased 100 AA-rated bonds issued by COW Corp. Melissa purchased the bonds at 105 percent of par value, and they're currently trading in the market at 104. If the coupon rate is 7½ percent, how much annual interest does Melissa receive?

(A) $37.50

(B) $75.00

(C) $3,750.00

(D) $7,500.00

The correct answer is (D). This question is a nice, easy one after you wade through the information you don't need. You need only the number of bonds and the coupon rate to figure out the answer. Don't let yourself get distracted by the AA rating, the purchase price, or the market price; that information is there to confuse you.

Melissa purchased 100 bonds at $1,000 par (remember that you can assume $1,000 par) with a coupon rate of 7½ percent, so do the math:

$$100 \text{ bonds} \times \$1{,}000 \text{ par} \times 7\tfrac{1}{2} = \$7{,}500.00$$

Answer (C) would have been correct if the question had asked for the semiannual interest.

Following bond issue and maturity schedules

Bond certificates can not only be in different forms, but also be scheduled with different types of maturities. Maturity schedules depend on the issuer's needs. The following list presents an explanation of the types of bond issues and maturity schedules:

- **Term bonds:** Term bonds are all issued at the same time and have the same maturity date. Short-term corporate bonds have initial maturities of three years or less; medium-term, four to ten years; and long-term more than ten years. If a company issues $20 million worth of term bonds, for example, they all mature in 30 years. Because of the large payment that's due at maturity, most corporations that issue this type of bond have what is called a *sinking fund*. (More on that in the next paragraph.) Most corporations issue term bonds because they're able to lock in a set coupon rate for a set period of time.

  A corporation creates a sinking fund when it sets aside money over time in order to retire its debt. Investors like to see that a sinking fund is in place because it lowers the likelihood of *default* (the risk that the issuer can't pay interest or par value back at maturity). The likelihood of default is determined by credit rating services such as Moody's and Standard & Poor's; for more on that topic, see "Considering bond credit ratings" later in this chapter.

- **Serial bonds:** In this type of bond issue, a portion of the outstanding bonds matures at regular intervals. (Perhaps 10 percent of the entire issue matures yearly.) Serial bonds are usually issued by corporations and municipalities to fund projects that provide regular income streams. Most municipal (local government) bonds are issued with serial maturities.

  A serial bond that has more bonds maturing on the final maturity date is called a *balloon issue*.

TIP

A typical SIE exam question may ask "Which of the following types of bonds is most likely to have a sinking fund?" The answer is term bonds; they're the ones in which the entire bond issue has one maturity date and, therefore, require the issuer to pay a lot of money at one time.

Comparing secured and unsecured bonds

The assets of the issuer may or may not back bonds. For test purposes, assume that bonds backed by *collateral* (assets that the issuer owns) are considered to be safer for the investor. Such *secured bonds* (bonds backed by collateral) involve a pledge from the issuer that a specific asset, such as property, would be sold to pay off the outstanding debt in the event of default. *Unsecured bonds,* as the name implies, involve no such pledge. Obviously, with all else being equal, secured bonds normally have a lower yield than unsecured bonds.

The SIE exam tests your knowledge of several types of secured bonds:

- **Mortgage bonds:** These bonds are backed by property that the issuer owns. In the event of default or bankruptcy, the issuer must liquidate the property to pay off the outstanding bonds. Mortgage bonds may be open- or closed-end. With an *open-end* mortgage bond, the issuer may borrow more money by using the same property as collateral. With a *closed-end* mortgage bond, the issuer can't borrow more money by using the same property as collateral.
- **Equipment trusts:** These bonds are issued mainly by transportation companies and are backed by equipment they own (airplanes, oil rigs, trucks, and so on). If the company defaults on its bonds, a trustee would sell the assets backing the bonds to satisfy the debt.
- **Collateral trusts:** These bonds are backed by financial assets (stocks and bonds) that the issuer owns. A *trustee* (a financial institution the issuer hires) holds the assets and would sell them to pay off the bonds in the event of default.

As I imply previously, unsecured bonds are the opposite of secured bonds: They aren't backed by any assets whatsoever — only by the good faith and credit of the issuer. If a reputable company that has been around for a long time issues the bonds, the bonds aren't considered to be too risky. If they're issued by a relatively new company or one with a bad credit rating, hold onto your seat! Again, for SIE exam purposes, assume that unsecured bonds are riskier than secured bonds. Here's the lineup of unsecured bonds:

- **Guaranteed bonds:** These bonds are backed by a firm other than the original issuer, often a parent company. If the issuer defaults, the guarantor pays off the bonds. As such, the rating of the bonds is tied to the rating of the guarantor.
- **Debentures:** These bonds are backed only by the issuer's good word (not backed by collateral) and written agreement (the indenture) stating that the issuer will pay the investor interest when due (usually, semiannually) and reach par value at maturity. They are sometimes called *subordinated debentures* because they are the last creditors to be paid in the event of corporate bankruptcy.
- **Income (adjustment) bonds:** These bonds are the riskiest of all. The issuer promises to pay par value back at maturity and will make interest payments only if earnings are high enough. Companies in the process of reorganization usually issue these bonds at a deep discount. (The bonds might sell for $500 and mature at par, or $1,000, for example.) For test and real-world purposes, you shouldn't recommend these bonds to investors who are looking for stable income and can't afford to take a lot of risk.

Because secured bonds are considered to be safer than unsecured bonds, secured bonds normally have lower coupon rates. You can assume that for the SIE, the more risk an investor takes, the more reward they will receive. Remember the saying "More risk equals more reward." More reward may be in the form of a higher coupon rate or a lower purchase price. Either or both may lead to a higher yield for the investor.

Check out the following question for an example of how the SIE may test your knowledge of the types of bonds.

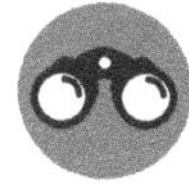

A 62-year-old investor has 50 percent of their portfolio invested in common stock of up-and-coming companies. The other 50 percent of their portfolio is invested in a variety of stocks of more-secure companies. This investor would like to start investing in bonds. If their main concern is the safety of the investment, which of the following bonds would you least likely recommend?

(A) Collateral trust bonds

(B) Mortgage bonds

(C) Equipment trust bonds

(D) Income bonds

The answer you're looking for is (D). This problem includes a lot of garbage information that you don't need to answer the question. One of your jobs (should you decide to accept it) is to dance your way through the question and cherry-pick the information that you do need. The last sentence is usually the most important one for answering a question. This investor is looking for safety; therefore, you'd be least likely to recommend income bonds because they're usually issued by companies in the process of reorganizing. As a side note, if you become this investor's broker, ensure they don't have 100 percent of their investments in stock. At age 62, they should have a decent amount of their portfolio invested in fixed-income securities such as bonds.

When you're comparing short-term and long-term debt securities, short-term bonds from the same issuer are considered to be safer because the investor isn't tying up their money for as long a period. Because of the extra risk long-term bondholders are taking for tying up their money for a longer period, long-term bondholders generally (except in rare cases) receive a higher coupon (interest rate) for taking that additional risk.

Making Basic Bond Price and Yield Calculations

Although there's not a lot of math on the SIE exam, it does test your knowledge of bond prices and bond yields and how to calculate them. In this section, I review the relationship between bond prices and bond yields. Outstanding bond prices typically don't remain static. As you can imagine, they, too, are affected by things like supply and demand, corporate rating change (see "Deciding the Best Investment: Comparing Corporate Bonds" later in this chapter), interest rate changes, whether the bond was purchased at a discount (below par value) or a premium (above par value), and so on.

The relationship between outstanding bond prices and yields is an *inverse* (opposite) one. You can assume for SIE exam purposes that if interest rates decrease, outstanding bond prices increase, and vice versa. Suppose that a company issues bonds with a 7 percent coupon rate for $1,000. After the bonds are on the market, interest rates decrease. Now the company can issue bonds with a 6 percent coupon rate. Investors with the 7 percent bonds are in a very good position and can demand a premium for their bonds should they decide to sell them in the market.

Rates down ⇓ = Prices up ⇑

Rates up ⇑ = Prices down ⇓

As a side note, when an investor sells their bonds between coupon dates, they're entitled to accrued interest. Suppose that this investor owned a bond paying $30 interest every 6 months. If they sold that bond halfway between coupon dates, they'd be entitled to receive $15 from the purchaser on top of the selling price. Calculations for accrued interest (broken down on a daily basis) aren't part of the SIE exam but are covered in detail in some of the top-off exams, such as the Series 7.

The following sections review the types of bond yields and how the SIE exam tests this topic.

Nominal yield (coupon rate)

The *nominal yield* (NY) is the easiest yield to understand because it's the coupon rate on the face of the bonds. For exam purposes, you can assume that the coupon rate will remain fixed for the life of a bond. If you have a 5 percent bond, the bond will pay $50 per year interest (5% × $1,000 par value) for the life of the bond. When a problem states that a security is a 5 percent (or 6 percent or whatever) bond, it's giving the nominal yield.

Current yield

The *current yield* (CY) is the annual rate of return on a security. The CY of a bond changes when the market price changes. You can determine the CY by dividing the annual interest by the market price:

$$\text{Current yield (CY)} = \frac{\text{annual interest}}{\text{market price}}$$

The following question involves bond yields.

EXAMPLE

Monique Moneybags purchased one XYZ convertible mortgage bond at 105. Two years later, the bond is trading at 98. If the coupon rate of the bond is 6 percent, what is the current yield of the bond?

(A) 5.7%

(B) 6.0%

(C) 6.1%

(D) Cannot be determined

The correct answer is (C). Yes, I'm giving you a question with a lot of unnecessary information. All I can tell you is that unfortunately, you'll have to get used to it. The securities exam creators are notorious for inserting useless (and sometimes misleading) information into the questions to daze and confuse you. In this case, you need only the annual interest and the market price to calculate the answer. Use the following formula to get your answer:

$$\text{CY} = \frac{\text{annual interest}}{\text{market price}} = \frac{\$60}{\$980} = 6.1\%$$

The annual interest is $60 (6% coupon rate × $1,000 par value), and the current market price is $980 (98% of $1,000 par). The facts that the bond is convertible (bondholders can trade it for common stock; see "Popping the top on convertible bonds" later in this chapter) or a mortgage bond (backed by the issuer's property) and that it was purchased at 105 ($1,050) are irrelevant.

TIP

"Cannot be determined," as tempting as it may be, is almost never the correct answer on the SIE exam.

Yield-to-maturity (basis)

The *yield-to-maturity* (YTM) is the yield an investor can expect if holding the bond until maturity. The YTM takes into account not only the market price, but also the par value, the coupon rate, and the amount of time until maturity. When someone yells to you, "Hey, what's that bond yielding?" (all right, maybe I run in a different circle of friends), they're asking for the YTM. The formula for YTM is as follows:

$$\text{YTM} = \frac{\text{annual interest} + \text{annual accretion or} - \text{annual amortization}}{(\text{market price} + \text{par value})/2}$$

$$\text{annual accretion} = \frac{\text{par value} - \text{market price}}{\text{years until maturity}}$$

$$\text{annual amortization} = \frac{\text{market price} - \text{par value}}{\text{years until maturity}}$$

I wouldn't worry about committing the preceding equations to memory. The amount of math you'll need on the SIE exam is pretty small. But it's important that you understand the concepts of measurement and the meanings of terms such as YTM, yield to call, total return, and yield to worst.

TIP

Accretion and amortization (the adjustment of the bond price toward par over the amount of time until the bond matures), as in the earlier equation, aren't tested on the SIE exam, but you need to be able to calculate them on some of the corequisite exams. (Accretion is used when a bond is purchased at a price below par value and amortization is used when a bond is purchased at a price above par value.) The preceding equation should help you visualize how YTM works.

Yield to call

The *yield to call* (YTC) is the amount that the investor receives if the bond is called by the issuer prior to maturity, which requires the bondholders to surrender their bonds for par value and sometimes above. The calculations are similar to those for the YTM (see the preceding section), but you substitute the call price for the par value. Your chances of needing to know this on the SIE exam are even more remote than those of needing the YTM calculations.

Yield to worst

To determine the *yield to worst* (YTW), you have to calculate the yield-to-maturity and YTC for all the call dates (if there's more than one) and choose the lowest. If you get a question on YTW, knowing the definition should be enough to get you by.

Total return

The *total return* calculates the full return on a particular investment over a given period of time. As with the other yields noted, you'll likely not need to calculate it, but you'll need to understand it. The total return provides you a percentage of gain or loss of an investment. To determine the total return, you need to follow these steps:

1. Determine the initial cost of the investment.
2. Calculate the total amount of interest or dividends received over the time of investment.

3. Add the interest or dividends to the selling price.
4. Divide that number by the initial cost of the investment and subtract 1.

Basis point

A *basis point* is one of the easier calculations. Basis points are typically used in the bond market, mutual funds, and exchange-traded funds (ETFs). Basis points are simply 1/100th of a percent. If the yield on a Treasury bond (T-bond) lowers 1.2 percent to 1.1 percent, it is said to have moved ten basis points. Also, when comparing expenses on a fund (see Chapter 9), people often refer to the fund expenses by basis points. If you're comparing two funds, one fund's expenses might be 0.15 percent and the other's 0.13 percent for a difference of 0.02 percent or two basis points.

Accrued interest

When investors purchase outstanding bonds in the market, they may have to pay an additional cost besides the market price (and, of course, your commission). The additional cost is called accrued interest. *Accrued interest,* which is due when bonds are purchased between coupon dates, is the portion of the interest still due to the seller. As you may remember, most bonds pay interest once every six months. If an investor holds onto a bond for 87 days out of a 180-day six-month period (for corporate and municipal bonds), they are entitled to 87/180 of that next interest payment; that's accrued interest.

REMEMBER

Although you won't be required to calculate accrued interest when taking the SIE (not so with the Series 7), you should understand the concept and that for *corporate* and *municipal bonds*, accrued interest is calculated using *30-day months and 360 day years*. When calculating accrued interest on *U.S. government bonds and notes*, you have to use *actual days in a month and a 365-day year*.

Accrued interest is calculated from the trade date, up to, but not including the settlement date.

Deciding the Best Investment: Comparing Corporate Bonds

As you grind your way through SIE exam questions, you may be asked to determine the best investment for a particular investor. You need to look at the question carefully for clues to help you choose the correct answer. (Is the investor looking for safety, for example, or is the investor close to retirement?) Consider several factors, including credit rating, callable and put features, and convertible features. Certainly, the investor's investment objectives (if stated) have to take center stage.

Considering bond credit ratings

The institutions that rate bonds are most interested in the likelihood of *default* (the likelihood that the interest and principal won't be paid when due). For the exam, you can assume that the higher the credit rating, the safer the bond and, therefore, the lower the yield.

There are others (Fitch, A.M. Best, DBRS, and so on), but the two main bond credit rating companies for corporate and municipal bonds are Moody's and Standard & Poor's (S&P). S&P ratings of BB and lower and Moody's ratings of Ba and lower are considered to be *junk bonds* or *high-yield bonds,* which have a higher likelihood of default, as Table 7-1 explains. ***Note:*** Different sources may show some slight variations in how S&P and Moody's ratings compare, but the relationships shown here are the most common.

TABLE 7-1 **Bond Credit Ratings (by Quality)**

Quality	S&P	Moody's
Highest	AAA	Aaa
High	AA	Aa
Upper medium	A	A
Lower medium	BBB	Baa
Speculative (junk)	BB	Ba
Speculative (junk): Interest or principal payments missed	B	B
Speculative (junk): No interest being paid	C	Caa
In default	D	D

As if these categories weren't enough, S&P can break down each category even further by adding a plus (+) or minus (–) sign after the letter category. The plus sign represents the high end of the category, and the minus sign designates the lower end of the category. If you see no plus or minus sign, the bond is in the middle of the category. Moody's can break down a category further by adding a 1, 2, or 3. The number 1 is the highest ranking, 2 represents the middle, and 3 is the lowest. The top four ratings are considered to be *investment grade* (AAA, AA, A, and BBB for S&P; Aaa, Aa, A, and Baa for Moody's), and the letter ratings below that are considered to be *junk bonds* or *high-yield bonds.*

TIP

S&P uses all capital letters (AAA, AA, and so on). Additionally, S&P has an ampersand (&) between the "S" and the "P" in its name. Think of the ampersand as being like a plus sign to help you remember that S&P uses pluses and minuses within its categories.

Here's a typical bond-ratings question.

EXAMPLE

Which of the following S&P bond ratings are in order from highest to lowest?

(A) A+, AA, A–, BBB+

(B) A+, A–, AA, BBB+

(C) BBB+, A+, AA, A–

(D) AA, A+, A–, BBB+

The correct answer is (D). When you're answering this type of question, always look at the letters first. The only time pluses or minuses come into play is when two answers have the same letters, as in answers (A) and (B). The highest choice is AA, followed by A+ because it's higher than A–, which is even higher than BBB+.

Contrasting callable and putable (put) bonds

Your mission for the SIE exam is to know which bonds are better for investors and when bonds are likely to be called or put. As you may know, bonds can be issued in callable and put forms:

- **Callable bonds:** A *callable bond* is a bond that the issuer has the right to buy back (call from investor) at the price stated on the indenture (deed of trust). All callable bonds must have a *call provision* that stipulates the *call date* (the first date the bonds can be called), and the *call price* (the price investors will receive if the bonds are called). Callable bonds are riskier for investors because investors can't control how long they can hold onto the bonds. To compensate for this risk, they usually receive a higher coupon rate (more risk = more reward).

  Most callable bonds are issued with call protection. *Call protection* is the amount of time (usually, several years) that an issuer has to wait before calling its bonds (such as five years after issuance). Some callable bonds also have a *call premium,* which is an amount over par value that an issuer has to pay if it calls its bonds in the year(s) immediately following the expiration of the call protection.

  If a *make whole call provision* is included, it allows the issuer to call the bonds provided that the issuer makes a lump-sum payment to investors that includes not only payment for the bond but also the present value of any future interest payments investors will miss because of the call.

  Another type of bond that can be callable is a step coupon bond. Also known as *stepped coupon bonds* or *step-up coupon securities, step coupon bonds* typically start at a low coupon rate, but the coupon rate increases at predetermined intervals, such as every five years. The issuer typically has the right to call the bonds at par value at the time the coupon rate is due to increase.

- **Put bonds:** *Put bonds* are better for investors. Put bonds allow the investor to "put" the bonds back (redeem them) to the issuer at any time at the price stated on the indenture. Because the investors have the control, put bonds are (of course) rarely issued. Because these bonds provide more flexibility to investors (who have an interest in the bond and stock prices), put bonds usually have a lower coupon rate.

There's a direct correlation between interest rates and when bonds are called or put. Issuers call bonds when interest rates decrease; investors put bonds when interest rates increase. Check out the following question to see how this process works.

Issuers would more likely call their bonds when interest rates are

(A) increasing

(B) decreasing

(C) staying the same

(D) fluctuating

The correct answer is (B). Being adaptable when taking the SIE exam can certainly help your cause. In this question, you have to look from the issuer's point of view, not the investor's. An issuer would call bonds when interest rates decrease because it could redeem the bonds with the higher coupon payments and issue bonds with lower coupon payments to save money. Conversely, investors would put their bonds back to the issuer when interest rates increase so they could invest their money at a higher interest rate.

You can assume for SIE exam purposes that if interest rates increase, bond yields increase.

Popping the top on convertible bonds

Bonds that are convertible to common stock are called *convertible bonds.* Convertible bonds are attractive to investors because investors have an interest in the bond price as well as the price of the underlying stock. *Parity* occurs when a convertible bond and its underlying stock (the stock it's convertible into) are trading equally (that is, when a bond trading for $1,100 is convertible into $1,100 worth of stock).

TIP

If a convertible bond is trading below parity (below the value of the underlying shares it covers), it would make financial sense for an investor to convert. It costs the investor nothing to convert their bonds to the underlying stock.

In the event that you have to answer a question about convertible bonds to determine whether they're worth converting to the underlying stock, you can use the following formula:

$$\text{conversion ratio} = \frac{\text{par value}}{\text{conversion price}}$$

REMEMBER

You see this same equation in Chapter 6 relating to convertible preferred stock.

You can use the conversion ratio to calculate the parity price:

$$\text{parity price of the bond} = \text{market price of the stock conversion ratio}$$

or

$$\text{parity price of the stock} = \frac{\text{market price of the bond}}{\text{conversion ratio}}$$

EXAMPLE

ABCD convertible bonds are convertible into 25 shares of common stock. If the stock trades at 36, what is the parity price of the bond?

(A) $36

(B) $40

(C) $80

(D) $900

The correct answer is (D). When you get a parity-price question, you have to determine where the stock and the bond (or convertible preferred stock) are trading equally. In this case, you were already given the conversion ratio, which is the amount of shares the bond is convertible into (25). So using that information, you can plug the information given into the following equation:

$$\text{parity price of the bond} = \text{market price of the stock} \times \text{conversion ratio}$$
$$\text{parity price of the bond} = \$36 \times 25 \text{ shares} = \$900$$

Examining U.S. Government Securities

On the SIE and companion exams, you need to know the basic types of U.S. government securities, their initial maturities, and certain characteristics.

As you may already know, the U.S. government also issues bonds. U.S. government bonds are considered to be the safest of all securities. (Yes, you did read that correctly: the *safest of all securities.* I feel that this statement is worth repeating.) How can U.S. government securities be so safe when the government is running such a large deficit? Guess what — I don't know, and you don't need to know either. I can only assume that the U.S. government can always print more currency to make payments on its securities if needed. But even U.S. government securities are subject to certain risks, such as interest risk, reinvestment risk, purchasing power risk, and so on. (See Chapter 13.)

These days, all U.S. government securities are issued and held in electronic (book-entry) form. Because Treasury bonds have maturities of up to 30 years, however, some are still out there in paper form.

TIP

With government bonds, you use some of the same types of calculations you use for corporate bonds.

Understanding the types of U.S. government securities

Table 7-2 gives you an overview of types of U.S. government securities and their specifics. Memorize all the information in the following table so that you can ace U.S. government securities questions on the SIE exam. Individual investors can purchase U.S. government securities directly through `www.treasurydirect.gov`, through a bank, or through a broker. The securities are issued in electronic form, so investors don't receive the actual bond certificate.

TABLE 7-2 U.S. Government Securities and Time until Maturity

Security	Initial Maturity	Characteristics
Treasury bills (T-bills)	4, 6, 8, 13, 17, 26, or 52 weeks; considered to be short-term U.S. debt securities	Issued at a discount and mature at par. The difference between the purchase price and par is considered to be interest, even though no interest payments were made. Minimum purchase is $100.
Treasury notes (T-notes)	2, 3, 5, 7, or 10 years; considered to be intermediate-term U.S. debt securities	Pay interest every 6 months. Minimum purchase is $100.
Treasury bonds (T-bonds)	20 or 30 years; considered to be long-term U.S. debt securities	Pay interest every 6 months. Minimum purchase is $100.
T-STRIPS (Separate Trading of Registered Interest and Principal of Securities)	6 months to 30 years	Considered to be zero-coupon securities (issued at a discount and mature at par) and don't receive interest payments. Purchase price varies. The minimum face value must be $100.
TIPS * (Treasury Inflation-Protected Securities)	5, 10, or 30 years	Pay interest every 6 months. Par value and interest payments adjust according to inflation or deflation. Minimum purchase is $100.

**TIPS are tied to the Consumer Price Index (CPI), which measures inflation. The par value changes according to inflation. If inflation is high (prices of goods and services are increasing), the par value increases. If we're in a period of deflation (prices on goods and services are decreasing), the par value decreases. Because investors are getting a percentage of par value as their interest payments, the interest payments vary along with the par value.*

REMEMBER

For the SIE exam, keep in mind that the interest received on U.S. government securities is exempt from state and local taxes. The interest received on municipal bonds is exempt from federal taxes (although I get into that topic a little more in Chapter 8). Chapter 15 gives you the scoop on taxes.

Looking at agency securities

Agency bonds are ones issued by a U.S. government-sponsored agency or government-sponsored entity (GSE). The bonds are backed by the U.S. government, but not all are guaranteed by the full faith and credit of the U.S. government except for Government National Mortgage Association (GNMA) bonds, which are directly backed. As such, agency bonds (although almost as safe) are considered to be riskier than U.S. government bonds and notes such as T-bonds, T-notes, and T-bills. Not all U.S. government agency securities are exempt from SEC registration. GSEs include the following:

- **GNMA** (Government National Mortgage Association, or Ginnie Mae): GNMAs are the only agency securities backed by the full faith and credit of the U.S. government. GNMAs support the U.S. Department of Housing and Urban Development (HUD). GNMAs are considered *asset-backed securities* (backed by mortgages), which typically are sold based on their *average life expectancy*, rather than their stated life expectancy (typically 30 years). Even though many people have a 30-year mortgage, the average life might be only 17 years or so based on refinancing and people selling their homes.
- **FNMA** (Federal National Mortgage Association, or Fannie Mae): FNMA is a publicly held corporation that is responsible for providing capital for certain mortgages. As such, FNMA may purchase conventional mortgages, Department of Veterans Affairs mortgages, U.S. Federal Housing Association mortgages, and so on. FNMA is privately owned and publicly held but is still a GSE.
- **FHLMC** (Federal Home Loan Mortgage Corporation, or Freddie Mac): As a public corporation, Freddie Mac was designed to create a secondary market for mortgages. Freddie Mac purchases residential mortgages from financial institutions and packages them into mortgage-backed securities that are sold to investors.
- **FFCS** (Federal Farm Credit System): The FFCS consists of lending institutions that provide financing and credit to farmers. It's a GSE but is privately owned. The FFCS sells securities to investors and in turn loans the funds raised to farmers. The FFCS is overseen by the Farm Credit Administration.
- **SLMA** (Student Loan Marketing Association or Sallie Mae): SLMA isn't involved in providing mortgages but provides a secondary market for student loans. As such, SLMA purchases student loans and repackages them as short- and medium-term debt securities for sale to investors.

TIP

Certain mortgage-backed securities are susceptible to reinvestment risk because many homeowners refinance when interest rates fall (*prepayment risk*). In that case, holders of mortgage-backed securities get paid back sooner than expected and are reinvesting at a lower interest rate. In addition, if interest rates stay the same or increase, homeowners won't refinance as often, and holders of mortgage-backed securities may end up having to hold their investment for a longer period than expected (*extension risk*).

Playing It Safe: Short-Term Loans or Money Market Instruments

Your SIE exam will likely include a question or two on money market instruments. *Money market instruments* are relatively safe short-term loans that can be issued by corporations, banks, the U.S. government, and municipalities. Most of these instruments have maturities of one year or less; they're usually issued at a discount and mature at par value. The following list reviews some basic characteristics of money market instruments to help you earn an easy point or two on the SIE exam:

- **Repurchase agreements:** Repurchase agreements (*repos*) are a contract between a buyer and a seller. The seller of the securities (usually, T-bills) agrees to buy them back at a previously determined price and time. Repos are short-term loans.
- **Federal funds:** Federal funds are loans between banks to help meet reserve requirements. Federal funds are usually overnight loans for which the rates change constantly depending on supply and demand.

REMEMBER

Reserve requirements are the percentage of deposits that member banks must hold each night as a regulatory protection device. Banks that aren't able to meet their reserve requirements may borrow from other banks at the fed funds rate. For more info on the fed funds rate and other tools that the Federal Reserve Board uses to influence money supply, see Chapter 13.

- **Corporate commercial paper:** Commercial paper is unsecured short-term corporate debt. Commercial paper is issued at a discount and matures at par value. Commercial paper is issued with an initial maturity of 270 days or less and is exempt from SEC registration.
- **Brokered (negotiable) certificates of deposit (CDs):** Brokered CDs are low-risk investments that originate from a bank and are outsourced to broker-dealers to sell to investors. Unlike typical CDs, which are purchased directly from a bank, brokered CDs can be traded in the market. Negotiable CDs that require a minimum investment of $100,000 are often called *jumbo CDs*.
- **Eurodollars:** *Eurodollars* are American dollars held by a foreign bank outside the United States. This situation is usually the result of payments made to overseas companies. Eurodollars are not to be confused with Eurodollar bonds (dollar-denominated bonds issued and held overseas).
- **Banker's acceptances (BAs):** A BA is a time-draft (short-term credit investment) created by a company whose payment is guaranteed by a bank. Companies use BAs for importing and exporting goods.
- **T-bills:** The U.S. government issues T-bills at a discount, and they have initial maturities of 4, 6, 8, 13, 17, 26, or 52 weeks. T-bills are somewhat unique in that they're sold and quoted on a discount-yield basis (YTM). U.S. government securities — and especially T-bills — are considered to be the safest of all securities.

Here's what a question on money market instruments might look like.

EXAMPLE

SNK Surfboard Company wants to import boogie boards from an Italian manufacturer in Sicily. SNK would use which of the following money market instruments to finance the importing of the boogie boards?

(A) T-bills

(B) Collateral trust bonds

(C) Repurchase agreements

(D) Banker's acceptances

The correct answer is (D). You can eliminate (B) right away because collateral trust bonds aren't money market instruments; they're secured long-term bonds. A BA is like a postdated check that's used specifically for importing and exporting goods.

TIP

Word association can help you here. If you see *importing, exporting,* or *time-draft*, your answer is probably BA.

Testing Your Knowledge

Now that you've discovered what you need to know about corporate and U.S. debt securities as far as the SIE exam goes, it's time to try some additional questions (besides the ones within the chapter). Read carefully so that you don't make any careless mistakes.

Practice questions

1. A corporate bond indenture includes which of the following?

I. The coupon rate

II. The maturity date

III. Par value

IV. Any collateral securing the bond

(A) I and II

(B) I, II, and III

(C) I, II, and IV

(D) I, II, III, and IV

2. Declan K. has 100 DEF corporate bonds with a coupon rate of 4½ percent. The bonds were purchased at 98 percent of $1,000 par each. How much interest will Declan receive the next time they get paid?

(A) $2,205

(B) $2,250

(C) $4,410

(D) $4,500

3. Which of the following types of corporate bond issues is most likely to have a sinking fund?

(A) Term

(B) Series

(C) Serial

(D) None of the above

4. All of the following are types of secured bonds **except**

(A) mortgage bonds

(B) collateral trusts

(C) income bonds

(D) guaranteed bonds

5. Which of the following is the formula that determines the current yield of a bond?

(A) Current yield = Semiannual interest divided by the market price

(B) Current yield = Semiannual interest divided by the par value

(C) Current yield = Annual interest divided by the market price

(D) Current yield = Annual interest divided by par value

6. Melissa R. Corporation has issued $6 million worth of 30-year callable bonds with a par value of $1,000, a coupon rate of 5¼ percent, and 7 years call protection. Melissa R. Corporation would least likely call the bonds when interest rates are generally

   (A) increasing

   (B) decreasing

   (C) remaining the same

   (D) none of the above

7. Which of the following are possible maturities for a U.S. Treasury bill?

   (A) 4 weeks and 16 weeks

   (B) 4 weeks, 8 weeks, and 16 weeks

   (C) 4 weeks, 8 weeks, and 26 weeks

   (D) 4 weeks, 8 weeks, 16 weeks, and 26 weeks

8. Which of the following U.S. government securities has interest payments that vary according to inflation or deflation?

   (A) T-bills

   (B) T-STRIPS

   (C) TIPS

   (D) T-notes

9. Which of the following securities are money market instruments?

   I. Banker's acceptances

   II. T-bills

   III. Commercial paper

   IV. Treasury notes

   (A) I and II

   (B) I, II, and III

   (C) II, III, and IV

   (D) I, II, III, and IV

10. Which of the following are direct obligations of the U.S. government?

   (A) T-bills and T-STRIPS

   (B) T-bills, GNMA, and FNMA

   (C) GNMA, FNMA, and T-STRIPS

   (D) T-bills, GNMA, and T-STRIPS

11. The last transaction in HIJ 6.50s 2035 was at 99. These HIJ bonds sold

   (A) at par value

   (B) at a discount

   (C) at a premium

   (D) cannot be determined

12. For callable bonds, the call provision must stipulate which of the following factors?

(A) The date of maturity

(B) The market value

(C) The call date and coupon rate

(D) The call price and call date

13. When issued, which of the following debt securities would mature in one year or less?

(A) SLMA bonds

(B) Money market securities

(C) U.S. government-issued Treasury notes

(D) Call options

14. When computing dollar prices and accrued interest on municipal bonds, they are typically calculated using

(A) a 30-day month and a 360-day year

(B) a 30-day month and a 365-day year

(C) actual days in a month and a 360-day year

(D) actual days in a month and a 365-day year

15. When would the stability of a portfolio of debt securities be the greatest?

(A) During a time of rising interest rates

(B) During a time of falling interest rates

(C) If the maturities of the debt securities are long-term

(D) If the maturities of the debt securities are short-term

16. These securities are typically traded based on their average life instead of their stated maturity dates.

(A) U.S. government bonds

(B) Asset-backed securities

(C) Corporate callable bonds

(D) Industrial development bonds

Answers and explanations

1. **D.** The indenture of a bond includes the date that the bond matures, the coupon rate, par value (typically, $1,000), collateral securing the bond (if any), and any callable or convertible features.

2. **B.** The coupon rate is based on the par value of the bonds, not the purchase price or market value. Declan purchased $100,000 par value of bonds with a coupon rate of 4½ percent. This means that Declan will receive $4,500 (4½% × $100,000) in interest per year. But you can assume (unless you're told differently in the question) that bonds pay interest semiannually (every six months). So you need to divide the annual interest by 2 to get $2,250 ($4,500/2).

3. **A.** Although all the choices listed may have a sinking fund (a fund for which the issuer sets aside money to pay the bonds off at maturity), term bonds are the ones most likely to have one. Term bonds are issues in which all the bonds are issued at the same time and have the same maturity date.

4. **C.** This question is an *except* question, so you're looking for the one that's not secured. Income bonds are ones issued by a corporation that's in trouble and needs to reorganize. In this case, the issuing corporation would issue these bonds at a deep discount and not make interest payments unless earnings are high enough. Income bonds are considered to be extremely risky and aren't suitable for most investors.

5. **C.** The current yield of a security is the annual rate of return divided by the market price of the security. So if the market price changes, so does the current yield.

6. **A.** A lot of information thrown into this question is meant to confuse you. The question just wants you to know when an issuer would least likely call its bonds. The whole idea of callable bonds is that issuers want the right to call their bonds if interest rates decrease because then they can issue bonds with lower coupon rates. So they'd least likely call their bonds when interest rates are increasing.

7. **C.** T-bills have initial maturities of 4, 6, 8, 13, 17, 26, and 52 weeks. T-bills are short-term U.S. government securities that are issued at a discount and mature at par value.

8. **C.** TIPS pay interest every six months, like T-notes and T-bonds, but have an interest payment that increases or decreases depending on inflation or deflation.

9. **B.** Money market instruments are debt securities that mature in one year or less. They include repurchase agreements, federal funds, commercial paper (some may mature in more than a year), brokered CDs, Eurodollars, BAs, and T-bills.

10. **D.** All the choices listed are directly backed by the U.S. government except for FNMA securities. FNMA is a publicly held corporation that provides capital for certain mortgages. It's privately owned but is still government-sponsored.

11. **B.** Remember par value for a bond is 100 (100 percent of $1,000 par). In this case, the bonds sold at a purchase price of 99 (99 percent of $1,000), so they sold at a discount from par value.

12. **D.** Although the indenture of the bond will provide the par value, coupon rate, and date of maturity, the call provision would provide the call price (what the issuer would pay the holder if calling the bonds) and also the first date that the bonds can be called.

13. **B.** Although call options typically mature in one year or less, they aren't debt securities, so you can count that one out. Out of the other choices, the only debt securities that mature in one year or less at the time of issuance are money market securities.

14. **A.** Logically, you should be able to throw out answers (B) and (C) because there is no way to make them work. If you calculate using 30-day months, it would have to work out to a 360-day year, not 365. Likewise, if you're using actual days in a month, it would have to work out to a 365-day year. Unlike U.S. government securities, which use actual days in a month and a 365-day year, municipal bonds typically compute using 30-day months and 360-day years.

15. **D.** Remember, when interest rates change, short-term debt securities typically change more quickly in price, but long-term debt securities change more in price. Therefore, an investor holding shorter-term debt securities would be holding securities that are more stable in price than someone holding a portfolio of long-term debt securities.

16. **B.** Asset-backed securities, such as GNMAs, are typically traded based on their average life. Asset-backed securities are ones that are backed by assets such as loans, mortgages, and accounts receivable. So, for arguments sake, say an individual takes out a 30-year mortgage; the average life of that mortgage may be 17 years due to that individual moving or refinancing the loan.

IN THIS CHAPTER

» Understanding municipal bond basics

» Comparing general obligation bonds with revenue bonds

» Reviewing other types of municipal bonds

» Recognizing sources of municipal bond information

» Checking your knowledge

Chapter 8

Municipal Bonds: Securities Issued by Local Governments

Municipal bonds are securities that state governments, local governments, and U.S. territories issue. The municipality uses the money it borrows from investors to fund and support projects, such as roads, schools, sewer systems, hospitals, and so on. Municipal bonds may also be issued to raise money for operating budgets. In most cases, the interest received from these bonds is federally tax-free to investors.

Even though you're most likely to spend a majority of your time selling equity securities (stocks), for some unknown reason, the SIE and some of the corequisite exams, such as the Series 7, test heavily on municipal securities. If you've flipped ahead, you may have noticed that this chapter isn't one of the biggest in the book. Why is that? Well, I cover a lot of the bond basics, such as par value, maturity, types of maturities (term, serial, and balloon), and so on, in Chapter 7. Also, you can find some of the underwriting information in Chapter 5.

In this chapter, I cover the SIE exam topics that are going to be tested relating to municipal bonds. This chapter and the real exam focus mainly on the differences between general obligation bonds and revenue bonds. The chapter wraps up with an exam to test your knowledge.

General Obligation (GO) Bonds: Backing Bonds with Taxes

Most SIE municipal test questions are on general obligation (GO) bonds. The following sections help you prepare.

General characteristics of GOs

REMEMBER

When you're preparing to take the SIE exam, you need to recognize and remember a few items that are specific to GO bonds:

- **They fund nonrevenue-producing facilities.** GO bonds aren't self-supporting because municipalities issue them to build or support projects that don't bring in enough (or any) money to help pay off the bonds. GOs fund schools, libraries, police departments, fire stations, and so on.
- **They're backed by the full faith and credit (taxing power) of the municipality.** The taxes received from the people living in the municipality back GO bonds.
- **They often require voter approval.** Because the generous taxes of the people living in the municipality back the bonds, those same taxpayers have the right to vote on the project when a municipality reaches their statutory debt limit.

The following question tests your knowledge of GO bonds.

EXAMPLE

Which of the following projects are **more** likely to be financed by general obligation bonds than revenue bonds (discussed later in this chapter)?

(A) A new municipal hospital and a public sports arena

(B) A new junior high school and a new library

(C) A new municipal hospital and a new junior high school

(D) A new municipal hospital, a new junior high school, and a new library

The correct answer is (B). Remember that GO bonds are issued to fund nonrevenue-producing projects. A new municipal hospital and a public sports arena will produce income that can back revenue bonds. But a new junior high school and a new library need the support of taxes to pay off the bonds and, therefore, are more likely to be financed by GO bonds.

Analyzing GO bonds

The SIE exam tests your ability to analyze different types of municipal securities and help a customer make a decision that best suits their needs. You should be able to analyze a GO bond as you'd analyze other investments. But because they're backed by taxes rather than sales of goods and services (as most corporations are), GO bonds have different components you need to look at when analyzing the marketability and safety of the issue.

Ascertaining marketability

Many items can affect the marketability of municipal bonds, including the characteristics of the issuer, factors affecting the issuer's ability to pay, and municipal debt ratios. You certainly want to steer investors away from municipal bonds that aren't very marketable unless those investors are willing to take extra risk. Here's a list of some of the other items that can affect a bond's marketability:

- **Quality (rating):** The higher the credit rating, the safer the bond and, therefore, the more marketable it is.
- **Maturity:** Typically, the shorter the maturity, typically the more marketable the bond issue is.
- **Call features:** Callable bonds are less marketable than non-callable bonds.

  REMEMBER

  Callable bonds give the issuer the right to call (redeem) the bonds from the holder at certain points before the maturity date, which is riskier to investors.
- **Interest (coupon) rate:** Everything else being somewhat equal, bonds with higher coupon (interest) rates are more marketable.
- **Dollar price:** All else being equal, the lower the dollar price, the more marketable the bond is.
- **Issuer's name (local or national reputation):** Bonds are more marketable when the issuer has a good reputation for paying off its bonds on time. Also, if they have a national, instead of just local, reputation for paying their debt on time, their debt securities will be more marketable.
- **Sinking fund:** If the issuer has put money aside to pay the bonds off at or prior to maturity in the open market, the bonds are more marketable because the default risk is lower.
- **Insurance:** If the bonds are insured against default, they're considered to be very safe and are much more marketable. Bond insurance is considered to be a *credit enhancement.*

Dealing with debt

One factor that influences the safety of a GO bond is the municipality's ability to deal with debt. After you consider the issuer's name, you can look at previous issues that the municipality had and find out whether it was able to pay off the debt in a timely manner.

In addition to the municipality's name (and credit history), you want to look at its current debt (the debt the municipality owes directly) and its net overall debt (including the debt the issuer owes directly and overlapping debt). *Overlapping debt* is debt that an issuer owes for being part of a larger state and local government. In other words, a town is part of a county and, in turn, is part of a state.

Bringing in taxes, fees, and fines

Taxes — one of life's little certainties — are another factor that influence the safety of GO bonds. Property taxes (collected by local municipalities, not states) and sales taxes are the driving forces behind paying back investors. So, in general, the higher the property values and the larger the tax base, the safer the municipal bond issue is. GOs are also backed by traffic fines, licensing fees, sales taxes, and so on.

REMEMBER

Municipal GO bonds are backed by the huge taxing power of a municipality, so GO bonds usually have higher ratings and lower yields than revenue bonds. Because investors aren't taking as much risk, they don't get as much reward, or *yield.*

Revenue Bonds: Raising Money for Utilities and Such

Unlike the tax-backed GO bonds (see the preceding sections), *revenue bonds* are issued to fund municipal facilities that will generate (or ideally will generate) enough income to support the bonds. These bonds raise money for certain utilities, toll roads, airports, hospitals, student grants offered by some states, and so on.

A municipality can also issue *industrial development revenue bonds* (IDBs or IDRs) to finance the construction of a facility for a corporation that moves into that municipality. Even though a municipality issues IDBs, they're backed by lease payments made by a corporation. Because the corporation is backing the bonds, the credit rating of the bonds is derived from the credit rating of the corporation.

REMEMBER

Because IDBs are backed by a corporation rather than a municipality, IDBs are generally considered to be the riskiest municipal bonds. Additionally, because these bonds are issued for the benefit of a corporation, not a municipality, the interest income may not be federally tax-free to investors who are subject to the *alternative minimum tax* (AMT).

General characteristics of revenue bonds

REMEMBER

Before taking the SIE exam, you need to recognize and remember a couple of items that are specific to revenue bonds:

- **They don't need voter approval.** Because revenue bonds fund a revenue-producing facility and, therefore, aren't backed by taxes, they don't require voter approval. The revenue that the facility generates should be sufficient to pay off the debt.
- **They require a feasibility study.** Before issuing revenue bonds, the municipality hires consultants to prepare a feasibility study. The study answers the question "Does this project make sense?" The study includes estimates of revenue that the facility could generate, along with any economic, operating, or engineering aspects of the project that would be of interest to the municipality.

Analyzing revenue bonds

As with any investment, you need to check out the specifics of the security. When you're gauging the safety of a revenue bond, for example, you want to see whether it has a *credit enhancement* (insurance), which provides a higher degree of safety. You also want to look at *call features* (whether the issuer has the right to force investors to redeem their bonds early). You can assume that if a bond is callable, it has a higher yield than a non-callable bond because the investor is taking more risk. (The investor doesn't know how long they can hold onto the bond.)

For SIE exam purposes, and if you ever sell one or more revenue bond, you also need to be familiar with the revenue-bond-specific items in this section. Municipal revenue bonds involve covenants, wonderful little promises that protect investors by holding the issuer legally accountable. Table 8-1 shows some of the promises that municipalities make on the municipal bond indenture.

TABLE 8-1 Revenue Bond Covenants

Type of Covenant	Promises That the Municipality Will . . .
Rate covenant	Charge sufficient fees to people using the facility to be able to pay expenses and the debt service (principal and interest on the bonds)
Maintenance covenant	Adequately take care of the facility and any equipment so the facility continues to earn revenue
Insurance covenant	Adequately insure the facility

TIP

If you see the word *covenant* on the SIE exam or any of the corequisite exams, immediately think of revenue bonds.

Other factors that provide investors a certain degree of comfort are that municipalities must provide financial reports and that they are subject to outside audits for all their revenue bond issues.

The Primary Market: Bringing New Municipal Bonds to Market

As you can imagine, like corporations and partnerships, municipalities need help selling their issues. To that end, they can choose their underwriter(s) directly, the way almost all corporations and Direct Participation Programs (DPPs) do it, or through a competitive (bidding) process:

- **Negotiated offering:** In this type of offering, the issuer chooses the underwriter(s) (a group of underwriters is called a *syndicate*) directly, with no competition from other underwriters. Like most corporations, municipalities that issue revenue bonds or IDRs typically choose the underwriter(s) directly, although they have the option of taking bids. Like many corporations, municipalities often have a relationship with one or more underwriters that they're comfortable working with. Because revenue bonds aren't backed by taxing power the way GOs are, the issuers aren't obligated to get the best price or coupon rate for their bond issue.
- **Competitive offering:** Because GO bonds are backed by the taxing power of the municipality, the municipal issuers are responsible for getting the best deal for the taxpayers who live in their municipality. To ensure the best deal, they post an advertisement known as a *Notice of Sale* in the *Daily Bond Buyer* (the main source of information about new municipal bonds), saying that they're accepting bids on a new issue of bonds. At this point, interested underwriters submit a good-faith deposit (to prove their sincerity) and their bids to the issuer. As you may suspect, the winner of the bid will be the underwriter that presents the lowest cost to the taxpayers backing the bond. The lowest cost could be the result of issuing the bond with a lower coupon rate and/or agreeing to pay more to purchase the bonds. Don't be too concerned about the underwriters that don't win; they'll get their good-faith deposit back.

REMEMBER

The Notice of Sale contains all bidding information about new municipal issues. Besides just saying that it's taking bids, the issuer gives bidding details. It tells potential underwriters where to submit bids, the amount of the good-faith deposit, whether it's expecting bids on the basis of net interest cost (NIC) or true interest cost (TIC, which considers the time value of money), the amount of bonds to be issued, the maturity of bonds to be issued, and so on. It's the responsibility of the underwriters to determine the coupon rate (based on the credit history of the issuer, the amount of outstanding debt, the size of the issue, the tax base, and so on) and selling price of the issue.

An underwriter needs to be able to sell the issue and still make a profit, so the selling price and the coupon rate have to be attractive to investors. You should remember that the difference between the cost the issuer pays for the security and the amount it receives from investors is called the *spread*. For argument's sake, suppose that the underwriter agrees to purchase the bonds for $990 each from the issuer and then reoffer them to the public for $1,000 each; the spread is $10 per bond. The underwriter's profit lies within that spread.

MUNICIPAL ADVISERS

Municipal advisers are firms or professionals that provide professional advice on bond sales and other financial advice to state and local governments. They help the state or local government decide the timing, structure, terms, amount, coupon rate, maturity schedule, and other aspects of borrowing money (issuing debt securities).

Allocation of orders

Under Municipal Securities Rulemaking Board (MSRB) rules, all syndicates must establish an allocation of orders. The allocation of orders states which orders are to be filled first — a priority provision. The allocation of orders must be supplied to customers who request it. The allocation of orders is in the syndicate agreement (agreement among underwriters) and must be signed by all syndicate members. The typical allocation of orders is as follows:

1. Presale orders

   These orders are entered before the date when the securities were officially available for sale.

2. Syndicate (group-net) orders

   In this case, the syndicate member receiving the order credits the sale to all the syndicate members, so all members profit.

3. Designated orders

   For designated orders, the buyer specifies which syndicate member is to profit from the sale.

4. Member orders

   If any securities are left after the presale, syndicate, and designated orders, syndicate members may purchase them for their own portfolios.

Definitions for new issues

The information contained in this section would be covered under the last section as MSRB Rule G-9. Because the rule has to do with the underwriting of municipal securities, however, it makes more sense to cover it in this section. The following list provides some of the terms specifically related to municipal bond underwritings.

- **Date of sale:** The *date of sale* is the date when the bids are submitted to the issuer for competitive offerings. For negotiated offerings, this date is when the syndicate signs the final contract. In both cases, the syndicate manager sends a commitment wire to the other syndicate members on the date of sale.
- **Presale period:** The *presale period* is the period preceding the date of sale.
- **Order period:** The *order period* is the time (established by the syndicate manager) during which syndicate members may solicit customers.
- **Underwriting period:** The *underwriting period* begins when the first order is submitted to the syndicate or when the securities are purchased from the issuer, whichever happens first. The underwriting period ends when the issuer delivers securities to the syndicate or the syndicate sells all the securities purchased from the issuer, whichever happens last.

Examining Other Types of Municipal Bonds on the Test

Along with standard revenue and GO bonds (see the earlier sections on these topics), you're required to know the specifics of the following bonds:

- **Special tax bonds:** These bonds are secured by one or more taxes other than ad valorem (property) taxes. The bonds may be backed by sales taxes on fuel, tobacco, alcohol, business license taxes, and so on.
- **Special assessment (special district) bonds:** These bonds are issued to fund the construction of sidewalks, streets, sewers, and so on. Special assessment bonds are backed by taxes only on the properties that benefit from the improvements. In other words, if people who live a few blocks away from you get new sidewalks, they'll be taxed for it, not you.
- **Double-barreled bonds:** These bonds are a combination of revenue and GO bonds. Municipalities issue these bonds to fund revenue-producing facilities (toll bridges, water and sewer facilities, and so on), but if the revenue taken in isn't enough to pay off the debt, tax revenue makes up the deficiency.
- **Limited-tax general obligation (LTGO) bonds:** These bonds are GO bonds for which the taxes backing the bonds are limited. LTGO bonds are secured by all revenue of the municipality that isn't used to back other bonds. The amount of property taxes municipalities can levy to back these bonds is limited, however. If the bond is backed by an unlimited tax pledge, the municipality can raise property tax rates to ensure that the bonds can be paid off, which is good for investors but bad for homeowners.
- **Public housing authority (PHA) bonds:** These bonds, also called new housing authority (NHA) bonds, are issued by local housing authorities to build and improve low-income housing. These bonds are backed by U.S. government subsidies, and if the issuer can't pay off the debt, the U.S. government makes up any shortfalls.

TIP

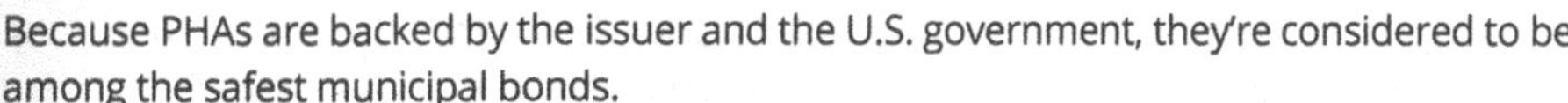

Because PHAs are backed by the issuer and the U.S. government, they're considered to be among the safest municipal bonds.

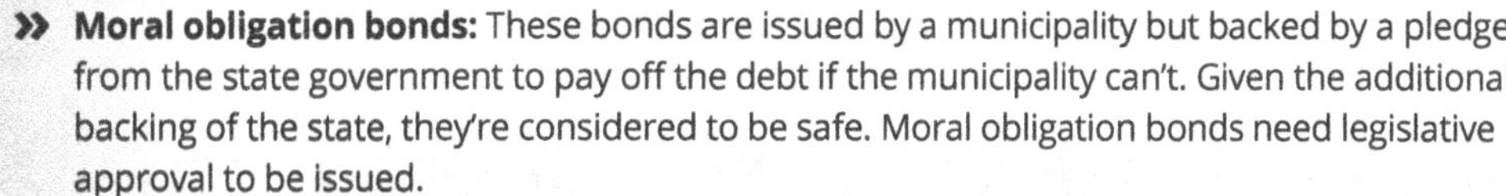

- **Moral obligation bonds:** These bonds are issued by a municipality but backed by a pledge from the state government to pay off the debt if the municipality can't. Given the additional backing of the state, they're considered to be safe. Moral obligation bonds need legislative approval to be issued.

REMEMBER

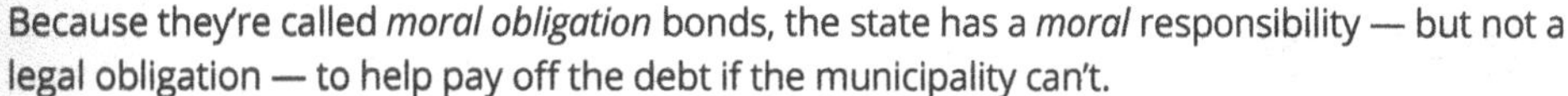

Because they're called *moral obligation* bonds, the state has a *moral* responsibility — but not a legal obligation — to help pay off the debt if the municipality can't.

The following question tests your ability to answer questions about the safety of municipal bonds.

EXAMPLE

Rank the following municipal bonds in order from safest to riskiest.

I. Revenue bonds

II. Moral obligation bonds

III. Public housing authority bonds

IV. Industrial development revenue bonds

(A) I, II, III, IV

(B) III, II, I, IV

(C) II, III, IV, I

(D) II, IV, III, I

The correct answer is (B). Remember that PHA bonds are considered to be the safest municipal bonds because they're backed by U.S. government subsidies. (This question's easy, because only one answer starts with III.) Next-safest are moral obligation bonds, which are also considered to be very safe because the state government has a moral obligation to help pay off the debt if necessary. Next come revenue bonds, which are backed by a revenue-producing facility. IDRs are considered to be the riskiest municipal bonds because although they're technically municipal bonds, they're backed only by lease payments made by a corporation.

Taxing Build America Bonds (BABs): Taxable Municipal Bonds

Although the interest on most municipal bonds is federally tax-free and sometimes triple tax-free (the interest is exempt from federal, state, and local taxes), you need to be aware that some bonds issued and backed by a municipality are taxable. These bonds were created under the Economic Recovery and Reinvestment Act of 2009 and are called *Build America Bonds* (BABs). The idea behind the BABs is to help municipalities raise money for infrastructure projects such as tunnels, bridges, roads, and so on. These bonds have either a higher coupon rate than most other municipal bonds because the municipality receives tax credits from the federal government or are more attractive because the investors receive tax credits from the federal government. As a result, these municipal bonds become more attractive to all investors, even ones with lower income-tax rates.

Even though the BAB program expired in 2010, plenty of these bonds are still out there, so you'll be tested on them. The two types of BABs are as follows:

- **Tax Credit BABs:** Investors in these bonds receive tax credits equal to 35 percent of the coupon rate.
- **Direct Payment BABs:** When a municipality issues Direct Payment BABs, it receives reimbursements from the U.S. Treasury equal to 35 percent of the coupon rate. As a result, Direct Payment BABs tend to have a higher coupon rate than Tax Credit BABs.

Municipal Notes: Securing Short-Term Financing

When municipalities need short-term (interim) financing, municipal notes come into play. These notes bring money into the municipality until other revenue is received. Municipal notes typically have maturities of one year or less (usually, three to five months). Know the different types of municipal notes listed here for the SIE exam:

- **Tax anticipation notes (TANs):** These notes provide financing for current operations in anticipation of future taxes, such as ad valorem taxes, that the municipality will collect.
- **Revenue anticipation notes (RANs):** These notes provide financing for current operations in anticipation of future revenue that the municipality will collect.
- **Tax and revenue anticipation notes (TRANs):** These notes are a combination of TANs and RANs.

- **Grant anticipation notes (GANs):** These notes provide interim financing for the municipality while it's waiting for a grant from the U.S. government. The notes are paid off from the grant funds.
- **Bond anticipation notes (BANs):** These notes provide interim financing for the municipality while it's waiting for long-term bonds to be issued.
- **Construction loan notes (CLNs):** These notes provide interim financing, typically for the construction of housing projects. The notes are typically paid back by the money the issuer receives from issuing longer-term bonds.
- **Tax-exempt commercial paper (CP):** These short-term notes are usually issued by organizations such as universities with permission of the government. This debt obligation usually lasts up to 270 days to help the organization cover its short-term liabilities.
- **Variable-rate demand note:** These notes have a variable (floating or fluctuating) interest rate and have a put option (an option to sell back to the issuer). This gives the holder the ability to periodically (typically daily or weekly) return the note to the issuer at the stated value.

REMEMBER

AON (all-or-none) is an order qualifier (fill an entire order at a specific price or not at all) or type of underwriting; it's not a municipal note, no matter how much the "N" of "AON" makes it look like one.

Municipal notes aren't rated the same as municipal or corporate bonds (AAA, AA, A, and so on). Municipal notes have ratings as follows (from best to worst):

- **Moody's:** MIG 1, MIG 2, MIG 3, MIG 4
- **Standard & Poor's:** SP-1, SP-2, SP-3
- **Fitch:** F-1, F-2, F-3

Taking a Closer Look at Municipal Fund Securities

Municipal fund securities are similar to investment company securities (see Chapter 9) but are exempt from that definition under section 2(b) of the Investment Company Act of 1940. Municipal fund securities are established by municipal governments, municipal agencies, or educational institutions but don't represent loans to the government. Included in municipal fund securities are Section 529 savings plans, Achieving a Better Life Experience (ABLE) accounts, and Local Government Investment Pools (LGIPs).

Note: Rule G-45 requires dealers underwriting ABLE programs or 529 savings plans (not LGIPs) to submit information such as plan descriptive information, assets, asset allocation information for each plan available, contributions, performance data, and so on, semiannually and performance data annually through the Electronic Municipal Market Access (EMMA) system. MSRB's EMMA system is designed to provide market transparency to help protect market participants.

Section 529 plans (529 savings plans)

Section 529 savings plans are specialized educational savings accounts available to investors. These plans are also known as *qualified tuition plans* (QTPs) because they're designed to allow money to be saved for qualified expenses for higher education (colleges, postsecondary trade and vocational schools, postgraduate programs, and so on). As of 2018, the MSRB has also added as qualified higher education expenses tuition at an elementary or secondary public, religious, or private school. A Section 529 plan has an owner (the one who sets up and contributes to the plan — typically, a parent) and a beneficiary (the one who benefits from the plan — typically, a child or relative of the person who set up the plan). The contribution allowance varies from state to state, and contributions are made from after-tax dollars. Withdrawals of the amount invested plus interest received is tax-free, meaning that the earnings grow on a tax-deferred basis, and no tax is due if earnings are used for qualified educational expenses. Investors must receive an official statement or offering circular before opening the account.

You should note the following:

- Contribution levels may vary from one state to another.
- No income limits are placed on the investors in a 529 plan.
- Contributions are typically used to acquire units in a state trust. The assets must be invested in a manner consistent with the trust's investment objectives.
- Many investors contribute monthly, although they aren't required to do so.
- Any account balances that are unused (if, for example, the beneficiary decides not to go to college or goes to a cheaper local college) can be transferred to another immediate family related beneficiary (parents, kids, and/or siblings).
- The assets in the account always remain under the control of the owner (donor) even after the beneficiary becomes of legal age (18, in most states).
- In some cases, plans can be set up as prepaid tuition plans, which allow investors to prepay college at a locked-in rate, or college savings plans, which allow owners to invest as they see fit (aggressively, moderately, or conservatively).

Note: If a registered representative is recommending a 529 savings plan to a customer, they should explain the potential state tax deduction they will receive on their contributions. Remember, the contribution amount and deductibility amount varies from state-to-state.

ABLE (Achieving a Better Life Experience) accounts

ABLE (Achieving a Better Life Experience) programs are designed for people with provable disabilities and their families. Because of the extra needs and expenses (educational, housing, transportation, health, assistive technology, legal fees, and so on) involved in taking care of people with disabilities, ABLE accounts allow people to invest after-tax dollars in an ABLE account. Any earnings or distributions are tax-free as long as they're used to pay for qualified disability expenses for the beneficiary.

ABLE accounts may be opened by the eligible person, a parent or guardian, or a person granted power of attorney on behalf of the person with the disability. After the account is opened, anyone can contribute. As with higher education savings plans (see the preceding section), the investments may be conservative, moderate, or aggressive. Many states have annual contribution caps and maximum account balances. ABLE accounts may be opened for a disabled person even if they are receiving other benefits, such as Social Security disability, Medicaid, or private insurance. To be eligible, the onset of the disability must have been discovered before the person reached age 26.

LGIPs (Local Government Investment Pools)

LGIPs are established by states to provide other government entities (cities, counties, school districts, and so on) a short-term investment vehicle for investing their funds. Because these pools are set up by state governments for state entities, LGIPs are exempt from registration with the U.S. Securities and Exchange Commission (SEC). As a result, no prospectus is required, but LGIPs have disclosure documents to cover investment policies, operating procedures, and so on. Although they aren't money market funds, they're similar in the fact that many of them operate like those funds. Like money market funds, LGIPs typically set the net asset value (NAV) at $1, and normally, the money is invested safely, although it doesn't have to be. LGIPs may be sold directly to municipalities or through municipal advisers hired by the municipal issuers.

Understanding the Taxes on Municipal Bonds

Municipal bonds typically have lower yields than most other bonds. You may think that because U.S. government securities (T-bills, T-notes, T-bonds, and so on) are the safest of all securities, they should have the lowest yields. That's not necessarily so, because municipal bonds have a tax advantage that U.S. government bonds don't have: The interest received on municipal bonds, with a few exceptions (see the earlier section "Taxing Build America Bonds (BABs): Taxable Municipal Bonds") is federally tax-free. (The interest on most U.S. government securities is free of state taxes.)

Comparing municipal and corporate bonds equally

The *taxable equivalent yield* (TEY) tells you what the interest rate of a municipal bond would be if it weren't federally tax-free. You need the following formula to compare municipal bonds and corporate bonds equally:

$$\text{taxable equivalent yield (TEY)} = \frac{\text{municipal yield}}{100\% - \text{investor's tax bracket}}$$

Because the investor's tax bracket comes into play with municipal bonds, municipal bonds are better suited for investors in higher tax brackets.

The following question tests your TEY knowledge.

Mrs. Stevenson is an investor who's in the 32 percent tax bracket. Which of the following securities would provide Mrs. Stevenson the BEST after-tax yield?

(A) 5 percent GO bond

(B) 6 percent T-bond

(C) 7 percent equipment trust bond

(D) 7 percent mortgage bond

The right answer is (A). If you were to look at this question straight up without considering any tax advantages, the answer would be (C) or (D). But you have to remember that the investor has to pay federal taxes on the interest received from the T-bond, equipment trust bond, and mortgage bond but doesn't have to pay federal taxes on the interest received from the GO municipal bond. So, you need to set up the TEY equation to compare all the bonds equally:

$$\text{taxable equivalent yield (TEY)} = \frac{\text{municipal yield}}{100\% - \text{investor's tax bracket}} = \frac{5\%}{100\% - 32\%} = \frac{5\%}{68\%} = 7.35\%$$

Looking into the SIE examiners' heads, you have to ask yourself, "Why would they be asking me this question?" Well, they want to make sure that you know that the interest received on municipal bonds is federally tax-free. Therefore, if you somehow forget the formula, you're still likely to be right if you pick a municipal bond as the answer when you get a question like the preceding one.

Note: Although this situation is less likely, the SIE may ask you to determine the *municipal equivalent yield* (MEY), which is the yield on a taxable bond after taxes. When you have that yield, you can compare it with a municipal bond to determine the best investment for one of your customers. The formula for the municipal equivalent yield is as follows:

$$\text{MEY} = \text{municipal yield} \times (100 - \text{investor's tax bracket})$$

Scot-free! Taking a look at triple tax-free municipal bonds

Bonds that U.S. territories (and federal districts) issue are triple tax-free; the interest is not taxed on the federal, state, or local level. These places include

- Puerto Rico
- Guam
- U.S. Virgin Islands
- American Samoa
- Washington, D.C.

Additionally, in most cases (a few exceptions exist), if you buy a municipal bond issued within your own state, the interest will be triple tax-free.

TIP

Unless you see the U.S. territories or Washington, D.C. in a municipal bond question, don't assume that the bonds are triple tax-free. Even if the question states that the investor buys a municipal bond issued within their own state, don't assume that it's triple tax-free unless the question specifically states that it is.

REMEMBER

The tax advantage of municipal bonds applies only to interest received. If investors sell municipal bonds for more than their cost basis, they have to pay taxes on the capital gains.

Following Municipal Bond Rules

Yes, unfortunately, the SIE tests you on rules relating to municipal bonds. Rules are part of life and part of the SIE exam. This section covers just a few rules that are specific to municipal securities, but if you're itching for more regulations, don't worry — you can see plenty more rules in my favorite chapter: Chapter 16.

Confirmations

All confirmations of trades must be sent or given to customers at or before the completion of the transaction (settlement date). Municipal securities settle the regular way (one business day after the trade date, or T+1). The following items are included in the confirmation:

- The broker-dealer's name, address, and phone number
- The capacity of the trade (whether the firm acted as a broker or dealer)
- The dollar amount of the commission (if the firm is acting as a broker)
- The customer's name
- Any bond particulars, such as the issuer's name, interest rate, maturity, and call features (if any)
- The trade date, time of execution, and settlement date
- Committee on Uniform Securities Identification Procedures (CUSIP) identification number (if there is one)
- Bond yield and dollar price
- Any accrued interest
- The registration form (registered as to principal only, book entry, or fully registered)
- Whether the bonds have been called or pre-refunded

Each broker, dealer, or municipal securities dealer must report to the MSRB all transactions in municipal securities through the Real-Time Reporting System (RTRS). The RTRS makes public reports on market activity and prices. In addition, the MSRB assesses transaction fees to make sure that they're in line with MSRB rules. The information of a transaction must be reported promptly. Exempt from the reporting process are transactions in securities without a Committee on Uniform Security Identification Procedures (CUSIP) number, transactions in municipal fund securities, and interdealer transactions (over the counter trades between one financial institution and another).

Advertising and record keeping

A brokerage firm has to keep all advertising for a minimum of three years, and these ads must be easily accessible (not in a bus storage locker) for at least two years.

The MSRB requires a principal (manager) to approve all advertising material of the firm before its first use. The principal must ensure that the advertising is accurate and true.

REMEMBER

Advertising includes any material designed for use in the public media. Advertising includes offering circulars, market and form letters, summaries of official statements, and so on. Preliminary and final official statements aren't considered to be advertising because they're prepared by the issuer; therefore, they don't require approval from a principal.

Gifts

According to MSRB rules, municipal securities dealers can't give customers gifts valued at more than $100 per year. (The board kind of has this thing against bribery.) Business expenses are exempt from the rule.

TIP

If you get a question on the SIE exam relating to what qualifies as a gift, remember that business expenses are exempt. Business expenses can be airline tickets (for the customer to meet with you, not for the customer to vacation in the Bahamas), hotel expenses (for the customer's lodging while they're meeting with you), business meals, and so on. You should note that FINRA gift rules fall directly in line with MSRB's gift rules.

Commissions

Although no particular guideline states what percentage broker–dealers can charge (as with The 5% Markup Policy; see Chapter 16), all commissions, markups, and markdowns must be fair and reasonable, and policies can't discriminate among customers. The items that firms should consider follow:

- The market value of the securities at the time of the trade.
- The total dollar amount of the transaction. Although you're usually going to charge more money for a larger transaction, the percentage charged is usually lower.
- The difficulty of the trade. If you had to jump through hoops to make sure that the trade was completed, you're entitled to charge more.
- The fact that you and the firm that you work for are entitled to make a profit (which, of course, is the reason you got involved in the business to begin with).

You can't take into account a client's race, ethnicity, religion, gender, gender identity, sexual orientation, disability, age, or accent, or how much you like (or dislike) the client.

Gathering Municipal Bond Info

As with other investments, you need to be able to locate information if you're going to sell municipal securities to investors. You may find that information about municipal bonds isn't as readily available as it is for most other securities. Some municipal bonds are relatively *thin* issues (not many are sold or traded) or may be of interest only to investors in a particular geographic location. This section reviews some of the information that you have to know to ace the SIE exam.

The bond resolution (indenture)

A *bond resolution* (indenture) provides investors contract terms including the coupon rate, years until maturity, and collateral backing the bond (if any). Almost every municipal bond comes with a bond indenture, which is printed on the face of most municipal bond certificates. A bond indenture isn't required by law, but it makes the bonds more marketable because it serves as a contract between the municipality and a trustee that's appointed to protect the investors' rights. Included in the indenture are the *flow of funds* (how the money collected from the revenue-producing project is distributed) and any assets that may be backing the issue.

Legal opinion

Printed on the face of municipal bond certificates, the legal opinion is prepared and signed by a municipal bond counsel (attorney). The purpose of the legal opinion is to verify that the issue is legally binding on the issuer and conforms to tax laws. Additionally, the legal opinion may state that interest received from the bonds is tax-exempt.

If a bond is stamped *ex-legal,* it doesn't contain a legal opinion.

Official statement

Municipal bonds don't have a prospectus; instead, municipalities usually provide an official statement. Like prospectuses, official statements come in *preliminary* and *final versions.* The preliminary version of the statement doesn't include an offering price or coupon rate. The *official statement* (OS) is the document that the issuer prepares or has prepared; it states what the funds will be used for, provides information about the municipality, and offers details how the funds will be repaid. The official statement also includes:

- The offering terms
- The underwriting spread (basically, who gets what)
- A description of the bonds
- A description of the issuer
- The offering price
- The coupon rate
- The feasibility statement (for revenue bonds — how much sense the project makes)
- The legal opinion (unless stamped ex-legal)

Any dealer selling municipal securities to a customer during the issue's underwriting period (see "The Primary Market: Bringing New Municipal Bonds to Market" earlier in this chapter) must deliver a final official statement, if there is one, to a customer by the settlement of the transaction. If a dealer is selling a new issue to another dealer, it must deliver the official statement to the purchasing dealer within one business day.

"G" That's a Whole Lot of Rules

Yes, there are a lot of "G" rules. You'll have to study even more before you take some of the corequisite exams, such as the Series 7. Some of these rules would be taller than you if they were printed out, even if you're tall enough to give Shaquille O'Neal a run for his money.

The following list isn't as huge as it could be because many of the rules are already covered throughout this book. But you're not expected to know the minute details of each rule — just the main idea. Fortunately, many of the rules just make sense. Also, don't worry about the rule numbers; pay more attention to the rule.

- **Rule G-2** (standards of professional qualifications): Before effecting any transaction (solicitation, negotiation of terms, or execution of a trade) in — or inducing or attempting to induce the purchase or sale of — any municipal security, the dealer and every person associated with that dealer must be qualified in accordance with MSRB rules.
- **Rule G-3** (professional qualification requirements): Broker-dealers that conduct a business in general securities must have at least one associated person qualified as a municipal securities principal to oversee and supervise their municipal securities business.

- **Rule G-7** (information concerning associated persons): Associated persons (municipal securities sales principal, municipal securities principal, general securities principal engaging in municipal securities business, municipal securities representative, limited representatives, and so on) must provide their employer a form U-4 or MSD-4 for bank dealers. A U-4 form is an application form sent to the Central Registration Deposit (CRD) along with the applicant's fingerprints. Included in the form are the applicant's address, work history, arrest record (if any — ideally not), education, previous addresses, and so on. A copy of the form must be kept by the employer. In addition, the employer is responsible for calling previous employers to find out whether the information in the form is accurate. In the event that the applicant's information changes any time during employ, the employer is responsible for updating the information.
- **Rules G-8 and G-9** (books and records requirements): All brokers, dealers, and municipal securities dealers must keep records regarding municipal securities business. Among the many items they have to keep are the following:
  - Records of original entry (blotters): Itemized daily records of all purchases and sales of municipal securities
  - Account records: Account records for each customer account
  - Securities records: Separate records showing all municipal securities positions
  - Subsidiary records: Records of municipal securities in transfer, municipal securities borrowed or loaned, municipal securities transactions not completed by the settlement date, and so on
  - Put options and repurchase agreements
  - Records for agency transactions
  - Records concerning primary offerings
  - Copies of confirmations (for more on confirmations, see Chapter 16)
  - Customer account information
  - Customer complaints
  - Records concerning political contributions

TIP

You aren't expected to remember the entire preceding list. Just get a general feeling for what's required. It looks as though the MSRB wants the broker–dealer or municipal securities dealer to maintain records of just about everything.

- **Rule G-9** (preservation of records): MSRB's record-keeping requirements are very similar to (but not exactly the same as) FINRA's requirements. Most records have to be kept for four or six years. To keep you from pulling your hair out (this coming from a bald man), look at the record-keeping requirements in Chapter 16, where I note how the MSRB rules and FINRA rules differ.
- **Rule G-10** (delivery of investment brochure): Broker–dealers and municipal securities dealers must send yearly written statements (which may be electronic) to each customer, stating that they're registered with the SEC and MSRB. The statement must also include the web address for the MSRB and a statement of how to receive an investment brochure on the website describing customer protections and how to file a complaint to the proper authority. The same information holds true of municipal advisers, who must also send yearly statements with the same information as well as provide information on how to get the client brochure on the MSRB website.
- **Rule G-13** (quotations): According to MSRB rules, all quotations for municipal securities published or distributed by any broker–dealer, municipal securities dealer, or person associated with a broker–dealer or municipal securities dealer must be bona fide (genuine).

» **Rule G-17** (conduct of municipal securities and municipal adviser activities): Municipal securities broker-dealers, municipal securities dealers, municipal advisers, agents, and so on shall deal fairly with all people and not engage in dishonest, deceptive, or unfair practices.

» **Rule G-18** (best execution): When entering into a municipal securities transaction with a customer or customer of another broker, dealer, or municipal securities dealer, a broker must use reasonable diligence to attempt to get the best price for the security (lowest buying price or highest selling price for the customer). This rule is similar to Rule G-30, but G-30 includes markups, markdowns, and commission.

» **Rule G-21** (advertising): Advertisements by municipal securities dealers, brokers, and dealers can't contain false or misleading statements. Advertisements include published material used in electronic or other public media, promotional literature (written or electronic) made available to customers or the public, circulars, market letters, seminar text, press releases, and so on. Preliminary official statements, official statements, offering circulars, and so on aren't considered to be advertisements.

» **Rule G-25** (improper use of assets): Brokers, dealers, and municipal securities dealers shall not make improper use of municipal securities or funds held on behalf of another person. In addition, no broker, dealer, or municipal securities dealer can make a guarantee against loss, and they may not share directly or indirectly in the profit or losses in a customer's account. An associated person may set up a partnership or joint account with a customer and share in the profits or losses based on the contribution made into the account. In that case, a proportionate sharing agreement should be in place.

» **Rule G-30** (pricing and commissions): If buying or selling municipal securities for a customer on a principal basis (for or from the dealer's inventory), the aggregate price (including the markdown or markup) must be fair and reasonable. If buying or selling municipal securities on an agency basis for a customer, the broker-dealer is responsible for making a reasonable effort to obtain the best price for the customer, and the commission charged must be fair and reasonable in relation to prevailing market conditions.

» **Rule G-34** (CUSIP numbers, new issue, and market information requirements): For new issues of municipal bonds (whether negotiated or competitive offerings), the managing underwriters must apply to CUSIP to receive identification numbers for the bonds for each maturity, if more than one. For negotiated offerings in which the underwriter is chosen directly, the managing underwriter must apply before the pricing of the new municipal issue. For competitive offerings, the managing underwriter must apply after winning the bid. In the event that the municipal issuer hired an adviser, the municipal adviser must apply no later than the business day after the notice of sale is published.

» **Rule G-37** (political contributions and prohibitions on municipal securities business): This rule prohibits brokers, dealers, municipal securities dealers, and municipal advisers from engaging in municipal adviser business with municipal entities if they've made political contributions to officials of such municipal entities. If a political contribution was made as described in the first sentence, they're not allowed to engage in municipal securities business with that municipal entity for a period of two years after the contribution. *Municipal finance professionals* (MFPs) are allowed to make political contributions of up to $250 per election to a candidate they're entitled to vote for.

» **Rule G-47** (time of trade disclosure): Brokers, dealers, and municipal securities advisers may not trade a municipal security (buy from or sell to) with a customer (whether solicited or unsolicited) without providing all material information about the trade. The information must be provided before or at the time of sale and can be disclosed orally or in writing.

If you're dying to know, you can view a complete list of what the MSRB considers to be material information at `www.msrb.org/Rules-and-Interpretations/MSRB-Rules/General/Rule-G-47.aspx`. It shouldn't be necessary to commit this information to memory.

Testing Your Knowledge

Other than the TEY formula, there wasn't much in the way of math in this chapter. Anyway, here's a 15-question quiz to help you get a feel for the type of municipal securities questions you're likely to see on the SIE exam.

Practice questions

1. Which of the following municipal securities could have a rating of MIG 2?

   (A) PNs and TRANs

   (B) PNs, tax-exempt commercial paper, and TRANs

   (C) PNs, TRANs, and IDRs

   (D) Tax-exempt commercial paper, TRANs, and IDRs

2. Which of the following is **not true** about general obligation bonds?

   (A) They are backed by the taxing power of the municipality.

   (B) They are issued to fund revenue-producing facilities.

   (C) They are subject to a debt ceiling.

   (D) They need voter approval to be issued.

3. A municipal securities broker–dealer sells 100 GO bonds to a customer on a principal basis. How much of a markup may the broker–dealer charge?

   (A) 5% of the selling price

   (B) 8% of the selling price

   (C) 8 1/2% of the selling price

   (D) Whatever is fair and reasonable

4. Which of the following documents include all relevant information about a municipal issuer?

   (A) Official statement

   (B) Notice of sale

   (C) Prospectus

   (D) Indenture

5. A special assessment bond is backed by

   (A) a private user

   (B) excise taxes

   (C) charges on the benefitted property

   (D) a revenue-producing facility

6. According to MSRB rules, brokerage firms must keep all municipal securities advertising

   (A) for a minimum of three years and easily accessible for a minimum of one year

   (B) for a minimum of three years and easily accessible for a minimum of two years

   (C) for a minimum of six years and easily accessible for a minimum of one year

   (D) for a minimum of six years and easily accessible for a minimum of two years

7. Municipal bonds issued by each of the following would be triple tax-free **except**

(A) Hawaii

(B) Guam

(C) Washington, D.C.

(D) Puerto Rico

8. Municipal bonds settle the regular way in

(A) 1 business day after the trade date

(B) 2 business days after the trade date

(C) 3 business days after the trade date

(D) 4 business days after the trade date

9. Under MSRB rules, how often must broker-dealers and municipal securities dealers send out investment brochures to their customers stating that they are registered with the SEC and MSRB?

(A) Once, before the customer opening the account

(B) Once, within 60 days of the customer opening the account

(C) Once, any time before the first transaction

(D) Once a year

10. According to MSRB rules, which of the following are considered to be forms of advertising?

I. Market letters

II. Seminar text

III. Official statements

IV. Offering circulars

(A) I only

(B) I and II

(C) I, II, and III

(D) I, II, III, and IV

11. What is the taxable equivalent yield for an investor purchasing a 5 percent municipal bond if they're in the 24 percent tax bracket?

(A) 5%

(B) 5.88%

(C) 6.14%

(D) 6.58%

12. All of the following are types of municipal notes **except**

(A) PN

(B) TRAN

(C) AON

(D) CLN

13. Which of the following **is not** a type of municipal fund security?

(A) Section 529 plans

(B) ABLE accounts

(C) LGIPs

(D) LTGOs

14. All things being equal, which of the following municipal bonds would most likely have the lowest coupon rate?

(A) Special assessment bonds

(B) LTGOs

(C) PHAs

(D) IDRs

15. Under MSRB rules, all syndicates must establish an allocation of orders, which states which orders are to be filled first. Place the typical allocation of orders in order from first to be filled to last to be filled.

(A) Presale, syndicate, designated, member

(B) Member, designated, syndicate, presale

(C) Designated, member, syndicate, presale

(D) Syndicate, presale, member, designated

16. Which type of security provides holders with a floating interest rate, a stated maturity date, and an option to put the security back to the issuer on a daily or weekly basis?

(A) Fixed annuities

(B) Build America Bonds

(C) Variable-rate demand notes

(D) GNMAs

Answers and explanations

1. **B.** MIG (Moody's Investment Grade) ratings are for municipal notes (short-term municipal securities). Municipal notes include TANs, RANs, TRANs, GANs, BANs, CLNs, PNs, and tax-exempt commercial paper. IDRs (Industrial Development Revenue bonds) are long-term debt securities issued by a municipality backed by a private user.

2. **B.** If you look at (A) and (B), they more or less contradict each other, so it makes sense that one of them is the answer. General obligation (GO) bonds are backed by the municipality's taxing power while revenue bonds are backed by money collected from revenue-producing facilities. Therefore, (B) is the correct answer for this question.

3. **D.** There is no set rule as far as the percentage that a municipal broker–dealer may charge when buying or selling municipal securities. Because this trade was executed out of the broker–dealer's inventory, you would expect that the amount that the broker–dealer would charge would be relatively low. The rule is "whatever is fair and reasonable," meaning that if the broker–dealer expended a lot of effort getting the securities, they would not be in violation if charging extra.

4. **A.** Municipal bonds don't have a prospectus. Instead, they have an official statement. Official statements, like prospectuses, come in preliminary and final versions. If prepared, an official statement would contain things like the offering terms, a description of the bonds being offered, a description of the issuer, the bond offering price, the coupon rate, and the maturity.

5. **C.** A special assessment (special district or special purpose) bond is backed on taxes on the properties that benefit from the improvement(s).

6. **B.** Under MSRB rules, all municipal securities advertising must be kept on file for a minimum of three years and kept easily accessible for at least two years.

7. **A.** U.S. territory bonds and bonds issued by federal districts are triple tax-free (exempt from federal, state, and local tax). Bonds issued by the state of Hawaii are not, however. The triple tax-free bonds you should be aware of are the ones issued by Puerto Rico, Guam, U.S. Virgin Islands, American Samoa, and Washington, D.C.

8. **A.** Municipal securities trades settle the regular way in one business day after the trade date (T+1, which is trade date plus one business day).

9. **D.** Broker–dealers and municipal securities dealers must send yearly statements to their clients, which may be in electronic form (emails and such). These statements must let the clients know that their firm is registered with the SEC and MSRB. The statement must let clients know their protections, how they can make a complaint to the proper authority, and so on.

10. **B.** Advertisements include promotional literature (written and electronic), circulars, market letters, seminar text, press releases, and so on. Preliminary official statements, official statements, offering circulars, and so on are not considered to be advertisements.

11. **D.** Because the interest received on municipal bonds is federally tax-free, you have to determine the taxable equivalent yield to be able to compare municipal bonds and corporate bonds equally. So, when you're using the taxable equivalent yield (TEY) formula, you're looking at what a corporate bond would have to yield to be equal to this municipal bond after taxes. See the following formula:

$$\text{TEY} = \frac{\text{municipal yield}}{100\% - \text{investor's tax bracket}} = \frac{5\%}{100\% - 24\%} = \frac{5\%}{76\%} = 6.58\%$$

So, for this investor in the 24 percent tax bracket, buying a 5 percent municipal bond is equivalent to purchasing a 6.58 percent corporate bond after taxes.

12. **C.** Municipal notes are short-term (one year or less) debt securities issued by municipalities to cover a short-term need. These include TANs, RANs, TRANs, GANs, BANs, CLNs, PNs, and tax-exempt commercial paper. AON (all-or-none) is an order qualifier and not a type of municipal note.

13. **D.** Section 529 plans (qualified tuition plans), ABLE (Achieving a Better Life Experience) accounts, and LGIPs (Local Government Investment Pools) are all types of municipal fund securities. LTGOs (Limited-Tax General Obligation) bonds are general bonds issued in which the backing municipality is limited on the property taxes they can collect from the people in their municipality backing the bond.

14. **C.** Remember, more risk equals more reward, so in most cases, riskier bonds are going to have a higher coupon rate and safer bonds a lower coupon rate. Out of the choices given, PHA (Public Housing Authority) bonds are the safest because they are backed by U.S. government subsidies.

15. **A.** Typically, a syndicate sets up the way their orders are to be filled as follows: presale, syndicate (group-net), designated, member.

16. **C.** Variable-rate demand notes are municipal securities that have a variable interest rate as well as a put option, which allows the holder to sell the bond back to the issuer at a stated value.

3 Diving Deeper: Taking a Look at More Complex Securities

IN THIS PART . . .

Understand the role of investment companies in helping investors diversify their portfolios.

Become versed in limited partnerships — their formation, function, structure, tax advantages, and tax disadvantages.

Examine direct participation programs (DPPs) and real estate investment trusts (REITs).

Get to know options — investment vehicles that allow investors to buy and sell securities at a fixed price.

IN THIS CHAPTER

» Taking advantage of management investment companies

» Understanding face-amount certificate companies and UITs

» Looking at annuities

» Taking a brief look at life insurance

» Checking your knowledge

Chapter 9
Delivering Diversification with Packaged Securities

Diversification is key when you're helping customers set up a portfolio of securities, and it's fairly easy when your customer has a good deal of money to invest. But what if an investor has limited resources? Certainly, such investors can't afford to buy hundreds of shares and/or debt securities of several companies, and you don't want to limit your customer to only one investment opportunity (heaven forbid it should go belly up). Packaged securities to the rescue! These securities — such as open-end funds, closed-end funds, face-amount certificate companies, unit investment trusts, and annuities — offer variety within one security by investing a customer's money in a diversified pool of securities — for a cost, of course. A bit of profit-driven teamwork can ensure your customers' investments are much safer than, say, playing slot machines or daily scratch-offs.

In this chapter, I cover topics relating to investment companies and annuities. Open-end (mutual) funds and closed-end funds are only the beginning. I discuss face-amount certificate companies and trusts such as unit investment trusts. I also give you a look at life insurance products and wrap it all up by giving you a small quiz at the end of the chapter.

Looking at Investment Company Registration

As with other nonexempt securities, investment companies must register with the U.S. Securities and Exchange Commission (SEC). You need to understand certain specifics about the registration process when taking the SIE. When registering with the SEC, investment companies must disclose

» Whether the investment company will be open- or closed-end

» The names and addresses of affiliated people

» Whether the company plans to raise money by borrowing
» Whether they plan on investing in commodities or real estate
» How they plan on investing (a single industry, many industries, debt securities, and so on)
» Conditions under which the investment plan can change (a vote of shareholders, for example)
» The business experience of each director and officer

Diversifying Through Management Investment Companies

In general, investment companies are those whose business is investing in securities. As such, they take the money received from investors and invest in a large number of different securities. Each investor shares in the profits or losses based on their interest in the investment company. The Investment Company Act of 1940 divides investment companies into three main types: management companies, face-amount certificate companies, and unit investment trusts (UITs). This section focuses on management companies, which are the more heavily tested areas of this chapter. I cover the other types in the aptly named "Contemplating Other Investment Company Options" section later.

Management companies are by far the most familiar type of investment company. The securities held by the management companies tend to be actively managed by portfolio managers, although they might be passive where a portfolio manager makes the initial choices but doesn't actively trade the account. As a subclassification of management companies, they are either *diversified* or *nondiversified*. To be diversified, a company must spread out at least 75 percent of its assets in the following way:

» The management company can't own more than 10 percent of the outstanding shares of a company.
» No more than 5 percent of the management company's money can be invested in one company's securities. However, through appreciation, one company may grow to more than 5 percent, which is fine, but the fund may not purchase any more of that company's securities unless it drops below 5 percent.

REMEMBER

Because the diversified portion relates to only 75 percent of the management company's assets, the other 25 percent can be invested in any way. Whether the management company is diversified or nondiversified must be in the prospectus (for more on what a prospectus is, see Chapter 5).

Comparing open- and closed-end funds

Management companies are either open-end or closed-end funds. Make sure that you know the difference.

Open-end (mutual) funds

An *open-end fund* is more commonly known as a *mutual fund*. Like closed-end funds, mutual funds invest in many different securities to provide diversification for investors. The key difference is that mutual funds are constantly issuing and redeeming shares (shares are redeemed with the issuer and not sold in the market), which provides liquidity for investors. Because open-end fund shares are continuous offerings of new shares, a mutual fund prospectus must always be available. You need to understand the makings of the net asset value and the public offering price when taking the SIE exam:

- **Net asset value (NAV):** Fortunately, the NAV or net asset value per share is determined the same way for both open- and closed-end funds: by dividing the value of the securities held by the fund by the number of shares outstanding. With mutual funds, however, the NAV is the bid price. When investors redeem shares of a mutual fund, they receive the next computed NAV (usually at the end of the day). This is also known as the *redemption value*. Mutual funds can never trade below the NAV.
- **Public offering price (POP):** For mutual funds, the public offering price (the ask price) is the NAV plus a sales charge. If a mutual fund doesn't charge a sales charge, it's called a *no-load fund*. However, they can charge a 12b-1 fee up to 25 basis points (explained in more detail shortly).

REMEMBER

Because mutual funds are new issues, investors must receive a statutory prospectus and/or receive a *summary prospectus* and have access to the statutory prospectus. Prospectuses for mutual funds include their holdings, investment strategy, fees, expenses, graphs of the fund's performance, and so on. Every prospectus for every security must contain a disclosure stating that the SEC doesn't approve of the issue. I assume that this disclosure is the SEC's way of not being sued if investors lose money. The SEC just clears the issue for sale to investors.

If the fund provides a summary prospectus, it must include items such as the fund's name and ticker symbol, the class of shares, the fund's investment strategies, investment objectives, costs of investing, investment advisers, financial compensation, risks, and performance. The summary prospectus may include an application that investors can use to purchase shares. Potential investors can also request a full prospectus before investing. If an investor purchases via a summary prospectus, the investor must either receive or be provided online access to a full prospectus.

On an ongoing basis, funds must include in their prospectus annual report graphs comparing the performance of the fund with a proper index (Standard & Poor's [S&P] 500, Nasdaq composite, and so on), items and/or strategies that may have affected the performance in the past year, and the name of the fund's manager.

Note: Expenses of a mutual fund include salaries for the board of directors; management (investment adviser) fees for the person or people who make the investment decisions for the fund; custodial fees for safeguarding assets (cash, securities, and so on) held by the fund; transfer agent fees for keeping track of investors, sending distributions, and sending proxies; and 12b-1 fees, if any. *12b-1 fees* are fees paid by a mutual fund out of the fund assets to cover promotional expenses such as advertising, printing, and mailing of prospectuses to new investors, and so on. If there are 12b-1 fees, they must be included in the prospectus.

Closed-end funds

Unlike open-end funds, closed-end funds have a fixed number of shares outstanding (hence the word *closed*). Closed-end funds act more like common stock than open-end funds because they issue new shares to the public; after that, the shares are bought and sold in the market. Because they trade in the market, they're often called *publicly traded funds*. Although the net asset value of closed-end and open-end funds is calculated the same way, the public offering price is determined a little differently:

- **NAV:** The NAV or net asset value per share is the parity price at which the fund should be trading. You determine it by taking all of the assets owned by the fund, subtracting the liabilities, and dividing by the number of shares outstanding. Closed-end funds may trade at a discount or premium compared to the NAV — based on supply and demand.

» **Public offering price (POP or ask price):** For closed-end funds, after the initial public offering (IPO) the public offering price (the ask price) depends not only on the NAV but also supply and demand for the issue. Investors of closed-end funds pay the POP (current market price) *plus* a broker's commission in an agency transaction.

Note: Although closed-end funds aren't purchased from and redeemed with the issuer, most offer a high degree of liquidity, based on the number of shares. After the initial offering, they can be purchased or sold either on an exchange (called exchange-traded funds or ETFs) or over the counter (OTC).

Open and closed: Focusing on their differences

You can expect at least a question or two on the SIE exam relating to investment companies to test you on the differences between open-end and closed-end funds. Table 9-1 should help you zone in on the major distinctions.

TABLE 9-1 Comparing Open-End and Closed-End Funds

Category	Closed-End	Open-End
Capitalization	One-time offering of securities (fixed number of shares outstanding).	Continuous offering of new shares (no fixed number of shares outstanding).
Pricing the fund	Investors purchase at the current market value (POP) plus a commission.	Investors purchase at the NAV plus a sales charge.
Issues	Common stock, preferred stock, and debt securities.	Common stock only.
Shares purchased	Shares can be purchased in full only.	Shares can be purchased in full or fractions (up to three decimal places).
Purchased and sold	Initial public offerings (IPOs) go through underwriters; after that, investors purchase and sell shares either over-the-counter or on an exchange (no redemption).	Shares are sold and redeemed by the fund only.

REMEMBER

The key difference between open-end and closed-end funds is the method of capitalization. An open-end (mutual) fund is a continuous offering of new securities, whereas a closed-end fund is a one-time offering of new securities.

Keeping your customer's investment objectives in mind

Unlike investors in face-amount certificate companies and unit investment trusts (see "Contemplating Other Investment Company Options" later in this chapter), investors of open-end and closed-end funds have many choices. Investors may be looking for safety, growth, a combination, and so on. This section gives you a glimpse into those investment choices.

REMEMBER

The single most important consideration for customers who invest in packaged securities is the fund's investment objectives. This feature surpasses even the sales charge or management fees. If you become a registered rep, one of your primary jobs will be to help investors decide which type of fund would be best for them. The test designers want to know you can handle that job. Comparing like-type funds is secondary. So, without further ado, here are the major types (although variables within each fund can make a fund riskier or safer, I've placed the list in the normal order from safest to riskiest):

- **Money market fund:** This fund (as you've probably guessed) invests in money market instruments (short-term debt securities). You need to know the specifics of this fund more than other types of funds. Here are the key points:
  - They usually provide a check-writing feature (you're given a checkbook) as a way of redeeming shares.
  - They're always no-load (there's no sales charge).
  - They compute dividends daily and credit them monthly.
  - There's no penalty for early redemption.
- **Income fund:** The primary objective of an income fund is to provide current revenue (not growth) for investors. This type of fund invests most of its assets in a diversified portfolio of (a) debt securities that pay interest and in preferred and (b) common stock of companies that are known to pay consistent dividends in cash.

  Income funds are considered much safer (more conservative) investments than growth funds. You can assume for SIE exam (and real-life) purposes that income funds are better investment choices for retirees and investors who are looking for a steady cash flow without much risk.

- **Balanced fund:** A balanced fund is a combination of a growth fund and an income fund. Balanced funds invest in common stocks, preferred stocks, long-term bonds, and short-term bonds, aiming to provide both income and capital appreciation while minimizing risk. These funds don't get hammered too badly when the market is bearish but typically underperform when the market is bullish.
- **Growth fund:** This fund is exactly what you'd expect it to be; growth funds invest most of their assets in a diversified portfolio of the common stock of relatively new and existing companies, looking for big increases in the stock prices. Growth funds offer a higher potential for growth but usually at a higher risk for the investor. This type of fund is ideal for an investor who's looking for long-term capital appreciation potential.

  Because of the inherent risk of investing in growth funds, they're better for younger investors who can take the risk because they have more time to recover their losses.

  Some growth funds are labeled as *aggressive growth funds* because the securities they invest in are even riskier than those of a standard growth fund.

- **Specialized (sector) fund:** A specialized or sector fund is a type of fund that invests primarily in the securities of a single industry. A specialized fund may invest only in financial services, healthcare, automotive stocks, technology securities, and so on. Because specialized funds are limited in their investments, you can assume that in many cases, they're a little riskier (more volatile) than the average fund.
- **International or global fund:** An international fund invests in companies based anywhere outside of the investor's home country. A global fund invests in securities located anywhere in the world, including the investor's home country. Although international and global funds may be good to round out a portfolio, they aren't without their risks. Along with the risk that investors face by just investing in securities in general, holders of international and global funds also face currency risk, which is the risk that the currency exchange rate between the U.S. and foreign issuers will hurt investors. There's also the additional risk that politics in a particular country will harm the value of the fund.
- **Index fund:** This type of fund invests in securities that are similar to a particular stock or bond index. Rather than being actively managed, these types of funds are passively managed, which means investors can expect lower or no management fees. Investors can expect that the NAV of the fund will increase or decrease based on the movement of the benchmark index (S&P 500, DJIA, and so on) the fund mimics.

Hedge funds: What are they?

You've probably heard about hedge funds but aren't exactly sure what they are. For the SIE exam, you do need to know a little bit about them. Because they aren't open- or closed-end funds, unit investment trusts, or face-amount certificate companies, they are an exception to the standard definition of investment company under the Investment Company Act of 1940. In addition, because they are considered *private* equity and are *only* open to sophisticated (accredited) investors, they are exempt from SEC registration. Hedge funds often require a very high initial investment — sometimes $500,000 or more — and therefore have limited or no liquidity. In addition, many have *lock-up provisions*, which means that investors cannot redeem or sell shares during the lock-up time.

Hedge funds hold a pool of investments and are professionally managed like mutual (open-end) funds but have a lot more flexibility. Hedge funds are typically much more aggressive in nature and may buy securities on margin, sell securities short, purchase or sell options, trade in currency, and so on in an attempt to maximize gains. I guess you can almost think of them as a "whatever it takes to make money" type of fund.

TIP

Don't let the variety of funds distract you too much. So many different funds are out there that the choices could drive you crazy. I list the main types, but funds can invest by objective (as previously listed) or composition, such as with foreign stock funds (which invest in foreign securities), tax-exempt funds (which invest in municipal bonds), U.S. government funds, and so on. The composition of the fund should help you match it with your customer's objectives. A customer primarily looking for safety and income might invest in a U.S. government bond fund.

Dealing with discounts

Investors who have the extra funds available may be able to receive a reduced sales charge for large dollar purchases. Breakpoints (see the next sections) and the letter of intent (see the next sections) are available to investors of open-end funds and unit investment trusts. Because closed-end funds, after the initial offering, are traded in the market, investors do not receive breakpoints. Dollar cost averaging and fixed share averaging are most often used for open-end fund purchases but may apply to other investments as well.

FUND OF A FUND

A fund of funds (FOF) is a fund that invests in other funds, as opposed to individual securities. Many funds are actually funds of funds, such as funds of hedge funds and *lifecycle funds*. Lifecycle funds are also called *targeted* or *age-based* funds. The idea behind lifecycle funds is to automatically adjust the composition of the fund so that investors take less risk as they get older. Typically, younger investors can afford to take more financial risk and, therefore, invest a larger percentage of their portfolio in equity securities and a lesser percentage in fixed-income securities. As investors grow older, the percentages should change so that a larger percentage of the portfolio is in fixed-income securities and a lesser percentage is in equity securities. Lifecycle funds are set up with targeted retirement dates. Investors choose the lifecycle fund that matches their retirement date, and the fund adjusts its holdings occasionally so that equity funds gradually decrease and funds that invest in fixed-income securities gradually increase.

Breakpoints

Funds have an investment adviser (portfolio manager) who gets paid a percentage of the value of the securities held in the fund. Therefore, one way to entice investors to spend more is to reduce the sales charge when they spend a certain minimum amount of money. That's where the breakpoint comes in.

Management investment companies divide purchase amounts into different tiers. Within a certain range, investors all pay the same sales charge percentage. But when investors spend and/or the account grows enough to put them in the next tier (when they hit the *breakpoint*), they get a reduced percentage sales charge. Breakpoints have no set schedule, so they vary from fund to fund.

Another discount, *rights of accumulation (ROA)*, allows shareholders to receive a reduced sales charge when the amount of the funds held (based on their current price, not purchase price) plus the amount purchased is enough to reach a breakpoint. There is no time limit for rights of accumulation.

Here are a few key points for you to remember for the SIE exam:

- Breakpoints must be disclosed in the prospectus.
- Breakpoints aren't available to partnerships or *investment clubs* (several people pooling money to receive reduced sales charges).
- Breakpoints are generally available to individual investors, joint accounts with family members, UGMA accounts, and corporations.

Breakpoint sales

As an agent, you're responsible for letting investors know about the existence of breakpoints. A *breakpoint sale* occurs when you induce a sale just below the level where an investor would receive a breakpoint or an additional sales discount. As shown in Table 9-2, you would make more money if a client purchased $23,000 worth of a fund instead of $25,000 because of the discounted sales charge the customer would receive at $25,000. It's your responsibility to let the client know that by investing $2,000 more, they can reach a breakpoint. Not disclosing breakpoints and inducing sales just below breakpoints are violations.

TABLE 9-2 Breakpoints for AylDec Growth Fund

Purchase Amount	Sales Charge
$1–$24,999	5%
$25,000–$49,999	3%
$50,000–$99,999	2%
$100,000 and up	1.5%

Letters of intent

A *letter of intent* (LOI) signed by an investor allows them to receive a breakpoint (quantity discount) right away with the initial purchase, even if the investor hasn't yet deposited enough money to achieve the breakpoint. This document states that as long as the investor deposits enough within a 13-month period, they will receive the discounted sales charge right away.

Here are a few specifics about the letter of intent that you need to know for the SIE:

- The investor has *13 months* after the first deposit to live up to the terms of the letter of intent in order to maintain the reduced sales charge.
- The LOI may be *backdated for up to 90 days*, meaning that it may apply to a previous purchase. However, remember that if the LOI applies to a previous purchase, the 13-month period starts from the date of that previous transaction.
- While the investor is under the letter of intent, shares are held in escrow to pay for the difference in the sales charge. If the investor doesn't live up to the terms of the obligation, the fund sells the shares held in escrow.

Here's how a letter of intent may work. Suppose that an investor purchased $10,000 worth of AylDec Growth Fund two months ago and is investing another $10,000 into the fund right now. They believe that they'll keep investing in AylDec Growth Fund and would like to get a reduced sales charge for investments of $25,000 and up (see Table 9-2 for the breakpoints).

An investor signs a LOI and wants to apply it to their previous purchase. Because their previous purchase was two months ago, the investor has only another 11 months to invest the remaining $5,000 into AylDec Growth Fund. The investor will receive the 3 percent sales charge on their $10,000 investment right now, which will be reduced by the overage they paid on the initial investment of $20,000. In other words, they'll pay only $100 sales charge on the current investment ($300 for this transaction minus the $200 overpaid from the previous investment) when they invest the $10,000. As long as the investor deposits the additional $5,000 by the end of the LOI's time frame, they'll pay the 3 percent sales charge. However, if they don't live up to the terms of the agreement, AylDec Growth Fund will sell the shares held in escrow to pay for the difference in the sales charge.

REMEMBER

Investors may redeem their shares at any time, even if they're under a LOI.

Figuring the sales charge and public offering price of open-end funds

You need to know two basic formulas to determine the sales charge and public offering price of open-end funds. Yes, every chapter seems to have more formulas, but these formulas are pretty straightforward and shouldn't cause you too many sleepless nights.

Sales charge percent

The sales charge, which is set at a maximum of 8½ percent, is part of the public offering price (POP), or ask price, not something tacked on afterward like a sales tax. One of the tricks for calculating the sales charge (or *load*) for open-end funds is remembering that the POP equals 100 percent. Therefore, if the sales charge is 8 percent, the NAV is 92 percent of the POP. The formula for determining the sales charge percentage is as follows:

$$\text{sales charge} = \frac{\text{ask} - \text{bid}}{\text{ask}} = \frac{\text{POP} - \text{NAV}}{\text{POP}}$$

The following question tests your expertise in calculating the sales charge of a mutual fund.

EXAMPLE

ABC Aggressive Growth Fund has a net asset value of $9.60 and a public offering price of $10.00. What is the sales charge percent?

(A) 3.4 percent

(B) 3.75 percent

(C) 4 percent

(D) 4.35 percent

The right answer is (C). The first thing you have to do is set up the equation. Start with the POP of $10.00 and subtract the NAV of $9.60 to get $0.40. Next, divide the $0.40 by the POP of $10.00 to get the sales charge of 4 percent:

$$\text{sales charge} = \frac{\text{POP} - \text{NAV}}{\text{POP}} = \frac{\$10.00 - \$9.60}{\$10.00} = \frac{\$0.40}{\$10.00} = 4\%$$

TIP

To help you remember that the ask (offer) price of a fund is the same as the POP, remember to ask your POP about it.

Public offering price (POP)

When taking the SIE exam, you may be asked to figure out the POP of a mutual fund when you're given only the sales charge percent and the NAV.

REMEMBER

The sales charge is already part of the POP, so the sales charge is *not* equal to the sales charge percent times the NAV. Use the following formula to figure out how much an investor has to pay to buy shares of the fund when you know only the NAV and the sales charge percentage:

$$\text{public offering price} = \frac{\text{net asset value}}{100\% - \text{sales charge}}$$

Classifying the load

As I explain earlier in this chapter, most mutual funds charge a sales charge (also known as a *load*) that's built into the POP. Most charge up front, but some charge constantly; some charge when redeeming; and some don't charge a load at all. Depending on how investors are charged, mutual funds are broken into classes:

- **Class A (front-end load):** The investor pays the load when purchasing shares of the fund. These funds typically are better for long-term investors because they usually have lower expense ratios, and they have breakpoints for large dollar purchases.
- **Class B (back-end load):** The investor pays the load when redeeming shares of the fund. These funds have higher expense ratios than Class A but often convert to Class A if held for many years. Very few mutual fund companies offer Class B shares at this point.
- **Class C (level load):** The investors pay a periodic fee (usually, annually) over the time period that they hold the fund. These funds have higher expense ratios than Class A and have an exit fee, which is often eliminated after a year or two. These funds typically are the best option for short-term investors.
- **No-load:** Investors don't pay a sales charge but may be charged some sort of transaction fee. Unlike load mutual funds, no-load funds may not charge a 12b-1 fee greater than 25 basis points.

Contemplating Other Investment Company Options

A couple of other types of investment companies — face-amount certificate companies and unit investment trusts (UITs) — aren't as popular as they used to be. Unfortunately, even though you may never sell any, you do need to know them for the SIE exam. You probably won't see more than a question or two on these topics. But exchange-traded funds (ETFs) are becoming increasingly popular, so your chance of seeing a question on ETFs and/or inverse ETFs is pretty high.

Face-amount certificate companies

A *face-amount certificate* is a type of packaged security that's similar to a zero-coupon bond (see Chapter 7); investors make either a lump-sum payment or periodic payments in return for a larger future payment. The issuer of a face-amount certificate guarantees payment of the face amount (a fixed sum) to the investor at a preset date. Very few face-amount certificate companies are around today, which is why the SIE exam doesn't include many questions about this type of packaged security.

Unit investment trusts

A *unit investment trust* (UIT) is a registered investment company that purchases a fixed (unmanaged) portfolio of income-producing securities (typically, bonds) and holds them in trust, which means that a UIT acts as a holding company for its investors. Then the company issues redeemable shares (units) that represent investors' interest in the trust. Unlike mutual funds, UITs are set up for a specific period of time and have a set termination date. Any capital gains, interest, and/or dividends are passed on to shareholders at regular intervals.

UITs have a finite number of shares outstanding and are distributed in the primary market at the initial public offering (IPO) price. Because a limited number of shares are outstanding and must be redeemed with the issuer or sponsor, liquidity is very limited.

Like mutual (open-end) funds, UITs can be purchased by type, such as growth, income, balanced, international, and so forth.

Here are the two main categories of these trusts that you should be familiar with for the exam:

- **Fixed investment trusts:** These companies invest in a portfolio of debt securities, and the trust terminates when all the bonds in the portfolio mature.
- **Participating trusts:** These companies invest in shares of mutual funds. The mutual funds that the trust holds don't change, but the securities held by the underlying mutual funds do.

REMEMBER

Because the portfolio of securities is fixed, UITs don't employ investment advisers and, therefore, have no investment adviser fees during the life of the trust. Nice break!

Exchange-traded products (funds and notes)

Exchange-traded products (ETPs), which you're likely to encounter on the exam, include ETFs and exchange-traded notes (ETNs). ETPs are considered to be alternatives to investing in mutual funds; they not only provide diversification, like mutual funds, but can also be sold short and purchased on margin. Investors should be aware, however, that they'll typically be charged a commission for buying and selling ETPs, which can really cut into any potential profits.

Most ETFs are *passive*, meaning that they're designed to be a single security that tracks certain indices such as the S&P 500, the S&P 100, the Dow Jones Industrial Average (DJIA), Nasdaq securities, and so on. Some ETFs are *active*, meaning that the securities they hold may change. Quite often, ETFs are designed to mirror securities held by certain mutual funds.

Exchange-traded funds

Exchange-traded funds (ETFs) are typically registered as open-end funds but act more like closed-end funds. They either passively track an index (such as the S&P 500 or DJIA) or another benchmark or are actively managed. ETFs, as the name implies, are actively traded on an exchange. ETFs provide investors with diversification along with ease of trading, the ability to sell short, and purchase shares on margin. Although ETFs can include investments across many asset classes, their main focus is on stocks (equity funds) and bonds (bond funds).

Inverse ETFs (also known as *short ETFs* or *bear ETFs*) are exchange-traded funds that are designed using many derivative products (options, for example) to attempt to profit from a decline in the value of the underlying index (the S&P 500, for example). Inverse ETFs can be used to profit from a decline in a broad market index or in a specific sector, such as the energy or financial sectors.

When compared to mutual funds, ETFs have some distinct advantages, including the ability to purchase shares on margin, ease of trading, and lower operating costs. Mutual funds have *forward pricing* — meaning that purchases or redemptions take place at the next computed public offering price (POP) or net asset value (NAV) — but ETFs can be traded any time throughout the day at the current bid or ask price.

A couple of disadvantages exist when comparing ETFs to mutual funds: Investors are typically charged commissions when buying and selling and, because they are so easy to trade, investors are more likely to trade excessively instead of holding their positions. (There are some commission-free ETFs but they usually have higher expense ratios.)

Leveraged ETFs are designed to attempt to return a *multiple* of the daily return of a benchmark index (the S&P 500, for example) that it tracks. (Think *multiplication* as in two times the daily return or three times the daily return.) Most leveraged and inverse ETFs are designed to achieve their objectives on a daily basis, which means that the securities held by the fund are changed more often than other funds.

Note: Because of the risk of inverse ETFs and leveraged ETFs, they are not long- or intermediate-term investments. In addition, because of the risk of these investments, it has to be determined by the firm if a customer is suitable for these investments prior to a recommendation. If a firm determines that a particular leveraged ETF or inverse ETF is suitable for recommendation, they have to determine which customers are suitable.

Exchange-traded notes

ETNs have characteristics of ETFs and fixed-income securities. ETNs are unsecured debt securities issued by a bank or financial institution. Their return is linked to a particular market index. ETNs don't provide dividends or coupon payments, so investors receive income at a specified maturity date. Because ETNs are traded on an exchange, they may be purchased on margin or sold short. If an investor holds an ETN until the maturity date, the investor receives a principal amount based on the performance of the index the note is tracking. Because ETNs are debt securities, they would be negatively impacted if the issuer's credit rating is downgraded. ETNs are not suitable for all investors because they're typically quite complex and carry many risks.

Investment company rules 17a-6 and 17a-7

There are certain additional rules for affiliated persons, advisers, officers, and/or directors of investment companies — specifically Rules 17a-6 and 17a-7. Please note the following important points:

- According to *Rule 17a-6*, affiliated persons of investment companies (persons affiliated with the manager of the fund, the custodian bank, and owners of 5 percent or more of the outstanding shares of the fund) are not allowed to trade securities within the fund's portfolio of securities. However, affiliated persons are certainly allowed to buy and redeem shares of the fund like regular public investors.
- *Rule 17a-7* says that advisers, officers, or directors may trade securities held by funds within the same family of funds (for example, trading securities held from the portfolio of securities of one of Fidelity's Large Value Funds to one of Fidelity's Large Blend Funds or vice versa).

REMEMBER

As with other securities, all investment company advertisements released by a broker–dealer must be approved by a registered principal of the firm.

Adding Annuities to a Portfolio

Annuities are similar to mutual funds, except annuities are designed to provide supplemental retirement income for investors and are typically more expensive than mutual funds. Life insurance companies issue annuities, and these investments provide guaranteed payments for the life of the holder. The SIE exam tests you on the two basic types of annuities: fixed and variable. Because variable annuities are considered securities and fixed annuities are not (because of the guaranteed payout by the insurance company), most of the annuity questions on the SIE exam are about variable annuities.

REMEMBER

Gather very specific information about your client before making recommendations. In addition, before recommending annuities, make sure you really understand the ins and outs and know what you're talking about. Annuities have been under the watchful eye of state insurance commissions and the SEC due to inappropriate recommendations from some brokers. Annuities typically aren't recommended for younger clients (most annuity purchasers are older than 50), for clients older than 75, or for a client's entire investment portfolio. For information on portfolio and securities analysis, see Chapter 13.

Looking at fixed annuities

The main thing for you to remember about *fixed annuities* is that they have fixed rates of return that the issuer guarantees. Investors pay money into fixed annuities, and the money is deposited into the insurance company's general account. After the investor starts receiving payments from the fixed annuity (usually monthly), the payments remain the same for the remainder of the investor's life. Because of the guaranteed payout, fixed annuities are *not* considered securities and, therefore, are exempt from SEC registration requirements and from the Investment Company Act of 1940. Therefore, whereas sellers of fixed annuities must have an appropriate insurance license, a securities license is not required.

Because the payouts associated with a fixed annuity remain the same, they're subject to *purchasing power risk* (the risk that the investment won't keep up with inflation). An investor who received payments of $1,000 per month in the 1970s may have been able to survive; however, that amount today is not even likely to pay your monthly grocery bill.

Focusing on variable annuities

Insurance companies introduced variable annuities as a way to keep pace with (or hopefully exceed) inflation. In a fixed annuity, the insurance company bears the investment risk; however, in a variable annuity, the investment risk is borne by the investor. Because the investors assume the investment risk, variable annuities are considered securities and must be registered with the SEC. All variable annuities have to be sold with a prospectus, and only individuals who hold appropriate securities and insurance licenses can sell them.

The money that investors deposit is held in a *separate account* (separate from the insurance company's other business) because the money is invested differently. The separate account is invested in securities such as common stock, bonds, mutual funds, and so on, with the hope that the investments will keep pace with or exceed the inflation rate.

The *assumed interest rate* (AIR) is a projection of the performance of the securities in the separate account over the life of the variable annuity contract. If the assumed interest rate is 4 percent and the performance of the securities in the separate account is equal to 4 percent, the investor receives the payouts that they expect. However, if the securities outperform the AIR, the investor receives higher payouts than expected. And unfortunately, if the securities held in the separate account underperform the AIR, the investor gets lower payouts than expected.

Putting money into (and receiving money from) annuities

Investors have choices when purchasing annuities and getting distributions. Investors may choose a lump-sum payment or multiple payments, depending on their needs. Investors also have a choice regarding how they want to get their distributions at retirement.

The pay-in (accumulation) phase

Payments into both fixed and variable annuities are made from after-tax dollars, meaning that the investor can't write the payments off on their taxes. However, payments into both fixed and variable annuities grow on a tax-deferred basis. (They aren't taxed until the money is withdrawn.) If an investor has contributed $80,000 into a variable annuity that's now worth $120,000, the investor is taxed only on the $40,000 difference because they have already paid taxes on the contribution. If an annuitant dies during the pay-in phase, most annuity contracts require a *death benefit* to be paid to the annuitant's beneficiary. The death benefit is typically the greater of all the money in the account or some guaranteed minimum.

Note: During the pay-in phase, an investor of a variable annuity purchases *accumulation units*. You can think of the accumulation units as being similar to shares of a mutual fund.

Investors have a few payment options to select when purchasing fixed or variable annuities. Here's the rundown of options:

- **Single payment deferred annuity:** An investor purchases the annuity with a lump-sum payment, and the payouts are delayed until some predetermined date.

» **Periodic payment deferred annuity:** An investor makes periodic payments (usually monthly) into the annuity, and the payouts are delayed until some predetermined date; this is the most common type of annuity.

» **Immediate annuity:** An investor purchases the annuity with a large sum, and the payouts begin right away or within a couple months.

Most annuities in which investors are making scheduled deposits provide a *waiver of premium* during the pay-in phase if the annuitant becomes disabled or is confined to long-term care.

Getting the payout

Investors of both fixed and variable annuities have several payout options. These options may cover just the *annuitant* (investor) or the annuitant and a survivor. No matter what type of payout option the investor chooses, they will be taxed on the amount above the contribution. The earnings grow on a tax-deferred basis, and the investor is not taxed on the earnings until withdrawal at retirement.

Note: During the payout phase (annuity phase) of a variable annuity, accumulation units are converted into a fixed number of *annuity units*. Investors receive a fixed number of annuity units periodically (usually monthly) with a variable value, depending on the performance of the securities in the separate account.

The kind of annuity (fixed or variable) and the payout options selected partly determines the payment amounts to the annuitant. So, when purchasing an annuity, the individual has to decide which of the following payout options works best for them:

» **Life (straight life) annuity:** This type of payment option provides income for the life of the *annuitant* (the individual covered by the annuity); however, after the annuitant dies, the insurance company stops making payments. This type of annuity is riskiest for the investor because if the annuitant dies earlier than expected, the insurance company gets to keep the leftover annuity money. Because it's the riskiest type of annuity for the annuitant, it has the highest payouts of all the options. As with joint life with last survivor annuities, life annuity payment amounts are based on the age and sex of the annuitant(s).

» **Life annuity with period certain:** This payout option guarantees payment to the annuitant for a minimum number of years (10, 20, and so on). For example, if the annuitant were to purchase an annuity with a 20-year guarantee and die after 7 years, a named beneficiary would receive the payments for the remaining 13 years.

» **Joint life with last survivor annuity:** This option guarantees payments over the lives of two individuals. As you can imagine, this type of annuity is typically set up for an individual and their spouse. When one spouse dies, the other spouse receives payments until their death. Because this type of annuity covers the lifespans of two individuals, it has the lowest payouts.

All annuities have a *mortality guarantee*. This guarantee means that the investor receives payments as long as they live, even if it's beyond their life expectancy.

Being mindful of the early withdrawal penalty

As with most other retirement plans, annuity investors are hit with a 10 percent early withdrawal penalty if they withdraw the money before age 59½. Yes, that's correct — the 10 percent penalty is added to the investor's tax bracket. Typically, annuities include a waiver of the 10 percent penalty in cases such as the need to cover long-term care expenses, death, or disability.

Understanding the Investment Component of Variable Life Insurance Products

You may wonder what life insurance is doing in the SIE, which is mainly about investments. Well, the answer is that certain life insurance products (specifically, *variable life* [VLI] and *variable universal life* [VUL]) have an investment component. Like variable annuities, variable life and variable universal life insurance policies have a separate account for investing. That separate account is kept separate from the insurance company's general fund. You won't need to know too much about the aforementioned insurance products, so I'll keep it brief.

REMEMBER

Persons selling variable annuities, variable life insurance, and variable universal life insurance must have not only an appropriate securities license but also an insurance license. Before recommending any of the previously mentioned products, you should do an analysis of the client's needs and make appropriate recommendations.

Variable life

Variable life policies have a fixed premium. As with variable annuities, the investor chooses the investments held in a separate account. The death benefit (face amount) on the policy is fixed to a minimum but not to a maximum. The death benefit may increase depending on the performance of the securities held in the separate account. If the separate account performs poorly, there may be limited or no cash value built up. Policyholders may borrow up to 75 percent of the cash value.

Variable universal life

Unlike variable life policies, variable universal life policies do not have fixed premiums. As such, they are sometimes called flexible premium variable life policies. As with variable life policies, the investors can pick the securities held in the separate account. In this case, since the premium is not fixed and the securities held in the separate account may perform poorly, the minimum death benefit and cash value are not guaranteed.

TIP

Variable annuities, variable life insurance, and variable universal life insurance may be referred to as *variable contracts* on the exam.

Testing Your Knowledge

This chapter touched base with some basics about different types of investment companies, annuities, life insurance, and so on. There are 15 questions here, so go ahead and see how you do. Good luck!

Practice questions

1. Which of the following is **true** of mutual funds?

   (A) They are a one-time offering of new securities and the shares must be sold in the market.

   (B) They are a one-time offering of new securities and the shares are redeemed with the issuer.

   (C) The issuer continuously offers new shares and the shares must be sold in the market.

   (D) The issuer continuously offers new shares and the shares are redeemed with the issuer.

2. For an investment company to be considered diversified, what is the maximum percentage of outstanding shares that the investment company can own of another company?

   (A) 1 percent.

   (B) 5 percent.

   (C) 10 percent.

   (D) 15 percent.

3. A fund that uses leverage, options, short sales, as well as other speculative investment strategies in an attempt to maximize gains is called a

   (A) balanced fund.

   (B) growth fund.

   (C) aggressive growth fund.

   (D) hedge fund.

4. Which of the following is **true** about a letter of intent?

   (A) It remains in effect for 13 months and it may be backdated for up to 90 days.

   (B) It remains in effect for 13 months and shares may be held in escrow.

   (C) It may be backdated for up to 90 days and shares may be held in escrow.

   (D) It remains in effect for 13 months, it may be backdated for up to 90 days, and the shares may be held in escrow.

5. What is the maximum sales charge for a mutual fund?

   (A) 8 percent, which is built into the public offering price.

   (B) 8 percent, which is added to the public offering price.

   (C) 8½ percent, which is built into the public offering price.

   (D) 8½ percent, which is added to the public offering price.

6. Which of the following is exempt from the Investment Company Act of 1940?

   (A) Mutual funds.

   (B) Closed-end funds.

   (C) Fixed annuities.

   (D) Variable annuities.

7. Which of the following is **true** of private-equity funds?

(A) They are exempt from SEC registration and they may purchase private companies.
(B) They are exempt from SEC registration and they may not purchase private companies.
(C) They must be registered with the SEC and they may purchase private companies.
(D) They must be registered with the SEC and they may not purchase private companies.

8. A _____________ fund only invests in a specific industry.

(A) sector.
(B) hedge.
(C) balanced.
(D) growth or aggressive growth.

9. Open-end funds may issue

(A) common stock.
(B) preferred stock.
(C) bonds.
(D) all of the above.

10. TUV Balanced Fund has a net asset value of $21.40 and a public offering price of $22.60. What is the sales charge percent?

(A) 5.15 percent.
(B) 5.30 percent.
(C) 5.60 percent.
(D) 5.66 percent.

11. FerdCo Communications Fund has a NAV of $14.20 and a POP of $15.02. FerdCo offers breakpoints for large dollar purchases. If FerdCo is only charging a 4 percent sales charge for purchases between $20,000 and $30,000, how many shares would Smith receive if purchasing $25,000 worth?

(A) 1,597.225 shares.
(B) 1,662.882 shares.
(C) 1,664.447 shares.
(D) 1,690.331 shares.

12. Which of the following can be purchased on margin?

(A) ETFs.
(B) Mutual fund Class A shares.
(C) Lifecycle funds.
(D) Money market funds.

13. All of the following are ways a variable annuity can be purchased **except**

(A) Immediate annuity.

(B) Payment deferred immediate annuity.

(C) Single payment deferred annuity.

(D) Periodic payment deferred annuity.

14. Which of the following life insurance products has a **fixed** premium?

(A) Variable life.

(B) Variable universal life.

(C) Both (A) and (B).

(D) Neither (A) nor (B).

15. Which of the following are **true** about variable annuities?

I. Investors purchase accumulation units during the pay-in phase.

II. Investors purchase annuity units during the pay-in phase.

III. If the performance of the securities held in the separate account exceeds the assumed interest rate, payouts increase.

IV. Payments to variable annuities are made from pretax dollars.

(A) I and III.

(B) I, III, and IV.

(C) II and III.

(D) II, III, and IV.

Answers and explanations

1. **D.** Mutual funds are open-end funds. Mutual fund issuers continuously offer new shares. Holders sell their shares by redeeming them with the issuer. By contrast, the issuer of a closed-end fund would sell the securities once, and then they would be traded in the market.

2. **C.** According to the Investment Company Act of 1940, out of the 75 percent that must be diversified, a diversified investment company may not own more than 10 percent of outstanding shares of another company. In addition, the investment company cannot invest more than 5 percent of its diversified assets into one issuer's securities.

3. **D.** Hedge funds are the most speculative (riskiest) type of fund. Hedge funds are available to accredited investors and are allowed to execute trades that other funds cannot.

4. **D.** Letters of intent allow mutual fund investors to receive a breakpoint (discounted sales charge for large dollar purchases) right away as long as they purchase enough of the fund within 13 months to receive the breakpoint. It may be backdated for up to 90 days so that the 13-month period can apply to a previous purchase. The issuer may hold shares in escrow to make sure the investor lives up to the terms of the letter of intent.

5. **C.** The maximum sales charge for a mutual fund is 8 1/2 percent of the amount invested. This means that investors make their purchase at the public offering price, which already has the sales charge built in.

6. **C.** Fixed annuities are not considered investment companies since the payout is guaranteed by the issuing insurance company.

7. **A.** Private-equity funds are only available to sophisticated (accredited) investors and are exempt from SEC registration. As part of their investment strategy, they may purchase private companies and/or purchase enough shares of public companies to gain control.

8. **A.** Sector funds invest in specific industries, such as automotives, pharmaceutical, energy, technology, and so on.

9. **A.** Open-end (mutual) funds may only issue common stock. Conversely, closed-end funds may issue common stock, preferred stock, and bonds.

10. **B.** With mutual funds, the sales charge is built into the public offering price (POP), so you have to subtract the net asset value (NAV) from the POP and then divide that by the POP. Check out the following equation:

$$\text{sales charge} = \frac{\text{POP} - \text{NAV}}{\text{POP}} = \frac{\$22.60 - \$21.40}{\$22.60} = \frac{\$1.20}{\$22.60} = 5.3\%$$

11. **D.** Because this investor is depositing enough to receive a breakpoint, the investor will not be paying the regular POP (public offering price). So, to determine what this investor will be paying per share, you have to calculate their POP. Look at the following equation:

$$\text{POP} = \frac{\text{NAV}}{100\% - \text{sales charge}} = \frac{\$14.20}{100\% - 4\%} = \frac{\$14.20}{96\%} = \$14.79 \text{ per share}$$

Okay, you got the difficult part of the question completed. Now all you have to do is divide the dollar purchase by Smith's cost per share. Don't let the fact that you may end up with fractional shares confuse you because you're allowed to purchase fractional shares of mutual funds.

$$\frac{\$25{,}000 \text{ invested}}{\$14.79 \text{ per share}} = 1{,}690.331 \text{ shares}$$

12. **A.** ETFs (Exchange-Traded Funds) can be purchased on margin, which provides investors with a leveraged position with increased risk. All of the other choices listed must be paid for in full. Since mutual funds are new securities, they may not be purchased on margin but are marginable after being held for 30 days.

13. **B.** (A), (C), and (D) are all possible ways of purchasing a variable annuity. However, an insurance company is not going to let you collect on an annuity when not a single payment has been made, as stated in (B).

14. **A.** Variable life insurance has a fixed premium, and the death benefit is fixed as to a minimum but not a maximum. If the securities held in the separate account outperform the expected return, the death benefit increases. Unlike variable life, variable universal life has a flexible premium. In this case, if the securities held in the separate account underperform, the death benefit and cash value are not guaranteed.

15. **A.** Looking at all of the answer choices, you see that III has to be true because it's in all of the answers. When an investor purchases an annuity, they're purchasing accumulation units. During the payout phase, the accumulation units are converted into annuity units. Unlike many retirement plans, purchases of annuities are made from after-tax dollars — in other words, they can't be written off on your taxes.

IN THIS CHAPTER

- » Understanding the specifics of DPPs
- » Distinguishing a limited partner from a general partner
- » Getting a handle on the paperwork and taxes involved
- » Looking at the different types of DPPs
- » Mitigating real estate risk with REITs
- » Testing your knowledge

Chapter 10 Working with Direct Participation Programs (DPPs) and REITs

Direct participation programs (DPPs) can raise money to invest in real estate, oil and gas, equipment leasing, and so on. More commonly known as limited partnerships, these businesses are somewhat similar to corporations (stockholder-owned companies). Limited partnerships, however, have some specific tax advantages (and disadvantages) that a lot of other investments don't have. According to tax laws, limited partnerships aren't taxed directly; the income or losses are passed directly through to the investors.

DPPs were once known as tax shelters because of the tax benefits to investors, but tax law changes have taken away a lot of these advantages. As a result, DPPs have somewhat fallen out of favor for investors (though not entirely for the SIE exam designers).

In this chapter, I explain the differences between limited and general partners, as well as the types of partnerships, their particular risks, and their potential rewards. The info here can help you examine those risks and rewards and determine the suitability of DPPs for investors. I also explain two inevitable facts of life as they apply to partnerships: the filing of paperwork and the payment of taxes. Finally, I explain the ins and outs and some of the specifics you need to know about real estate investment trusts (REITs). Unlike mutual funds that invest in a pool of securities, REITs invest in real estate. If you can't wait, they're discussed toward the end of the chapter. At the very end, I test your knowledge with a quick chapter quiz.

Searching for Identity: What DPPs Are (and Aren't)

Just as stockholders are owners of a corporation, limited (and general) partners are owners of a direct participation program. The key difference for people investing in DPPs is that they're *illiquid*, so investors can expect that their investment dollars will be tied up for a long period of time, although they receive tax advantages for doing so. Most DPPs (at least the ones you'll be tested on) are set up for real estate projects, oil and gas projects, or equipment leasing.

The Internal Revenue Service (IRS) determines whether an enterprise is a corporation or a limited partnership. For a limited partnership to be considered (and taxed) as a limited partnership, it has to avoid at least two of the following corporate characteristics (usually, the last two):

- **Having a centralized management:** Corporations have management in one place. The challenges of managing a limited partnership from several locations make this corporate trait quite difficult for a partnership to avoid.
- **Providing limited liability:** Corporate shareholders have limited liability; well, so do limited partners. The liability of corporate shareholders is limited to the amount invested, and the liability of limited partners, providing they don't take an active management role, is limited to the amount invested plus a portion of any recourse loans taken out by the partnership. Providing limited liability is pretty much unavoidable.
- **Having perpetual (never-ending) life:** Unlike corporations, which hope to last forever, limited partnerships are set up for a defined period of time. Limited partnerships are dissolved at a predetermined time, such as when their goals are met or after a set number of years.
- **Having free transferability of partnership interest:** DPPs are difficult to get into and out of. Unlike shares of stock, which can be freely bought and sold by anyone, limited partners not only have to pass the scrutiny of a registered rep, but also require the approval of the general partner. DPP investors (limited partners) must show that they have enough money to invest initially and have liquidity in other investments in the event that the partnership needs a loan.

For SIE exam purposes, you need to remember that the easiest corporate characteristics for a partnership to avoid are perpetual life (continuity of life) and free transferability of shares; the most difficult to avoid are providing limited liability and having a centralized management.

The DPP Characters: General and Limited Partners

By law, limited partnerships require at least one limited partner and one general partner. Limited partners are the investors, and general partners are the managers. When you're looking at general and limited partners, you want to focus on who can and can't do what.

General partners are responsible for the day-to-day decision-making (overseeing operations, deciding when to buy or sell, choosing what to invest in, and so on) for the partnership. Limited partners (the investors) provide the bulk of the money for the partnership but, unlike general partners, they can't make any of the partnership's investment decisions. Table 10-1 lays out the key points to remember about general and limited partners for the SIE.

TABLE 10-1 Comparing General and Limited Partners

Category	General Partners	Limited Partners
Decision-making	Are legally bound to make decisions in the best interest of the partnership; make all the partnership's day-to-day decisions	Have voting rights but can't make decisions for the partnership
Tasks	Buy and sell property for the partnership; manage the partnership's assets	Provide capital; vote; can keep general partners in check by reviewing books
Liability and litigation	Have unlimited liability (can be sued and held personally liable for all partnership debts and losses)	Have limited liability (limited to the amount invested and a proportionate share of any recourse loans taken by the partnership); can inspect all the partnership books; can sue the general partner or can sue to dissolve the partnership
Financial involvement	Maintain a financial interest in the partnership	Provide money contributed to the partnership, recourse debt of the partnership, and nonrecourse debt for real estate DPPs
Financial rewards	Receive compensation for managing the partnership	Receive their proportion of profits and losses
Conflicts of interest	Can't borrow money from the partnership; can't compete against the partnership (can't manage two buildings for two different partnerships in close proximity, for example)	None; can invest in competing partnerships

Partnerships are usually set up as *tenants in common* (TIC). Each limited partner owns an undivided interest in the property held by the partnership. In addition, in the event that one of the limited partners dies, their partnership interest will be passed to a beneficiary or to their estate.

Pushing Through Partnership Paperwork

You'll need to know about certain paperwork that's specific to limited partnerships. The following sections explain the three documents necessary for a limited partnership to exist.

Partnership agreement

The *partnership agreement* is a document that includes the rights and responsibilities of the limited and general partners. Included in the agreement are basics that you would probably guess, such as the name of the partnership, the location of the partnership, the name(s) of the general partner(s), and so on. In addition, the partnership agreement addresses the general partner's rights to

- Charge a management fee for making decisions for the partnership
- Enter the partnership into contracts
- Decide whether cash distributions will be made to the limited partners
- Accept or decline limited partners

Certificate of limited partnership

The *certificate of limited partnership* is the legal agreement between the general and limited partners, which is filed with the U.S. Securities and Exchange Commission (SEC) for public offerings and the secretary of state in the home state of the partnership. The certificate of limited partnership includes basic information such as the name of the partnership and its primary place of business, the names and addresses of the limited and general partner(s), and the following items:

- The objectives (goals) of the partnership and how long the partnership is expected to last
- The amount contributed by each partner, plus future expected investments
- How the profits are to be distributed
- The roles of the participants
- How the partnership can be dissolved
- Whether a limited partner can sell or assign their interest in the partnership

If any significant changes are made to the partnership, such as adding new limited partners, the certificate of limited partnership must be amended accordingly.

Subscription agreement

The *subscription agreement* is an application form that potential limited partners have to complete. The general partner uses this agreement to determine whether an investor is suitable to become a limited partner. The general partner has to sign the subscription agreement to officially accept an investor into the DPP.

One of your jobs as a registered rep is to prescreen the potential limited partner to make sure that the partnership is a good fit for that person. Consider the following questions:

- Does the investor have enough money to invest (net worth and annual income)?
- Does the investor have enough cash or liquidity in other investments in case the partnership needs more money?
- Is the investor okay with tying up their money for a long period of time?
- Can the investor handle the risks?

Also, you need to review the agreement to ensure (to the best of your ability) that the information the investor provides is complete and accurate. Besides the investor's payment, the subscription agreement has to include items such as the investor's net worth and annual income, a statement explaining the risks of investing in the partnership, and a power of attorney that allows the general partner to make partnership investment decisions for the limited partner. The subscription agreement is typically sent in with some form of payment from the potential limited partner.

Passive Income and Losses: Looking at Taxes on Partnerships

DPPs used to be called tax shelters because DPPs flow through (or pass through) not only income, but also losses to investors. (Corporations flow through only income.) Before 1986, investors could write off these losses against income from other investments, such as capital gains. Then

Congress stepped in because it felt that this write-off was too much of an advantage for investors (or our elected officials felt that the IRS wasn't collecting enough money) and decided to give DPPs their own tax category. Now, because investors aren't actively involved in earning the income, taxes on DPPs are classified as *passive income* and *passive losses*. (See Chapter 15 for more info on taxes and types of income.)

REMEMBER

The key thing to remember for SIE purposes is that investors can write off passive losses only against passive income from other DPP investments.

Evaluating DPPs

DPPs can be offered publicly or privately. Public offerings of DPPs must be registered with the SEC, whereas private offerings (offerings to mostly wealthy investors) are not. Typically, publicly offered DPPs have a lower unit (buy-in) cost than that of privately offered DPPs.

Certainly, direct participation programs provide some advantages, but they also have additional risks that investors don't face with other types of investments, such as having to lend additional money to the partnership if necessary. Therefore, when evaluating whether an investment in a DPP may be right for one of your clients, you need to determine whether investing in a partnership is wise for that client, and as their representative, you also need to consider the following items:

- The economic soundness of the program. In other words, do you think it will be profitable?
- The expertise (track record) of the general partner.
- The basic objectives of the program.
- The start-up costs involved.
- Leverage and other revenue considerations.

Checking Out Types of Partnerships

Partnerships can be formed to run just about any sort of business that you can imagine, including business development companies (BDCs), small-cap debt and equity, and so on. However, the SIE exam focuses on the big three: real estate, equipment leasing, and oil and gas. You need to be able to identify the risks and potential rewards of each of the following types of partnerships.

REMEMBER

Because of the risks associated with some types of DPPs, investors should have the ability to tie up their money for a long period of time and recover from a loss of all the money invested in case the partnership never becomes profitable.

Building on real estate partnership info

Real estate limited partnerships (RELPs) include programs that invest in raw land, new construction, existing properties, or government-assisted housing. You need to know the differences among the types of programs, along with their risks and potential rewards. Here are the types of real estate DPPs, from safest to riskiest:

- **Public housing (government-assisted housing programs):** This type of real estate DPP develops low-income and retirement housing. The focus of this type of DPP is to earn consistent income and receive tax credits. The U.S. government (through subsidies), via the U.S. Department of Housing and Urban Development (HUD), makes up any deficient rent payments. Appreciation potential is low, and maintenance costs can be high, but the DPP does benefit from some level of government security. Public-housing DPPs are backed by the U.S. government and, therefore, are typically considered to be the safest real estate DPPs.

- **Existing properties:** This type of DPP purchases existing properties with the intent of generating a regular stream of rental income. Because the properties already exist, this DPP generates immediate cash flow. The risks with this type of DPP are that the maintenance or repair expenses will eat into the profit and that tenants won't renew their leases. The properties already exist and are producing income, so risk for this type of DPP is relatively low.
- **New construction:** This type of DPP purchases property for the purpose of building. After completing the construction, the partnership's goal is to sell the property and structure at a profit after all expenses. Building costs may be more than expected, and the partnership doesn't receive income until the property is sold, but the DPP can benefit from appreciation on both the land and the structure. Although this investment is speculative (risky), it's not as risky as a raw-land DPP.
- **Raw land:** This type of DPP invests in undeveloped land in anticipation of long-term capital appreciation, which means raw-land DPPs don't actually build on or rent out the property. The partnership hopes that the property purchased will appreciate in value so that the DPP can sell the property for more than the purchase price plus all expenses.

Raw-land DPPs are considered to be the riskiest (most speculative) real estate DPPs because the partnership doesn't have any cash flow (no rental or sales income) or tax deductions. In addition, the value of the land may not increase; it may actually decrease. Also, investors cannot claim depreciation deductions because land cannot be depreciated.

The main thing to remember with real estate DPPs is that depending on which type you invest in, they can provide capital growth potential through the appreciation of property held by the DPP; cash flow for DPPs that hold rentals; tax deductions for mortgage interest, depreciation, and capital improvements; and tax credits for DPPs that hold government-assisted housing.

Gearing up with equipment leasing

Although you may be tested on equipment leasing programs on the SIE exam, it's typically the least-tested type of DPP on securities exams. Equipment leasing programs purchase equipment (trucks, heavy machinery, airplanes, railroad cars, computers, you name it) and lease it out to other businesses. The objective is to obtain a steady cash flow and *depreciation* write-offs. The two types of leasing arrangements you need to be aware of are the operating lease and the full payout lease:

- **Operating lease:** This type of equipment leasing program purchases equipment and leases it for a short period of time. The DPP doesn't receive the full value of the equipment during the first lease. This type of arrangement allows the DPP to lease the equipment several times during the life of the machinery.
- **Full payout lease:** This type of equipment leasing program purchases the equipment and leases it out for a long period of time. The DPP receives enough income from the first lease to cover the cost of the equipment and any financing costs. Usually, the initial lease lasts for the useful life of the equipment.

The main point to remember about equipment leasing is that the operating lease is riskier, because the equipment becomes less valuable or outdated over time and, therefore, less rentable.

Strengthening your grasp on oil and gas

Oil and gas partnerships include programs that produce income, are speculative in nature, or are a combination of the two. You need to know how the types of programs differ, along with their risks and potential rewards. Oil and gas partnerships also have certain tax advantages that are unique:

- **Intangible drilling costs (IDCs):** IDCs are write-offs for drilling expenses. The word *intangible* is your clue that you're not talking about actual equipment. These costs include wages for employees, fuel, repairs, hauling of equipment, insurance, and so on. IDCs are usually completely deductible in the tax year in which they occur. IDC deductions are only for drilling and preparing a well for the production of oil and gas.
- **Tangible drilling costs (TDCs):** TDCs are write-offs on items purchased that have salvage value (items that can be resold). All oil and gas DPPs have TDCs, which include costs for purchasing items such as storage tanks and well equipment. These costs aren't written off immediately but are *depreciated* (deducted) over several years.

REMEMBER

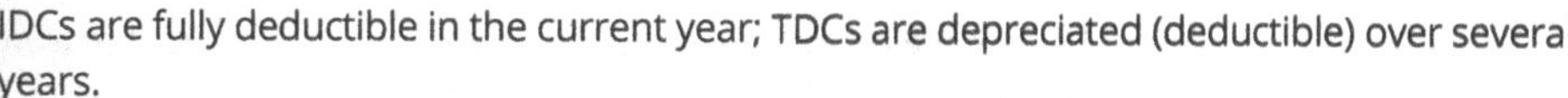

IDCs are fully deductible in the current year; TDCs are depreciated (deductible) over several years.

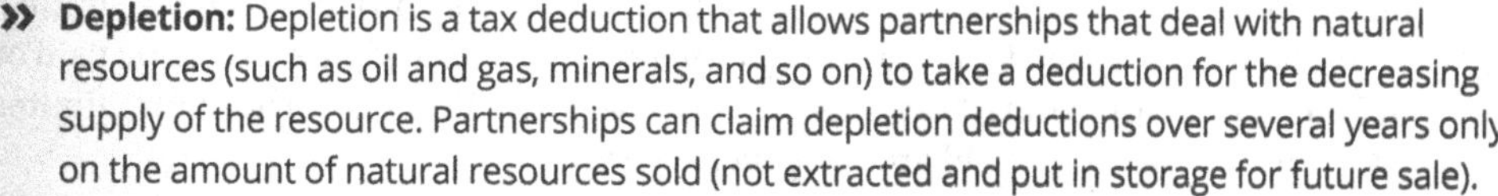

- **Depletion:** Depletion is a tax deduction that allows partnerships that deal with natural resources (such as oil and gas, minerals, and so on) to take a deduction for the decreasing supply of the resource. Partnerships can claim depletion deductions over several years only on the amount of natural resources sold (not extracted and put in storage for future sale).

REMEMBER

Depletion deductions are only for DPPs that deal with natural resources. On the SIE exam, the only DPP with depletion deductions that you need to be concerned about is oil and gas.

When investing in oil, partnerships can pioneer new territory, drill near existing wells, buy producing wells, or try a combination of those methods. For SIE-exam purposes, exploratory programs are the riskiest oil and gas DPPs because oil may never be found, and income programs are the safest oil and gas DPPs. To make your life easier (I hope), I've composed a DPP comparison chart (see Table 10-2) to help you focus on the main points of each type of oil and gas DPP.

TABLE 10-2 Advantages and Risks of Various Oil and Gas DPPs

Type	Objective	Advantages	Risks
Exploratory (wildcatting)	To locate and drill for oil and/or gas in unproven, undiscovered areas	Long-term capital appreciation potential; high returns for discovery of new oil or gas reserves	Riskiest oil and gas DPP because new oil reserves may never be found; high IDCs because the DPP isn't working with producing wells
Developmental	To drill near producing fields (in proven areas) with the hope of finding new reserves	Long-term capital appreciation potential with less risk than exploratory programs; oil and/or gas will likely be found	The property's expensive; the drilling costs may be higher than expected; the risk of dry holes (nonproducing wells) is still somewhat high; medium level of IDCs
Income	To provide immediate income by purchasing producing wells	The partnership generates immediate cash flow; the least risky of the oil and gas DPPs; no IDCs	High initial costs; the well could dry up; oil and/or gas prices could go down
Combination	To provide income to help pay for the cost of finding new oil reserves	The ability to offset the costs of drilling new wells by using income generated by existing wells	Carries the risks of all the programs combined

The following question concerns different DPP investments.

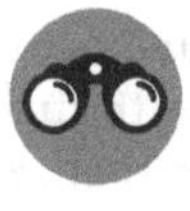

EXAMPLE

Ayla has money invested in a limited partnership that's expected to have a significant amount of income over the next one to two years. Which of the following programs would **best** help Ayla shelter the **most** of that income?

(A) Oil and gas exploratory

(B) Raw land purchasing

(C) Equipment leasing

(D) Existing real estate property

The answer you want is (A). Oil and gas exploratory programs spend a lot of money attempting to find and drill for oil. These programs have high IDCs, which are fully tax-deductible when the drilling occurs. Therefore, the oil and gas exploratory programs have the largest write-offs in the early years, which could help Ayla offset some or all of their passive income from the other limited partnership.

REMEMBER

Unlike corporations, DPPs have an ending date. That date could be predetermined as placed in the partnership agreement, when a project is completed (such as when buildings are built and sold, oil is found and the land is sold, equipment is sold, and so on), or when the limited partners vote to dissolve the partnership. When the partnership is dissolved, the first to be paid out of the partnership assets are secured creditors; then general creditors are paid; next, limited partners are paid; and the last to be paid are the general partners.

Reducing Real Estate Risk with REITs

A real estate investment trust (REIT) invests in real estate–related projects such as properties, mortgage loans, and construction loans. REITs pool the capital of many investors to manage property and/or purchase mortgage loans. Like other trusts, they issue shares to investors representing their interest in the trust. REITs registered with the SEC are known as *public REITs*, and those that aren't registered with the SEC are known as *private REITs*. In addition, REITs may be listed on an exchange or can trade over the counter. (See Chapter 14 for more info on markets.) They also provide real estate diversification and liquidity for investors.

REITs are distributed in the primary market at the initial public offering (IPO) price. Unlike mutual funds, which are redeemed with the issuer, REITs are traded (bought and sold) in the secondary market (the sale of outstanding securities) to other investors. In addition, REITs have a finite number of shares outstanding, like closed-end funds. Because REITs are traded in the secondary market, their price may be at a discount or premium to the net asset value (NAV; see Chapter 9), depending on profitability and investor sentiment.

Types of REITs include the following:

- **Equity REITs:** They take equity positions in real estate properties; the income is derived from rent collected or profits made when the properties are sold. Equity REITs typically hold income-producing properties like apartments, shopping malls, vacation resorts, and so on.
- **Mortgage REITs:** They are used to purchase construction loans and mortgages. The trust receives the interest paid on the loans and in turn passes it on to the owners of the trust (the investors).

» **Hybrid REITs:** These are a combination of equity and mortgage REITs. Hybrid REITs generate income derived from rent and capital gains (like equity REITs) and interest (like mortgage REITs).

As for taxation, REITs can avoid being taxed like a corporation if

» At least 75 percent of the income comes from activities related to real estate.

» At least 75 percent of the REIT's assets are in real estate, government securities, and/or cash.

» At least 90 percent of the net income received is distributed to shareholders (who pay taxes on the income). Which means that, unlike corporations that are taxed at the corporate level and investors who are taxed on the cash dividends, there's no double taxation with REITs if they follow these rules. So, for individuals investing in REITs, they have *tax-advantaged income.*

WARNING

Don't get REITs confused with real estate limited partnerships. Limited partnerships, such as RELPs, pass on (the industry term is *pass through*) income and losses to investors to claim on their own personal tax return; REITs only pass income and gains through to investors, not losses or write-offs.

REITS may be sold as private placements, nonlisted, or listed. Check out the following list of specifics:

» **Private (private placement) REITs:** REITs may be sold privately. Private REITs are exempt from SEC registration, and their shares don't trade on a national securities exchange, such as the New York Stock Exchange. As such, they're not subject to the same disclosure requirements as exchange-listed or public nonlisted REITs. Private REITs are exempt from SEC registration under Regulation D of the Securities Act of 1933. (See Chapter 5.) In general, private REITs can be sold only to accredited investors and institutional investors. Because they aren't sold on an exchange and can't be sold to just any investor, private REITs aren't liquid investments.

» **Registered nonlisted REITs:** Registered nonlisted REITs are also known as public nonlisted REITs (PNLRs). PNLRs are registered with the SEC but don't trade on a major exchange. PNLRs are similar to listed REITs in every way, including disclosure requirements, except that they're not as liquid. PNLRs may be purchased and sold over the counter and some issuers have periodic (daily or less frequent) repurchase options that allow investors to sell shares back to the issuer at the NAV.

» **Listed REITs:** As you can imagine, listed REITs are ones that have to register with the SEC and are also listed on one or more national exchanges. So listed REITs provide the highest degree of liquidity to investors.

Don't kill yourself worrying too much about REITs (not that you would); you won't get more than one or two questions on the SIE relating to REITs.

Testing Your Knowledge

This chapter gives you a brief glimpse of limited partnerships and real estate investment trusts. Even in some of the top-off exams like the Series 7, there isn't a tremendous amount of material to cover. Following is a ten-question quiz. Have fun!

Practice questions

1. Which of the following is **not true** of real estate investment trusts?

   (A) They may trade at a discount to the NAV.

   (B) They may invest in construction loans.

   (C) They are redeemable securities.

   (D) None of the above.

2. When making a public offering, which of the following documents is a limited partnership required to file with the SEC?

   (A) Certificate of limited partnership

   (B) Agreement of limited partnership

   (C) Subscription agreement

   (D) All of the above

3. Passive income can be written off against which of the following?

   (A) Passive losses

   (B) Capital losses

   (C) Both (A) and (B)

   (D) Neither (A) nor (B)

4. Which of the following types of oil and gas partnerships is the riskiest?

   (A) Exploratory

   (B) Developmental

   (C) Income

   (D) Combination

5. Which of the following documents must be signed by a general partner to accept a new limited partner?

   (A) Partnership welcome form

   (B) Certificate of limited partnership

   (C) Agreement of limited partnership

   (D) Subscription agreement

6. Which of the following corporate characteristics are the easiest for a limited partnership to avoid?

   (A) Having perpetual life and having centralized management

   (B) Having perpetual life and having free transferability

   (C) Providing limited liability and having centralized management

   (D) Providing limited liability and having free transferability

7. Which of the following is a benefit of investing in a direct participation program?

   (A) Professional management

   (B) Pass through of income and losses

   (C) Limited liability

   (D) All of the above

8. Which of the following partnership documents includes the rights and responsibilities of the general and limited partners?

(A) Certificate of limited partnership

(B) Subscription agreement

(C) Partnership agreement

(D) Both (A) and (C)

9. Depletion deductions may be claimed for

(A) equipment leasing programs

(B) raw land real estate programs

(C) exploratory oil and gas programs

(D) income oil and gas programs

10. Which of the following real estate investment trusts have income that is derived at least partially from rent collected?

I. Equity REITs

II. Mortgage REITs

III. Hybrid REITs

(A) I and III

(B) II and III

(C) I and II

(D) I, II, and III

Answers and explanations

1. **C.** REITs are a one-time offering of securities, and after the IPO, they must be purchased and sold in the market. They're not redeemed with the issuer, like mutual funds.

2. **A.** A limited partnership must file a certificate of limited partnership with the SEC before making a public offering.

3. **A.** Passive income is income received from a limited partnership. Passive income can be written off against passive losses but not capital losses.

4. **A.** Exploratory programs are the riskiest because the partnership is drilling in unproven areas trying to find oil. As with other investments, typically, the more risk investors take, the more potential reward. For this type of program, the risks are greatest, but if the partnership finds oil, the rewards should be much higher than those of other oil and gas programs.

5. **D.** To officially accept a new limited partner to the partnership, a general partner must sign the subscription agreement.

6. **B.** For a partnership to not be taxed as a corporation, it must avoid at least two corporate characteristics. The easiest corporate characteristics for a partnership to avoid are having a perpetual life (partnerships are set up for a finite period of time) and having free transferability to partnership interest. Because of the approval process, limited partnerships are some of the most difficult investments to get into and out of.

7. **D.** All the choices listed are benefits of investing in a limited partnership. Investors are certainly getting (or hoping for) professional management by way of a general partner. Also, because a partnership isn't taxed as a corporation, the gains and losses are passed through to investors. In addition, limited partners' losses are limited to the amount invested plus any recourse loans (for real estate DPPs only).

8. **C.** The partnership agreement lays out the rights and responsibilities of the limited and general partner(s).

9. **D.** To claim depletion deductions, the partnership has to be depleting a natural resource. Of the choices given, only oil and gas programs deal with a natural resource. Exploratory programs (ones that are looking for oil) don't have depletion deductions until they actually hit oil and start pulling it from the ground, like income programs.

10. **A.** Both equity REITs and hybrid REITs, which are a combination of equity and mortgage REITs, derive part of their income from rent collected from property that is owned.

IN THIS CHAPTER

» Understanding the specifics of options

» Feeling comfortable with an options chart

» Calculating the maximum loss, maximum gain, and breakeven points

» Discovering more about option rules

» Taking a chapter quiz

Chapter 11

Options: Understanding the Elements of Puts and Calls

Welcome to the wonderful world of options. I'm sure you've heard stories about the difficulty of options. Put your mind at ease; I'm here to make your life easier. Maybe I'm a little warped, but options are my favorite part of the SIE exam!

You don't have to do a lot of calculations related to options on the SIE, but the ones that you do have to do are relatively simple. More of the option questions on this exam are about understanding the terminology and rules. But in this chapter, I make facing any math questions you may encounter as simple as possible for you. At the end of this chapter, you get a chance to test your knowledge of options with a chapter quiz.

TIP

Many more-complex options strategies exist — straddles, spreads, combinations, and so on — but you won't need to calculate any of them on the SIE exam. If you're planning to take the Series 7 exam after this one, however, be prepared.

Acquainting Yourself with Option Basics

Options are just another investment vehicle that (ideally) more-savvy investors can use. Options may be used for *hedging* to protect a securities position or for *speculation*, when looking to trade or exercise an option at a profit.

An owner of an *option* has the right, but not the obligation, to buy or sell an underlying security (stock, bond, and so on) at a fixed price; as derivatives, options draw their value from that underlying security. Investors may either *exercise* the option (buy or sell the security at the fixed price), trade the option in the market, or let it expire.

All option strategies, whether simple or sophisticated, when broken down are made up of simple call and/or put options. After going over how to read an option, I explain a basic call option and help you figure out how to work with that before moving on to a put option. Next, I discuss options that are in-, at-, or out-of-the-money and the cost of options. After you've sufficiently mastered the basics, the rest (the more-difficult strategies later in this chapter) becomes easier.

Reading an option

To answer SIE questions relating to options, you have to be able to read an option. The following example shows you how a monthly option may appear on the real exam:

Buy 1 XYZ Apr 60 call at 5

Here are the seven elements of the option order ticket and how they apply to the example:

1. **Whether the investor is buying or selling the option: Buy**

   When an investor buys (or *longs, holds,* or *owns*) an option, they are in a position of power; that investor controls the option and decides whether and when to exercise the option. If an investor is selling *(shorting* or *writing)* an option, they are obligated to live up to the terms of the contract and must either purchase or sell the underlying stock if the holder exercises the option.

2. **The contract size: 1**

   You can assume that one option contract is for *100 shares* of the underlying stock. Although this idea isn't as heavily tested on the SIE exam, an investor may buy or sell multiple options (for example, five) if they're interested in having a position in more shares of stock. If an investor owns five option contracts, they're interested in 500 shares of stock, which you will need to know in more detail when taking other exams such as the Series 7.

3. **The name of the stock: XYZ**

   In this case, XYZ is the underlying stock that the investor has a right to purchase at a fixed price.

4. **The expiration month for the options: Apr**

   All options are owned for a fixed period of time. Investors can purchase options with daily, weekly, and monthly maturities as well as long-term options (*long-term equity anticipation securities*, known affectionately as LEAPS). In the preceding example, the option will expire in April — more specifically, at 11:59 p.m. EST (10:59 p.m. CST) on the third Friday in April. (All monthly options expire on the third Friday of the expiration month.)

   REMEMBER

   EST (Eastern Standard Time) is generally easier to recall than CST (Central Standard Time) and is more often tested.

5. **The strike (exercise) price of the option: 60**

   When the holder (*purchaser* or *owner*) *exercises* the option, they use the option contract to make the seller of the option buy or sell the underlying stock at the strike price. (See the next step for info on determining whether the seller is obligated to buy or sell.) In this case, if the holder were to exercise the option, the holder of the option would be able to purchase 100 shares of XYZ at $60 per share.

6. **The type of option: call**

   An investor can buy or sell a call option or buy or sell a put option. Calls give holders the right to buy the underlying security at a set price, whereas puts give holders the right to sell. So, in the example scenario, the holder has the right to buy the underlying security at the price stated in the preceding step.

7. **The premium: 5**

   Of course, an option investor doesn't get to have the option for nothing. An investor buys the option at the premium. In this case, the premium is 5, so a purchaser would have to pay $500 (5 × 100 shares per option), and the seller would receive the $500.

Looking at call options: The right to buy

A *call option* gives the holder (owner) the *right*, but not the obligation, to buy 100 shares of a security at a fixed price and the seller the *obligation* to sell the stock at the fixed price. (If the seller does not own 100 shares of the underlying security, they would have to purchase them in the market to be able to fulfill their obligation.) Owners of call options are bullish (picture a bull charging forward) because the investors want the price of the stock to increase. If the price of the stock increases above the strike price, holders can either exercise the option (buy the stock at a good price) or sell the option for a profit. By contrast, sellers of call options are neutral or bearish (imagine a bear hibernating for the winter) because they want the price of the underlying stock to either stay the same or decrease.

Assume that Ms. Smith buys 1 DEF Oct 40 call option. Ms. Smith bought the right to purchase 100 shares of DEF at 40. If the price of DEF increases to more than $40 per share, this option becomes very valuable to Ms. Smith because she can purchase the stock at $40 per share and sell it at the market price or sell the option at a higher price.

If DEF never eclipses the 40 strike (exercise) price, the option doesn't work out for poor Ms. Smith, and she doesn't exercise the option. However, it does work out for the seller of the option, because the seller receives a premium for selling the option, and the seller gets to pocket that premium.

Checking out put options: The right to sell

You can think of a put option as being the opposite of a call option (see the preceding section). The holder of a *put option* has the right to sell 100 shares of a security at a fixed price, and the writer (seller) of a put option has the obligation to buy the stock if exercised. Owners of put options are bearish because the investors want the price of the stock to decrease (so they can buy the stock at market price and immediately sell it at the higher strike price or sell their option at a higher premium). However, sellers of put options are bullish (they want the price of the stock to increase), because that would keep the option from going in-the-money (see the next section) and allow them to keep the premiums they received.

Assume that Mr. Jones buys 1 ABC October 60 put option. Mr. Jones is buying the right to sell 100 shares of ABC at 60. If the price of ABC decreases to less than $60 per share, this option becomes very valuable to Mr. Jones. If you were in Mr. Jones's shoes and ABC were to drop to $50 per share, you could purchase the stock in the market and exercise (use) the option to sell the stock at $60 per share, which would make you (the new Mr. Jones) very happy.

If ABC never drops below the 60 strike (exercise) price, the option doesn't work out for Mr. Jones and he doesn't exercise the option. However, it does work out for the seller of the option, because the seller receives a premium for selling the option that they get to keep.

Getting your money back: Options in-, at-, or out-of-the-money

To determine whether an option is in- or out-of-the-money, you have to figure out whether the investor would be able to get at least some of their premium money back if the option were exercised.

REMEMBER

You can figure out how much an option is in-the-money or out-of-the-money by finding the difference between the market value and the strike price. Here's how you know where in-the-money an option is:

» When an option is *in-the-money,* exercising the option lets investors sell a security for more than its current market value or purchase it for less — a pretty good deal.

The *intrinsic value* of an option is the amount that the option is in-the-money; if an option is out-of-the-money or at-the-money, the intrinsic value is zero.

» When an option is *out-of-the-money,* exercising the option means investors can't get the best prices; they'd have to buy the security for more than its market value or sell it for less. Obviously, holders of options that are out-of-the-money don't exercise them.

» When the strike price is the same as the market price, the option is *at-the-money;* this is true whether the option is a call or a put.

Call options — the right to buy — go in-the-money when the price of the stock is above the strike price. Suppose that an investor buys a DEF 60 call option and that DEF is trading at 62. In this case, the option would be in-the-money by two points (the option's intrinsic value). If that same investor were to buy that DEF 60 call option when DEF was trading at 55, the option would be out-of-the-money by five points (with an intrinsic value of zero).

A put option — the right to sell — goes in-the-money when the price of the stock drops below the strike price. For example, a TUV 80 call option is in-the-money when the price of TUV drops below 80. The reverse holds as well: If a put option is in-the-money when the price of the stock is below the strike price, it must be out-of-the-money when the price of the stock is above the strike price.

WARNING

Don't take the cost of the option (the premium) into consideration when determining whether an option is in-the-money or out-of-the-money. Having an option that's in-the-money is not the same as making a profit. (See the next section for info on premiums.)

TIP

Use the phrases *call up* and *put down* to recall when an option goes in-the-money. *Call up* can help you remember that a *call* option is in-the-money when the market price is *up,* or above the strike price. *Put down* can help you remember that a *put* option is in-the-money when the market price is *down,* or below the strike price.

The following question tests your knowledge of options being in- or out-of-the-money.

EXAMPLE

Which **two** of the following options are in-the-money if ABC is trading at 62 and DEF is trading at 44?

(A) An ABC Oct 60 call option and a DEF May 40 put option

(B) An ABC Oct 60 call option and a DEF May 50 put option

(C) An ABC Oct 70 call option and a DEF May 40 put option

(D) An ABC Oct 70 call option and a DEF May 50 put option

The correct answer is (B). Start with the strike (exercise) prices. You're *calling up* or *putting down* from the strike prices, not from the market prices. Because call options go in-the-money when the market price is above the strike price, Statement I is the only one that works for ABC. An ABC 60 call option would be in-the-money when the price of ABC is above 60. ABC is currently trading at 62, so that 60 call option is in-the-money. For the ABC 70 call option to be in-the-money, ABC would have to be trading higher than 70. Next, use *put down* for the DEF put options, because put options go in-the-money when the price of the stock goes below the strike price. Therefore, Statement IV makes sense because DEF is trading at 44, and that's below the DEF 50 put strike price but not the 40 put strike price.

When people purchase an option, it is said that they are *long* the option. An investor who is long an option has paid the premium for the option so they need the option to go in-the-money (the price of the underlying security to go in the correct direction) enough for them to not only recoup their premium but also make a few dollars.

When someone is *short* an option, it means that they sold the option. This means that they are on the opposite side of the transaction than the person who is long the option. In this case, the seller received a premium for selling the option. So, someone who is short an option is doing so for income and is hoping that the option expires out-of-the-money so that they get to keep the premium.

Paying the premium: The cost of an option

The *premium* of an option is the amount that the purchaser pays for the option. The premium may increase or decrease depending on whether an option goes in- or out-of-the-money, gets closer to expiration, and so on. The premium is made up of many different factors, including

- Whether the option is in-the-money (see the preceding section)
- The amount of time the investor has to use the option
- The volatility of the underlying security
- Investor sentiment (for example, whether buying calls on ABC stock is the cool thing to do right now)

One of the simple options math questions you may run across on the SIE exam requires you to figure out the time value of an option premium. *Time value* has to do with how long you have until an option expires. There's no set standard for time value, such as every month until an option expires costs buyers an extra $100. However, you can assume that if two options have everything in common except for the expiration month, the one with the longer expiration will have a higher premium. Ideally, the following equation can help keep you from getting a pit in your stomach:

$$P = I + T$$

In this formula, P is the premium or cost of the option, I is the intrinsic value of the option (the amount the option is in-the-money), and T is the time value of the option.

Here's how you find the time value for a BIF Oct 50 call option if the premium is 6 and BIF is trading at 52: Call options (the right to buy) go in-the-money when the price of the stock goes above the strike price (*call up* — see the preceding section). Because BIF is trading at 52 and the option is a 50 call option, it's two points in-the-money; therefore, the intrinsic value is two.

Because the premium is six and the intrinsic value is two, the premium must include four as a time value:

$$P = I + T$$
$$6 = 2 + T$$
$$T = 4$$

The following question tests your knowledge of using the formula $P = I + T$.

EXAMPLE

Use the following chart to answer the next question.

Stock	Strike Price	Calls		Puts	
LMN		July	Oct	July	Oct
40.50	30	13	14.5	0.25	0.50
40.50	40	2.5	4.5	1.5	2.75
40.50	50	0.25	0.75	10.5	12

What is the time value of an LMN October 30 call?

(A) 2.5

(B) 4

(C) 6.25

(D) 9.5

The answer you're looking for is (B). I threw you a curveball by giving you a chart similar to what you may see on the SIE exam. I hope you're able to find the premium that you need to answer the question. Most of the exhibits you get on the SIE are simple, and solving the problem is just a matter of locating the information you need.

In the chart, the first column shows the price of the stock trading in the market, the second column shows the strike prices for the options, and the rest of the chart shows the premiums for the calls and puts and the expiration months. Scan the chart under the October calls, which is in the fourth column; then look for the 30 strike price, which is in the first row of data. The column and row intersect at a premium of 14.5.

Now you need to find the intrinsic value (how much the option is in-the-money). Remember that call options go in-the-money when the price of the stock is above the strike price (call up). This is a 30 call option, and the price of the stock is 40.50, which is 10.5 above the strike price. Plug in the numbers, and you find that the premium includes a time value of 4:

$$P\,(\text{premium}) = I\,(\text{intrinsic value}) + T\,(\text{time value})$$
$$14.5 = 10.5 + T$$
$$T = 4$$

Incorporating Standard Option Math

I'm here to make your life easier. Prep courses use several different types of charts and formulas to figure out things such as gains or losses, breakeven points, maximum gain or loss, and so on. I believe that the easiest way is to use the options chart that follows. It's a simple Money Out,

Money In chart that you can use to plug in numbers. What's great about this chart is that you don't even necessarily have to understand what the heck is going on to determine the answers to most options questions. As this chapter progresses, I show you how incredibly useful the options chart can be.

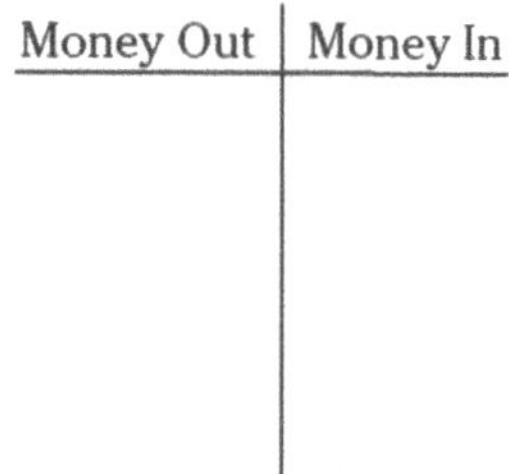

If it looks basic, it is — and that's the idea. Any time an investor spends money, you place that value in the Money Out side of the options chart, and any time an investor receives money, you place the number in the Money In side of the chart.

Calls same: Buying or selling call options

The most basic options calculations involve buying or selling call or put options. Although using the options chart may not be totally necessary for the more basic calculations (such as the one that follows in the next section), working with the chart now can help you get used to the tool so you'll be ready when the SIE exam tests your sanity with more-complex calculations.

As you work with options charts, you may notice a pattern when determining maximum losses and gains. Table 11-1 gives you a quick reference concerning the maximum gain or maximum loss an investor faces when buying or selling call options. Notice that the buyer's loss is equal to the seller's gain (and vice versa).

TABLE 11-1 Maximum Gains and Losses for Call Options

Buying or Selling	Maximum Loss	Maximum Gain
Buying a call	Premium	Unlimited
Selling a call	Unlimited	Premium

TIP

The key phrase to remember when working with call options is *calls same*, which means that the premium and the strike price go on the same side of the options chart.

Buying call options

The following steps show you how to calculate the maximum loss and gain for holders of call options (which give the holder the right to buy). I also show you how to find the breakeven point. Here's the order ticket for the example calculations:

Buy 1 XYZ Oct 40 call at 5

1. **Find the maximum loss (maximum potential loss or maximum possible loss).**

   The holder of an option doesn't have to exercise it, so the most they can lose is the premium. The premium is five, so this investor purchased the option for $500 (5 × 100 shares per option); therefore, you enter that value in the Money Out side of the options chart (think "money out of the investor's pocket"). According to the chart, the maximum loss (the most this investor can lose) is $500.

Money Out	Money In
$500	

2. **Determine the maximum gain (maximum potential gain or maximum possible gain).**

   To calculate the maximum gain, you have to exercise the option at the strike price. The strike price is 40, so you enter $4,000 (40 strike price × 100 shares per option) under its premium (which you added to the chart when calculating maximum loss); exercising the call means buying the stock, so that's Money Out. When exercising call options, always put the multiplied strike price under its premium. (Remember *calls same:* The premium and the strike price go on the same side of the options chart.)

Money Out	Money In
$500	
$4,000	

   Because you've already determined the maximum loss, look at the Money In portion of the options chart. The Money In is empty, so the maximum gain (the most money the investor can make) is unlimited.

When you see a question about the breakeven point, the SIE examiners are asking, "At what point does this investor not have a gain or loss?" The simplest way to figure out this point for a call option is to use *call up* (remember that call options go in-the-money when the price of the stock goes above the strike price — see the earlier section "Getting your money back: Options in-, at-, or out-of-the-money"). When using *call up*, you add the strike price to the premium:

$$\text{strike price} + \text{premium} = 40 + 5 = 45.$$

For this investor, the breakeven point is 45. This number makes sense because the investor paid $5 for the option, so the option has to go $5 in-the-money for the investor to recoup the amount they paid. *Note*: The breakeven point is always the same for the buyer and the seller.

Selling call options

Here, I show you how to find the maximum gain and loss, as well as the breakeven point, for sellers of call options. Here's the order ticket for the example calculations:

Sell 1 ZYX Oct 60 call at 2

1. **Determine the maximum gain.**

   The seller makes money only if the holder fails to exercise the option or exercises it when the option is in-the-money by less than the premium received. This investor sold the option for \$200 (2 × 100 shares per option); therefore, you enter that amount in the Money In side of the options chart. According to the chart, the maximum gain (the most that this investor can make) is the \$200 premium received. ***Note:*** The exercised strike price of \$6,000 (60 × 100 shares) doesn't come into play when determining the maximum gain in this example because the holder of the option would exercise the option only if it were in-the-money.

Money Out	Money In
	\$200

2. **Find the maximum loss.**

   To calculate the maximum loss, you need to exercise the option at the strike price. The strike price is 60, so you enter \$6,000 (60 strike price × 100 shares per option) under its premium. The \$6,000 goes in the Money In side of the options chart because this investor had to sell the stock to the holder at the strike price (60 × 100 shares). When exercising call options, always enter the multiplied strike price under its premium. (Remember *calls same:* The premium and the strike price go on the same side of the options chart.)

Money Out	Money In
	\$200
	\$6,000

   You've already determined the maximum gain; now look at the Money Out portion of the options chart. The Money Out is empty, so the maximum loss (the most money the investor can lose) is unlimited.

When you see a question about the breakeven point, the examiners are asking you, "At what point does this investor not have a gain or loss?" The simplest way to figure this out for a call option is to use *call up*. When using *call up*, you add the strike price to the premium:

$$\text{strike price} + \text{premium} = 60 + 2 = 62$$

For this investor, the breakeven point is 62. This makes sense because the investor received \$2 for the option, so the option has to go \$2 in-the-money for this investor to lose the amount that they received for selling the option. Call options go in-the-money when the price of the stock goes above the strike price.

Puts switch: Buying or selling put options

Fortunately, when you're calculating the buying or selling of put options (which give the holder the right to sell), you use the options chart in the same way but with a slight change (see the preceding section for info on call options). Instead of using *calls same* as you do with call options, you use *puts switch* — in other words, you place the premium and the strike price on opposite sides of the options chart.

Table 11-2 serves as a quick reference regarding the maximum gain or maximum loss an investor faces when buying or selling put options.

TABLE 11-2 Maximum Gains and Losses for Put Options

Buying or Selling	Maximum Loss	Maximum Gain
Buying a put	Premium	(Strike – premium) × 100 shares
Selling a put	(Strike – premium) × 100 shares	Premium

Buying put options

This section explains how to find the maximum loss, maximum gain, and the breakeven point for buyers (holders) of put options. Here's the ticket order for the calculations:

Buy 1 TUV Oct 55 put at 6

1. **Find the maximum loss.**

   Exercising an option is, well, optional for the holder, so buyers of put options can't lose more than the premium. Because this investor purchased the option for $600 (6 × 100 shares per option), you enter that value in the Money Out side of the options chart. The maximum loss (the most that this investor can lose) is the $600 premium paid.

Money Out	Money In
$600	

2. **Determine the maximum gain.**

   To find the maximum gain, you have to exercise the option at the strike price. The strike price is 55, so you enter $5,500 (55 strike price × 100 shares per option) on the opposite side of the options chart. (Remember *puts switch:* The premium and the strike price go on opposite sides of the options chart.) Exercising the option means selling the underlying stock, so that $5,500 is Money In.

Money Out	Money In
$600	$5,500

You've already determined the maximum loss; now look at the Money In portion of the options chart. Because you find $4,900 more Money In than Money Out ($5,500 – $600), the maximum gain is $4,900.

The breakeven point is the security price where the investor doesn't have a gain or loss. The simplest way to figure out this point for a put option is to use *put down* (put options go in-the-money when the price of the stock goes below the strike price). When using *put down*, you subtract the premium from the strike price:

strike price – premium = 55 – 6 = 49

For this investor, the breakeven point is 49. The investor paid $6 for the option, so the option has to go $6 in-the-money in order for this investor to recoup the amount that they paid. As with call options, the breakeven point is always the same for the buyer and the seller.

Selling put options

The following steps show you how to calculate the maximum gain and loss for the seller of a put option. I also demonstrate calculations for the breakeven point. Here's the ticket order for the example:

Sell 1 TUV Sep 30 put at 8

1. **Determine the maximum gain.**

   The seller makes money only if the holder of the option fails to exercise it. This investor sold the option for $800 (8 × 100 shares per option); you put that number in the Money In side of the options chart. The maximum gain (the most this investor can make) is $800.

Money Out	Money In
	$800

2. **Find the maximum loss.**

   To calculate the maximum loss, you have to exercise the option at the strike price. The strike price is 30, so you place $3,000 (30 strike price × 100 shares per option) on the opposite side of the options chart. (Remember *puts switch:* The premium and strike price go on opposite sides of the options chart.)

Money Out	Money In
$3,000	$800

> You've already determined the maximum gain; now look at the Money Out portion of the options chart and compare it to the Money In. The maximum potential loss for this investor is the $2,200 difference between the Money Out and the Money In.

You calculate the breakeven point for buying or selling puts the same way: You use *put down* (the strike price minus the premium) to figure out the breakeven point:

$$\text{strike price} - \text{premium} = 30 - 8 = 22$$

For this investor, the breakeven point is 22. Because this investor received $8 for the option, the option has to go $8 in-the-money for this investor to lose the amount they received for selling the option. Put options go in-the-money when the price of the stock goes below the strike price (put down).

Trading options: Opening and closing transactions

Although some investors hold onto their options long enough to actually exercise them, more often, investors trade options the way that they trade other investments. On the SIE exam, not only do you need to know the difference between opening and closing transactions, but you also have to be able to calculate the profit or loss for an investor trading options. This process is actually pretty easy when you break it down.

Putting things back where you found them: Doing opposite transactions

When distinguishing between opening and closing transactions, your key is to know whether this transaction is the first time or the second time the investor is buying or selling an option: The first time is an *opening*, and the second time is a *closing*. Regardless of whether it is an opening or closing transaction, it must be placed on the order ticket.

Here are your opening transactions:

- **Opening purchase:** An opening purchase occurs when an investor first buys a call or a put.
- **Opening sale:** An opening sale is when an investor first sells a call or a put.

If an investor already has an option position, the investor has to close that position by doing the opposite — through a closing transaction. If the investor originally purchased the option, they have to sell to close it. By contrast, if they originally sold the option, they have to purchase to close. Here are the two types of closing transactions:

- **Closing purchase:** A closing purchase occurs when an investor buys themselves out of a previous option position that they sold. For example, if an investor sold an XYZ Oct 40 call (opening sale), they would have to buy an XYZ Oct 40 call to close out the position. The second transaction is a closing purchase.

» **Closing sale:** A closing sale occurs when an investor sells themselves out of a previous option position that they purchased. For example, if an investor bought an ABC Sep 60 put (opening purchase), they would have to sell an ABC Sep 60 put to close out the position. The second transaction is a closing sale.

REMEMBER

When determining opening or closing transactions, whether the transactions are both calls or both puts doesn't matter.

The following question tests your knowledge of opening and closing transactions.

EXAMPLE

Mr. Kollen previously bought 1 XYZ Oct 65 call at 8 when the market price of XYZ was 64. XYZ is currently trading at 69, and Kollen decides that now would be a good time to sell the option that they previously purchased. The second option order ticket would be marked

(A) opening sale

(B) opening purchase

(C) closing sale

(D) closing purchase

The right answer is (C). This is the second time that Mr. Kollen does something with the option that he owns; therefore, the move has to be a closing transaction, and you can immediately eliminate (A) and (B). Mr. Kollen has to sell himself out of the position because he owns the option. The second order ticket would have to be marked *closing sale.*

Tricks of the options trade: Calculating gains and losses

In addition to knowing how to mark the order ticket, you have to be able to figure out an investor's gain or loss when trading options. This task isn't difficult after you master the options chart. The key thing to remember is that when an investor closes, they do the opposite of what they did before.

The following question tests your mastery of options trades.

EXAMPLE

Mrs. Wegner purchased 100 shares of DPY stock at $50 per share. Two weeks later, Mrs. Wegner sold 1 DPY Oct 55 call at 6. Mrs. Wegner held that position for three months before selling the DPY stock at $52 per share and closing the DPY Oct 55 call at 4. What is Mrs. Wegner's gain or loss on the transactions?

(A) $400 gain

(B) $400 loss

(C) $600 gain

(D) No gain or loss

The correct answer is (A). This question introduces stock trades as well as options transactions, but that's no problem. The options chart works for questions involving actual stocks and options or just options.

When you approach the transactions one at a time, the problem-solving process is actually pretty straightforward. Mrs. Wegner purchased 100 shares of DPY stock at $50 per share for a total of $5,000; therefore, you enter $5,000 in the Money Out side of the options chart. Next, she sold the DPY 55 call for a premium of 6, so you need to enter $600 (6 × 100 shares per option) on the Money In side of the chart because she received money for selling that option.

Three months later, Mrs. Wegner sold the stock for $5,200 ($52 per share × 100 shares) and received money for selling the stock. Place the $5,200 in the Money In side of the options chart. When closing the option, the customer has to do the opposite of what they did before. Originally, Mrs. Wegner sold the option, so to close, she has to buy the option (make a closing purchase). She purchased the option for $400 (4 × 100 shares per option), so enter $400 in the Money Out side of the options chart. All that's left for you to do is total up the two sides. Mrs. Wegner has $5,800 in and $5,400 out for a gain of $400.

Money Out	Money In
$5,000	$600
$400	$5,200
$5,400	$5,800

Got it covered: Stock/option contracts

When an investor purchases or sells option contracts on securities they actually own, that investor is choosing an excellent way to protect (hedge) against loss or to bring additional funds into their account, which would only be a partial hedge. The most common form is when an investor sells *covered call options.*

If an investor is selling a call option against a security that they own, the investor is considered to be *covered.* They're covered because if the option is exercised, they have the stock to deliver.

Take the following position as an example:

Buy 100 shares of QRS at $47 per share

Sell 1 QRS Dec 55 call at 4

1. **Find this investor's maximum potential loss.**

   Place the purchases and sales in the options chart. This investor purchased 100 shares of QRS stock at $47 per share for a total of $4,700. That's money spent, so enter $4,700 in the Money Out side of the options chart. Next, this investor sold 1 QRS Dec 55 call for a total premium of $400 (4 × 100 shares per option) and received money for selling that option, so you enter $400 in the Money In section of the options chart.

Money Out	Money In
$4,700	$400

This investor has more Money Out than Money In, so the investor's maximum potential loss is $4,300 ($4,700 minus $400).

2. **Determine the investor's maximum potential gain.**

   Placing the two transactions (in this case the stock purchase and the option sale) in the options chart helps you calculate the maximum gain as well as the maximum loss. To find the maximum gain, you need to exercise the option. You always exercise at the strike price, which in this case is 55. Take the $5,500 (55 × 100 shares per option) and place it under its premium. (Remember *calls same:* The exercised strike price and the premium go on the same side of the chart.) Total the two sides and you find that the Money In is $1,200 more than the Money Out, so that's the investor's maximum potential gain.

Money Out	Money In
$4,700	$400
	$5,500
$4,700	$5,900

When the investor is covered, finding the breakeven point is nice and easy for stock and options. Although you can use the options chart, you really don't need to in this example case. First, look at how much the investor paid for the stock; then look at how much more they paid or received for the option. Find the difference, and you have your breakeven point:

$47 stock price – $4 option premium = $43 breakeven point

Because this investor paid $47 per share for the stock and received back $4 per share for selling the option, this investor would need to receive another $43 per share to break even.

REMEMBER

Here's how to find the breakeven point for stock and options:

- **If the investor purchased twice** (bought the stock and bought a *protective put* option), add the stock price and the premium.
- **If the investor sold twice** (sold short the stock and sold an option), add the stock price and the premium.
- **If the investor had one buy and one sell** (for example, bought the stock and sold the option or sold short the stock and bought the option), subtract the premium from the stock price.

Index options

Besides buying or selling options on an individual stock, you can also buy or sell index options. Index options allow investors to speculate on (or hedge against) the price movement of market or segments of the market. Like indexes themselves, index options can be broad-based or narrow-based. The main broad-based index options are the S&P 500 Index Options (SPX), the S&P 500 Volatility Market Index (VIX), and the S&P 100 Index Options (OEX). Narrow-based index options include options on the energy sector (IXE), financial sector (IXM), healthcare sector (IXV), technology sector (IXU), and so on.

Note: The Chicago Board Options Exchange (CBOE) VIX is a measure of how volatile investors believe that the S&P 500 index will be over the next 30 days. Typically, the higher the expectation of volatility, the higher the VIX premiums.

Premiums of index options

Like standard stock options, the pricing unit for index options is 100. This means that, like standard stock options, you multiply the premium by 100 to get the actual cost.

Exercises in cash

Unlike regular stock options in which, when the option is exercised, the underlying security must be delivered, index options are settled in *cash*. This makes sense because it would be very difficult for investors to buy and deliver all the securities covered by an index. If the holder of an index call option exercises their option, they will receive the in-the-money amount multiplied by 100 based on the closing price at the *end of the trading day*, not the current value at the time of exercise.

Trading hours, settlement, and expiration dates

Narrow-based index options trade until 4:00 p.m. Eastern Time, and broad-based index options trade until 4:15 p.m. Eastern Time. Like equity options, the settlement date for index options is the next business day.

REMEMBER

Index options are either broad-based or narrow-based. So, people may buy or sell index options based on how they believe the market will perform overall (broad-based) or just how a segment of the market will perform (narrow-based). In this case, the same strategy of buying calls and selling puts if you're bullish and buying puts and selling calls if you're bearish still applies. However, investors can also use index options to hedge (protect) a portfolio against a market decline. If an investor has a diverse portfolio of securities, they may decide to purchase an OEX or SPX put to protect themselves in the event that the market declines. Also, an investor who has a large portfolio of healthcare sector stocks may purchase IXV put options to protect themselves in the event that healthcare stocks are falling out of favor. There are even index options that only last a week *(weeklys)* that allow investors a way to trade index options based on economic news or earnings reports that may have a sudden impact on the market or a segment of the market.

TIP

You'll find that buyers and sellers of index options can incorporate most of the same strategies as equity option buyers and sellers. These strategies include covered writing, hedging, protective puts, straddles and combinations, and uncovered call or put writing.

Gaining Additional Option Wisdom

To help you get a deeper understanding of options, you need to know a few additional things that you will most certainly see on the real-deal SIE exam. Some of these items include who issues the options, what an ROP is, what a risk disclosure document is, and so on.

Clearing through the OCC

The Options Clearing Corporation (OCC) is the issuer and guarantor of all listed options. The OCC decides which options will trade as well as their strike prices. In addition, when an investor decides to exercise their option, it's the OCC that randomly decides which firm on the other end will be responsible for fulfilling the terms of the option.

REMEMBER

The OCC does not determine the premium for options; the premium is determined by investors based on supply and demand, the option's intrinsic value (how much it's in-the-money — or away from the money based on the exercise price and the price of the underlying security), and the amount of time until the option expires.

That's ODD: Options risk disclosure document

Because options have a risk that is greater than almost any other investment, all investors must receive an options risk disclosure document (Options Disclosure Document or ODD) and a copy of amendments (if any) prior to their first options transaction (at the time of or before the account is approved). This ODD explains to investors option terminology and strategies as well as the potential rewards and risks involved in investing in options, such as the chance of losing all money invested or, if selling call options, facing an unlimited maximum loss potential. In addition to the risks, the ODD must also explain tax rules related to options, transaction costs, margin requirements, a special statement for uncovered option writers, and so on.

Getting the go-ahead: Registered options principal

Because of the extra risk of investing in options, all new accounts and option order tickets must be approved and signed by a registered options principal (ROP) — a manager with a Series 4 license, in other words. The registered options principal determines the amount of risk that each investor can take. Certainly, sophisticated investors with a lot of money are able to handle more risk than new option investors with a limited supply of funds.

Options account agreement

Within 15 days after approval of the account by an ROP, the customer must sign and return an options account agreement (OAA, sometimes just called an options agreement). Basically, the OAA just states that the customer has read the ODD, understands the risk associated with trading options, and will abide by the rules and regulations regarding options trading. Should anything change (such as the customers, investment objectives, financial situation, and so on), the customer agrees to notify the firm. If the OAA is not received within 15 days after approval of the account, the customer cannot open any new options positions.

Order ticket

You can find out more about what is required on an order ticket in Chapter 16. However, a few things are required on an order ticket that are unique to options. Besides the option that is being bought or sold, you have to write down whether the customer is establishing a long position (if they're buying) or a short position (if they're selling). In addition, for option sellers, you need to put down whether the seller is covered or uncovered (naked). The seller of a call option is considered covered if they own the underlying security or own an option on the same security with the same or longer expiration that will be in-the-money first. And, of course, an uncovered (naked) position is when the seller owns neither the underlying stock nor an option on the same security that will be in-the-money first with an equal or longer expiration date.

Last trade, last exercise, and expiration of an option

Unlike stock certificates, options do expire after a certain period of time. In addition, investors are limited as to when they can trade and exercise an option. Here's the timeline to keep in mind:

- **Last trade:** The last time an investor can trade an option is 4:00 p.m. Eastern Time on the business day of expiration.

- **Last exercise:** The last time an investor can exercise an option is 5:30 p.m. Eastern Time on the business day of expiration. If an option is in-the-money by at least 1 point at expiration, it will be automatically exercised. A vast majority of options (all equity [single-stock] and exchange-traded fund options) can be exercised any time up 'til expiration — this is known as *American style*. However, there are also *European-style* options that can be exercised only on the expiration date. European-style options include capped index options and some foreign currency options. Even though a European-style option can be exercised only at expiration, it can still be traded at any time.
- **Option expiration:** Options expire at 11:59 p.m. Eastern Time on the third Friday of the expiration month.

Exercise and assignment

When taking the SIE exam, you are expected to have a basic understanding of how options are exercised and assigned. Options are cleared through the OCC. Here's how an option is *exercised:*

> When a client wants to exercise an option they own, they contact their broker-dealer. The broker-dealer contacts the OCC. The trade settles in two business days after the OCC is notified because when the investor is exercising an option, they are actually trading stock (the right to buy or sell stock). Stock trades settle in two business days, so exercises of options settle in two business days. However, trades of options settle in *one* business day.

The steps involved look like this:

1. **Client #1 tells their broker-dealer (Broker A) to exercise the option.**
2. **Broker A notifies the Options Clearing Corporation.**
3. **The Options Clearing Corporation chooses the *contra broker* (the broker-dealer on the other side of the transaction — Broker B) randomly.**
4. **Broker B *assigns* a client (chooses the client — Client #2) either randomly, first-in-first-out (FIFO), or by any other method that is fair and reasonable.**

   However, Broker B cannot choose the assignment based on size (the one with the most options, the one with the least options, and so on).
5. **Client #2 sends the proceeds (stock or cash) to Broker B.**
6. **Broker B sends the proceeds directly to Broker A (the OCC doesn't handle stock or cash).**

So, if you were to look at a flow chart, it would look something like this:

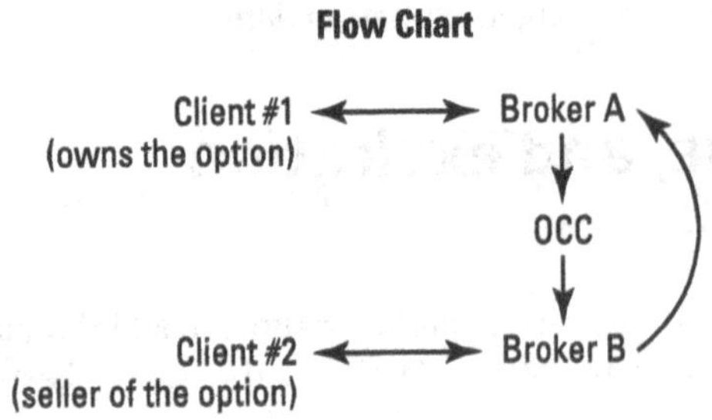

Flow Chart

Client #1 (owns the option) ⟷ Broker A

OCC

Client #2 (seller of the option) ⟷ Broker B

REMEMBER

Although most exercises of options are settled by the delivery of the underlying security, there are some that are settled by the delivery of *cash*. Specifically, *index options* (options on an index of securities) and *foreign currency options* are always settled in cash. This just makes sense because investors can't be expected to deliver an entire index for index options nor be expected to deliver the underlying foreign currency for foreign currency options.

Additional definitions

For some reason, the SIE exam writers decided you need to know some additional option-specific definitions. I cover several of them earlier in this chapter, but there are several more that you need to be aware of. I will try to make this as painless as possible.

- **Aggregate exercise price:** The exercise (strike) price of an option multiplied by the number of units (usually shares) of the underlying security covered by the option contract (usually 100 shares).
- **Class of options:** All option contracts of the same type (puts or calls) covering the same underlying security or index.
- **Clearing member:** A FINRA member that has been admitted to membership in the OCC (Options Clearing Corporation).
- **Closing sale transaction:** An option transaction in which the seller wants to reduce or eliminate a long position. So, for argument's sake, say an investor is long (owns) 1 ABC Oct 40 call. To close that position, the investor would short (write or sell) the 1 ABC Oct 40 call.
- **Conventional index option:** An option that overlies a basket (nine or more equity securities) or index of securities providing that no one security comprises more than 30 percent of the basket or index.
- **Conventional option:** Any option contract not issued or subject to issuance by the OCC or an OCC-cleared OTC option.
- **Delta neutral:** An equity options position that has been fully hedged. For example, owning 100 shares of ABC stock and owning an at-the-money put on ABC stock. Basically, offsetting long and short positions.
- **Net delta:** The number of shares that must be maintained (either long or short) to offset the risk the investor is facing by having an equity option position.
- **Opening writing (opening sale) transaction:** The initial sale of an option in which the seller receives the premium paid.
- **Outstanding:** An option contract that has been neither closed (closing sale) nor exercised and has not reached the expiration date.
- **Series of options:** All option contracts that are of the same class, same expiration date, and same exercise price and that cover the same number of units of the underlying security or index.
- **Type of option:** Either a call or a put.

Some additional option rules

Yes, I know . . . even more? Don't blame me; I didn't design the test. Anyway, as with the preceding section, I think a quick perusal of the following items will give you enough of a general understanding of some of the additional rules that you should be able to pick them out of any multiple-choice questions posed on the exam.

- **Position limits:** A number placed on the amount of option contracts that a person can hold or write on the same side of the market (bullish or bearish) on the same security. This will be covered more in depth if you are taking the Series 7.
- **Exercise limits:** A number placed on the amount of option contracts that a person can exercise on the same side of the market (bullish or bearish) within five consecutive business days. This will be covered in more detail if you are taking the Series 7 exam.
- **Limit on uncovered short positions:** FINRA may decide to limit the amount of uncovered short positions on option contracts of a given class if deemed necessary for the protection of investors.
- **Restrictions on option transactions and exercises:** As with the limit on uncovered short positions, FINRA may also place restrictions on option transactions or the exercise of option contracts in one or more series of options of any class when deemed necessary to help maintain a fair and orderly market.
- **Open order on the "ex-date" (ex-dividend date):** Since the underlying stock price will be lowered due to a dividend, the OCC will adjust option contracts accordingly unless otherwise instructed by the customer.
- **Confirmations:** Members are responsible for providing a written confirmation of each option transaction for each customer's account. The confirmation must include the type of option (call or put); the underlying security or index; the expiration month; the exercise (strike) price; the number of option contracts; the premium, trade, and settlement dates; whether it was a purchase or sale (long or short); opening or closing transaction; whether it was done on a principal or agency basis; the amount of commission; and so on. (There's more on confirmations in Chapter 16 — yippee!)
- **Statements of account (account statements):** All clients must receive account statements at least monthly if there has been any trading in the account for the previous month and at least quarterly (once every three months) when there has been no trading in the previous month. The account statements must show the security and money positions, entries, interest charges, and any other charges assessed against the account. (Account statements are covered in more detail in Chapter 16.)
- **Opening of accounts:** In order to open an options account for a client, the client must receive an ODD, and you must exercise due diligence by getting the customer's investment objectives, employment status, estimated annual income, estimated net worth, estimated liquid net worth, marital status, number of dependents, age, investment experience and knowledge, and so on. In addition, the account and all transactions must be approved by a registered options principal (ROP), branch office manager, or limited principal-general securities sales supervisor. All options accounts must be approved or disapproved within ten business days. Note that all options accounts may not be approved for all transactions — depending on the client, they may be approved for buying covered writing, uncovered writing, spreading, discretionary transactions, and so on.
- **Options account agreement (OAA):** Within 15 days of the approval of the account, a member must obtain from the customer a written account agreement, which states that the customer understands that they are aware of and agrees to be bound by FINRA rules regarding options trading.
- **Uncovered short option contracts:** Since uncovered short option contracts are the riskiest of all option contracts, member firms must create standard rules for evaluating the suitability of customers who plan on writing uncovered options.
- **Maintenance of records:** Each member must keep a current log, index, or other file for options-related complaints. Each complaint should be easily identified and easy to retrieve if necessary. Each complaint file (hopefully there aren't many) must contain the identification of

the complaint, the date the complaint was received, the name of the registered rep handling the account, a description of the complaint (such as a commission that they believe is too high), action taken (if any), and so on.

- **Discretionary account:** As with any discretionary account in which the client gives you the right to trade their account without pre-approval, it must be approved by a principal (manager). Options discretionary accounts must be approved in writing by a registered options principal (ROP) or limited principal-general securities sales supervisor, and written approval must be received from the client. In addition, discretionary accounts must be reviewed frequently by an ROP.
- **Suitability:** You may not recommend any option transaction(s) to a customer unless you believe that the transaction is suitable for the customer. Remember that you should already know the customer's investment objectives, financial information, and so on. In other words, you should not be recommending a risky option transaction for someone you deem incapable of handling the risk.
- **Supervision of accounts:** Members conducting an options business must have a written supervisory system in place to adequately address the public customer's option business. In addition, each branch office must have either a registered options principal or a limited principal-general securities sales supervisor in order to conduct options business.
- **Fingerprinting:** Individuals (directors, officers, employees, temporary personnel, consultants, vendors, independent contractors, service providers, and so on) who would have access to the CBOE facilities must be fingerprinted for identification and processing.

Testing Your Knowledge

As I said at the beginning of the chapter, this is really just an introduction to options, so the more-complex strategies are covered in subsequent exams. Take your time and read carefully. I give you a good mix of questions in this chapter quiz without too much math needed to answer the questions. Good luck.

Practice questions

1. Which of the following are bearish options strategies?

   (A) Buying calls and buying puts

   (B) Buying calls and selling calls

   (C) Buying puts and selling calls

   (D) Buying puts and selling puts

2. A customer owns call options on ABC common stock. ABC announces a cash dividend. What happens on the ex-dividend date?

   (A) The strike price is reduced to reflect the dividend.

   (B) The strike price remains the same.

   (C) The strike price is increased to reflect the dividend.

   (D) The strike price remains the same unless the customer instructs the OCC to change the strike price.

3. What are possible outcomes for the writer of a covered call option?

(A) Unlimited profit and unlimited loss

(B) Unlimited profit and limited loss

(C) Limited profit and unlimited loss

(D) Limited profit and limited loss

4. Declan is opening a new options account at a broker–dealer. Declan must return the signed options account agreement

(A) before the account is approved

(B) within 15 days after approval of the account

(C) any time before the first transaction

(D) sometime before receiving the risk disclosure document

5. An investor is long 1 GHI Oct 30 call. If GHI has a current market value of 33, which of the following is **true**?

(A) The option is out-of-the-money.

(B) The option is at-the-money.

(C) The option is in-the-money.

(D) The call has a negative intrinsic value.

6. An investor reads in the newspaper that JKL Dec 60 puts are trading for 6 when JKL is at 64. What is the time value of these options?

(A) 0

(B) 2

(C) 4

(D) 6

7. Which of the following is **true** regarding option contracts?

I. The OCC sets the contract size.

II. The OCC sets the strike prices.

III. The OCC sets the premiums.

IV. The OCC sets the expiration dates.

(A) I and III

(B) I, II, and IV

(C) II and III

(D) I, II, III, and IV

8. Melissa previously wrote 10 MKR Aug 45 puts for 6 each when the market price of MKR was 46. MKR is currently trading at 41 and the options are one week away from expiration. Melissa would like to buy her way out of that position. If she does, how would the second option order ticket be marked?

(A) Opening sale

(B) Opening purchase

(C) Closing sale

(D) Closing purchase

9. Who is the issuer and guarantor of all listed options?

(A) OAA

(B) OCC

(C) ODD

(D) FINRA

10. When is the last time an investor can exercise an option contract?

(A) 4:00 p.m. EST on the third Friday of the expiration month

(B) 5:30 p.m. EST on the third Friday of the expiration month

(C) 11:59 p.m. EST on the third Friday of the expiration month

(D) 11:59 p.m. CST on the third Friday of the expiration month

11. What is the breakeven point for an investor who writes a Sep 40 call for 3?

(A) 37

(B) 40

(C) 43

(D) 34

12. What is the maximum potential loss for an investor who shorted 1 XYZ Oct 40 put for 6?

(A) 3,400

(B) 4,000

(C) 4,600

(D) Unlimited

13. What is the breakeven point for an investor who is long 1 ABC Jan 60 put, which was purchased for 4?

(A) 56

(B) 60

(C) 64

(D) 66

14. Which **two** of the following options are in-the-money if TUV is trading at 43?

(A) TUV 40 calls and TUV 50 calls

(B) TUV 40 calls and TUV 50 puts

(C) TUV 40 puts and TUV 50 calls

(D) TUV 40 puts and TUV 50 puts

15. Before opening an options account, a customer must receive an

(A) OAA

(B) OCC

(C) ODD

(D) All of the above

16. Which **two** of the following options are **true** of an investor who writes a call option?

   I. The maximum potential gain is the premium.

   II. The maximum potential loss is the premium.

   III. The breakeven point is the premium added to the strike price.

   IV. The breakeven point is the premium subtracted from the strike price.

   (A) I and III

   (B) I and IV

   (C) II and III

   (D) II and IV

17. If an S&P 500 index call option is in-the-money at expiration, settlement is made by delivery of

   (A) cash

   (B) a percentage of all of the S&P 500 index stocks

   (C) an exchange-traded fund (ETF) that tracks the S&P 500

   (D) longer-term S&P 500 index call options

18. An investor buys 1 TUV Oct 45 put for a premium of $4 and simultaneously buys 100 shares of TUV stock for $45 per share. At expiration, the stock would have to be selling at what price per share for the investor to be able to break even?

   (A) $4

   (B) $41

   (C) $45

   (D) $49

Answers and explanations

1. **C.** If you are bearish on a particular security, you want the price of it to decrease. If you are buying a call option without any other underlying positions, you want the price of the underlying security to increase. Therefore, if you purchase a put, you want the price of the underlying security to decrease. You have to remember that the buyer and seller want opposite things to happen. So, if the buyer of a call wants the price of the underlying security to increase, the seller wants it to decrease. Stating that, buyers of puts and sellers of calls with no other positions are bearish.

2. **A.** For investors with options positions, the strike (exercise) price would be lowered as a result of a dividend on the underlying security on the ex-dividend date.

3. **D.** When writing (selling) a covered call option, you are selling a call option on a security that you already own. The purpose of this is to provide income on the security that you own by receiving the premium for the call option sold. However, this comes at a cost. If the price of the security owned increases to the point where it will be profitable for the purchaser of the option to exercise that option, they will be buying the underlying security from you at the exercise price. This limits your upside potential. In addition, if the option is exercised, the loss is limited because you don't have to purchase the security in the market; you already own the security, which would have to be delivered.

4. **B.** The options account agreement (OAA or options agreement) must be signed and returned within 15 days after approval of the account. The customer would first receive an options risk disclosure document (ODD or options disclosure document), and then the account would be approved by an options principal. Once approved, the customer has 15 days to sign and return the options account agreement.

5. **C.** Call options go in-the-money when the price of the underlying security trades above the strike (exercise) price. In this case, the underlying stock price is at 33 and the strike price of the option is 30, so it's 3 points in-the-money. In case you were wondering, there is no such thing as negative intrinsic value, which is answer (D).

6. **D.** The premium of an option is made up of intrinsic value (how much the option is in-the-money) and time value (the longer the time until expiration, the higher the time value). To determine the time value, use the following equation:

$$P\,(\text{premium}) = I\,(\text{intrinsic value}) + T\,(\text{time value})$$
$$6 = 0 + T$$
$$T = 6$$

Since put options go in-the-money when the price of the underlying security goes below the strike price, this option has no intrinsic value because the price of the stock is above the strike price. This means that the premium is made up of time value only.

7. **B.** The OCC (Options Clearing Corporation) sets the contract sizes, the strike prices, and the expiration dates for all options. However, the premium is based off of the intrinsic value (how much the option is in-the-money) and time value (the amount of time until the option expires).

8. **D.** When Melissa originally sold (wrote) the options, it was an initial or opening transaction. Since Melissa sold those options, it's an opening sale. To get out of that position, Melissa would need to close the options. So, since they have to purchase the options, it is a closing purchase.

9. **B.** The OCC (Options Clearing Corporation) is the issuer and guarantor of all listed options. The OCC decides which securities will have options, their strike prices, and their expiration dates. In addition, the OCC guarantees that option holders will be able to exercise their options.

10. **B.** The last trade of an option is 4:00 p.m. EST on the third Friday of the expiration month. The last exercise is 5:30 p.m. EST on the third Friday of the expiration month. And, options expire 11:59 p.m. EST on the third Friday of the expiration month.

11. **C.** When buying or selling a call option with no other positions, you need to add the premium to the strike (exercise) price to get the breakeven point. In this case, it doesn't matter whether this investor was purchasing or selling the option because both break even at the same price.

    $$40 + 3 = 43$$

12. **A.** The easiest way to determine the maximum potential loss for this question is to use an options chart.

Money Out	Money In
$4,000	$600

    Since the investor shorted (sold) the option for $600 (6 × 100 shares per option), they received $600, so you have to put that on the "Money In" side of the chart. That tells you that their maximum potential gain is $600. To determine the maximum potential loss, you have to exercise the option. So, you exercise at the strike (exercise) price of 40. This means that you have to put $4,000 (40 strike price × 100 shares per option) on the opposite side of its premium because puts switch (the exercised premium goes on the opposite side of the chart from its premium). Now you see that there is $3,400 more Out than In ($4,000 – $600), so that's the maximum potential loss.

13. **A.** When buying or selling a put option with no other positions, you need to subtract the premium from the strike (exercise) price to get the breakeven point. In this case, it doesn't matter whether this investor was purchasing or selling the option, because both break even at the same price.

    $$60 - 4 = 56$$

14. **B.** Call options go in-the-money when the price of the underlying stock goes above the strike price, and put options go in-the-money when the price of the underlying stock goes below the strike price. Therefore, TUV 40 calls and TUV 50 puts are both in-the-money.

15. **C.** Before a customer opens an options account, they must receive an ODD (options risk disclosure document). This is the document that explains all of the risks of investing in options so that customers will understand what they're getting into.

16. **A.** When writing (selling) an option with no other position, the maximum potential gain is the premium received. To determine the breakeven point for a call option, *call up*, which means to add the premium to the strike price.

17. **A.** Index options are settled in cash by multiplying the in-the-money amount by 100 per option.

18. **D.** This investor purchased a protective put to limit their potential downside loss. You could set this up in an options chart but in this case, it's probably not necessary. This investor purchased the stock for $45 per share, and since options are for 100 shares, they purchased the option for $4 per share. This means that they spent $49 ($45 + $4) per share to purchase both positions. This means that their breakeven point is $49.

4

Playing Nicely: Serving Your Client's Needs and Following the Rules

IN THIS PART . . .

Scrutinize customers' accounts and monitor market conditions that can affect their investments.

Familiarize yourself with the markets where securities trade.

Get an overview of income tax breaks and learn to distinguish long-term from short-term capital gains and losses for income tax purposes.

Review the essential rules for the care and protection of your customers' accounts.

IN THIS CHAPTER

» Understanding the information needed when opening accounts

» Knowing your customer

» Grasping the ins and outs of margin accounts

» Determining when you can call a potential customer

» Taking a chapter quiz and checking your answers

Chapter 12

Customer Accounts: Proper Handling of Accounts

If you're going to have a successful business, you have to be able to open accounts. Beyond "smiling and dialing," you need to know what to do when you hook your first whale. Next, you need to get the account form filled out. The account form and conversations with your customers and potential customers help you make appropriate recommendations. Ideally, the securities you recommend will do well, and your customers will rent a van with a huge speaker on top so they can drive through town telling everyone how great you are.

In this chapter, I cover topics related to opening accounts. First, I help you understand the information required on a new account form. Then I go over investment objectives, cover margin accounts, and finally discuss when you can call potential customers. I also include a couple of example questions throughout the chapter and more practice questions at the end to give you an idea of potential questions you may see on the exam.

Following Protocol When Opening Accounts

The SIE examiners seem to be focusing more and more on handling customer accounts. You need to know what to do to open accounts, how to take customer orders, the rules for sending out confirmations, and so on.

Filing the facts on the new account form

When you're opening any new account for a customer, you first need to fill out a *new account form* — an internal document used to compile basic information about customers for compliance purposes. Getting this information is your responsibility (or the responsibility of the broker–dealer).

Here's a list of the items that need to be on the new account form:

- The name(s) and address(es) of the individual(s) who'll have access to the account as well as a trusted contact person aged 18 or older (especially if the person opening the account is 65 or older) (A trusted contact person isn't mandatory but is highly encouraged.)
- The customer's date of birth. (The customer must be of legal age to open an account.)
- Contact telephone number(s).
- Marital status and number of dependents (if any).
- Whether the person opening the account or any immediate family member is employed or associated with the securities industry, and if so, how.
- The type of account the customer is opening (cash, margin, retirement, day trading, prime brokerage, delivery versus payment [DVP]/receive versus payment [RVP], advisory or fee-based, discretionary, options, and so on).
- The customer's Social Security number (if the customer is an individual) or tax ID number (if the customer is a business).
- The customer's occupation, employer, address of employer, and type of business (certain limitations are placed on customers who work for banks, broker–dealers, insurance companies, self-regulatory organizations [SROs], and so on).
- Domestic or foreign residency and/or citizenship (including ID info per the customer's driver's license, passport, state ID, government ID, and so on).
- Bank references and the customer's net worth, liquid net worth, tax rate, and annual income.
- Whether the customer is an insider of a company. (By insider, I mean a senior officer, director, or individual who owns more than 10 percent of the issuer's voting shares.)
- Financial investment experience.
- The signature of a principal (manager).

Broker–dealers may, in accordance with the Patriot Act, also require a customer to provide proof of identification. The Patriot Act was enacted in 2001 to help identify and catch terrorists. As part of the Patriot Act, broker–dealers should:

- Keep records of the information used to identify the customer via customer identification programs (CIPs). Financial institutions use CIPs to verify the identity of customers who want to conduct financial transactions.
- Verify that a customer doesn't appear on any list of known terrorists or terrorist organizations. (The Office of Financial Assets Control [OFAC], which is a U.S. Treasury Department Agency, keeps this list.)

REMEMBER

If anything changes (such as a customer's address or marital status), the new account form needs to be updated. Additionally, only individuals who are legally competent may open accounts — meaning you have to pay close attention to the investor's age and/or mental or physical ability. The Financial Industry Regulatory Authority (FINRA) has additional rules specifically put in place for older people and/or those with some sort of disability; these rules, regarding "financial exploitation of specified adults," are covered in Chapter 16.

TIP

In the course of filling out a new account form, be sure to ask whether your client is accredited. (See Chapter 14 for more on the topic of accredited investors.) If a client is, in fact, accredited, they're potentially able to handle more risk than non-accredited retail investors.

The following question tests your knowledge about opening a new account.

EXAMPLE

Which of the following people must sign a new account form?

(A) The customer and the customer's spouse

(B) A principal only

(C) The customer and a principal

(D) The customer, the registered representative, and a principal

The correct answer is (B). When you're opening a new account for a customer, the new account form requires only a principal's (manager's) signature. Make sure you don't assume extenuating circumstances. Surprisingly, you need the customer's signature on a new account form only if the customer is opening a margin account. Additionally, you need the spouse's signature only if the account you're opening is a joint one. Because the question doesn't say that the account is a margin or joint account, you can't assume that it is.

Gathering other important customer info

REMEMBER

You should be able to gather the information you need for making recommendations based on the customer's account form and your conversations with the person. It is your duty to know your customer (also conveniently called the "Know-Your-Customer [KYC] Rule") so you can make recommendations that are suitable and can handle the account effectively. Your recommendations should be fair and reasonable based on the customer's profile and within the customer's financial ability. Basically, don't recommend buying $100,000 of (extremely risky) penny stocks to a customer who's risk-averse and/or has limited funds. In the event that your customer doesn't provide you with enough information to make an appropriate recommendation, you can still take unsolicited orders. Some of the things you should know (or attempt to find out) to make accurate recommendations are

- The customer's age
- Other investments they might have
- Their financial situation and needs (Are they buying a house soon or paying for one or more of their kids to go to college, for example?)
- Their tax rate (Municipal bonds are more suitable for investors with a high tax rate.)
- Their investment objectives, such as retirement funding, generating current income, preservation of capital, capital growth, total return (growth and income), tax-advantaged investments, liquidity, speculation, trading profits, and long-term versus short-term risk
- Their investment experience (How much do you need to explain to them?)
- Their time horizon (expected time to reach a financial goal, if any)
- Their risk tolerance (Should you recommend speculative securities or only safer ones?)
- Their liquidity needs (Should you recommend only securities that they can get in and out of easily?)

Word on the street: Street name accounts

A *street name account* is an account registered in the name of the broker–dealer with an ID number for the benefit of the customer. Most firms put new customer accounts in street name format to make trading easier. Street name accounts give the investor a certain degree of privacy and help facilitate the trading of securities because the brokerage firm, not the customer, signs the certificates.

Because the securities are still owned by the investor, any gains and losses in the account are going to be the investor's, not the brokerage firm's.

You need to know a few rules about street name accounts for the SIE:

- You need a written statement from the customer attesting to the ownership of the account.
- With the exception of margin accounts, which must be in street name, a street name account may be changed by the customer to a regular account at any time.
- All margin accounts must be in street name.

Selecting the Appropriate Type of Account

Investors can open many types of accounts through a broker–dealer. Besides knowing a customer's investment profile, you also need a basic understanding of the types of accounts for the SIE exam. Fortunately, most of them are pretty straightforward.

Single and joint accounts

Some investors prefer to share; others like to go it alone. Whatever their preference, adults can open accounts that fit their needs:

- **Single (individual) accounts:** Naturally, this account is in the name of one person. The key thing for you to remember is that individuals may not open accounts in other people's names without written permission (power of attorney).
- **Joint accounts:** This account is in the name of more than one person. All individuals named on the account have equal trading authority for the account. For SIE exam purposes, you need to be familiar with two types of joint accounts:
  - *Joint tenants in common (JTIC):* With this type of account, when one tenant of the account dies, their portion of the account becomes part of their estate, which is governed by the decedent's will or state law. JTICs are usually set up for two or more unrelated investors. JTIC accounts are often set up for estate-planning purposes.
  - *Joint tenants with rights of survivorship (JTWROS):* With this type of joint account, when a joint tenant named on the account dies, their portion of the account passes on to the surviving joint tenant(s). These accounts are usually set up almost exclusively for married couples or otherwise related persons. In states where *community property laws* exist (currently, Arizona, California, Idaho, Louisiana, Nevada, New Mexico, Texas, Washington, and Wisconsin), investments acquired during the marriage are automatically presumed to be jointly owned by both spouses.

The following question tests your knowledge of account types.

EXAMPLE

All the following people may open a joint account **except**

(A) two friends

(B) a husband and wife

(C) a parent and minor son

(D) three people who work together

The right choice here is (C). A joint account is an account in the name of more than one adult. Choices (A), (B), and (D) are all possible for joint accounts, but an account opened for a minor must be a custodial account, which I discuss in the next section.

Trust accounts

Trust accounts are managed by one party (the trustee) for the benefit of another party. A specific type of trust account that you're most likely to see on the SIE exam is a custodial account. A *custodial account* is set up for a child who's too young to have their own account. A custodian (adult) makes the investment decisions for the account. Any adult can open a custodial account for a minor, so the people named on the account don't have to be related although they're typically parents.

REMEMBER

Custodial accounts for minors are trust accounts and may be referred to on the SIE exam as UGMA or UTMA accounts because they fall under the Uniform Gifts to Minors Act or Uniform Transfer to Minors Act. A *UTMA account* is an extension of the UGMA account that allows gifts in addition to cash and securities to be transferred to the minor. The additional gifts allowed are art, real estate, patents, and royalties.

Additionally, because minors are too young to make investment decisions for themselves, some rules are specific to custodian accounts:

- There can only be one custodian and one minor per account.
- The minor is responsible for the taxes. (The minor's Social Security number is registered for the account.)
- The account is registered in the name of the custodian for the benefit of the minor. (The custodian is responsible for endorsing all certificates.)
- The account can't be held in street name (in the name of the broker-dealer with an ID number; see the earlier section "Word on the street: Street name accounts").
- Because of the additional risk, securities can't be traded on margin or sold short.
- Anyone may give a gift of cash or securities to the minor. The gift is irrevocable (can't be refused by the custodian).
- If an account receives rights, the custodian can't let the rights expire. (See Chapter 6 for more info on rights.) Because rights have value, a custodian can exercise or sell the rights.

REMEMBER

UGMA accounts are for minors, so as soon as a minor reaches the age of majority, which is determined by the minor's state of residence, the UGMA account is terminated, and the account is transferred to a single account in the name of the (former) minor.

Discretionary accounts

Decision-making can be stressful, and some investors don't want to deal with it. With a *discretionary account*, an investor can give you (the registered rep) the right to make trading decisions for the account. All discretionary accounts need a *written power of attorney* signed by the investor, which gives trading authorization to the registered rep. Although this may sound wonderful, to keep reps honest, these discretionary accounts are scrutinized more than other accounts.

REMEMBER

If a customer places an order but doesn't specify the security, the number of shares or units, and/or whether the customer wants to buy or sell, you need a written power of attorney. If you don't have a written power of attorney, you can't do anything but decide when to place the order (timing). Suppose that one of your customers calls you and says that they want to sell 100 shares of ABC common stock, and you believe you can get them a better price later in the day. The customer can give you verbal permission to place the order at your discretion. This type of order is called a *market not held order* and is usually good only for the rest of the day.

Here are some specific rules for discretionary orders that you're likely to see on the SIE exam:

- Each discretionary order must be marked as *discretionary* on the order ticket.
- As with other orders, principals must sign each order ticket.
- A principal needs to review discretionary accounts regularly to make sure reps don't trade excessively to generate commissions — a practice referred to as *churning*.

REMEMBER

A *fiduciary* is anyone who can legally make decisions for another investor. Examples of fiduciaries are custodians (UGMA accounts), a registered rep having power of attorney, an executor of an estate, a trustee, and so on. Fiduciaries are subject to the *Prudent Man* or *Prudent Investor Rule*, which means that they must invest the principal client's money in securities designated by their state's *legal list*. As you can imagine, legal lists are filled with safer investments. If their state does not have a legal list, fiduciaries should invest in securities that only a prudent person who's seeking reasonable income and preservation of capital would invest in.

Corporate accounts

Only incorporated businesses can open corporate accounts. If you're opening a corporate account, you need to obtain the tax ID number of the corporation, which is similar to an individual's Social Security number. Additionally, you need to obtain a copy of the *corporate resolution*, which lets you know whom you should be taking trading instructions from (so you don't get a call like "Hi, I'm Joe Blow, the janitor for XYZ Corporation, and I'd like to purchase 1,000 shares of ABC for our company").

If a corporation wants to open a margin account (accounts that entail borrowing some money from the broker-dealer to purchase securities; see the "Cash or margin account" section later in the chapter), you also need a copy of the corporate charter (bylaws). The corporate charter has to state that the corporation is allowed to purchase securities on margin.

REMEMBER

An *unincorporated association* (sometimes called a *voluntary organization*) is a group of two or more individuals who form an organization for a specific purpose (in this case, investing). If an unincorporated association has too many characteristics of a corporation, such as having a board of directors, limited liability, and so on, it may be treated and taxed at a higher rate, as though it were a corporation.

Institutional accounts

Accounts set up by institutions such as banks, mutual funds, insurance companies, pension funds, hedge funds, and investment advisers are considered institutional accounts. Their role is to act as specialized investors on behalf of others.

Partnership accounts

Two or more individual owners of a business that's not set up as a corporation may set up a partnership account. All partnerships must complete a partnership agreement, which the broker–dealer has to keep on file. The *partnership agreement*, like a corporate resolution, states who has trading authorization for the account so you know whom you're supposed to be taking orders from.

Accounts can be opened for many reasons other than to just buy and sell stocks. They may be opened to trade options (which I cover in Chapter 11), or they may be opened to provide a family member with a means to pay for their education (such as the Section 529 savings plans I discuss in Chapter 8); or maybe they're set up to provide income for retirement. (Chapter 15 has the inside information on retirement income.) In addition, if you're registered as an investment adviser, you may be setting up a fee-based account rather than one in which you make a commission on trades (see the following section). No matter which type of account you open, unless you're otherwise directed by the client, portfolio diversification is key.

Cash or margin account

When one of your clients is opening a *cash account*, it means that they must pay for each trade in full. It doesn't mean that they have to drop off a suitcase full of cash; the trades are typically paid for via check or wire transfer. When a customer opens a cash account, they cannot purchase securities on margin.

INVESTMENT ADVISERS

If you're working for a broker–dealer as an agent, you'll receive commission when one of your clients makes a trade using your expert services. However, there is a different way to make money other than commission (or markups or markdowns, if your employer trades securities from inventory). More and more broker–dealers are requiring their agents to get a Series 66 (for those with a Series 7 license) or 65 license, which allows them to receive a fee for giving investment advice. To do so, you have to pass an exam and be registered as an investment adviser under the Investment Advisers Act of 1940. Advisers must have a written contract that explains to clients how and when fees will be charged. Fees may be charged as a percentage of managed assets for every time the adviser offers services or as wrap fees, whereby a client is charged fees for unlimited trading, advice, and/or custody of funds and securities. People who provide investment advice that is incidental to their business (teachers, accountants, lawyers, and so on) do not have to register as investment advisers.

Working with Margin Accounts

You don't necessarily need to have all of the funds available to buy securities. Thanks to the wonder of *margin accounts*, you can borrow money from a broker–dealer to purchase securities or borrow the securities themselves. Margin accounts allow customers to buy more securities (or sell more securities short) from you (as a registered rep) than they otherwise would, thus leading to more money in your pocket (a greater commission). This is a great thing if the margined securities are going the customer's way because it can increase their potential profit substantially. However, margin accounts are not without an additional degree of risk (which a lot of people found out back in 1929 when the market crashed and many economists blamed the crash on the number of securities purchased on margin). Margin accounts are great if the securities held in the account are going in the right direction but horrible if they aren't.

Disclosures and agreements: Getting margin paperwork out of the way

Because purchasing or selling short on margin involves extra risk, all customers must receive a *risk disclosure document*, which outlines those risks and some of the broker–dealer's rules. Besides receiving the margin risk disclosure document, the customer must sign a *margin agreement* before any securities can be purchased or sold short on margin. The margin agreement is broken down into three main sections:

- **The credit agreement:** Because the investors are borrowing money from the broker-dealer to purchase the securities, they're going to be charged interest on the money borrowed. The required credit agreement discloses the terms for that borrowing, including the interest rate charged, the broker-dealer's method of computation, and situations under which the interest rate may change.
- **The hypothecation agreement:** This required agreement states that all the margined securities must be held in street name (in the name of the broker-dealer for the benefit of the customer). In addition, it allows the broker-dealer to use a portion of the customer's margined securities as collateral for a bank loan *(rehypothecation)*. The hypothecation agreement also allows the broker-dealer to sell securities from the account in the event that the customer's equity falls below a certain level. When the securities held in a margin account go in the wrong direction, customers lose equity at a much faster rate than those who purchased the securities for cash.
- **The loan consent form:** The loan consent agreement (loan consent form) gives permission to the broker-dealer to lend a customer's margined securities to other investors or broker-dealers, typically for the short sale of securities. Although the credit agreement and hypothecation agreement are mandatory, investors may opt out of the loan consent agreement.

REMEMBER

Besides receiving the paperwork listed previously, investors opening margin accounts also receive a *margin risk disclosure document*. Some of the things included in that document let the client know that they can lose more money than deposited into the margin account, the firm can force the sale of securities or other assets in the account without contacting the client, the client cannot choose which securities in the account are liquidated, the firm can increase the house maintenance requirement in the account at any time, a client is not entitled to additional time to meet a margin call, and so on.

Introducing long and short margin accounts

As the heading here says, at this point, I'm only introducing long and short margin accounts. You will need to know some basics for the SIE exam, but a majority of the calculations related to margin accounts will be covered in some top-off exams like the Series 7.

In margin accounts, investors either borrow some money to buy securities or borrow the securities themselves. As a result, margin accounts come in two varieties: long and short.

As you may remember, *long* means *to buy*. With a *long margin account*, the customer buys securities by coming up with a certain percentage of the purchase price of the securities (typically 50 percent) and borrowing the balance from the broker-dealer. These optimistic investors are hoping for a bull market, because they want to sell the securities sometime later for a profit.

With a *short margin account*, investors are borrowing securities to immediately sell in the market. The process sounds a bit backward, but investors are selling things they don't actually own yet. Ideally, for this bearish customer, the price of the security will decrease so they can purchase the shares in the market at a lower price and then return them to the lender. The basics of buying low and selling high are there, but the customer is hoping to sell high before buying low.

REMEMBER

When a customer buys securities, they can purchase the securities in a cash or margin account, but when a customer sells short securities, the transaction *must* be executed in a margin account.

Regulation T: Following the Fed's rules for purchasing margin accounts

The Securities Exchange Act of 1934 gives the Federal Reserve Board (FRB) the authority to regulate the extension of credit to customers in the securities industry. In addition to Regulation T (see the following section), the FRB decides which securities can be purchased on margin. (Chapter 13 can tell you more about the FRB and its role in influencing money supply.)

Regulation T is the FRB rule that covers the credit broker-dealers may extend to customers who are purchasing securities. Currently for margin accounts both long and short, Regulation T (Reg T) requires customers to deposit at least 50 percent of the current market value of the securities purchased on margin, and the balance is borrowed from the broker-dealer.

REMEMBER

Regulation T is currently set at 50 percent; however, firms not willing to take as much risk may increase the *house margin* requirement to 55 percent, 60 percent, 65 percent, and so on. When you're taking the SIE and subsequent exams, you should assume 50 percent unless the question states a different percentage.

Regulation T applies not only to margin accounts, but also to cash accounts. (See Chapter 16.) When customers are purchasing securities in cash accounts, they must pay for the trade by the settlement date (one business day after the trade date, T+1). This delay is an extension of credit; therefore, it falls under Regulation T.

Reg T also identifies which securities can be purchased on margin and which ones can't.

Making margin call

A *margin call* (also known as a *Fed call, federal call,* or *Reg T call*) is the broker-dealer's demand for a customer to deposit money in a margin account when purchasing or shorting (selling short) securities. If a customer is buying securities on margin, the customer may deposit fully paid securities in lieu of cash to meet the margin call.

For both long and short margin accounts, the margin call is the dollar amount of securities purchased (or shorted) multiplied by Regulation T (50 percent). So, for example, if an investor purchases $50,000 worth of securities on margin, the margin call would be $25,000. Here's how you figure that:

$$\text{margin call} = \text{the current market value of the securities} \times \text{Reg T}$$
$$\text{margin call} = \$50{,}000 \times 50 = \$25{,}000$$

Opening a margin account: The initial requirements

The initial margin requirements for short and long accounts apply to the *first* transaction in a margin account only. After the account is established, the investor can purchase or short securities just by depositing Regulation T of the current market value of the securities purchased.

For an initial purchase in a margin account, customers must deposit a minimum of equity in their margin accounts. Currently, Regulation T calls for a minimum deposit of 50 percent of the current market value of the securities purchased. However, FINRA and the New York Stock Exchange (NYSE) call for a minimum deposit of $2,000 or for the customers to pay for the securities in full. (See the section "Starting long accounts," later in this chapter, for more on how this works.)

TIP

When you're taking the SIE, pay attention to the wording of the question. Phrases like "opens a margin account," "in an initial transaction in a margin account," and so on indicate that the question is asking for the initial margin requirement rather than a margin call. (See the preceding section for info on margin calls.)

REMEMBER

The following sections are based on the initial margin requirements for regular long and short margin accounts. If an investor wants to open a *day trading account,* the initial margin requirement is $25,000, and the investor must keep at least $25,000 in equity to continue trading. A day trading (pattern day trader) account is one in which the investor buys and sells the same security on the same day or sells short and buys the same security on the same day at least four times in five consecutive days.

Starting long accounts

To open a long margin account, the customer is required to deposit Regulation T or $2,000, whichever is greater. The exception to this rule occurs when a customer is purchasing less than $2,000 worth of securities on margin. In this case, the customer pays for the transaction in full. It certainly wouldn't make sense for a customer to purchase $1,000 of securities on margin and pay $2,000 when they could pay $1,000 if it were purchased in a cash account. Even if the customer pays in full, the account is still considered a margin account because the customer can make future purchases on margin as soon as they have more than $2,000 in equity.

Table 12-1 shows you how Regulation T (50% of the current market value) and the FINRA/NYSE requirements affect how much customers have to deposit when opening long margin accounts.

TABLE 12-1 Deposit Requirements for Long Margin Accounts

Dollar Amount of Purchase	Regulation T Requirement	FINRA/NYSE Requirement	Amount Customer Must Deposit
$6,000	$3,000	$2,000	$3,000
$3,000	$1,500	$2,000	$2,000
$1,000	$500	$1,000	$1,000

REMEMBER

In short, here's how much an investor has to deposit:

Purchase Price	Amount Owed
Initial purchase < $2,000	Full purchase price
$2,000 ≤ initial purchase ≤ $4,000	$2,000
Initial purchase > $4,000	Reg T (50% of market value)

Opening short accounts

The minimum deposit for short accounts is fairly easy to remember. The $2,000 minimum required by the FINRA and NYSE applies to short margin accounts. Because of the additional risk investors take when selling short securities, the $2,000 minimum always applies, even if the customer is selling short only $300 worth of securities. In this case, the customer must deposit 50 percent of the current market value of the securities or $2,000, whichever is greater. Here's the breakdown:

Shorting Price	Amount Owed
Initial sale ≤ $4,000	$2,000
Initial sale > $4,000	Reg T (50% of market value)

Obeying the Telephone Consumer Protection Act of 1991 (Telephone Act of 1991)

Because this chapter is about opening customer accounts, it makes sense to cover the Telephone Act of 1991. So if you're opening the account, you likely called them first unless you happen to be lucky enough to have a customer call you to open an account. To make sure that certain standards are used when calling potential customers (such as not calling them at midnight), the Telephone Act of 1991 was created. When you're dealing with *potential customers* on the phone, you need to know these rules:

- You can't make calls before 8 a.m. or after 9 p.m. local time of the potential customer.
- You have to give your name, company name, company address, and phone number.

» If you get a potential customer who's tired of being called, you should place that person on a *do not call list.* Each firm must maintain its own do not call list and have the U.S. government's National Do Not Call List available.

» Although fax machines are becoming more obsolete, you may not send unsolicited ads by fax machine.

REMEMBER

The Telephone Act of 1991 *does not* apply to existing customers (customers who have executed a trade or had a security in the firm's account in the previous 18 months) or calls from nonprofit organizations. Existing customers who want to be placed on the "do not call" list after opening an account cannot be solicited but can be updated on the status of their account.

Testing Your Knowledge

Okay, so you're feeling good about what you need to know for the SIE about different types of accounts. Here's a ten-question quiz to test your expertise. Good luck!

Practice questions

1. AylDec Corporation would like to open a margin account at Guess Right Broker–Dealer. To open the account, Guess Right would need

   I. to fill out a new account form

   II. a copy of the corporate resolution from AylDec

   III. a copy of the corporate charter from AylDec

   IV. a signed copy of the margin agreement

   (A) II and IV

   (B) I and IV

   (C) I, II, and IV

   (D) I, II, III, and IV

2. In an initial transaction in a margin account, Alyssa Hudson purchases 100 shares of Hopeful Corporation common stock at $12 per share. How much must Alyssa deposit to meet the margin requirement?

   (A) $600

   (B) $1,200

   (C) $2,000

   (D) Cannot be determined

3. All of the following are true about UGMA accounts **except**

   (A) parents of a minor can be joint custodians.

   (B) securities held in the account cannot be sold short or traded on margin.

   (C) gifts of securities to the minor are irrevocable.

   (D) they can't be held in street name.

4. Which of the following **does not** have to be included on a new account form?

(A) The customer's signature

(B) The registered representative's signature

(C) The customer's marital status and number of dependents

(D) The customer's bank references

5. According to the Telephone Act of 1991, which of the following is **true**?

(A) You may not make calls to potential customers before 8 a.m. or after 9 p.m.

(B) You may not make calls to potential customers before 8 a.m. or after 9 p.m. local time of the customer.

(C) You may not make calls to potential customers before 9 a.m. or after 8 p.m.

(D) You may not make calls to potential customers before 9 a.m. or after 8 p.m. local time of the customer.

6. Which of the following documents are required for an investor opening a margin account?

(A) A credit agreement and a hypothecation agreement

(B) A credit agreement and a loan consent form

(C) A hypothecation agreement and a loan consent form

(D) A credit agreement, a hypothecation agreement, and a loan consent form

7. Which **two** of the following are **true**?

I. If an investor of a joint tenants with rights of survivorship account dies, their portion of the account is transferred to their estate.

II. If an investor of a joint tenants with rights of survivorship account dies, their portion of the account is transferred to the remaining account holder(s).

III. If an investor of a joint tenants in common account dies, their portion of the account is transferred to their estate.

IV. If an investor of a joint tenants in common account dies, their portion of the account is transferred to the remaining account holder(s).

(A) II and IV

(B) I and IV

(C) II and III

(D) II and IV

8. A customer opens a short margin account by selling short 200 shares of DIM common stock at $17 per share. What is the margin call?

(A) $1,700

(B) $2,000

(C) $3,400

(D) Cannot be determined

9. To make proper recommendations to a client, you should know their

(A) age and liquidity needs

(B) time horizon and tax bracket

(C) age, tax bracket, and liquidity needs

(D) age, time horizon, tax bracket, and liquidity needs

10. The Patriot Act requires broker–dealers to identify their investors through

(A) CIPs

(B) DIMs

(C) LLPs

(D) All of the above

11. The tax ID of ________________ is required for the opening of an UTMA account.

(A) both parents

(B) at least one parent

(C) the minor

(D) the custodian

12. John Smith has a joint account with sisters Mirabelle and Elyse. If the account was set up as a joint with tenants in common, which of the following is true?

(A) Since John and siblings are not married, they could not have set up an account as joint with tenants in common.

(B) John and the two sisters must share equally in the assets of the account.

(C) If any of the siblings die, that individual's portion of the account is divided equally among the two remaining siblings.

(D) Ownership of the decedent's assets in the account are governed by their will (if any) or by the laws in the state in which they live.

Answers and explanations

1. **D.** For any new account, a new account form must be filled out by the broker–dealer. Because this is a margin account, a margin agreement must be signed and the broker–dealer must obtain a copy of the corporate charter (bylaws), which would need to state that the corporation is allowed to purchase or sell short on margin. In addition, because the account is a corporate account, you need to know who in that corporation has the authority to trade the account; that's where the corporate resolution comes in.

2. **B.** The key to this question is that it is an initial transaction in a margin account. So in this case, the customer purchased $1,200 (100 shares × $12) of securities. Reg T (50 percent) of that amount would be $600 ($1,200 × 50%). That would be the correct answer if it were an existing margin account. Because Alyssa is just opening the margin account, however, Alyssa would either have to deposit the Reg T amount if over $2,000, $2,000, or pay in full if the purchase is less than $2,000, which in this case it is. Therefore, Alyssa would have to deposit $1,200.

3. **A.** Regarding UGMA (Uniform Gifts to Minors Act), you can only have one minor and one custodian per account. So in this case, even though the minor may have two parents, they can't be joint custodians.

4. **A.** Although the registered representative's and principal's signatures have to be on a new account form, the customer's does not. This allows the registered rep to make a trade with a customer right away without having to have the customer fill out, and ideally return, the new account form.

5. **B.** The rule is that you can't call potential customers (cold calling) before 8 a.m. or after 9 p.m. local time of the customer. If a potential client doesn't want to be called anymore, you must place them on your firm's do not call list.

6. **D.** The credit agreement, hypothecation agreement, and loan consent form are all part of the margin agreement that must be signed by new clients who want to open a margin account. In the event that it is a corporation that is opening the margin account, you would also need a corporate charter (bylaws), which would spell out whether the corporation was allowed to buy or short securities on margin.

7. **C.** When an investor of an account set up as joint tenants with rights of survivorship dies, their portion of the account goes to the remaining survivor(s). This is the type of account typically set up by a married couple. If the account is set up as joint with tenants in common, if an investor dies, their portion of the account would go to their estate.

8. **B.** Because this investor is opening a short margin account, they must deposit either the Reg T amount or $2,000, whichever is greater. Because 50 percent of the Reg T amount ($3,400 × 50% = $1,700) is less than $2,000, this investor must come up with $2,000 to meet the call.

9. **D.** Besides the information required on a new account form, you should gain any knowledge about your client that you can to help you make better investment recommendations. The customer's age is important because, in most cases, the older people get, the less risk they should take. So for older investors, you may want to rebalance their portfolio so they have more debt securities than a younger investor would. The time horizon is typically the amount of time until someone retires, but it could be something like the number of years until the investor plans on buying a house and so on. The tax bracket is important because

if the tax bracket is high, you may want to recommend tax-advantaged investments like municipal bonds. Liquidity needs are how easy it is for the investor to sell the securities in a hurry if needed. In this case, you wouldn't recommend investments like limited partnerships.

10. **A.** As part of the U.S. Patriot Act, all broker–dealers are required to help identify terrorists or potential terrorists through CIPs (Customer Identification Programs).

11. **C.** An UTMA (Uniform Transfer to Minors Act) account is an account set up for a minor who (by law) is too young to make investment decisions on their own. It is an account set up for one minor and one custodian, who must make investment decisions in the best interest of the minor. All profits and/or losses in the account are the minor's and, therefore, the firm is required to have the tax ID of the minor.

12. **D.** With a joint with rights of survivorship account, if one investor dies, the surviving individual(s) of the account would split the individual's portion of the account. However, with a joint with tenants in common account, if one investor dies, their portion of the account goes to their estate.

IN THIS CHAPTER

» Doing some fundamental analysis

» Showing what a technical analyst does

» Looking at the money supply

» Understanding economic indicators

» Reviewing some economic terms and principles you need to know

» Trying some practice questions

Chapter 13
Securities Analysis: Doing Some Market Research

In terms of choosing securities, throwing darts at a list of stocks seems to have fallen out of favor. So has drawing company names out of a hat. But, hey, no problem. Your psychic powers may not be the most reliable, but you still have tons of tools that can help you get a good idea of where the market's heading and how certain securities may perform.

One of your main jobs as a registered representative is to figure out the best investments for your clients based on their investment objectives and your research. To help lead people down the path to riches, you have to analyze each client's portfolio and the market and try to find a good fit. In many cases, firms hire analysts to provide registered reps investment information, which helps you (as the registered rep) determine the best recommendations for each customer.

In this chapter, I cover topics relating to securities analysis and money supply. The majority of this chapter is about analyzing companies and the market and seeing what happens with the money supply. Don't worry, though — I don't leave out technical and fundamental analysis. I just focus on the information that can help you get the best score on the SIE. At the end, you get to test your knowledge with a quick chapter quiz.

Getting to Know Your Securities and Markets: Securities Analysis Basics

Although many brokerage firms have their own analysts, you do need to know some of the basics of securities analysis to pass the SIE and corequisite exams. Besides, the more you know about securities analysis, the better you'll be able to understand the analysts and the more informed you'll sound when talking to your customers and potential customers. In this section, I cover investment risks that your customers face and show you the differences between technical and fundamental analysis.

Regarding systematic and nonsystematic risk

Investors face many risks (and many rewards) when investing in the market. You need to understand the risks because this knowledge cannot only make you sound like a genius, but also help you score higher on the SIE exam.

Systematic risk

Systematic (undiversifiable or market) risk is the risk that securities can decline due to political, social, or economic factors — changes in the economy, natural disasters, government policy, and so on. Examples of systematic risks are the housing crisis of 2008 and the COVID-19 pandemic. Both of those major events impacted the economy and market tremendously. Systematic risk is a risk that could affect the whole market. Systematic risks include the following:

- **Market risk:** The risk of a security or securities declining due to regular market fluctuations or negative market conditions. All securities have market risk.
- **Interest rate risk:** The risk of bond prices declining with increasing interest rates. (Use the idea behind the seesaw from Chapter 7: When interest rates increase, outstanding bond prices decrease.) All bonds, even zero-coupon bonds, are subject to interest risk.
- **Reinvestment risk:** The risk that interest and dividends received will have to be reinvested at a lower rate of return; zero-coupon bonds, T-bills, T-STRIPS, and so on have no interperiod reinvestment risk (until maturity) because they don't receive interest payments.
- **Purchasing power (inflation or inflationary) risk:** The risk that the return on the investment is less than the inflation rate. Long-term bonds (even Treasury bonds) and fixed annuities have high inflation risk. To avoid inflation risk, investors should consider purchasing Treasury Inflation-Protected Securities (TIPS), equity securities, variable annuities, and so on.

Nonsystematic risk

Nonsystematic (unsystematic, unique, or diversifiable) risk is more industry- or firm-specific. The good news is that this type of risk can be eliminated through diversification. You've probably heard the expression "Don't put all your eggs in one basket." Well, the same holds true for investing. Suppose that one of your customers has everything, or a large portion of their investment money, invested in DIMP Corporation common stock, and DIMP files for bankruptcy; now you have to tell your customer they've lost all (or at least a large portion of) their investment money.

- **Business risk:** The risk of a corporation failing to perform up to expectations.
- **Political (geopolitical) risk:** The risk that the value of a security could suffer due to instability or political changes in a country (such as the nationalization of corporations).
- **Default risk (credit risk):** The risk of default or that the principal and interest aren't paid on time; Moody's, Standard & Poor's, and Fitch are the main bond-rating companies.
- **Regulatory risk:** The risk that changes in the regulatory climate (rulings by the Food and Drug Administration, Environmental Protection Agency, and so on) will have a detrimental effect on certain securities in the market.

- **Legislative risk:** The risk that changes in state or federal law will affect certain securities in the market.
- **Currency (exchange rate) risk:** The risk that an investment's value will be affected by a change in currency exchange rates; long-term investors who have international investments are the ones most affected by currency risk.

REMEMBER

Many investors buy and sell currencies in an attempt to take advantage of currency exchange rates. The initial currency to be traded (the base currency) would be exchanged for another currency (the counter currency). To determine the amount of counter currency they would receive, they would look at the spot exchange rate.

- **Liquidity (marketability) risk:** The risk that the security is not easily traded without affecting the price of the security; long-term bonds and limited partnerships have more liquidity risk.
- **Capital risk:** The risk of losing all money invested (for options [Chapter 11] and warrants [Chapter 6]); because options and warrants have expiration dates, purchasers may lose all money invested at expiration. To reduce capital risk, investors should buy high-quality stocks or investment-grade (higher rated) bonds.
- **Prepayment risk:** The type of risk mostly associated with real estate investments such as mortgage-backed securities (Chapter 7); mortgage-backed securities have an average expected life when first issued, but if mortgage interest rates decrease, more investors will refinance, and the bonds will be pre-paid earlier than expected.
- **Timing risk:** The risk of an investor buying or selling a security at the wrong time, thus failing to maximize profits.

TIP

When taking the real exam and practice exams, you should always pay close attention to the investor's risk tolerance, financial considerations, nonfinancial considerations, and risk(s) mentioned in order to determine the best investment for a particular customer.

Strategies for mitigating risk

Certainly, all investments have a certain degree of risk. Younger investors, sophisticated investors, and wealthy investors can all afford to take more risk than the average investor. However, when you are talking to your clients, you should help them make decisions that will help them mitigate their risk. Those in charge of coming up with questions for the SIE exam would expect you to be able to navigate the whole risk topic effectively, so you can be sure that some questions will address the following topics directly.

Diversification

Consider again the customer mentioned in the earlier section "Nonsystematic risk" who has everything invested in DIMP Corporation common stock. All of a sudden, DIMP Corporation loses a big contract or is being investigated. Your customer could be wiped out. However, if your customer had a diversified portfolio, DIMP Corporation would likely be only a small part of their investments, and they wouldn't be ruined. This is the reason that having a diversified portfolio is so important.

There are many ways to diversify, including the following:

- **Geographical:** Investing in securities in different parts of the country or world.
- **Buying bonds with different maturity dates:** Buying a mixture of short-term, intermediate-term, and long-term debt securities.

» **Buying bonds with different credit ratings:** Purchasing high-yield bonds (bonds with a low credit rating, also known as *junk bonds*) in combination with highly rated bonds with lower returns so that you get a mixture of high returns with the safety of the highly rated bonds.

» **Investing in stocks from different sectors:** Assuming different sectors may perform better than others at certain times, it definitely makes sense to look at different sectors when considering which securities to buy. By spreading your investments out among these different sectors, you can manage your risk and ideally make a profit if one or more sectors happen to be performing well. Sectors include financials, utilities, energy, healthcare, industrials, technology, and so on.

» **Type of investment:** Investing in a mixture of different types of stocks, bonds, direct participation programs (DPPs), real estate, options, and so on.

TIP

There are certainly many more ways to diversify a portfolio than the ones listed previously; use your imagination. In addition, they aren't mutually exclusive. Remember that mutual funds (packaged securities) and exchange-traded funds (ETFs) provide a certain amount of diversification within an individual holding. This is why smaller investors who may not be able to afford to diversify their portfolio are ideal candidates for mutual funds.

Portfolio rebalancing

Say that you and one of your clients determine that it is best for them to have a portfolio of 50 percent equity securities and 50 percent debt securities. After setting up and purchasing the portfolio, one year later, due to appreciation, your client has 60 percent in equity securities and 40 percent in debt securities. At that point, your client may decide to rebalance their portfolio by selling some equity securities and purchasing more debt securities to help maintain their original desired level of asset allocation (50–50). As a matter of fact, a subset of mutual funds known as *asset allocation funds* will rebalance the portfolio of securities held by the fund without needing to contact the shareholders.

REMEMBER

Typically, as investors age, they can't afford to take as much risk and should change their asset allocation to include fewer equity securities and more debt securities.

Hedging

I'm sure you've heard the saying "Hedge your bets." In the gamblers' world, this may mean taking insurance to protect oneself against the possibility of the dealer getting a 21 when playing blackjack. It means that you are trying to reduce your risk. The problem is that by doing so, you may be limiting your upside potential. In the investors' world, there are several ways to hedge, depending on what you're investing in.

You can hedge (protect) your investments against market volatility (the risk that the market will fluctuate in price) by having a diversified portfolio. In this case, although some of your investments may be subject to big swings in price, others will remain stable or increase when the market decreases. A well-diversified portfolio may include short- and long-term bonds of varying credit risk, cash equivalents (in other words, money market funds), all sorts of equity securities (value, growth, large-cap, small-cap, and so on), real estate investments, commodities, precious metals, and so on.

To hedge against credit risk (the risk that bond issuers will default), you can purchase some more secure debt securities issued by the U.S. government (T-bills, T-notes, T-bonds, and so forth), debt securities issued by local governments (municipal bonds and municipal notes), debt securities by higher-rated corporations, and so on.

To hedge against the risk that a security doesn't keep pace with inflation, you can purchase stocks (best answer in for an SIE question), variable annuities, real estate, commodities (raw materials or agricultural products), or even Treasury Inflation-Protected Securities (TIPS).

REMEMBER

Just as there are many types of risk (as you can see in the previous sections "Systematic risk" and "Nonsystematic risk"), there are different ways to hedge against risk, depending on which risk you're concerned about. The preceding are just a few examples. Options can also be used to hedge against the risk of a security you own going in the wrong direction. The best way to limit risk for most investors is to have a diversified portfolio. You must also understand that in most cases, older investors can't afford to take as much risk. For SIE exam purposes, the main thing you need to remember is that *hedge* means to protect.

Deciding what to buy: Fundamental analysis

Although most analysts use some combination of fundamental analysis and technical analysis to make their securities recommendations, for SIE exam purposes, you need to be able to differentiate between the two types. This section discusses fundamental analysis; I cover technical analysis later in the section "Deciding when to buy: Technical analysis."

Fundamental analysts perform an in-depth analysis of companies. They look at the management of a company and its financial condition (balance sheets, income statements, the industry, management, earnings, and so on) and compare with other companies in the same industry. They can also compare many years of financial statements to help determine whether a company is heading in the right direction. In addition, fundamental analysts look at the overall economy and industry conditions to determine whether an investment is good to buy.

REMEMBER

In simplest terms, fundamental analysts decide *what to buy.*

A fundamental analyst's goal is to determine the value of a particular security and decide whether it's underpriced or overpriced. If they believe the security is underpriced, a fundamental analyst recommends buying the security; if they believe the security is overpriced, they recommend selling outright or selling the security short.

The following sections explain some of the fundamental analyst's tools of the trade and how to use them.

Balance sheet components

The *balance sheet* provides an image of a company's financial position at a given point in time. The SIE exam tests your ability to understand the components of a balance sheet (see Figure 13-1) and how financial moves that the company makes (buying equipment, issuing stock, issuing bonds, paying off bonds, and so on) affect the balance sheet. In general, understanding how a balance sheet works is more important than being able to name all the components.

REMEMBER

People call this statement a balance sheet because the assets must always balance out the liabilities plus the stockholders' equity.

Assets	**Liabilities**
Current assets Fixed assets Intangible assets	Current liabilities Long-term liabilities
	Stockholder's equity (net worth) Par value (common) Par value (preferred) Paid-in capital Treasury stock Retained earnings

FIGURE 13-1: Components of a balance sheet.

Assets are items that a company owns. They include

- **Current assets:** Owned items that are easily converted into cash within the next 12 months; included in current assets are cash, marketable securities, accounts receivable, inventory, and any prepaid expenses (like rent or advertising).

  Note: Fundamental analysts also look at methods of inventory valuation, such as *LIFO* (last-in-first-out) or *FIFO* (first-in-first-out). In addition, they look at the methods of depreciation, which are either *straight line* (depreciating an equal amount each year) or *accelerated* (depreciating more in earlier years and less in later years).
- **Fixed assets:** Owned items that aren't easily converted into cash; included are property, building(s), furniture, and equipment. Because many fixed assets wear down or become outdated over time, they can be depreciated (except for land). Therefore, accumulated depreciation is usually deducted from fixed assets.
- **Intangible assets:** Owned items that don't have any physical properties; included are items such as trademarks, patents, formulas, copyrights, goodwill, and so on. (Created when a corporation purchases or merges with another company, *goodwill* is the dollar amount paid above the fair market value to purchase that company.)

Liabilities are what a company owes. They may be current or long-term:

- **Current liabilities:** Debt obligations that are due to be paid within the next 12 months; included in current liabilities are *accounts payable* (what a company owes in bills), wages, debt securities due to mature, short-term *notes payable* (the balance due on money borrowed), declared cash dividends, and taxes.
- **Long-term liabilities:** Debt obligation due to be paid after 12 months; included in long-term liabilities are mortgages, bank loans, outstanding corporate bonds, and long-term notes.

Stockholders' equity (net worth) is the difference between the assets and the liabilities (basically, what the company is worth). This value includes

- **Par value of the common stock:** The arbitrary amount that the company uses for bookkeeping purposes; if a company issues 1 million shares of common stock with a par value of $1, the par value on the stockholders' equity portion of the balance sheet is $1 million.
- **Par value of the preferred stock:** The value that the company uses for bookkeeping purposes (usually $100 per share but could be $25, $50, or some other number); if the company issues 10,000 shares of preferred stock at $100 par, the par value of the stockholders' equity portion of the balance sheet is $1 million.

REMEMBER

Unlike common stock, preferred stock has a par value that is typically $100 and a stated dividend rate; preferred stock shareholders would also receive money prior to common stockholders in the event of corporate bankruptcy.

- **Additional paid-in capital:** The amount over par value that the company receives for issuing stock; if the par value of the common stock is $1 but the company receives $7 per share, the additional paid-in capital is $6 per share. The same theory holds true for the preferred stock.
- **Treasury stock:** Stock that was outstanding in the market but was repurchased by the company.
- **Retained earnings:** The amount of net earnings the company holds after paying out dividends (if any) to its shareholders.

Income statement components

An income statement tells you how profitable a company is currently. *Income statements* list a corporation's expenses and revenue for a specific period of time (quarterly, year-to-date, or yearly). When comparing revenue and expenses, you should be able to see the efficiency of the company and how profitable it is.

Again, I don't think you need to actually see a detailed income statement from a company, but knowing the components of an income statement is important. Take a look at Figure 13-2 to see how an income statement is laid out. Most of the items are self-explanatory.

Net sales
\- Cost of goods sold (earnings before interest, taxes, depreciation, and amortization) (EBITDA)
\- Operating expenses (including depreciation)
Operating profit (earnings before interest and taxes) (EBIT)
\- Interest expenses
Taxable income (earnings before taxes) (EBT)
\- Taxes
Net income (earnings after taxes) (EAT)
\- Preferred dividends
Earnings available to common stockholders
\- Common dividends
Retained earnings

FIGURE 13-2: Components of an income statement.

Deciding when to buy: Technical analysis

Technical analysts look at the market to identify patterns and measure indicators in an attempt to predict whether the market and/or particular securities will become or remain bullish or bearish. They look at trend lines, trading volume, market sentiment, market indices (Standard & Poor's [S&P] 500, Dow Jones Industrial Average [DJIA], and so on), options volatility, market momentum, available funds, index futures, new highs and lows, the advance-decline ratio, odd lot volume, short interest, put-to-call ratio (options trading), and so on. These analysts believe that history tends to repeat itself and that past performance of securities and the market indicate its future performance.

REMEMBER

Fundamental analysts decide *what to buy*, and technical analysts decide *when to buy* (timing).

Technical analysts chart not only the market, but also market sectors and individual securities. Technical analysts try to identify market patterns and patterns of particular securities in an attempt to determine the best time to purchase or sell. Even though a security's price may vary a lot from one day to another, the prices tend to head in a particular direction (up, down, or sideways) and create a *trend line* over a period of time.

Benchmarks and indices

If you watch news stations, read the newspaper, listen to the radio, and so on, you can't help but see or hear about the DJIA or the Nasdaq being up or down. Well, those are indices (indexes) or benchmarks. Benchmarks are typically used to evaluate the performance of individual investments or a group of investments. Most investors compare their investments with certain broad-based or narrow-based indices:

- **Narrow-based:** Narrow-based indices indicate the performance of a particular industry such as the Dow Jones Transportation Index.
- **Broad-based:** Broad-based indices are more indicative of the overall market. Broad-based indices measure securities from many industries.

TIP

There are certainly more indices than the ones listed, but for SIE exam purposes, you shouldn't need to memorize them — mainly understand what indices are and that they are often used as benchmarks.

Here are examples of some of the broad-based stock indices:

- **S&P 500 Index:** Includes 500 large-cap (companies that have a market capitalization above $10 billion) common stocks.
- **Wilshire 5000 Total Market Index:** The largest of all stock indexes; includes 5,000 listed common stocks.
- **Russell 2000 Index:** An index of 2,000 small-cap (companies that have a market capitalization between $300 million and $2 billion) companies.
- **Lipper Indexes:** Track the financial performance of different mutual funds based on their investment strategy; each Lipper Index tracks the performance of only the largest fund in each category (large-cap growth, mid-cap value, international fund, and so on).
- **Dow Jones Composite Average:** An index that tracks 65 stocks from some of the most prominent companies; the Dow Jones Composite is broken into
  - *Dow Jones Industrial Average (DJIA):* Tracks 30 stocks from the industrial sector; the DJIA is the index most commonly used to indicate the performance of the market in general.
  - *Dow Jones Transportation Average:* Tracks 20 stocks from the transportation sector
  - *Dow Jones Utility Average:* Tracks 15 stocks from the utility sector

TIP

Proponents of the *Dow Theory* believe that major market trends are confirmed if the Dow Jones Industrial Average and the Dow Jones Transportation Average are trending in the same direction (that is, both advancing or both declining). Logic dictates that if industrial companies are producing more goods, those same goods need to be transported.

Most of the indices listed here are weighted toward larger companies. This means that price movement of the larger companies has a greater impact on the particular index than a smaller company does.

Stages of the business cycle

The business cycle is the natural rise and fall of goods and services (gross domestic product, or GDP) that occur over time. The business cycle has four phases that will occur over and over:

- **Expansion** (*A* in Figure 13-3): *Expansion* is characterized by increasing demand for goods and services. During expansion, the stock market is generally increasing (bullish), property values are increasing, and industrial production is increasing. Expansion also can be characterized as recovery.
- **Peak** (*B* in Figure 13-3): The *peak* occurs at the top of the expansion phase and happens right before the economy starts to contract.
- **Contraction** (*C* in Figure 13-3): *Contraction* is characterized by higher levels of consumer debt, a stock market that is generally decreasing (bearish), a decreasing demand for goods and services, and an increasing number of bond defaults and bankruptcies.
- **Trough** (*D* in Figure 13-3): *Trough* is the lowest part of the contraction phase and happens right before the economy starts to expand (recover) again.

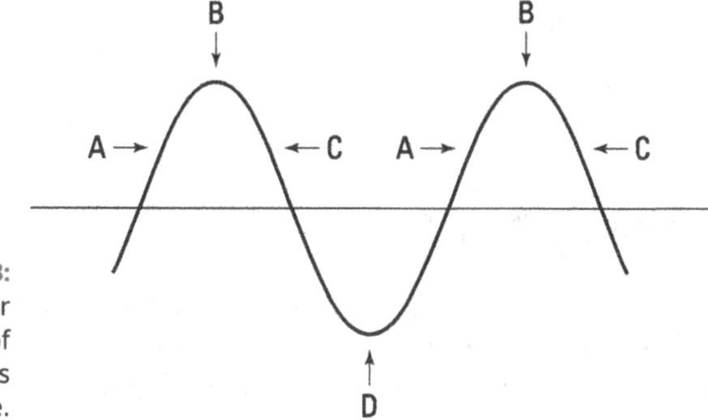

FIGURE 13-3: The four phases of the business cycle.

TIP

If asked to place these phases in order on the SIE exam, you can put them in order just as they're given in the preceding list.

Bullish versus bearish

When thinking of whether the market is bullish or bearish, think of the terms. You can think of bullish as charging ahead. So, if the market is bullish, it is generally increasing in value. If the market is bearish, it is generally hibernating or sleeping. When the market is bearish, it is generally decreasing in value.

Individuals can be bullish or bearish on the market in general or bullish or bearish on certain securities.

- **Bullish** strategies include buying individual stocks, buying mutual funds, buying call options, selling uncovered (naked) put options, and so on.
- **Bearish** strategies include selling short individual stocks, buying bearish funds (funds that generally increase in value in a declining market), buying inverse exchange-traded funds (ETFs), selling uncovered (naked) call options, buying put options, and so on.

Following the Green: Money Supply and Monetary Policy

The money supply heavily affects the market. If the money supply is higher than average, typically interest rates go down, people usually borrow more money, and people spend more money. That all sounds great, but the situation can lead to some negatives, such as higher inflation and the weakening of U.S. currency in relation to foreign currency. The Federal Reserve Board (the Fed or FRB) tries to do a balancing act to help the economy grow at a slow and steady rate. This section deals with how the money supply affects the market and the tools that the Fed uses to control the money supply.

REMEMBER

The Fed controls the monetary policy, but the *fiscal policy* is controlled by government politicians (the House, the Senate, and ultimately signed by the president). The fiscal policy is typically included in budget decisions and includes how much the U.S. government will borrow (and how), how much it will spend (and on what), how much money will be raised through taxes, and so on.

TIP

To put it in a nutshell, so to speak, you can think of monetary and fiscal policies like this:

- Monetary policy = money supply, interest rates
- Fiscal policy = borrowing, spending, taxes

Influencing the money supply

Changes in money supply can affect rates of economic growth, inflation, and foreign exchange, so knowing a bit about monetary policy can help you predict how certain securities will fare and how interest rates will change. Take a look at Table 13-1 to see what easing and tightening the money supply can do.

TABLE 13-1 Effects of Easing and Tightening the Money Supply

Category	Easing the Money Supply	Tightening the Money Supply
Economy	Easy money helps the United States avoid or get out of a recession. Consumers can borrow money at lower interest rates.	High interest rates slow the economy down because people aren't spending and investing as much money; the rate of small-business failure increases.
Market	As a result of lower interest rates, investors have more money to invest and can purchase more goods. Additionally, businesses don't have to pay as much interest to borrow money, which increases their profits. Both elements can lead to a bullish market.	High interest rates hurt the market because investors don't have extra money to invest. Additionally, corporations have to pay higher interest on loans and, therefore, report lower earnings. The market becomes bearish.
Inflation	Lower interest rates lead to higher inflation. If companies see that customers are spending money freely, they raise their prices.	A tighter money supply helps curb high inflation.
Strength of the U.S. dollar	The U.S. dollar weakens. U.S. exports increase because foreign currency strengthens (people can trade fewer units of foreign currency for more dollars); therefore, buying U.S. products is cheaper for foreign consumers. However, the U.S. dollar loses value for purchasing foreign goods, so foreign imports decrease.	The value of the U.S. dollar rises in relation to foreign currency. The U.S. dollar is subject to supply and demand, so if our money supply is tight, the value of our currency increases. Because the U.S. dollar is strong, importing foreign goods is cheaper for U.S. companies. However, U.S. exports decline because buying U.S. goods becomes more expensive for foreign companies.

When the money supply is eased (resulting in *easy money*), interest rates in general decrease. The Fed can ease the money supply by

- Buying U.S. government securities in the open market
- Lowering the discount rate, reserve requirements, and/or Regulation T (although changing Reg T isn't likely)
- Printing U.S. currency

Occasionally, the Fed has to tighten the money supply. (Remember that the Fed wants the U.S. economy to grow at a slow, steady pace.) When the money supply is tightened (resulting in *tight money*), interest rates across the board increase. The Fed can tighten the money supply by

- Selling U.S. government securities (pulling money out of the banking system)
- Increasing the discount rate, increasing reserve requirements, and/or raising Regulation T

The following section tells you more about these tools.

Opening the Federal Reserve Board's toolbox

The Fed has the authority on behalf of the U.S. government to lend money to banks; it determines the interest rate charged to banks for these loans. You probably remember the chairman of the Fed (currently, Jerome Powell) coming on TV to announce an increase or decrease in the *discount rate* (the rate the Fed charges banks for loans) and what a big deal it was. The rate the Fed charges affects the rates banks charge one another and their public customers. Because banks charge customers higher rates than the Fed charges banks, the Fed policy affects consumers as well (through credit card fees, mortgage loans, auto loans, and so on):

Fed $ → banks $ → customers $

The Fed has a few tools in its arsenal to help control the money supply. (The preceding section explains the effects of tightening and easing the supply.) Here's what you need to understand about these tools for the SIE:

- **Open market operations:** Besides the printing of money, this is the tool the Fed uses most often. *Open market operations* are the buying or selling of U.S. government bonds or U.S. government agency securities to control the money supply. Open market operations are performed by the Federal Open Market Committee (FOMC). If the Fed sells securities, it pulls money out of the banking system; if the Fed purchases securities in the open market, it puts money into the banking system.
- **The discount rate:** This value is the rate that the 12 Federal Reserve Banks charge member banks for loans. If the discount rate increases, the money supply tightens; by contrast, if the discount rate decreases, the money supply eases.
- **Reserve requirement:** The *reserve requirement* is the percentage of customers' money that banks are required to keep on deposit in the form of cash. In line with the theory of supply and demand, if the Fed increases the reserve requirement, banks have less money to lend to customers, so interest rates increase.
- **Regulation T:** *Reg T* is the percentage that investors must pay when purchasing securities on margin (see Chapter 12 for details). Regulation T is currently set at 50 percent, and it doesn't change very often. If the Fed raises the rate, investors have less cash, which tightens the money supply.

HOW THE FED IS SET UP

Here's a quick lesson in government: Congress established the Federal Reserve System in 1913 to stabilize the country's chaotic financial system. The Fed controls our money supply and, therefore, our economy.

The nation is divided into 12 Federal Reserve Districts, each with its own bank. Each bank prints currency to meet the business needs of its district, and each district is distinguished by a letter printed on the face of the bill.

The Federal Reserve Board in Washington is the parent organization that oversees and controls each of the 12 Federal Reserve District Banks. The members of the board, including the chairman, are nominated by the president of the United States, subject to confirmation by the Senate.

Exchange rates

Exchange rates are the rates at which one currency can be converted to another. As you can imagine, exchange rates are constantly changing as the value of currency in different countries appreciates, stays the same, or depreciates. Some investors even speculate in foreign currencies, hoping to be able to purchase a foreign currency when its value is low in the hope that it will appreciate so that they can sell it at a higher value. Certainly, many things can affect the value of a currency, such as a change in a country's social policies, taxing policies, economy, government, and so on.

TIP

You can assume for SIE exam purposes that the value of the U.S. dollar and foreign currency go in opposite directions. The exchange rate is considered to be a *floating rate* because it changes constantly.

U.S. balance of payments

The U.S. *balance of payments* (BoP) is an accounting of the United States' economic transactions with the world over a given period of time (typically quarterly or annually). The balance of payments may show a deficit (more money flowing out of the United States than in) or a credit (more money flowing into the United States than out). As such, the value of our currency (strong or weak dollar) greatly affects our balance of trade and, thus, the U.S. BoP.

If the U.S. dollar is strong in comparison with other currencies, it will be cheaper for Americans to buy foreign goods and services. Thus, more money will likely be going out of the United States.

If the U.S. dollar is weak in comparison with other currencies, it will be cheaper for foreign corporations, governments, individuals, and so on to purchase U.S. goods and services. As a result, more money will be flowing into the United States.

Reading Economic Indicators

Economic indicators are statistics that help show the performance or direction of the economy and help predict the direction of the economy in the near future. The economic indicators are broken into leading indicators, coincident indicators, and lagging indicators.

TIP

For the following sections, you should pay attention to the indicators toward the top of each indicator list because those are the ones most likely to be tested.

Leading indicators

Leading indicators are statistics that indicate how the economy is going to (or likely to) do in the future. Leading indicators include

- M2 money supply — the Federal Reserve's estimate of cash people have on hand plus, money available in checking accounts, savings deposits, money market instruments, and so on
- Stock prices
- Fed funds rate (rates that depository institutions [banks and credit unions] charge each other for overnight loans)
- Discount rate (the rate the Fed charges banks for loans)
- Reserve requirements (the percentage of customer deposits that the banks must hold)
- Housing; new construction (building permits)
- Unemployment claims
- Average hours per workweek
- Orders for durable goods (those not for immediate consumption)
- Consumer sentiment
- Yield curves (lines that plot interest rates for bonds of different maturities)

Coincident (coincidental) indicators

Coincident (coincidental) indicators are statistics that indicate how the economy is performing right now. Coincident indicators include

- Industrial production
- Personal income
- GDP
- Number of employees on nonagricultural payrolls and employment levels
- Retail sales

Lagging indicators

Lagging indicators are statistics that mirror leading indicators but reach their peaks and troughs somewhat later. Lagging indicators include

- The prime rate (the rate that banks charge their best customers for loans)
- Outstanding industrial and commercial loans
- Corporate profits
- Ratio of consumer credit to personal income
- Duration of employment — in other words, how long people stay at their jobs before they retire, become unemployed, or move on to a new job

» Unemployment rate

» Ratio of inventories to sales

GDP and GNP: Measuring goods and services

As you can imagine, gross national product (GNP) and gross domestic product (GDP) are closely related terms. When you are taking the SIE exam, you should understand the difference between the two. Because the SIE is mainly taken by U.S. residents, I focus on the GDP and GNP in U.S. terms. Analysts see high GNP and GDP as a good sign.

» **GDP:** To cut the information down to what you need to know for the SIE exam, think of the GDP as the total of all goods produced and all services provided by the United States in a one-year period.

» **GNP:** GNP includes the GDP plus the investments made by U.S. businesses and residents inside and outside the United States. However, the GNP doesn't count income earned by foreign businesses or residents in the United States. It also excludes products from overseas firms manufactured in the United States.

Because inflation occurs over time, the GDP and GNP are measured in *constant dollars,* which includes the cost of inflation. This is necessary to help determine whether the economy is expanding or contracting from year to year.

How Economic Factors Affect Securities

Economic factors affect securities differently. When taking the SIE exam, you are expected to understand how the economy affects *cyclical, defensive,* and *growth* companies.

Cyclical

A *cyclical* corporation is one in which the performance depends on the economy. If the economy is expanding, cyclical companies will do well. If the economy is contracting, cyclical companies will be heavily affected. Some examples of cyclical corporations are household appliances, automobile companies, tourism, construction, and manufacturing. Obviously, when the economy is not doing well, people will wait to buy that new refrigerator or that new car, wait to go on vacation, and so on. As such, cyclical companies' stock will likely decrease, and these companies may have problems paying interest on their debt securities.

Countercyclical stocks such as fast food, auto parts, discount retailers, and other investments such as precious metals may actually do better as the economy gets worse.

Defensive

Defensive corporations are ones whose sales remain relatively stable no matter how the economy performs. The corporations offer products or services that people will purchase even in a contracting economy. Examples of defensive companies include utilities, food, clothing, alcohol, tobacco, and cosmetics.

Growth

Growth companies, such as technology companies, are ones that are growing at a more rapid pace than comparable companies or the market as a whole. Growth companies are typically the newer companies and are more likely to do extremely well during periods in which the economy is expanding, but they underperform other stocks, such as value stocks, when the economy is contracting and the market is bearish. Because growth companies invest a lot of money back into their business, they typically don't pay much (or anything) in dividends.

Your Principal Economic Theory Primer

Economists follow principal economic theories. These theories are important because the administration that's in power typically nominates people to help run our economy who share their same beliefs. Economists typically believe in one of these theories, and there has been much debate about which one is best for the economy. Fortunately for you, you don't have to figure that out; you only need to understand the basics of each theory to help you pass the SIE exam. This list describes the three main economic theories that economists usually follow.

- **Keynesian (demand side):** The basis of the Keynesian theory is that government intervention through fiscal policy is good to help stimulate consumer demand for goods and services. Keynesian policy typically involves raising taxes, enabling deficit spending, borrowing money, and printing currency.
- **Supply side (Reaganomics):** Supply-side economics is the theory that the government should remain relatively inactive and the economy will grow by itself. According to this theory, the less regulation and the lower the taxes are, the more businesses will reinvest and the more people they will hire.
- **Monetarist:** Monetarists believe that the economy's performance is largely determined by the money supply (controlled by the Fed). The money supply can be used to fight inflation or to stimulate the economy.

Testing Your Knowledge

This chapter, probably more than any other one, requires you to think about what happens. What happens, for example, if the Fed raises interest rates? Or what happens if a company's liabilities increase? This type of analysis is important because it helps analysts and investors decide which securities to buy or sell.

As with other chapter questions, I try to give you a wide variety of potential questions you may see on the exam.

Practice questions

1. Which of the following are defensive industries?

   (A) Utilities and food

   (B) Tourism, household appliances, and food

   (C) Tourism and household appliances

   (D) Utilities, tourism, household appliances, and food

2. All of the following are examined by a fundamental analyst **except**

   (A) earnings per share

   (B) balance sheets

   (C) the industry

   (D) timing

3. All of the following are bearish positions **except**

   (A) buying inverse ETFs

   (B) selling uncovered call options

   (C) selling short

   (D) selling naked put options

4. Which of the following best describes the discount rate?

   (A) The interest rate that banks charge one another for overnight loans

   (B) The interest rate that the banks charge their best customers for loans

   (C) The interest rate that the Fed charges banks for loans

   (D) The interest rates charged in margin accounts

5. Melissa wants to invest in a retirement plan that protects against purchasing power risk. Which of the following would be the most suitable investment?

   (A) Municipal bonds

   (B) Common stock

   (C) Variable annuities

   (D) Fixed annuities

6. Looking at the stages of the business cycle, if the economy is expanding, what stages would you expect to follow, in order from first to last?

   (A) Trough, peak, contraction

   (B) Peak, contraction, trough

   (C) Contraction, peak, trough

   (D) Trough, contraction, peak

7. Which **two** of the following actions may the Fed take to ease the money supply?

I. Purchase T-bills

II. Sell T-bills

III. Increase reserve requirements

IV. Decrease reserve requirements

(A) I and III

(B) I and IV

(C) II and III

(D) II and IV

8. All of the following are leading indicators **except**

(A) the prime rate

(B) M2 money supply

(C) the discount rate

(D) stock prices

9. Which of the following is measured in constant dollars?

(A) The Fed funds rate

(B) The M2 money supply

(C) The prime rate

(D) GDP

10. Proponents of the Dow Theory look at

(A) the Dow Jones Composite Average and the DJIA

(B) the Dow Jones Utility Average and the Dow Jones Transportation Average

(C) the DJIA and the Dow Jones Transportation Average

(D) the Dow Jones Composite Average and the Dow Jones Utility Average

11. Zero-coupon bonds have no

(A) reinvestment risk

(B) purchasing power risk

(C) market risk

(D) interest risk

12. All of the following can be found on a corporation's balance sheet **except**

(A) fixed assets

(B) long-term liabilities

(C) retained earnings

(D) net income

13. Which of the following is a way an investor can diversify investments?

(A) Geographically
(B) Investing in stocks from different sectors
(C) Purchasing bonds with different maturity dates
(D) All of the above

14. A holder of which of the following securities is the most exposed to inflationary risk?

(A) U.S. Treasury bonds with ten years until maturity
(B) U.S. Treasury bills with one year until maturity
(C) Stocks issued by a utility company
(D) Pharmaceutical stocks

15. A registered representative from Missed Again Securities is reviewing one of their client's portfolios. They see that the client has 35 percent invested in TUV Energy Company, 15 percent invested in ETFs tracking the S&P 500, 35 percent in LMN Healthcare Company, 15 percent in U.S. government securities, and 10 percent in money market funds. Which of the following risks are built into this portfolio?

(A) Liquidity risk
(B) Political risk
(C) Credit risk
(D) Nonsystematic risk

16. Which of the following risks apply to both domestic and foreign debt securities?

(A) Regulatory
(B) Political
(C) Interest rate
(D) All of the above

17. The greatest investment risk that an investor would face when purchasing a variable annuity is

(A) interest rate risk
(B) market risk
(C) purchasing power risk
(D) credit risk

Answers and explanations

1. **A.** Defensive industries are ones that are pretty much resistant to economic downturns. These include utilities, food, clothing, alcohol, tobacco, cosmetics, and so on. Tourism and household appliance–related companies suffer during economic downturns and, therefore, are considered to be cyclical companies.

2. **D.** Fundamental analysts look at and compare companies. They do an in-depth analysis to help professionals decide which companies would be good or bad investments. So fundamental analysts help decide what to buy, whereas technical analysts look at the market and help professionals decide when to buy (timing).

3. **D.** Bearish strategies are ones in which you want the price of the security to decrease. Bearish strategies include selling short, buying bearish funds, buying inverse exchange-traded funds, selling uncovered (naked) call options, and so on. Selling naked (uncovered) put options is actually a bullish strategy because the investor who holds that position wants the price of the underlying security to increase.

4. **C.** The discount rate is the rate that the Fed charges banks for loans. These loans are typically overnight loans taken by banks to help them meet their reserve requirements.

5. **C.** You can cross off (A) and (B) right away because stocks and bonds are not retirement plans. Out of the two annuity plans, variable annuities do not have purchasing power (inflation) risk because the return is based on the performance of the securities held in the separate account. Ideally, the securities will outperform the rate of inflation.

6. **B.** If the economy is expanding, you would expect it to hit a peak at some point. After reaching the peak, the economy would start to contract until hitting the lowest point, which is the trough. After that, you would expect it to start all over again.

7. **B.** The Fed has a few tools to help ease or tighten the money supply including open market operations, adjusting the discount rate, changing reserve requirements, and raising or lowering Regulation T requirements. Of the choices given, the two that would ease (add money to) the money supply would be inserting money into the system by purchasing U.S. government securities like T-bills and lowering reserve requirements (the percentage of customer deposits banks have to hold each night).

8. **A.** Leading indicators are those that help give an indication of how the economy is going to do. The main leading indicators are M2 money supply, stock prices, the Fed funds rate, and the discount rate. The prime rate — the rate that banks charge their best customers for loans — is a lagging indicator. Lagging indicators go the same direction as the leading indicators but arrive a little later.

9. **D.** Both the GDP and GNP are measured in constant dollars. When measuring in constant dollars, they are factoring inflation into the equation to see whether the economy is actually expanding or contracting year to year.

10. **C.** Proponents of the Dow Theory logically believe that major market trends are confirmed if both the DJIA and the Dow Jones Transportation Average are going the same direction. In other words, companies not only have to be making a lot of goods, but also have to be transporting those goods to be considered a positive sign.

11. **A.** Reinvestment risk is the additional risk taken with interest or dividends received. Zero-coupon bonds are issued at a discount and mature at par value. These bonds do not make interest payments along the way, so there is nothing to reinvest.

12. **D.** The balance sheet is just a snapshot of the net worth (stockholders' equity) of a company. The balance sheet includes the company's assets, liabilities, and stockholders' equity. Net income is derived from a company's income statement. The income statement looks at a company's income minus expenses.

13. **D.** Diversification helps investors mitigate investment risk. All the choices listed are ways investors can lessen risk. When dealing with clients, you should always help them diversify their portfolio. It's the old "don't put all of your eggs in one basket" theory.

14. **A.** Inflationary risk (purchasing power risk) is the risk that inflation can pose to a security or portfolio over time. Treasury bonds (T bonds) have a longer maturity, and if inflation kicks in, the Fed is likely to raise interest rates. If interest rates increase, outstanding bond prices decrease. Longer-term bonds are affected more than shorter-term bonds, like Treasury bills.

15. **D.** This investor has 70 percent of their portfolio invested in two different companies (35 percent in TUV and 35 percent in LMN). Therefore, this customer has nonsystematic (unsystematic or diversifiable) risk built into their portfolio. Nonsystematic risk is the risk that a particular company or industry might do poorly and bring the value of the portfolio down substantially. Obviously, you would look at this portfolio and say that the investments in U.S. government securities, money market funds, and ETFs provide a certain degree of safety. However, those investments are only 30 percent of their portfolio. Therefore, you would likely recommend that the other 70 percent should be spread out to more than two companies.

16. **D.** All of the choices listed can apply to both domestic and foreign debt securities. Regulatory risk is the risk that law changes will affect the market. Political risk is the risk that politics in a particular country could negatively affect securities. Interest rate (money rate) risk is the risk that bond prices will decline due to increasing interest rates.

17. **B.** The greatest investment risk that an investor will face when purchasing a variable annuity is market risk. Variable annuities have a separate account where an investor chooses the securities held. The securities held in the account are subject to market risk, which is the risk that the securities can decline due to negative market conditions.

IN THIS CHAPTER

» Understanding the differences between the primary and secondary markets

» Comparing stock exchanges to the over-the-counter market

» Seeing the role of the broker-dealer

» Looking at order qualifiers

» Getting to know market participants

» Taking a chapter quiz

Chapter 14
Securities Markets: Taking Orders and Executing Trades

Part of your function as a registered rep is to understand and explain to customers (and potential customers) how the stock market works. I designed this chapter with that in mind (along with the fact that you need to know this stuff for the SIE, of course).

In this chapter, I cover the basics of exchanges and the over-the-counter (OTC) market, along with some of the active participants who help the market run smoothly (at least most of the time). Pay particular attention to the sections "Reviewing basic order types" and "Factoring in order features," because you'll definitely use that information every day after you pass the SIE and corequisite tests. The chapter wraps up with a short quiz.

Shopping at Primary and Secondary Markets

Depending on whether the securities are new or outstanding, they trade in either the primary or secondary market. This section deals with the differences between the two.

Buying new in the primary market

The primary market (new issue market) is where the issuer receives the proceeds from the sale of securities. This market's offerings are broken into two categories, depending on whether the company has ever issued securities before. A security that has never been offered or sold to the public is considered a *new issue*. Here are the three types of offerings on the primary market:

- **Initial public offering (IPO):** An IPO is the first time a corporation ever sells stock to the public to raise money. When a corporation is in the process of issuing securities for the first time, it's said to be *going public*. So, an IPO is the *first* primary offering.
- **Primary offering:** A primary offering is the issuer market, where the issuer is selling shares to raise money. Certainly, an IPO falls into that category. However, the corporation usually holds shares back for future use; it later pulls those securities out of storage and sells them in a subsequent (add-on, additional, or follow-up) offering, which is also a primary offering. A corporation may be authorized to sell 4 million shares of common stock, but in its IPO, it may sell only 1,800,000. At this point, 2.2 million new shares remain that have never been offered to the public. One year later, when the company needs to raise additional capital to build a new warehouse, it can sell some of the remaining 2.2 million shares in a subsequent primary offering.
- **Combined (split) offering:** This type of offering is a combination of new securities and a large block of outstanding or previously outstanding securities.

When securities are sold in the primary market, the bulk of the sales proceeds goes to the issuer and the balance goes to the entity or entities responsible for selling the securities to the public — the underwriter(s) and selling group members (if any) in other words.

Buying used in the secondary market

When the securities are already trading in the market, the sales proceeds go to another investor instead of to the issuer. The secondary market, also called the *aftermarket*, is where previously issued securities are purchased and sold. (See the following section for info on trading on exchanges versus OTC markets). The secondary market is broken down into the third and fourth market:

- **Third market:** The third market is comprised of exchange-listed securities trading over-the-counter (OTC) — traders are calling in their orders or ordering online. All NYSE, NYSE American, NYSE Arca, and most of the securities listed on other exchanges can be traded OTC.
- **Fourth market:** The fourth market is the trading of securities between institutions without the use of a brokerage firm. Fourth-market trades are reported on a FINRA Trade Reporting Facility (TRF).

Making the Trade

After securities are issued publicly, they may trade on an exchange or on the OTC market.

Auctioning securities at securities exchanges

Exchanges are auction markets, where bidders and sellers get together to execute trades. I'm sure you've seen movies or TV shows featuring the NYSE. It definitely looks very chaotic (and like it's a good place to have a heart attack or develop an ulcer). However, some sort of order is definitely there:

- All exchanges have a trading floor where all trades are executed.
- Each security listed on an exchange has its own *trading post* (location) on the floor where the auction takes place.
- Brokers looking to purchase or sell securities are surrounded by computers, which allow them to make trades. Trades may take place through a physical auction using the services of a designated market maker (DMM) or through computer trading.

The main exchange that the SIE tests you on is the NYSE, also known as the Big Board or Exchange, but there are others, such as NYSE Amex Equities (formerly the American Stock Exchange [AMEX]), Nasdaq, Chicago Board Options Exchange (CBOE), Boston Stock Exchange (formerly BSE, now Nasdaq OMX BX), and so on.

Listed securities are ones that satisfy minimum requirements and are traded on a regional or national exchange like the NYSE. Listed securities may trade on the exchange or in the OTC market discussed in the following section.

Although thousands of people may seem to be on the floor of the exchange, you don't need to be aware of too many titles. Most of the people on the floor of the exchange fall into one of three categories:

- **Floor brokers:** These individuals act as agents in executing buy or sell orders on behalf of their firms' customers. A floor broker may also facilitate buying and selling for their firm. Floor brokers receive buy or sell orders from their firms and either transfer the orders to a designated market maker (DMM) or trade with another floor broker.
- **Two-dollar brokers (independent brokers):** These brokers assist other floor brokers in getting their orders executed on busy days. (By the way, they're called *two-dollar brokers* because many, many years ago, they used to receive $2 per trade. Commissions may have gone up a bit since then.)
- **Designated market makers (DMMs; formerly specialists):** These market professionals manage the auction market trading for a particular security (or for a few securities, if not actively traded). Their purpose is to maintain a "fair and orderly market" in one or more securities. A DMM can act as a broker or a dealer (trading out of their own account) to help keep trading as active as possible. An important function of a DMM is to keep track of and execute limit orders on behalf of other exchange members.

Negotiating trades over the counter

The OTC market is a negotiated market. Instead of yelling out bid and ask prices, traders buy and sell securities by way of telephone or computer transactions. There's no central location for trading OTC securities. Thousands of securities — both listed and unlisted — are traded this way. In fact, *unlisted securities*, which aren't listed on an exchange, can only trade OTC.

The OTC equities market is divided into Nasdaq issues (issues that meet the Nasdaq listing requirements) and non-Nasdaq issues. Non-Nasdaq issues are unlisted and traded on the OTCQX or OTCQB, or in the OTC Pink Market.

REMEMBER

U.S. government and municipal bonds trade only OTC.

OTC market makers

Unlike exchanges where they have designated market makers, the OTC market has none. However, some firms (dealers) will make a market for particular securities and be willing to trade to and from their own inventory. If they wish to make a market in a security, they must receive FINRA's approval. OTC market makers create the inside market by offering to buy and sell securities. The inside market is the highest bid price (the most a market maker is willing to pay) for a security and the lowest ask or offer price (the most a market maker is willing to accept) for a security. In the Nasdaq system, you typically have several market makers for one security. Take a look at what happens when you have several market makers entering quotes for LMNO common stock:

Market Maker	BID	ASK	Size
DK Broker-Dealer	18.30	18.75	5 × 10
Golden Hammer BD	18.25	18.80	20 × 3
Cardinal Wing Securities	18.35	19.05	7 × 14

By looking at this chart, you can see that three market makers have entered quotes for LMNO Common stock as well as the size (how many round lots they're willing to buy and/or sell). To determine the inside market, look at the highest bid price, which was entered by Cardinal Wing Securities, and the lowest ask price, which was entered by DK Broker-Dealer. For LMNO, the inside market is currently 18.35–18.75. Looking at a Level I machine in the brokerage firm, you would see only the name of the security and the inside market price. If you were to give a quote to customers, you would have to let them know it's a subject quote (subject to change) because as buy and sell orders are placed, the inside market will change.

If you were placing an order to buy, you would buy at the lowest ask price. If you were placing an order to sell, you would sell at the highest bid price. The size of the market relates to how many round lots (100 shares) each market maker is willing to trade. So, if you look at DK Broker-Dealer, they're wanting to purchase five round lots (500 shares) and sell ten round lots (1,000 shares).

Understanding the Role of a Broker-Dealer

I guestimate that a large percentage of people taking the SIE exam will be working for a broker-dealer. For a firm to be considered a broker-dealer, it must buy and sell securities from its own account and act as an intermediary for securities not in inventory. Here are the differences between brokers and dealers:

- **Broker:** A firm is acting as a broker when it doesn't use its own inventory to execute a trade. A broker charges a *commission* (sales charge) for acting as an intermediary between a buyer and a seller.

  For SIE exam purposes, the terms *broker* and *agent* may be used interchangeably. A registered representative is sometimes called an agent or stockbroker because they act as an intermediary between buyers and sellers.

- **Dealer:** A firm is acting as a dealer when it uses its own inventory to execute a trade. When a dealer sells securities to a customer using its own inventory, it charges a *markup* (sales charge). When a dealer buys securities from a customer for its own inventory, it charges a *markdown* (reducing the price a customer receives by charging a sales charge). A firm becomes a dealer in the hopes that the securities it has in its own inventory will increase in price so that the dealer can benefit from the appreciation and subsequent sale of the securities.

The terms *dealer, principal,* and *market maker* may be used interchangeably on the SIE and corequisite exams.

Capacity refers to whether a firm is acting as a broker (agent) or dealer (principal), and it must always be disclosed on the *confirmation* (receipt of trade). If a firm is acting as a broker, the commission always needs to be disclosed on the confirmation. However, if a firm is acting as a dealer, the markup or markdown doesn't always have to be disclosed.

REMEMBER

A firm can't act as a broker and a dealer for the same trade. In other words, charging a markup (or markdown) and a commission on the same trade is a violation. (For info on rules and regulations, see Chapter 16.)

TIP

To help you remember the differences between a broker and a dealer, think of a real estate broker. A real estate broker (or agent) acts as an intermediary between sellers and buyers and charges a commission, just like a stockbroker does. Conversely, a dealer, like a used-car dealer, sells from their own inventory, charges a markup, and buys in the hopes of making a profit on that inventory.

An introducing broker

An introducing broker (IB) is a person or business that does not actually handle the transactions but just provides investment advice or counsel to investors. In general, an introducing broker will recommend trades to clients while handing over the job of executing the trade to a clearing firm. (See the next section.) In general, the IB and the clearing firm that executes the trade split the trading fees and/or commission.

A clearing (carrying) broker

Clearing brokers (clearing firms) handle orders to buy and sell securities. In addition, clearing brokers maintain custody of clients' assets (securities and cash). Clearing firms are responsible for segregating (separating) clients' cash and securities held in their custody.

A prime broker

Prime brokers are used mainly by institutional accounts or large retail clients. Prime brokerage accounts are ones set up for individuals or entities with more complex financial needs. Besides helping the client combine information from all firms they are using into one statement, they also provide services such as lending, leveraged trade execution, and cash management. Often, hedge funds use prime brokerage accounts.

Receiving and Executing Customer Orders

Here's where the rubber meets the road. You can receive several types of orders from customers along with numerous order qualifiers. This section explains the types of orders and how to execute them.

REMEMBER

Unlicensed associated persons *cannot* receive or execute orders for customers. In addition, they cannot discuss securities, recommend securities, talk about investment objectives, and so on. However, they may send out paperwork, answer phone calls, and so on. In order to discuss investment objectives, take orders, execute trades, and so on, the person must be licensed.

Reviewing basic order types

You can definitely expect a question or two on the SIE exam relating to *orders* (you know, the buying and selling kind). The following sections explore the most common order types.

Market order

A market order is for immediate execution at the best price available. A majority of the orders that you'll receive will be market orders. They come in two varieties:

- **Buy order:** When an investor places a market order to buy, they're not price-specific; the investor purchases the security at the lowest ask price (the lowest price at which someone's willing to sell the security). An investor who's purchasing a security wants the price to increase (after the sale, of course) and is establishing a bullish position.
- **Sell order:** When an investor places a market order to sell, they're not price-specific; they sell the security at the highest bid price (the highest price someone's willing to pay for the security).

Note: As with exchanges, the difference between the highest bid price and lowest ask (offer) price in the OTC market is known as the *spread*. Typically, the narrower the spread, the more actively traded the security.

REMEMBER

For investors looking to make a profit when they believe the price of a security is going to drop, there's always *selling short*. Selling short occurs when an investor sells securities they don't actually own. (The investor is actually borrowing securities from a lender to sell.)

Here's how selling short works: Say an investor borrows 100 shares of ABC stock and sells them short at $40 per share, thus receiving $4,000. The borrower doesn't owe the lender $4,000; they owe the lender 100 shares of ABC stock. After a month or two, when ABC is trading at $20 per share, the borrower can purchase the 100 shares for $2,000 and return them to the lender, making a nice $2,000 profit (excluding commission costs).

A short seller is bearish (wants the price of the security to decrease). If the price increases instead, the short seller has to buy the stock in the market at a higher price, thus losing money. Remember that all short sales must be executed in margin accounts. Short sales are subject to short-sale regulations under Regulation SHO. (See the nearby sidebar.)

Note: Investors may sell short for *speculation* (believing the price of the security will decrease), *hedging* (protecting a security or several securities in the event of a market decline), or *arbitrage* (taking advantage of a price disparity on the security in different markets).

REMEMBER

When you *purchase* a security, the most you can lose is the amount you invest. When you *short* a security, your maximum loss potential is unlimited because the price of the stock could keep climbing, in which case you'd have to spend more money to cover your short position. Additionally, because of the additional risk, all short sales must be executed in a margin account. Chapter 12 tells you a little more about margin accounts.

REGULATION SHO AND SHORT SALES

According to Regulation SHO, which covers the short sale of securities, all order tickets must be marked as *short sale* rather than *long sale*. (In this context, a long sale is one in which a customer is selling securities they actually own, rather than securities they've only borrowed.) Additionally, all brokerage firms must establish rules to locate, borrow, and deliver securities that are to be sold short. Brokerage firms must be sure that the security can be located and delivered on the date the delivery is due before executing the short sale.

Stop orders

A stop order is used for protection; it tries to limit how much an investor can lose. (On the other hand, it can also be used to lock in gains.) Depending on whether an investor has a long or short stock position, they may enter a buy stop order or a sell stop order:

- **Buy stop orders:** These orders protect a short position (when an investor sells borrowed securities). A buy stop tells you to buy a security if the market price touches a particular price or higher. Investors who are short the stock make money when the price of the stock decreases; however, if the price increases, they lose money. An investor who's short ABC stock currently trading at $25 could enter a buy stop order on ABC at $30. If ABC reaches $30 or more, the order is triggered, and the order becomes a market order for immediate execution at the next available price.
- **Sell stop orders:** These orders protect a long position (when an investor owns the stock involved); they tell you to sell a security if the market price touches a particular price or lower. Investors who are long stock make money when the price of the stock increases; if the price decreases, they lose money. Say an investor who is long DEF stock currently trading at $50 enters a sell stop order on ABC at $45. If DEF reaches $45 or below, the order is triggered, and the order becomes a market order for immediate execution at the next price, whether higher or lower than $45.

Limit orders

A customer who's specific about the price they want to spend or receive for a security places a limit order; this order says the customer doesn't want to pay more than a certain amount or sell for less than a certain amount. Depending on whether an investor is interested in buying or selling, they can enter a buy limit or a sell limit order:

- **Buy limit orders:** Investors who want to purchase a security place these orders. A buy limit order is a directive to buy a particular security at the limit price or lower. Suppose DEF stock is trading at $35 per share but one of your customers doesn't want to pay more than $30 per share. You could place a buy limit order at $30. If the price of DEF ever reaches $30 or less, chances are good that your customer will end up with the stock.
- **Sell limit orders:** Investors who want to sell a security place sell limit orders. A sell limit order is a directive to sell a particular security at the limit price or higher. Suppose one of your customers owns LMN stock, which is currently trading at $62 per share, but they want to receive at least $70 per share if they're going to sell it. This customer could place a sell limit on LMN at $70 per share. If LMN touches or goes above $70 per share, chances are good that the stock will be sold.

Stop limit orders

A *stop limit order* is a combination of a stop and limit order (see the preceding sections); it's a buy stop or sell stop order that becomes a limit order after the stop price is reached. An order that reads "sell 1,000 HIJ at 41 stop, 40.75 limit" means that the sell stop order will be triggered as soon as HIJ reaches $41 or below (the stop price). If this were just a stop order, the stock would be sold on the next trade (no matter what the price). But because this is a stop limit order, after the order is triggered, it becomes a limit order to sell at $40.75 or above (the limit price). In other words, this customer is interested in selling their stock if it drops to $41 but wants to receive at least $40.75 per share.

REMEMBER

Because stop and limit orders are price-specific, they may or may not be executed. Additionally, even if limit orders do reach or surpass the limit price, the order may not be executed if more orders were placed ahead of the investor's order.

Factoring in order features

Besides knowing the basic types of orders (market, stop, and limit; see "Reviewing basic order types"), you should have a handle on some additional features that may be added to the order to make your customers happy. A lot of them exist, but for the most part, the name of the order feature pretty much explains what it is:

- **Day:** If a day order hasn't been filled by the end of the trading day, it's canceled. All price-specific orders (stop and limit) are assumed to be day orders unless marked to the contrary. Most of the orders you'll receive will be market orders for immediate execution at the best price available (highest bid and lowest ask prices).
- **Good-'til-canceled (GTC):** Good-'til-canceled orders are also called *open orders* because the order is kept open until executed or canceled. Say that an investor wants to purchase ABC stock at $30. While the price of ABC is at $35, they enter an open buy limit order for ABC at $30. If the price of ABC ever hits $30 or below, the order will likely be executed; however, if the price of ABC never hits $30 or below, the order stays open until canceled.

  Note: An investor may specify that they want the order canceled next week, next month, in two months, and so on. Many exchanges no longer take GTC orders, but customers can place them with their broker-dealers, and they will handle it internally. In actual practice, because customers may forget about their GTC orders, many broker-dealers will set them to expire in 30 days, 60 days, 90 days, and so on.
- **Not held (NH):** This order gives the broker discretion about when to execute the trade. Typically, investors use not held orders when the broker believes they can get the customer a better price later in the day.

  Not held orders deal only with timing. For registered reps to choose the security, number of shares, and/or whether to buy or sell, the customer needs to open a discretionary account, which requires a written power of attorney. See "Discretionary versus nondiscretionary orders," later in this chapter, for details.
- **Fill or kill (FOK):** This order instructs a floor broker either to immediately execute an entire order at the limit price or better or to cancel it.
- **Immediate or cancel (IOC):** These limit orders are similar to FOK orders except that the order may be partially filled. Any portion of the order that's not completed is canceled.

- **All-or-none (AON):** These limit orders have to be executed either in their entirety or not at all. AON orders don't have to be filled immediately (several attempts to fill the order completely are allowed) and may be day orders or good-till-canceled orders.
- **At-the-open:** These orders are to be executed at the security's opening price. At-the-open orders can be market or limit orders, but if they aren't executed at the opening price, they're canceled. These orders allow for partial execution.
- **At-the-close (market on close):** This order is to be executed at the closing price (or as near as possible). If this order isn't completed, it's canceled.
- **Do not reduce (DNR):** This order says not to reduce the price of a stop or limit order in response to a dividend. Say that QRS stock is currently trading at $50 on the day prior to the ex-dividend date (the first day the stock starts trading without a previously declared dividend). If QRS previously announced a $0.50 dividend, the next day's opening price would be $49.50. If a customer had placed a DNR limit order to buy 1,000 shares of QRS at $45, the order wouldn't be reduced by the $0.50 dividend.
- **Alternative:** The alternative order is also known as a *one cancels the other order* or an *either/or order.* This type of order instructs the broker to execute one of two orders and then cancel the other. Say Smith owns stock at $60 per share. They enter a sell stop order at $55 for protection and a sell limit order at $70 in the event that the stock price increases. If one of the orders is executed, the other order is canceled immediately.
- **Bid wanted:** This order is an indication or notice that an investor or broker-dealer wants to sell a security at a specific price. Bid wanted is used most often when no current buyers of a security are available.
- **Offer wanted:** This order is an indication or notice that an investor or a broker-dealer wants to buy a particular security at a specific price. Offer wanted is used particularly when no current sellers of a security are available.

Following customers' orders or using your discretion

No matter whether a buy or sell order is involved, some customers will be willing to give you a little more input and freedom to make choices for them than others. Other customers are going to provide you with every detail of a trade (security, price, dollar amount, the whole shebang) without needing your input at all, which actually is a good thing.

REMEMBER

No matter what the type of order, or how it's communicated to you, your job and your firm's job is to get your customers the best price available for their orders. As such, your customers' orders cannot be split into multiple smaller orders for execution with the primary purpose of maximizing the amount of money (credits, commissions, gratuities, fees, and so on) that you or your firm makes. In addition, "reasonable diligence" must be used to get the customer the best price. Here are some of the factors involved to determine if reasonable diligence was used: the price of the security, the volatility of the security, the liquidity of the security, the size and type of transaction, the number of markets checked, and accessibility of the quotation.

Discretionary versus nondiscretionary orders

To be sure, most of the orders you will receive from your clients will be nondiscretionary orders. If one of your clients tells you to purchase 100 shares of ABC common stock, they are giving you a nondiscretionary order. It is nondiscretionary because they are giving you all the components of an order: purchase or sell, how many shares or dollar amount, and what security. If the client does not provide that information, it is considered discretionary, meaning that you must use your discretion. Here are some examples of discretionary orders:

> "*Buy or sell* 100 shares of ABC common stock"
>
> "Buy *as many shares* of ABC common stock as you think I should own"
>
> "Buy 100 shares of *pharmaceutical stock*"

REMEMBER

Discretionary orders may be executed by a registered rep or brokerage firm without prior verbal permission from the client. Because they don't require verbal approval, the registered rep is required to have a written power of attorney signed by the customer prior to executing any discretionary orders. The power of attorney remains in effect until the discretionary account is closed or the power of attorney is removed by the client. As you can imagine, discretionary orders must be marked as such on the order ticket. In addition, these accounts must be closely watched by a principal of the firm to make sure that there's no excessive trading (churning) for the purpose of generating commission.

TIP

A client may give you approval to place the order at a later time in the day without discretionary authority. Say a client tells you to purchase 100 shares of DIM stock at the market price. You may tell your client that you believe that the price will drop later in the day and you may be able to get them a better price. This is allowed as long as the customer gives verbal approval, and it's not considered a discretionary order.

Solicited versus unsolicited orders

As with nondiscretionary orders, most of the orders you receive from clients will be *solicited* by you, meaning that you may call up one of your clients and say, "DEF Corporation seems to be on the move, so I think it would be wise for you to buy 100 shares of DEF common stock." Because you called and suggested what the client should buy (or sell), you actually solicited that order.

Unsolicited orders are ones in which your client tells you what they want to buy or sell. You may not think that this is the best idea for them and may tell them that, but you are not going to turn down the order and lose commission. In this case, because it was not your suggestion, you need to mark the order ticket in the box that says "unsolicited." This basically takes you off the hook in the event that the client loses money on that particular investment.

Not All Are Created Equally: Recognizing Different Types of Investors

As a financial professional, you'll be working with all different types of investors: some smaller investors, some larger investors, corporations, and so on. Part of the SIE exam is knowing that you understand who's who when it comes to these different types of investors.

Retail investors

You are more likely to deal with retail investors than accredited or institutional investors. These are nonprofessionals who trade (buy or sell) for their own accounts. Retail investors typically purchase or sell a much smaller number of securities than accredited or institutional investors.

Accredited investors

Some investors just have access to more money or are considered more knowledgeable than others. The bigger investors are called accredited investors. As such, they are typically able to handle more risk than retail investors. Accredited investors include

- Financial institutions (banks, insurance companies, pension funds, and so on)
- Insiders (officers, directors, or owners of 10 percent or more of the outstanding shares of the corporation and their immediate family members)
- Investors who have an annual income of at least $200,000 (joint $300,000) for the previous two years and are expected to meet that requirement this year
- Investors who have a net worth of at least $1 million, excluding primary residence
- Reps registered and in good standing with the U.S. Securities and Exchange Commission (SEC), FINRA, and/or at least one state who have passed the Series 7, Series 65, Series 66, and/or the Series 82 exams
- Knowledgeable employees of private funds (hedge funds, private-equity funds, and so on) who have the ability to raise money privately
- Rural business investment companies (investment companies that raise money to invest in small rural businesses)
- Limited liability companies (LLCs) with more than $5 million in assets
- Family offices with at least $5 million in assets under management
- Corporations, partnerships, or organizations with a net worth of at least $5 million

Institutional investors

Institutional investors are the big guys. They are the ones that invest a lot of money on behalf of their entity. They are generally considered to be knowledgeable about the market. Institutional investors include

- Commercial banks
- Mutual funds
- Pension funds
- Insurance companies
- Real estate investment trusts
- Hedge funds
- Endowment funds

DEPOSITORY TRUST AND CLEARING CORPORATION

The DTCC provides safeguards to the world's financial markets. Its role is to provide clearing, settlement, institutional matching, asset servicing, collateral management, global data management, information services, and so on for equity securities, corporate bonds, municipal bonds, government securities, mortgage-backed securities, mutual funds, money market instruments, derivatives, and so forth. The DTCC is absolutely massive and processes more than 100 million financial transactions each trading day. Its key roles are to provide reliability to the global financial system, to provide after-trade services, to limit risk, to lower cost, to provide transparency, and to promote greater market efficiency. The services offered by the DTCC are

- Clearing services
- Matching, settlement, and asset services
- Collateral management
- Wealth management services
- Derivative services
- Data services

Testing Your Knowledge

So, you just learned about market participants and types of orders; it's time to see questions like those you'll experience on the SIE exam. Here's a small sampling of questions for you to ace.

Practice questions

1. Which two of the following are **true**?

   (A) Dealers charge a markup or markdown for trades; brokers charge a markup or markdown for trades.

   (B) Dealers charge a markup or markdown for trades; brokers charge commission for trades.

   (C) Dealers charge a commission for trades; brokers charge a markup or markdown for trades.

   (D) Dealers charge a commission for trades; brokers charge a commission for trades.

2. Which of the following best describes a third market trade?

   (A) Exchange-listed securities trading OTC

   (B) Exchange-listed securities trading on the exchange floor

   (C) Unlisted securities trading OTC

   (D) Institutional trading without using the services of a broker–dealer

3. Which of the following orders would protect a short position?

   (A) Buy limit

   (B) Sell limit

   (C) Buy stop

   (D) Sell stop

4. If an at-the-open order is not executed at the opening price, what happens to the order?

(A) It is canceled.

(B) It becomes a market order.

(C) It becomes a day order.

(D) It becomes a limit order.

5. An investor with no other positions would like to purchase ABC common stock, which is currently trading at $30.80. If this investor is interested in purchasing the stock for $28 or less, you should suggest the investor enters a

(A) buy stop limit order

(B) buy limit order

(C) buy stop order

(D) market order

6. Which of the following would be considered accredited investors?

I. Banks

II. An individual investor with a net worth of $2 million, excluding their primary residence

III. A corporation with a net worth of $10 million

IV. Insurance companies

(A) II and IV

(B) I and IV

(C) I, III, and IV

(D) I, II, III, and IV

7. Which **two** of the following are **true** of short sellers?

(A) They are taking a bullish position and they have a maximum gain potential that is unlimited.

(B) They are taking a bullish position and they have a maximum loss potential that is unlimited.

(C) They are taking a bearish position and they have a maximum gain potential that is unlimited.

(D) They are taking a bearish position and they have a maximum loss potential that is unlimited.

8. A not held order gives a broker discretion as to

(A) which security is traded

(B) the time at which a security is traded

(C) whether to purchase, sell, or sell short a security

(D) all of the above

9. Which of the following order features allows for partial execution?

(A) FOK

(B) AON

(C) IOC

(D) All of the above

10. Which **two** of the following are FALSE regarding unsolicited orders?

I. They cannot be accepted without prior approval from a principal.

II. They can be accepted without prior approval from a principal.

III. They must be limited in size.

IV. They are not limited in size.

(A) I and III

(B) I and IV

(C) II and III

(D) II and IV

11. Which of the following order features allows for partial execution?

(A) Sell 2,500 shares at $18.10 and buy 2,000 shares at $18.30

(B) Buy 2,000 shares at $18.10 and sell 2,500 shares at $18.30

(C) Sell 250 shares at $18.10 and buy 200 shares at $18.30

(D) Buy 200 shares at $18.10 and sell 250 shares at $18.30

12. Max and John have been married for several years. They have a combined income that has exceeded $300,000 per year for the last four years and is expected to at least be that much for the current year. They would be considered a(n)

(A) qualified institutional buyer (QIB)

(B) accredited investor

(C) institutional investor

(D) bank qualified investor

13. WXY Broker–Dealer charges a commission on a securities transaction. WXY Broker–Dealer has acted as a(n)

(A) agent

(B) principal

(C) market maker

(D) dealer

14. "Spread" in the over-the-counter (OTC) market refers to the difference between the

(A) highest bid and lowest ask price

(B) lowest offer price and highest ask price

(C) the opening and closing prices of a particular security

(D) the "when issued" ask price

15. Marvin Plimpton is an associated person but is not a licensed registered representative. Which of the following activities is Marvin permitted to engage in?

(A) Accepting unsolicited orders from a customer who resides in the same state

(B) Discussing the plusses and minuses of a particular investment to an existing customer of the firm

(C) Forwarding account opening forms to a new customer

(D) Discussing investment objectives with a potential customer prior to handing the customer over to a licensed registered representative

Answers and explanations

1. **B.** Most brokerage firms are broker–dealers, meaning that they act as an intermediary and deal out of their own inventory. When acting as a broker, a firm is buying or selling a security for a customer through another dealer. If executing a trade as a broker, the firm charges the customer a commission. Firms also act as dealers if they are buying and selling out of their own inventory. If acting as a dealer, the firm charges a markup when the customer buys and a markdown when the customer sells.

2. **A.** A third market trade is a trade of exchange-listed securities trading OTC. This type of trade takes place all the time.

3. **C.** Remember, stop orders are used for protection. So, in this case, you're looking for a stop order. Because the investor is short the security, they would have to buy themselves out of that position if the price of the security went in the wrong direction (up in this case). To protect a short position, an investor could enter a buy stop order.

4. **A.** At-the-open orders must be executed at the opening price; otherwise, the order must be canceled. At-the-open orders allow for partial execution.

5. **B.** Because this investor would like to purchase the stock at a particular price or better and is not currently short the stock, you should enter a buy limit order for ABC common stock at $28.

6. **D.** Actually, all of the choices listed are considered accredited investors. Accredited investors can handle more financial risk than average investors.

7. **D.** Short sellers are bearish because they want the price of the security they're purchasing to decrease. Because short sellers can lose money if the price of the security increases, their maximum loss potential is unlimited because there is nothing from keeping the price of the security from increasing more.

8. **B.** Not held orders have to do with the timing of an order. So, for not held orders, the customer must agree to whether they want to buy, sell, or sell short a security as well as the number of shares. A not held order is one in which the customer is giving you, their registered rep, discretion as to the time an order is placed. This may be a situation in which you think that you can get the customer a better price later in the day.

9. **C.** If you remember what the initials stand for, it makes the question a lot easier. FOK stands for fill or kill, which means that the entire order must be either filled immediately or killed (canceled). AON stands for all-or-none, which means that the entire order must be filled entirely (but not immediately) or none of the order gets executed. The one that allows for partial execution is an IOC (immediate or cancel) order, which means that the broker has to execute as much of the order as possible immediately and cancel the rest.

10. **A.** Remember, you're looking for false answers to this question. Unsolicited orders are ones in which the investor tells the registered rep which securities they want to purchase, sell, or sell short. Although orders must be approved by a principal, they don't have to be approved prior to the order being placed. In addition, there are no limits to the size of the order regarding unsolicited orders; they are only limited based on the investor's ability to pay.

11. **B.** The first price (18.10) is the bid price (the price at which the market maker is willing to purchase the security). The second price (18.30) is the ask price that the market maker is willing to accept when selling the security. The "20x25" represents the number of round lots the market maker is willing to buy or sell. Unless told differently, a round lot is 100 shares. Therefore, the market maker is willing to buy up to 2,000 shares at $18.10 and sell up to 2,500 shares at $18.30.

12. **B.** As a married couple, accredited investors are ones that have a joint income of at least $300,000 for the previous two years and that is expected to be at least $300,000 for the current year.

13. **A.** Brokers act as middlemen in a securities transaction. They're putting a buyer and seller together to make a trade. As such, they charge a commission. A good way to remember this is to think of a real estate agent or broker. Real estate agents or brokers charge a commission for selling someone else's house to a buyer.

14. **A.** The term "spread" refers the difference between the highest bid price (the most a market maker is willing to pay to purchase the security) and the lowest ask (offer) price (the least a market maker will take when selling the security). Typically, the narrower the spread, the more actively traded the security.

15. **C.** Since Marvin is not licensed, he cannot discuss anything relating to investments with an existing customer or potential customer. If he cannot do that, he certainly cannot accept orders (whether solicited or not) from a customer. However, he can do things such as sending account opening forms to a new customer.

IN THIS CHAPTER

» Outlining the breakdown of taxes and income

» Seeing how the IRS taxes securities

» Comparing the different types of retirement plans

» Taking a practice quiz

Chapter 15
Making Sure the IRS Gets Its Share

Yes, it's true what they say: The only sure things in life are death and taxes. Although taxes are an annoying necessity, investors do get tax breaks if they invest in securities for a long period of time — which means you, as a rep, need a good understanding of the tax discounts investors could potentially receive. Additionally, the SIE exam tests your ability to recognize the different types of retirement plans, the specifics about each one, and the tax advantages.

In this chapter, I cover tax categories and rules, from distinguishing among types of taxes to types of income. And although enjoying retirement isn't quite as certain as pushing up daisies, I explain Uncle Sam's claim on the cash investors put into 401(k)s, individual retirement accounts (IRAs), and other retirement plans. As always, you can count on some example questions and an exam at the end of the chapter to wrap it up.

Everything in Its Place: Checking Out Tax and Income Categories

The many lines you see on tax forms clue you in to the fact that the Internal Revenue Service (IRS) likes to break things into categories. The following sections explain progressive and regressive taxes, as well as types of personal income.

Touring the tax categories

The supreme tax collector (the IRS) has broken taxes into a couple of categories, according to the percentage individuals pay. Your mission is to understand the different tax categories and how they affect investors:

- **Progressive taxes:** These taxes affect high-income individuals more than they affect low-income individuals; the more taxable income individuals have, the higher their income tax bracket. Progressive taxes include taxes on personal income (see the next section), gift taxes, and estate taxes. The SIE contains more questions on progressive taxes than on regressive taxes.
- **Regressive taxes:** These taxes affect individuals earning a lower income more than they affect people earning a higher income; everyone pays the same rate, so individuals who earn a lower income are affected more because that rate represents a higher percentage of their income. Examples of regressive taxes are payroll taxes, sales taxes, property taxes, excise taxes, gasoline taxes, and so on.

Looking at types of income

The three main categories of income are earned, passive, and portfolio. (If you're especially interested in the details of how investments are taxed, you can find more information at `www.irs.gov`.) You need to distinguish among the different categories because the IRS treats them differently:

- **Earned (active) income:** People generate this type of income from activities that they're actively involved in. Earned income includes money received from salary, bonuses, tips, commissions, and so on. Earned income is taxed at the individual's tax bracket and based on their filing status.
- **Passive income:** This type of income comes from enterprises in which an individual isn't actively involved. Passive income includes income from limited partnerships (see Chapter 10) and rental property. When you see the words *passive income* on the SIE exam, immediately start thinking that the income comes from a direct participation program (DPP). Individuals can write off passive losses against any passive income to determine the net taxable income.
- **Portfolio income:** This type of income includes interest, dividends, and capital gains derived from the sale of securities. The following section tells you more about taxes on portfolio income. Portfolio income may be taxed at the investor's tax bracket or at a lower rate, depending on the holding period.

Noting Taxes on Investments

You need to understand how dividends, interest, capital gains, and capital losses affect investors. To make your life more interesting, the IRS has given tax advantages to people who hold onto investments for a long period of time, so familiarize yourself with the types of taxes that apply to investments and how investors are taxed.

Interest income

Interest income that bondholders receive may or may not be taxable, depending on the type of security or securities held:

- **Corporate bond interest:** Interest received from corporate bonds is taxable at all levels (federal, state, and local, where local taxes exist).
- **Municipal bond interest:** Interest received from most municipal bonds (except taxable municipals) is federally tax-free; however, investors may be taxed on the state and local levels, depending on where the investor lives and the municipality of the issuer of the bonds. (See Chapter 8.)
- **U.S. government securities interest:** Interest received from U.S. government securities, such as T-bills, T-notes, T-STRIPS, TIPS, and T-bonds, is taxable on the federal level but exempt from state and local taxes.

REMEMBER

Even though T-bills, T-STRIPS, and any other zero-coupon bonds don't generate interest payments (because the securities are issued at a discount and mature at par, which is the face value of the security), the difference between the purchase price and the amount received at maturity is considered interest and is subject to taxation.

Dividends

Dividends may be in the form of cash, stock, or product. The following sections discuss dividends in cash, in stock, and from mutual funds.

Cash dividends

Qualified cash dividends received from stocks are taxed at a maximum rate of 0 percent, 15 percent, or 20 percent, depending on the investor's adjusted gross income (AGI). Qualified dividends are ones in which the customer has held onto the stock for at least 61 days (91 days for preferred stock). The 61-day holding period starts 60 days prior to the *ex-dividend date* (the first day the stock trades without dividends). If the investor has held the stock for less than the 61-day holding period, the dividends are considered *nonqualified,* and investors are taxed at the rate determined by their regular tax bracket.

Note: There is currently an additional net investment tax of 3.8 percent for individual investors with a modified adjusted gross income above $200,000 ($250,000 for married couples).

Stock dividends

Stock dividends don't change the overall value of investment, so additional shares received are not taxed. (For details, see Chapter 6.) However, stock dividends do lower the cost basis per share for tax purposes. The cost basis is used to calculate capital gains and losses.

Dividends from mutual funds

Dividends and interest generated from securities that are held in a mutual fund portfolio are passed through to investors and are taxed as either *qualified* (see the earlier section "Cash dividends") or *nonqualified*. The type(s) of securities in the portfolio and the length of time the fund held the securities dictate how the investor is taxed. Here's how mutual fund dividends are taxed:

Federally Tax-Free	0, 15, or 20 Percent	Ordinary Income
Municipal bond funds	Stock funds	Corporate bond funds
	Long-term capital gains	Short-term capital gains

REMEMBER

One of the great things about owning mutual funds is that they're nice enough to let you know what taxes you're going to be subject to. At the beginning of each year (usually in January), you receive a statement from the mutual fund that lets you know how much you received the previous year in dividends, in short-term capital gains, and in long-term capital gains. The mutual fund also sends a copy of the statement to the IRS.

The mutual fund determines the long-term or short-term gains by its holding period, not the investors'. Also, remember that you're subject to capital gains tax and taxes on dividends each year even if the money is reinvested in the fund.

At the sale: Capital gains and losses

Capital gains are profits (*realized gains*) made when selling a security, and *capital losses* are losses incurred when selling a security. To determine whether an investor has a capital gain or capital loss, you have to start with the investor's cost basis. The *cost basis* is used for tax purposes and includes the purchase price plus any commission (although on the SIE exam, the test designers usually don't throw commission into the equation). The cost basis remains the same unless it's adjusted for things like stock splits, stock dividends, accretion, amortization, and so on.

REMEMBER

Accretion and amortization come into play when an investor purchases a bond at a price other than par. The bond cost basis will be adjusted toward par over the amount of time until maturity. You won't be asked to calculate it on the SIE exam.

Incurring taxes with capital gains

An investor realizes capital gains when they sell a security at a price higher than their cost basis. Capital gains on any security (even municipal and U.S. government bonds) are fully taxed on the federal, state, and local levels.

REMEMBER

A capital gain isn't realized until a security is *sold*.

Note: If the value of an investment increases, it's considered *appreciation* or an *unrealized* gain, and if the investor doesn't sell, the investor doesn't incur capital gains taxes. Mutual fund shareholders would be subject to taxation if the issuer sold securities held by the fund at a profit, even if the shareholder didn't sell any shares.

Capital gains are broken down into two categories, depending on the holding period of the securities:

- **Short-term capital gains:** These gains are realized when a security is held for *one year or less*. Short-term capital gains are taxed according to the *investor's tax bracket*.

» **Long-term capital gains:** These gains are realized when a security is held for *more than one year.* To encourage investors to buy and hold securities, long-term capital gains are currently taxed at a rate in line with cash dividends (0, 15, or 20 percent depending on the investor's adjusted gross income). For more information on capital gains and losses, visit the IRS website at `www.irs.gov/taxtopics/tc409`.

Note: If an investor purchased 100 shares of a particular security for $4,000 and later sold those shares for $6,000, the original $4,000 purchase price would be considered a *return of capital.* Only the $2,000 capital gain ($6,000 selling price minus the $4,000 purchase price) would be taxable. So, the taxes would be based upon the profit made (how much was made above the investor's cost basis).

Offsetting gains with capital losses

Certainly, no matter how much research has been done, not every investment is going to be profitable. An investor realizes a capital loss when selling a security at a value lower than the cost basis. Investors can use capital losses to offset capital gains and reduce the tax burden. Like capital gains, capital losses are broken into short-term and long-term:

» **Short-term capital losses:** An investor incurs these losses when they have held the security for *one year or less.* Investors can use short-term capital losses to offset short-term capital gains.

» **Long-term capital losses:** An investor incurs these losses when they have held the security for *more than one year.* Long-term capital losses can offset long-term capital gains.

When an investor has a net capital loss, they can write off up to $3,000 per year on their federal taxes against their earned income and carry the balance forward to the following year. Married couples filing jointly can write off $3,000 per year, and married couples filing separately can write off $1,500 per year each. For test purposes, assume $3,000 per year.

The following question involves capital-loss write-offs.

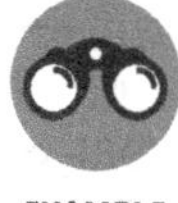
EXAMPLE

In a particular year, Jones realizes $30,000 in long-term capital gains and $50,000 in long-term capital losses. How much of the capital losses would be carried forward to the following year?

(A) $3,000

(B) $17,000

(C) $20,000

(D) $30,000

The correct answer is (B). Jones has a net capital loss of $20,000 (a $50,000 loss minus the $30,000 gain). Jones writes off $3,000 of that capital loss against the earned income and carries the additional loss of $17,000 forward to write off against any capital gains they may have in future years. In the event that Jones doesn't have any capital gains the following year, they can still write off $3,000 of the $17,000 against any earned income and carry the remaining $14,000 forward, which can be used to offset any capital gains the following year. The loss can be carried forward to subsequent years until used up or the investor dies.

The wash sale rule: Adjusting the cost basis when you can't claim a loss

To keep investors from claiming a loss on securities (which an investor could use to offset gains on another investment; see the preceding section) while repurchasing substantially (or exactly) the same security, the IRS has come up with the *wash sale rule*. According to this rule, if an investor sells a security at a capital loss, the investor can't repurchase the same security or anything convertible into the same security for 30 days prior to or after the sale and be able to claim the loss. An investor doesn't end up in handcuffs for violating the wash sale rule; they simply can't claim the loss on their taxes.

However, the loss doesn't go away if investors buy the security within that window of time; investors get to adjust the cost basis of the security. If an investor were to sell 100 shares of ABC at a $2-per-share loss and purchase 100 shares of ABC within 30 days for $50 per share, the investor's new cost basis (excluding commissions) would be $52 per share (the $50 purchase price plus the $2 loss on the shares sold), thus lowering the amount of capital gains they would face on the new purchase.

The following question tests your understanding of the wash sale rule.

EXAMPLE

If Melissa sells DEF common stock at a loss on June 2, for 30 days she can't buy which of the following securities without being subject to the wash sale rule?

(A) DEF common stock only

(B) DEF common stock and DEF preferred stock

(C) DEF common stock, DEF warrants, and DEF call options

(D) DEF common stock, DEF warrants, DEF call options, and DEF preferred stock

The answer you want is (C). You need to remember that Melissa sold DEF at a loss; therefore, she can't buy back the same security or anything convertible into the same security within 30 days to avoid the wash sale rule. Warrants give an investor the right to buy stock at a fixed price (see Chapter 6), and call options give investors the right to buy securities at a fixed price (Chapter 11). However, answer (C) is okay because DEF preferred stock is a different security and is not convertible into DEF common stock (unless it's convertible preferred, which it isn't; if it were convertible, the question would have told you so). For Melissa to avoid the wash sale rule, she can't buy DEF common stock, DEF convertible preferred stock, DEF convertible bonds, DEF call options, DEF warrants, or DEF rights for 30 days. However, she can buy DEF preferred stock, DEF bonds, or DEF put options (the right to sell DEF).

REMEMBER

Putting it in simple terms, the cost basis is the price an individual paid for an investment after taxes. This cost includes brokerage fees, trading costs, and loads (sales charges for mutual funds). Now, things can get a little more complex in the event of stock splits, mergers, and dividend payments. The main thing that you need to know for the SIE exam is that the cost basis is used for calculations to determine an investor's tax liability when selling securities. More recently, brokerage firms, mutual funds, and so on are required to provide investors information on their tax liability, such as the amount of short-term capital gains, long-term capital gains, dividends, interest, and so on.

Estate taxes

Estate tax is a tax on property that is passed along to someone's estate when the person dies. Inheriting securities is a little more straightforward than receiving gifts of securities. When an individual receives securities as a result of an inheritance, they *always* assume the fair market cost basis of the inherited securities on the date of the owner's death. Additionally, securities received by inheritance are always assigned a long-term holding characterization for tax purposes when sold. Estate taxes are covered a little more in depth in the Series 7 book.

Exploring Retirement Plan Tax Advantages

I place retirement plans with taxes because retirement plans give investors tax advantages. When you're reviewing this section, zone in on the differences and similarities among the different types of plans. The contribution limits are important but not as important as understanding the plan specifics and who's qualified to open which type of plan.

Qualified versus nonqualified plans

The IRS may dub employee retirement plans as qualified or nonqualified. The distinction concerns whether they meet IRS and Employee Retirement Income Security Act (ERISA) standards for favorable tax treatment.

Tax-qualified plans

A *tax-qualified plan* meets IRS standards to receive a favorable tax treatment. When you're investing in a tax-qualified plan, the contributions into the plan are made from pretax dollars and are excluded from your taxable income. Not only are contributions into the plan excluded from income, but the account also grows on a tax-deferred basis, so you aren't taxed until you withdraw money from the account at retirement. IRAs are examples of tax-qualified retirement plans. The two types of corporate tax-qualified retirement plans are defined contribution and defined benefit plans. These include 401(k)s, profit-sharing plans, and money-purchase plans. Most corporate pension plans are tax-qualified plans.

Because investors don't pay tax on the money initially deposited or on the earnings, the entire withdrawal from a tax-qualified plan is taxed at a rate determined by the investor's tax bracket, which is normally lower during retirement. Additionally, distributions taken before age 59 1/2 are subject to a 10 percent tax penalty (10 percent additional tax on early distributions) except in cases of death, disability, first-time home buying, educational expenses for certain family members, medical premiums for unemployed individuals, and so on.

Nonqualified plans

Obviously, a nonqualified plan is the opposite of a qualified plan. *Nonqualified plans,* such as deferred compensation plans, payroll deduction plans, and 457 plans, do not meet IRS and ERISA standards for favorable tax treatment. If you're investing in a nonqualified retirement plan, deposits are not tax-deductible (they're made from after-tax dollars); however, because you're dealing with a retirement plan, earnings in the plan do build up on a tax-deferred basis. People may choose to invest in nonqualified plans because either their employer doesn't have a qualified plan set up or the investment guidelines are not as strict (investors may be able to contribute more and invest in a wider choice of securities).

Because investors have already paid tax on the money initially deposited but not on the earnings, withdrawals from nonqualified plans are only partially taxed at the rate determined by the investor's tax bracket. The investor is taxed only on the amount that exceeds the amount of the contributions made.

IRA types and contribution limits

You'll likely be tested on a few different types of retirement plans and possibly the contribution limits. When you're looking at this section, understand the specifics of the types of plans and view the contribution limits as secondary. The contribution limits change pretty much yearly, and the SIE questions may not change that often. If you have a rough idea of the contribution limits, you should be okay. For updates and additional information, you can go to `www.irs.gov/retirement-plans/plan-participant-employee/retirement-topics-ira-contribution-limits`.

Traditional IRAs

IRAs (Individual Retirement Accounts or Individual Retirement Arrangements) are tax-qualified retirement accounts, so deposits in the account are made from pretax dollars. (They're tax-deductible.) IRAs are completely funded by contributions that the *holder of the account* makes. Regardless of whether individuals are covered by a pension plan, they can still deposit money in an IRA. Here's a list of some of the key points of IRAs:

- IRAs may be set up as *single life* (when the owner is the beneficiary of the account), *joint and last survivor* (when the sole beneficiary of the account is their spouse and the spouse is more than ten years younger than the owner), or *uniform lifetime* (when the spouse is not the sole beneficiary or the spouse is not more than ten years younger than the owner).
- Permissible investments for IRAs include stocks, bonds, mutual funds, U.S. gold and silver coins, and real estate.
- The maximum contribution per person as of 2026 (which increased from $7,000 from 2025) is $7,500 per year, with an additional catch-up contribution of $1,100 per person allowed for investors age 50 or older. Excess contributions are taxed at a rate of 6 percent per year until the excess is withdrawn.
- A husband and wife under age 50 can have separate accounts with a maximum contribution of $7,500 per year each, whether both are working or one is working.
- Contributions to the IRA are fully deductible for individuals not covered by employer pension plans.

  If investors are covered by a workplace retirement plan, deposits into an IRA may or may not be tax-deductible. Although I think that the chances of your being tested on the values are slim, as of 2026, if an individual is covered by a workplace retirement plan and earns up to $81,000 per year ($129,000 jointly), deposits made into an IRA are fully deductible. The deductions are gradually phased out and disappear when an individual earns more than $91,000 per year ($149,000 for married couples filing jointly).
- When an investor starts to withdraw funds from an IRA, the investor is taxed on the entire withdrawal (the amount deposited, which was not taxed, and the appreciation in value). The withdrawal is taxed as ordinary income.
- Withdrawals can't begin before age 59 ½, or investors have to pay an early withdrawal penalty of 10 percent added to the investor's rate according to their tax bracket. An investor isn't subject to the 10 percent tax penalty in cases of death, disability, first-time homebuyers, and a few other exceptions. (Obviously, dead retirees won't be making withdrawals, but their beneficiaries will be; in this case, the beneficiaries aren't hit with the 10 percent penalty.)
- Withdrawals must begin by April 1 of the year after the investor reaches age 73 (the *required beginning date*, or RBD). Investors who don't take their *required minimum distribution* (RMD) by that time are subject to a 50 percent tax penalty on the amount they should have withdrawn. The IRS provides minimum distribution worksheets to help you determine the amount that

needs to be withdrawn in order to avoid the penalty; you can find them at `www.irs.gov/retirement-plans/plan-participant-employee/required-minimum-distribution-worksheets`.

» Deposits in IRAs are allowed up to April 15 (Tax Day) to qualify as a deduction for the previous year's taxes.

Roth IRAs

Anyone whose income is below the IRS modified adjusted gross income limit can open a Roth IRA. The key difference between a traditional IRA and a Roth IRA is that withdrawals from a Roth IRA are not taxed. However, deposits made in the Roth IRA are not tax-deductible (made from after-tax dollars). Provided that the investor has held onto the Roth IRA for more than five years and has reached age 59½, they can withdraw money from the Roth IRA without incurring any taxable income on the amount deposited or on the appreciation in the account. So, in this case, all qualified distributions are excluded from federal income tax.

REMEMBER

As of 2026, the maximum that an individual may contribute to a traditional IRA and Roth IRA is $7,500 per year combined. There is also a catch-up contribution of $1,100 allowed for individuals age 50 and older, which means they can contribute up to $8,600 per year.

As of 2026, investors who have an adjusted gross income of more than $168,000 per year ($252,000 married, filing jointly) can't contribute to a Roth IRA.

Simplified employee pensions (SEP-IRAs)

An SEP-IRA is a retirement vehicle designed for small-business owners, self-employed individuals, and their employees. SEP-IRAs allow participants to invest money for retirement on a tax-deferred basis. Employers can make tax-deductible contributions directly to their employees' SEP-IRAs. As of 2026, the maximum employer contribution to each employee's SEP-IRA is 25 percent of the employee's compensation (salary, bonuses, and overtime) or $72,000 (subject to cost-of-living increases in the following years), whichever is less. Employees who are part of the plan may still make annual contributions to a traditional or Roth IRA.

401(k) and 403(b)

There are certainly a number of qualified retirement plans besides IRAs. 401(k)s and 403(b)s are two that you should know a little about before taking the SIE exam.

401(k) plans

As stated previously, a 401(k) is a corporate retirement plan. With this type of plan, employees can voluntarily contribute a percentage of their salary up to a certain amount each year (as such, it's a defined contribution plan). Because it's a qualified plan, the amount contributed by the employee to the 401(k) is excluded from the employee's gross income. In addition, in most cases, the employer matches the employee's contribution up to a certain amount (for example, 25 percent, 50 percent, and so on). The account grows on a tax-deferred basis, so everything withdrawn from the account at retirement is taxable.

Roth 401(k) plans

A Roth 401(k) has similarities between traditional 401(k) plans and Roth IRAs. As with a traditional 401(k), the contribution limits, which adjust yearly, are the same as well as the fact that they are both employer-sponsored plans. However, like a Roth IRA, contributions are made after taxes. So, withdrawals of contributions and earnings are not taxed as long as the account has been held for at least five years and the holder is at least 59½ years old (except in cases of death or disability). Unlike Roth IRAs, required minimum distribution (RMD) rules apply.

Note: Roth 401(k)s are like Roth IRAs because qualified distributions are excluded from federal income tax.

403(b) plans

These are salary reduction plans for public school (elementary school, secondary school, college, and so on) employees, tax-exempt organizations, and religious organizations. These plans are also known as *tax-sheltered annuities* (TSAs). As with 401(k)s, employees can elect to have a portion of their pay put into the retirement plan that's tax deferred. Like 401(k)s, the employer may match a percentage of the contributions. To be eligible, employees must be at least 21 years old and have been working for the employer for at least a year.

REMEMBER

Because the IRS wants to be able to collect taxes, the holders of IRAs (except for Roth IRAs) and other qualified-plan participants must start withdrawing money at a certain point. Plan participants must take a required minimum distribution (RMD) by April 1 of the year after they turn age 73, whether they need the money at that point or not. In addition, they must continue to take additional minimum distributions each subsequent year until all the money is out of the account.

Testing Your Knowledge

Following is a small sample of questions you may see related to taxes and retirement plans on the SIE exam. Read each question carefully. Good luck!

Practice questions

1. Which of the following are regressive taxes?

   (A) Gasoline and alcohol

   (B) Sales, income, and gasoline

   (C) Sales, gasoline, and alcohol

   (D) Sales, income, gasoline, and alcohol

2. All of the following are types of tax-qualified retirement plans **except**

   (A) 401(k)

   (B) profit-sharing

   (C) IRA

   (D) deferred compensation

3. Which of the following are **true** regarding Roth IRAs and Roth 401(k)s?

(A) Withdrawals from both are tax-free provided that investors have held the accounts for at least five years and have reached the age of 59½.

(B) There are no contribution limits.

(C) Contributions made to both are made pretax.

(D) All of the above.

4. An investor buys 1,000 shares of a stock at $30. If the stock increases in value to $50, how would the result be categorized?

(A) Profit

(B) Appreciation

(C) Capital gain

(D) Investment income

5. An individual investor who lives at home with their parents is covered by an employer pension plan. However, they would like more coverage at retirement and decide to put the maximum allowable contribution in an IRA. If their salary is $52,000 per year, which of the following is **true**?

(A) Contributions to the IRA are fully deductible.

(B) Contributions to the IRA are partially deductible.

(C) Contributions to the IRA are not deductible.

(D) Cannot be determined.

6. Which of the following is taxable for an investor for the year in which it occurs?

I. Stock dividends

II. Cash dividends

III. Interest received from corporate bonds

IV. Interest received from U.S. government bonds

(A) I, II, and III

(B) II and III

(C) II, III, and IV

(D) I, II, III, and IV

7. A customer purchased 100 shares of ABC stock at $40 per share on March 24. On March 24 of the following year, the customer sold the stock at $46 per share. Which **two** of the following are **true** regarding these transactions?

I. They would be taxed as a short-term capital gain.

II. They would be taxed as a long-term capital gain.

III. The gain would be taxed at the customer's tax bracket.

IV. The gain would be taxed at 0 percent, 15 percent, or 20 percent, depending on the customer's adjusted gross income.

(A) I and III

(B) I and IV

(C) II and III

(D) II and IV

8. According to the wash sale rule, if a customer sold a security at a loss, which of the following is **true**?

(A) The customer cannot purchase call options on the same security for 30 days before or after the sale and be able to claim the loss.

(B) The customer cannot purchase bonds by the same issuer for 30 days before and after the sale and be able to claim the loss.

(C) The customer cannot sell short the same security within 30 days before or after the sale and be able to claim the loss.

(D) The customer cannot purchase mutual funds holding the same security for 30 days before and after the sale and be able to claim the loss.

9. Which of the following types of retirement plans is a salary reduction plan set up for public school employees?

(A) SEP-IRAs

(B) 401(k)s

(C) 403(b)s

(D) Keogh plans

Answers and explanations

1. **C.** Regressive taxes are ones in which all individuals are charged the same percentage regardless of their income. Sales tax, gasoline tax, and alcohol tax are all regressive taxes. Income tax is a progressive tax because the higher your income, the higher the tax bracket.

2. **D.** Tax-qualified plans are ones that meet IRS standards for favorable tax treatment. If the plan is tax-qualified, contributions are made from pretax dollars. However, when the money is withdrawn, the entire amount, including the initial contributions plus any gains, is taxable. Tax-qualified plans include IRAs, 401(k)s, profit-sharing, money-purchase, and so on. Nonqualified plans are funded from after-tax contributions and include deferred compensation, payroll deduction, 457 plans, and so on.

3. **A.** Contributions to both Roth IRAs and Roth 401(k)s are made from after-tax dollars. So, withdrawals are tax-free provided that investors have held the accounts for at least five years and are at least 59½ years old.

4. **B.** In this case, because the investor didn't sell the security at a profit, in which case it would've been a capital gain, it is categorized as appreciation.

5. **A.** An investor can always contribute money to an IRA even if covered by an employer pension plan. However, whether it's deductible depends on the investor's earnings. As of 2026 (the amount increases yearly), an investor who makes up to $81,000 can contribute to an IRA and be able to deduct the full amount from their taxes.

6. **C.** Cash dividends, interest from corporate bonds, and interest from U.S. government bonds are all taxable for the year in which they occurred. However, stock dividends are not taxable because the investor didn't receive a payment, just more shares of stock, which lowered the cost basis.

7. **A.** This is a short-term capital gain because when a security is sold up to and including one year from the purchase date, it would be a short-term capital gain or loss. Because it is short-term, the gain would be taxed at the investor's tax bracket.

8. **A.** According to the wash sale rule, an investor who is selling a security at a loss cannot purchase the same security or anything convertible into the same security for 30 days prior or 30 days after the sale and be able to claim the loss. However, the loss isn't gone completely; it just means that the cost basis for the new securities purchased will be adjusted for the loss. So, if the investor sold ABC common stock at a loss, they wouldn't be able to purchase ABC call options on the stock because call options give the investor the right to purchase the underlying security.

9. **C.** 403(b) plans are set up for public school employees (elementary, secondary, college, and so on). They are considered salary reduction plans because the amount contributed by the employee reduces their salary so that they aren't taxed on the money contributed until it's taken out at retirement.

IN THIS CHAPTER

» Meeting the self-regulatory organizations

» Opening and handling customer accounts

» Playing by the rules

» Reviewing additional topics tested

» Checking your knowledge with a chapter quiz

Chapter 16
Rules and Regulations: No Fooling Around

First off, I'd like to apologize for having to include this chapter. Unfortunately, rules are a part of life and part of the SIE. When you're reading this, please remember that I didn't make the rules — but I do my best to make them as easy to digest as possible. Rules have become increasingly important on FINRA securities exams like the SIE, especially since the Patriot Act came into the picture.

In this chapter, I cover topics related to rules and regulations. First, I help you understand who the guardians of the market are and their roles in protecting customers and enforcing rules. I also place considerable emphasis on opening, closing, transferring, and handling customers' accounts. And, of course, I provide practice questions to guide you on your way. At the end, I give you a 24-question chapter quiz to help you test your knowledge.

Meeting the Market Watchdogs: Securities Regulatory Organizations

To keep the market running smoothly and to make sure investors aren't abused (at least too much), regulatory organizations stay on the lookout. Although you don't need to know all the minute details about each of them, you do have to know the basics.

The Securities and Exchange Commission

The U.S. Securities and Exchange Commission (SEC) is the major watchdog of the securities industry. Congress created the SEC to regulate securities markets and to protect investors from fraudulent and manipulative practices. All broker–dealers who transact business with investors and other broker–dealers must register with the SEC. And that registration means something: All broker–dealers have to comply with SEC rules or face censure (an official reprimand), limits on activity, their own suspension or suspension of one or more associated persons (such as a registered rep or principal), a fine, and/or having their registration revoked.

REMEMBER

SEC investigations may lead to a civil (financial) complaint being filed in a federal court. The SEC may seek disgorgement (taking away) of ill-gotten gains, civil money penalties, and injunctive relief (a cease-and-desist order from the court). If the matter is criminal in nature, the investigation is conducted by the U.S. attorney's office and the grand jury.

Among its other numerous functions, you need to be aware that the SEC also enforces the following acts:

» **The Securities Act of 1933:** The Act of 1933 requires the full and fair disclosure of all material information about a new issue.

» **The Securities Exchange Act of 1934:** The Act of 1934, which established the SEC, was enacted to protect investors by regulating the over-the-counter (OTC) market and exchanges, such as the New York Stock Exchange (NYSE). Chapter 14 tells you more about markets. In addition, the Act of 1934 regulates

- The extension of credit in margin accounts (see Chapter 12)
- The registration and regulation of brokers and dealers
- The registration of securities associations
- Transactions by insiders
- Customer accounts
- Trading activities

» **The Trust Indenture Act (TIA):** This act, formerly called the Trust Indenture Act of 1939, prohibits bond issues valued at more than $50 million (originally $5 million) from being offered to investors without an indenture. The trust *indenture* is a written agreement that protects investors by disclosing the particulars of the issue (the coupon rate, the maturity date, any collateral backing the bond, and so on). As part of the Trust Indenture Act, all companies must hire a trustee who's responsible for protecting the rights of bondholders.

» **The Investment Company Act of 1940:** This act regulates the registration requirements and the activities of investment companies.

» **The Investment Advisers Act of 1940:** This act requires the registration of certain investment advisers with the SEC. An investment adviser is a person who receives a fee for giving investment advice. Any investment adviser with at least $110 million of assets ($25 million in some states) under management or anyone who advises an investment company must register with the SEC. All other investment advisers have to register on the state level. The Investment Advisers Act of 1940 regulates

- Record-keeping responsibilities
- Advisory contracts
- Advertising rules
- Custody of customers' assets and funds

Self-regulatory organizations

As you can imagine, due to the unscrupulous nature of some investors and registered representatives, the SEC's job is overwhelming. Fortunately, a few self-regulatory organizations (SROs) are there to take some of the burden off of the SEC's shoulders. Although membership isn't mandatory, most broker–dealers are members of one or more SROs. SRO rules are usually stricter than those of the SEC.

The four types of SROs you need to know for the SIE are the FINRA, MSRB, NYSE, and CBOE:

- **Financial Industry Regulatory Authority (FINRA):** FINRA is the SRO responsible for the operation and regulation of the OTC market, investment banking (the underwriting of securities), NYSE trades, investment companies, limited partnerships, and so on. FINRA was created in 2007 and is a consolidation of the National Association of Securities Dealers (NASD) and the regulation and enforcement portions of the NYSE. FINRA is responsible for making sure that its members follow not only FINRA rules, but also the rules set forth by the SEC. Additionally, FINRA is responsible for handling complaints against member firms and may take disciplinary action if necessary. FINRA is also responsible for administering securities exams such as the SIE. (Now you know who to blame.) FINRA has strict rules (as the other SROs do, I suspect) regarding filing of misleading, incomplete, or inaccurate information concerning membership, the firm's registration, and the registration of member associates.
- **Municipal Securities Rulemaking Board (MSRB):** The MSRB was established to develop rules that banks and securities firms have to follow when underwriting, selling, buying, and recommending municipal securities. (Check out Chapter 8 for info on municipal bonds.) MSRB rules apply to individuals and firms conducting municipal securities business. So, the MSRB does not regulate issuers of municipal securities. The MSRB is subject to SEC oversight but does not enforce SEC rules.

  REMEMBER

  The MSRB makes rules for firms (and representatives) who sell municipal bonds but don't enforce them; it leaves enforcement up to FINRA.
- **NYSE:** The NYSE is the oldest and largest stock exchange in the United States. The NYSE is responsible for listing securities, setting exchange policies, and supervising the exchange and member firms. The NYSE has the power to take disciplinary action against member firms.
- **Chicago Board Options Exchange (CBOE):** The CBOE is an exchange that makes and enforces options exchange rules.

REMEMBER

Although SROs may be independent, they work together creating and enforcing rules. FINRA and NYSE can fine, suspend, censure (reprimand), and expel members; however, the FINRA and NYSE can't imprison members who violate the rules and regulations.

TIP

Look at SIE questions with the words *guarantee* or *approve* in them very carefully. The FINRA, SEC, NYSE, and so on do *not* approve or guarantee securities. Any statement that says that they do is false. In addition, because a firm is registered with (or didn't have its registration revoked by) an SRO, it does not mean that the SRO approves of the firm, its financial standing, its business, its conduct, and so on. As such, member firms and their associates may not claim that they've been approved by the SEC or any SRO.

State regulators

The North American Securities Administrators Association (NASAA) is devoted to investor protection. It is a voluntary association that consists of 67 regulators. NASAA even predates the creation of the SEC. Its key roles include

- Licensing stockbrokers, smaller investment adviser firms (ones managing less than $100 million in assets), and securities firms conducting business in the state.
- Registering securities on the state level.
- Investigating customer complaints and possible cases of investment fraud.
- Enforcing state securities laws. As such, the NASAA may fine, penalize, provide restitution to investors, assist in prosecuting investment-related criminals, and impose new conduct laws to correct problems as they arise.
- Examining investment adviser firms and broker-dealers to ensure compliance with securities laws and making sure they keep accurate client records.
- Reviewing offerings that are not exempt from state law.
- Providing education to investors regarding their rights and providing information so that they can make more informed financial decisions.
- Advocating for the passage of state securities laws.

TIP

When it comes to the SIE exam, don't go crazy trying to remember every minute detail regarding the NASAA; you'll have to know more when taking the Series 63, Series 65, or Series 66. Get a general feeling for what they do so that you're able to recognize them in a question.

Department of the Treasury/IRS

The U.S. Department of the Treasury (USDT) was established to manage U.S. government revenue. As such, the USDT oversees the printing of all paper currency and minting of all coins. In addition, it is responsible for collecting taxes through the Internal Revenue Service (IRS); it is responsible for managing U.S. government debt securities (T-bonds, T-notes, T-bills, and so on); it licenses banks; and it helps advise U.S. government branches regarding fiscal policy.

FINRA Registration and Reporting Requirements

Unless an individual is exempt from registration requirements, all brokerage firms have registration and reporting requirements that must be followed for their employees. Financial professionals must fill out U4 forms, be fingerprinted, pass necessary exams, take continuing education, and so on.

Filling out the U4 form

Persons wanting to register as financial professionals with FINRA (like you) must submit a *U4 form*. The application includes things like a ten-year employment history and a five-year residential history; if you're registered with another firm, how you're registering (Securities Trader,

Financial and Operations Principal, General Securities Representative, and a slew more); states you want to be registered in; and so on. In addition, applicants must submit their fingerprints.

All U4 forms (`www.finra.org/sites/default/files/form-u4.pdf`) must be thoroughly reviewed by a principal of the firm. *Background checks* must be performed, and the applicant's employers for the previous three years must be called to verify the applicant's employment history. The calls must be made within 30 days of the firm receiving the U4 form. Special scrutiny of the applicant is required if the applicant has previously worked in the securities industry. Information contained in the U4 form must be complete and not misleading.

The U4 form also contains an *arbitration disclosure*, which states that disputes between the applicant and the member firm will be settled by arbitration (essentially, you won't take the firm to court).

TIP

Although a lot of information listed here can disqualify a person, most of the information follows a common theme — which makes sense; you shouldn't have to memorize it all, in other words. However, I suggest you be aware of the ten-year disqualification rule if an individual has been *convicted* (not charged or accused) of a felony or certain misdemeanors. In addition, if a registrant includes misleading information or omits information, their registration will be denied.

Note: Nonregistered (unregistered) persons may not solicit customers or take orders. In addition, member firms are prohibited from paying commissions, fees, concessions, discounts, and so on to any person who is not registered. The failure of a member firm to register someone who should be registered will likely end in disciplinary action by FINRA. Nonregistered persons may handle basic questions. (What is your location? Can I leave a message? What are your hours?) In addition, they may send out literature, transfer calls, set up appointments, let customers know about upcoming seminars, and such. They can't be directly involved in securities business (opening accounts, taking trade orders, soliciting trades, giving quotes, and so on). In the event that a nonregistered person is to handle securities and/or money, they must be fingerprinted.

Grounds for disqualification

A person will be *statutorily disqualified* from membership from FINRA under the following circumstances:

- If they had a felony criminal conviction or certain misdemeanor convictions within the last ten years.
- If they have had a temporary or permanent injunction (no matter what the injunction's age) issued by a court involving a long list of unlawful investment activities.
- If they have been expelled, barred, or are currently suspended from membership or participation in another self-regulatory organization. This holds true even if the person has been barred with the right to reapply.
- If they have been barred or current suspension orders are coming from the SEC, Commodity Futures Trading Commission (CFTC), or any other appropriate authority or regulatory agency. As with the preceding rule, this holds true even if the person has been barred with the right to reapply.
- If they have been denied or had their registration revoked by the CFTC, SEC, or any other appropriate authority or regulatory agency.
- If it has been found that a member or person has made certain false statements in their application, in reports, or in proceedings before the SEC, SROs, or any other appropriate regulatory authority or agency.

» If any final order from a state securities commission (or from any agency or state officer performing similar functions), savings association, credit union, any state authority that examines or supervises banks, state insurance commission (or any office or agency performing similar functions), an appropriate federal banking agency, or the National Credit Union Administration.

- Bars said person from association with an entity (such as a broker-dealer, investment advisory firm, and so on) regulated by such commission, agency, authority, or officer, or from engaging in the business of banking, insurance, securities, savings association activities, or credit union activities.
- Constitutes a final order based on violations of any regulations or laws that prohibit manipulative, fraudulent, or deceptive conduct.

» If the SEC, CFTC, or any SRO finds that a person

- "Willfully" violated federal securities laws, "willfully" violated commodities laws, or "willfully" violated MSRB rules.
- "Willfully" aided, commanded, induced, abetted, counseled, or procured violations as set forth in the preceding rule.
- Failed to supervise another person who committed violations as set forth in rule number one.

Handing over your fingerprints

Under SEC Rule 17f-2 (you don't have to remember the rule number), all employees of a brokerage firm are required to be fingerprinted if they are involved in any of the following activities:

» Making sales

» Handling assets (cash and/or certificates)

» Accessing original books and records

» Supervising any of the preceding activities

Fingerprints are always required when a person is applying for registration. The fingerprints must be submitted as well as the U4 form. If FINRA doesn't receive the fingerprints within 30 days of the U4 being submitted, the applicant's registration will be deemed inactive.

REMEMBER

The information you provide and your investment professional history don't remain in a bubble. The Central Registration Depository's (CRD's) BrokerCheck (`https://brokercheck.finra.org/`) allows investors access to vital information that they may need to help them pick the right firm and the right professional, like you. Don't worry; it won't disclose your address, Social Security number, and the like. However, it will disclose complaints against you and your employer, where you and your employer are registered, exams you passed, how many years you've been in the business, if you were convicted or pled guilty to a crime, if you or your broker have been expelled from an SRO, and so on. If a member maintains a website, the site must provide a link to BrokerCheck.

Continuing education

Yes, even after you've passed your securities exams like this one, you're not done. You're required to take continuing education programs as required by FINRA. These are to make sure that you are up-to-date with any new laws and that you remember the existing ones. Two elements of continuing education are required: the firm element and the regulatory element.

Firm element

Member firms must have annual meetings covering the services and strategies offered by the firm. In addition, the meeting must cover any recent regulatory developments, if any. The meetings must be interactive and allow people to ask questions. All registered persons who have direct contact with the public must attend the meeting. All firms must have continuing and current education programs for their covered employees.

Regulatory element

All registered persons are required to take a computer-based training session covering FINRA regulations by December 31st of each year. In the event that the training isn't taken within the required period, the person's securities license(s) will be deactivated until it's completed. If the registered person's licenses have been deactivated for two years, the individual will be administratively terminated. If administratively terminated, the person must reapply for registration.

What happens when a rep resigns or is terminated

If you leave your firm for whatever reason, the member firm you were working for has to file a U5 form with the CRD within 30 days of the date you resigned or were terminated. You will also receive a copy for your records. The U5 form requires the member firm to provide an explanation of why you left or why you were terminated. If you're moving to a new member firm, your new employer must file a new U4 form and receive a copy of the U5 filed by your former employer.

Things sometimes change, so if something on your U4 or U5 form is or becomes inaccurate, your firm must update the information on the CRD. This could be something as simple as an address change or something a tad more complex — a violation of some kind or (Heaven forbid) a felony conviction.

Don't wait too long going from one firm to another. After a U5 form has been filed on your behalf, you have up to two years to get registered with another firm or you'll have to take your securities exams all over again. You certainly don't want that to happen.

Skipping a step: Who's exempt from FINRA registration

Certain individuals who work for a member firm are exempt from FINRA registration. These include

- Persons whose functions are solely clerical or ministerial
- Persons solely affecting transactions on the floor of a national securities exchange and who are registered with that exchange
- Persons whose function is solely and exclusively involved in transactions of municipal securities

- Persons whose function is solely and exclusively involved in transactions of commodities
- Persons whose function is solely and exclusively involved in transactions in securities futures, as long as that person is registered with a registered futures association

Adhering to reporting requirements

Under FINRA Rule 4530, member firms must report specified events, including quarterly statistical and summary information regarding customer complaints as well as copies of certain civil and criminal actions. Members must report promptly (no later than 30 days after the member knows or should've known about the event) if the member (or associated person of the member)

- Has been found to have violated any securities-related or non-securities-related investment laws or standards of conduct by a U.S. or foreign regulatory organization.
- Is the subject of a written customer complaint involving allegations of theft or misappropriation of funds or securities.
- Is the subject of a written customer complaint involving allegations of forgery.
- Has been named as a defendant or respondent in a proceeding brought by a U.S. or foreign regulatory body alleging a violation of rules.
- Has been denied registration, suspended, expelled, or disciplined by a U.S. or foreign regulatory organization.
- Is indicted, convicted of, or pleads guilty to any felony or certain misdemeanors in or outside the United States.

REMEMBER

The preceding list includes firm reporting requirements under Rule 4530, but firms are required to report certain other events, too. These include

- Outside business activities (covered in the following section).
- Private securities transactions — transactions outside the broker-dealer's normal business, in other words. For argument's sake, say that an associate of a firm has a client who wants to trade options but their firm doesn't trade options because it doesn't have an options principal. In this case, with the permission of their firm, they can accept the order from their client and do the trade through another firm.
- Political contributions and consequences for exceeding dollar contribution thresholds (see "Avoiding violations" later in the chapter).
- Felonies, financial-related misdemeanors, liens, bankruptcies.

Outside business activities

While you're building your business and getting new clients, you may feel the need to make a few extra bucks working another job. If so, you must notify your brokerage firm in writing. However, you don't need to receive written permission to work the other job. Your member firm may reject or restrict your outside work if it feels there is a conflict of interest. (Volunteering does not require written notification.)

Accounts at other broker-dealers and financial institutions

Although you probably won't do this, persons associated with a member firm may open an account at another member firm (executing firm) with prior written permission from the employing firm. The associated person must also let the executing firm know that they are working for another member firm. Duplicate confirmations and statements must be sent to the employing firm if requested.

Private securities transactions

When involved in a private securities transaction, associated persons must provide written notice to their employing firm. These take place when an associated person is involved in a securities transaction outside of their normal business and outside of their employing member firm.

If an associated person would like to enter into a private securities transaction, they must:

- Provide written notice to their employing firm
- Explain their role in the possible transaction
- Describe complete details of the possible transaction
- Disclose whether they will receive compensation (what type and/or dollar amount) for the transaction

Whether the associated person receives compensation or not, the employing firm must provide approval. Transactions for immediate family members in which the associated person does not receive compensation *are not* considered private securities transactions.

Trading by the Book When the Account Is Open

After you've opened a new account, you have to follow additional rules and regulations to keep working in the business. You need to know how to receive trade instructions and how to fill out an order ticket, as well as settlement and payment dates for different securities.

Filling out an order ticket

When you're working as a registered rep, completing documents such as order tickets will become second nature because you'll have them in front of you. When you're taking the SIE, you don't have that luxury, but you still need to know the particulars about what to fill out.

Getting the particulars on paper (or in binary form)

When your customer places an order, you have to fill out an order ticket. Order tickets may be on paper or entered electronically, which happens more often. Regardless of how you enter the order, it needs to contain the following information:

- The registered rep's identification number
- The customer's account number

» The description of the security (stocks, bonds, symbol, and so on)

» The number of shares or bonds that are being purchased or sold

» Whether the registered rep has discretionary authority over the account

» Whether the customer is buying, selling long (selling securities that are owned), or selling short (selling borrowed securities; see Chapter 12)

» For option tickets, whether the customer is buying or writing (selling), is covered or uncovered, and is opening or closing (see Chapter 11 for info on options)

» Whether it's a market order, good-'til-canceled (GTC) order, day order, and so on

» Whether the trade is executed in a cash or margin account

» Whether the trade was solicited or unsolicited

» The time of the order

» The execution price

Figure 16-1 shows you what standard paper order tickets may look like.

Designating unsolicited trades

Normally, you'll be recommending securities in line with a customer's investment objectives. If, however, the customer requests a trade that you think is unsuitable, it's your duty to inform them about it. You don't have to reject the order. (It's the customer's money, and when all is said and done, you're in the business to generate commissions.) If the customer still wants to execute the trade, simply mark the order as *unsolicited*, which takes the responsibility off your shoulders.

A trip to the principal's office: Securing a signature

Principals are designated managers of a firm. All brokerage firms must have *at least two principals* (unless the firm is a sole proprietorship). When you open or trade an account, you have to bring the new account form or order ticket to a principal to sign. Principals need to approve all new accounts, all trades in accounts, and all advertisements and sales literature; they also handle all complaints (lucky break for you!), oversee employees, and watch for potential red flags. (*Note:* A principal doesn't have to approve a prospectus or your recommendations to your customers.)

REMEMBER

Although you'll generally bring an order ticket to a principal right after taking an order, the principal can sign the order ticket later in the day. If you're questioned about this on the SIE exam, you want to answer that the principal needs to approve the trade on the same day, not before or immediately after the trade.

Proportionate sharing

Members or associated persons are prohibited from sharing in the profits or losses in a customer's account. An exception to this rule is if the associated person contributed to the account. In that case, the associated person needs a written authorization from the customer and principal and the profits and/or losses are shared by the customer and associated member based on the percentage contributed. Exempt from the rule of proportional sharing are accounts of immediate family (parents, mother-in-law, father-in-law, spouse, or children) of the associated member.

BUY

B	EXCHANGE	BRANCH	ACCOUNT No.	TYPE	R.R. No.	DAY OPEN
QUANTITY	SECURITY			PRICE LIMIT		EXECUTION PRICE

CUSTOMER NAME AND ADDRESS

SOLICITED _
UNSOLICITED _
DISCRET'Y A/C _

CANCEL

FUNDS, LOCATION

AMOUNT
INTEREST
COM.

BOUGHT FROM

NET

NEW | BROKERAGE | **SOARING SECURITIES** | CHECKED BY

SELL

S	EXCHANGE	BRANCH	ACCOUNT No.	TYPE	R.R. No.	LONG SHORT	DAY OPEN
QUANTITY	SECURITY			PRICE LIMIT			EXECUTION PRICE

CUSTOMER NAME AND ADDRESS

SOLICITED _
UNSOLICITED _
DISCRET'Y A/C _

CANCEL

AMOUNT

SECURITY LOCATION

INTEREST OR ST. TAX
SEC.

SOLD TO

COM.

NET

EXEC. BRKR. | BROKERAGE | **SOARING SECURITIES** | CHECKED BY

FIGURE 16-1: Buy and sell order tickets have spaces for the info you need to make a trade.

Checking your calendar: Payment and settlement dates

Securities that investors purchase have different payment and settlement dates. Here's what you need to know:

- **Trade date:** The day the trade is executed. An investor who buys a security owns the security as soon as the trade is executed, whether or not they have paid for the trade.
- **Settlement date:** The day the issuer updates its records and the certificates are delivered to the buyer's brokerage firm.
- **Payment date:** The day the buyer of the securities must pay for the trade.

TIP

Unless the question specifically asks you to follow FINRA or NYSE rules (which I doubt it will), assume the Fed *regular way* settlement and payment dates as they appear in Table 16-1. The FINRA and NYSE rules both require payment for securities to be made no later than the settlement date, but the Federal Reserve Board states that the payment date for corporate securities is four business days after the trade date.

TABLE 16-1 Regular Way Settlement and Payment Dates

Type of Security	Settlement Date (in Business Days after the Trade Date)	Payment Date (in Business Days after the Trade Date)
Stocks and corporate bonds	2 (T+1 — one business day after the trade date)	3
Municipal bonds	2 (T+1)	1
U.S. government bonds	1 (T+1)	1
Options	1 (T+1)	4

REMEMBER

Cash trades (which are same-day settlements) require payment for the securities and delivery of the securities on the same day as the trade date.

In certain cases, securities may not be able to be delivered as in the preceding chart. In these cases, the seller may specify that there's going to be a *delayed delivery*. There can also be a *mutually agreed upon* date in which the buyer and seller agree on a delayed delivery date prior to or at the time of the transaction.

The *when, as, and if issued (when-issued transaction)* method of delivery is used for a securities issue that has been authorized and sold to investors before the certificates are ready for delivery. This method is typically used for stock splits, new issues of municipal bonds, and Treasury securities (U.S. government securities). The settlement date for when-issued securities can be any of the following:

- A date to be assigned
- Two business days after the securities are ready for delivery
- On the date determined by FINRA

Safeguarding investor info: Regulation S-P

According to Regulation S-P, broker-dealers, investment companies, and investment advisers must "adopt written policies and procedures that address administrative, technical, and physical safeguards for the protection of customer records and information." This means that members must provide a way for securing customers' nonpublic personal information, such as Social Security numbers, bank account information, or any other personally identifiable financial information. Members must provide customers a notice of their privacy policies. Members may disclose a customer's nonpublic information to unaffiliated third parties unless the customer *opts out* and chooses not to have their information shared. A firm must include their policies to protect the security of a customer's nonpublic information in their customer privacy and opt-out notices. Members must make every effort to safeguard customers' information, including securing computers, encrypting emails, and so on.

Confirming a trade

A *trade confirmation* (receipt of trade) is the document you send to a customer after a trade has taken place. You have to send out trade confirmations after each trade, at or before the completion of the transaction (the settlement date). Here's a list of information included in the confirmation:

- The customer's account number
- The registered rep's ID number
- The trade date
- Whether the customer bought (BOT), sold (SLD), or sold short
- A description of the security purchased or sold
- The number of shares of stock or the par value of bonds purchased or sold
- The yield (if bonds)
- The Committee on Uniform Security Identification Procedures (CUSIP) number (a security ID number, in other words)
- The price of the security
- The total amount paid or received, not including commission or any fees
- The commission, which is added on purchases and subtracted on sales (if the broker-dealer purchased for or sold from its own inventory, the markdown or markup doesn't have to be disclosed)
- The *net amount,* or the amount the customer paid or received after adding or subtracting the commission (if the investor purchased or sold bonds, the accrued interest is added or subtracted during this calculation)
- Whether the trade was executed on a principal or agency basis (the capacity)

REMEMBER

You should recognize the items listed in the preceding list, which are required for most securities trades including municipal bonds. However, the MSRB tends to be a little stricter and also requires the following information:

- Whether the member acted as an agent for both the customer and another person for the same trade
- The time of execution for institutional accounts or transactions in municipal fund securities
- The settlement date
- Yield-to-maturity or yield-to-call, whichever is lower
- Final monies, including the total dollar amount of the transaction and accrued interest if applicable
- Whether there's any credit backing the securities (for revenue bonds, the source of revenue; or if there's insurance backing the bonds)
- Any special features of the bonds (callable, puttable, stepped coupon, book entry only, and so on)
- Information on the status of the securities (pre-refunded, called, escrowed to maturity, securities in default, and so on)
- Tax information (taxable, nontaxable, subject to alternative minimum tax, original issue discount)

PHYSICAL VERSUS BOOK ENTRY

Although many years ago almost all delivery of stock certificates and debt securities (bonds) was in physical form (meaning you actually received the certificate), most delivery and settlement now is in book-entry form. Even though you don't get to actually hold your oft-times cool-looking certificates, book entry helps save money and makes trading much easier. When purchasing securities via book entry, you will receive a receipt of trade, showing you own the securities but will not receive the actual certificates. A record of your trading activity is kept on the financial institution's books. When it comes time to sell the securities, nothing has to be transferred; it is just changed on the institution's books, and you receive confirmation (receipt) of the trade.

Acting in your customers' best interest

As part of your job, your clients' interest has to come before your own. So besides understanding your clients' needs, you need to follow and understand regulatory rules as well.

SEC Regulation BI (Best Interest) — Rule 15i-1

SEC Regulation BI was established recently to enhance the Securities Exchange Act of 1934. All broker–dealers are required to act in the best interest of their customers. In that regard, broker–dealers are required to comply with the following rules:

- They're required to disclose all relationships with their clients in writing. This includes letting clients know whether they're acting as a broker or dealer in a trade, disclosing fees for non-trade related services, the services they provide, and any potential conflicts of interest.
- They must provide a *Form CRS* (customer relationship survey) to each client prior to the initial recommendation to that client.
- They must use reasonable care, skill, and diligence when making recommendations to clients.
- They must establish procedures to disclose potential conflicts of interest to customers when making recommendations.
- They must establish procedures to enforce compliance with Regulation BI.

Financial exploitation of specified adults

With people living longer and the number of seniors increasing, FINRA recently created rules to help curb or handle cases of financial exploitations of specified adults (seniors — natural persons (living human being) aged 65 or older — and natural persons aged 18 or older who have mental or physical impairments that render them unable to protect their own interests). For specified adults, financial institutions must make a reasonable effort to get a *trusted contact person* whom they can contact regarding unusual trading activity in the account.

FINRA defines the term *financial exploitation* as:

A. "the wrongful or unauthorized taking, withholding, appropriation, or use of a Specified Adult's funds or securities"; or

B. "any act or omission by a person, including through the use of a power of attorney, guardianship, or any other authority regarding a Specified Adult to:"

a. "obtain control, through deception, intimidation or undue influence, over the Specified Adult's money, assets, or property"; or

b. "convert the Specified Adult's money, assets or property."

In the event that a member believes that the financial exploitation of specified adults has or may be taking place, Rule 2165 allows the member to place a temporary hold on the disbursements and trades (if needed) of the specified adult's funds or securities. If a temporary hold has been put in place, the member has up to two business days to contact all parties involved in the transaction as well as the trusted contact person (unless the member believes that they are involved in the exploitation) to describe the reason(s) for the temporary hold. The hold typically lasts up to 15 business days, which may be extended while being reviewed.

The SIE and other FINRA exams cover topics related to protecting seniors, including

- Firms' marketing and communications to investors age 65 and older
- Information required when opening an account for a senior
- Any disclosures provided to senior investors
- Complaints filed by senior investors as well as how the firm handles the complaints
- Supervision of registered reps as they communicate with senior investors
- The suitability and types of securities marketed and sold to senior investors
- The training of a firm's representatives as to how they are to handle the accounts of specified adults

FINRA created a helpline (844-57-HELPS) for seniors to provide support and assistance.

Borrowing from or lending to

Registered persons associated with a member firm are prohibited from borrowing money from a customer or lending money to a customer unless the member firm has written procedures allowing borrowing and lending money between registered persons and customers and one of the following applies:

- The customer is a member of the registered person's immediate family (spouse, mother, father, mother-in-law, father-in-law, children).
- The customer is a financial institution such as a bank that is in the business of providing credit, financing, or loans.
- The customer and the registered person are both registered under the same member firm.
- The customer and the registered person have a personal relationship outside the broker-customer relationship.
- The customer and the registered person have a business relationship outside the broker-customer relationship.

REMEMBER

This works only if the member firm allows borrowing from or lending to customers. The registered member would have to notify and get written approval from their firm prior to entering into a buying or lending arrangement unless it's not required in the firm's written rules.

Following up with account statements

An *account statement* gives the customer information about their holdings in the account along with the market value at the time the statement was issued. Customers are required under FINRA Rule 2231 to receive account statements quarterly (once every three months). The account statement needs to include all account activity, securities positions, and money balances during the period from the time the customer received the previous account statement. For mutual funds, no matter how much (or little) trading was done, a customer needs to receive an account statement semiannually (every six months).

REMEMBER

Customers may want to know how their accounts are doing, and they may wonder about the condition of the firm that they're working with. So upon request by a customer, a member firm must disclose its financial condition by delivering its most recent balance sheet (not income statement). The balance sheet may be delivered in paper form or in electronic form (email) if the customer agrees to the electronic delivery.

Keeping your dividend dates straight

When customers are purchasing securities of a company that's in the process of declaring or paying a dividend, you need to be able to tell those customers whether they're entitled to receive the dividend. Because stock transactions settle in one business day (T+1, trade date plus one), the customers are entitled to the dividend if they purchase the securities at least one day prior to the *record date.* Here's a list of the four need-to-know dates for the SIE exam:

- **Declaration date:** The day that the corporation officially announces that a dividend will be paid to shareholders. On the declaration date, the dividend amount, the record date, and the payment date, will be announced.
- **Ex-dividend date (ex-date):** The first day that the stock trades without dividends. An investor purchasing the stock on the ex-dividend date isn't entitled to receive the dividend; because stock transactions take one business day to settle, the ex-dividend date is automatically on the record date. In the event that the record date lands on a non-business day, the ex-dividend date is automatically one business day before the record date.

REMEMBER

The ex-dividend date is the day that the price of the stock is reduced by the dividend amount. (Chapter 6 tells you more about dividends and related calculations.) When a stock is purchased ex-dividend (on or after the ex-dividend date), the seller is entitled to the dividend, not the buyer. Because the dividend may not be paid for up to a month and sometimes longer, the buyer is required to sign a *due bill* indicating that the dividend belongs to the seller. In the case of a cash dividend, the due bill is in the form of a *due bill check,* which is payable on the date the dividend is paid by the issuer. In addition, if an investor buys a stock on time to receive a dividend but for some reason will not receive the certificates on time (by the record date), the seller must send a *due bill* to the buyer. A due bill states that the buyer is entitled to the rights of ownership even though they've not yet received the certificates.

- **Record date:** The day the corporation inspects its records to see who gets the dividend. To receive the dividend, the investor must be listed as a stockholder in company records.
- **Payment (payable) date:** The day that the corporation pays the dividend to eligible stockholders.

REMEMBER

The board of directors must announce three dates: the declaration date, the record date, and the payment date. The ex-dividend date doesn't need to be announced because it's automatically on the record date. However, mutual funds have to announce all four dates because they may set their ex-dividend date at any time (even on the record date).

The following question tests your ability to answer a dividend question.

EXAMPLE

Wedgie Corporation has just announced a 50-cent cash dividend. If the record date is Monday, March 9, when is the last day an investor can purchase the stock and receive the dividend?

(A) March 4

(B) March 6

(C) March 7

(D) March 8

The answer you're looking for is (B). For an investor to purchase the stock and receive a previously declared dividend, they must purchase the stock at least one business day before the ex-dividend (record) date. This question is a little more difficult because you have a weekend to take into consideration.

The ex-dividend date is March 9, which is the same as the record date. This investor has to buy the stock before the ex-dividend date in order to receive the dividend, so they have to buy it Friday, March 6 or before (because the 7th and 8th are Saturday and Sunday). The last day an investor can purchase the stock and receive the dividend is March 6.

REMEMBER

If a stock is sold short (if the investor is selling a borrowed security), the lender of the stock sold short is entitled to receive the dividend. (See Chapter 9 for details on margin accounts.) Also, the trades in the example problems are *regular way settlement* (one business day after the trade date); remember that cash transactions settle on the same day as the trade date. In the case of dividends, if an investor purchases stock for cash, they receive the dividend if they purchase the stock anytime up to and including the record date.

Handling complaints

It's bound to happen sooner or later, no matter how awesome you are as a registered rep: One of your customers is going to complain about something (like unauthorized trades, guarantees, and so on). Complaints aren't considered official unless they're in *writing.* If necessary, FINRA wants you to follow the proper procedure for handling complaints. The following sections cover formal and informal proceedings.

Code of procedure (COP)

The *code of procedure* is FINRA's formal procedure for handling securities-related complaints between public customers and members of the securities industry (broker–dealers, registered reps, clearing corporations, and so on). The public customer has the choice of resolving the complaint via the formal code of procedure or the informal code of arbitration. All complaints going through code of procedure must be responded to by the firm within 25 days after receipt of the customer complaint.

In the code of procedure, the FINRA's Department of Enforcement (DOE) is responsible for investigating suspected violations. In the event that the investigation leads to what the DOE believes is a violation, the DOE will hold a hearing. If the customer or member isn't satisfied with the results, they can appeal the decision to the FINRA board of governors. Decisions are appealable all the way to federal appellate courts.

Code of arbitration

The *code of arbitration* is an informal hearing (heard by neutral arbiter or a panel of arbiters) that's primarily conducted for disputes between members of the FINRA. Members include not only broker–dealers but also individuals working for member firms.

If you (a registered rep) have a dispute with the broker–dealer that you're working for, you can take the broker–dealer to arbitration. If a customer has a complaint against a broker–dealer or registered rep, the customer has the choice of going through code of procedure or code of arbitration, unless the customer has given prior written consent (usually by way of the new account form) stating that they will settle disputes only through arbitration.

The decisions in arbitration are binding and nonappealable, so they're less costly than court action. If a member firm or person associated with that member firm fails to comply with the terms of the arbitration (in the case of a loss) within 15 days of notification, FINRA reserves the right to suspend or cancel the firm's or person's membership.

Mediation

If an investor and/or broker–dealer are looking for a more informal way to handle disputes, they may voluntarily decide to go to mediation. Disputes settled through mediation are heard by an independent third party. Unlike arbitration, mediation is nonbinding.

Not all complaints end up going to arbitration, to mediation, or go through the code of procedure. Sometimes, the complaints are the result of miscommunication, such as instances in which the customer made a mistake, a customer feels they were charged too much commission, and so on. A lot of these complaints can be handled internally without the need for progression. However, all complaints need to be kept on file along with any action taken.

Disseminating info: Appropriate communications

To help promote their business and to keep customers up-to-date, member firms continually send out sales literature, publish ads, run commercials, send out research reports, have scripted seminars, and so on. As you can imagine, ads and such cannot omit material facts, exaggerate, or be fraudulent or misleading, and must also explain the potential risks along with the potential benefits. You've probably heard the disclaimers "Past performance does not indicate future performance" and "People can and do lose money" in radio ads. Believe me, they wouldn't put those in unless they had to.

FINRA divides communication into three categories:

- **Correspondence:** Any written communication (including electronic) distributed or made available to *25 or fewer* retail investors (ones that are not institutional investors) within a 30-calendar-day period.
- **Retail communication:** Similar to correspondence but made available to *more than 25* retail investors within a 30-calendar-day period.
- **Institutional communication:** Any written communication (including electronic) distributed or made available only to institutional investors, but not including a member's internal communications. Institutional investors include government entities, member firms and registered persons, employee benefit plans, a person acting solely on behalf of any such institutional investor, and so on.

REMEMBER

As with just about everything that happens at a brokerage firm, retail communications must be approved by a qualified principal of the firm. Research reports on particular securities must be approved by a supervisory analyst who has expertise in the particular product. Testimonials (if any) must be made by a person who has the knowledge and experience to have a valid opinion. Member firms are in many cases required to file retail communications with FINRA ten business days prior to first use. Members are required to keep the communications for a minimum of three years.

Keeping clear records

As you can imagine, member firms must keep certain records on file. Depending on which records they are, there are certain SEC retention requirements. The records do not necessarily need to be kept in printed format; they can be kept digitally as long as they are in a nonerasable format.

Corporate or partnership documents of the member firm must be kept for the *lifetime* of the firm. The documents must contain the list of officers, partners, and/or directors of the firm. Additionally, U4 forms of all active employees must be kept as long as the firm is in business.

The following records must be kept for a minimum of *six years:*

- **Blotters:** Blotters are records of original entry relating to the purchase and sale of securities, the receipt and delivery of securities, as well as the records of receiving or delivering cash.
- **Ledgers:** Customer account statements, which include trade settlement dates.
- **General ledgers:** A firm's financial statements, which must be updated monthly. A general ledger includes the firm's assets, liabilities, and net worth.
- **Position record:** A record of all the securities owned by the firm and its location.
- **Account record:** Terms and conditions of margin accounts and cash accounts.
- **Closed accounts:** Records of customers who've closed accounts.

Note: Like FINRA rules, MSRB rules require blotters, ledgers, closed accounts, and position records to be kept for six years. However, MSRB also requires records relating to the underwriting of municipal securities, complaints (FINRA, four years), supervisory records, and gift records to be kept for six years.

The following records must be kept for a minimum of *three years:*

- U4 forms, U5 forms, and fingerprints of former employees
- Trade confirmations
- Order tickets
- Advertisements
- Sales literature
- Dividends and interest received in each account
- Powers of attorney
- Speeches/public appearances
- Compliance procedure manuals

» Gifts
» Compensation records of associates

Note: MSRB rules require members to maintain certain records for *four years*. These include subsidiary ledgers, trades, confirmations, terms and conditions of customer accounts, checkbooks and canceled checks, delivery of official statements, public communications, and so on.

REMEMBER

Whether the records have to be kept for three years, six years, or whatever, they have to be easily accessible for two years (FINRA and MSRB).

As you can imagine, strict penalties are enforced for falsification, improper maintenance, or improper retention of records. FINRA reserves the right to inspect the books, records, and accounts of all member firms and their associates. All regulatory requests by FINRA for specified books, records, or accounts should be supplied by the member firm *promptly*.

Committing Other Important Rules to Memory

Brokers and investors must follow numerous rules to keep themselves from facing fines or worse. In this section, I list a few of the more important rules.

Sticking to The 5% Markup Policy

The 5% Markup Policy is more of a FINRA guideline than a rule. The policy was enacted to make sure that investors receive fair treatment and aren't charged excessively for broker–dealer services in the OTC market. The guideline says that brokerage firms shouldn't charge commissions, markups, or markdowns of more than 5 percent for standard trades.

The following trades are subject to the 5 percent markup policy:

» **Principal (dealer) transactions:** A firm buys securities for (or sells securities from) its own inventory and charges a markdown or markup.

» **Agency (broker) transactions:** A firm acts as a middleman (broker) and charges a commission.

» **Riskless (simultaneous) transactions:** A firm buys a security for its own inventory for immediate resale to the customer (riskless to the firm).

» **Proceeds transactions:** A firm sells a security and uses the money to immediately buy another security. You must treat this transaction as one trade. (You can't charge on the way out and on the way in.)

REMEMBER

The 5 percent markup policy covers *over-the-counter trades of outstanding, nonexempt securities with public customers.* If securities are exempt from SEC registration or if they're new securities that require a prospectus, they're exempt from the 5 percent policy. Additionally, if a dealer pays $20 per share to have a security in inventory (dealer cost), and the market price is $8 per share, the dealer can't charge customers $20 per share so that it doesn't take a loss.

Under extenuating circumstances, the brokerage firm may charge more. Justifiable reasons for charging more (or less) than 5 percent include

- Experiencing difficulty buying or selling the security because the market price is too low or too high.
- Handling a small trade. If a customer were to place an order for $100 worth of securities, you'd lose your shirt if you were to charge only 5 percent ($5); in this case, you wouldn't be out of line if you were to charge 100 percent. By the same token, if a customer were to purchase $1 million worth of securities, 5 percent ($50,000) would be considered excessive.
- Encountering difficulty locating and purchasing a specific security.
- Trading nonliquid securities.
- Executing transactions on foreign markets.

Note: The 5 percent markup policy is a guideline that member firms should use when making trades. However, firms may also charge customers for services performed other than trading securities. These services include collection of monies due for principal, interest, or dividends. They may also charge for the exchange or transfer of securities or the safekeeping of customers' securities. The main thing for you to remember is that the charges should be reasonable and not unfairly discriminatory.

Avoiding violations

It's up to your firm and you to understand violations and avoid them. FINRA expects its members and their representatives to "observe high standards of commercial honor and just and equitable principles of trade."

REMEMBER

You need to be aware of some violations not only for the SIE exam but also so you stay out of trouble. Of course, the entire book and this chapter are filled with rules and violations. However, some violations can be summed up in a sentence or two (or three); that's what this section is for. Some of the violations are more connected with broker–dealers, some with registered reps, and some with investment advisers. Violators are subject to sanctions such as fines, censures, suspensions, expulsions, and so on.

- **Commingling of funds:** Combining a customer's fully paid and margined securities or combining a firm's securities with customer securities.
- **Interpositioning:** Having two securities dealers act as agents for the same trade so that two commissions are earned on one trade.
- **Giving (or receiving) gifts:** Giving or receiving a gift of more than $100 per customer per year. Noncash business expenses (lunch, dinner, hotel rooms, travel expenses, occasional tickets to a sporting event, and so on) are exempt from this rule.
- **Making political contributions (paying to play):** Under the Investment Advisers Act of 1940, investment advisers are prohibited from providing investment advisory services for a fee to a government client for two years after a contribution is made. This rule applies not only to the adviser, executives, and employees making contributions to certain elected officials, but also to candidates who may later be elected. In addition, investment advisers are prohibited from soliciting contributions for elected officials or candidates if the investment adviser is seeking or providing government business.
- **Falsifying or withholding documents:** Firms cannot make up information or withhold needed documents from customers or any SRO.
- **Signatures of convenience:** Basically, forging a customer's signature even if approved by the customer is a violation.

- **Guarantees:** Members and associates are prohibited from making guarantees against loss in any securities transaction or in any securities account of a customer.
- **Improper use:** Members and associates are prohibited from making improper use of a customer's securities or funds.
- **Freeriding:** Allowing a customer to buy and then sell the same securities without paying for the purchase. Under Regulation T, if a customer purchases and sells the same security in a cash account without paying for the security, their account will be restricted for 90 days. For that 90-day period, the customer will have to pay in full before purchasing securities.
- **Backing away:** Failure on the part of a securities dealer to honor a firm quote.
- **Churning:** A violation whereby a registered rep excessively trades a customer's account for the sole purpose of generating commission.
- **Use of manipulative, deceptive, or other fraudulent devices:** Members are prohibited from inducing the sale or purchase of any security by means of manipulation, deception, or any other fraudulent device or contrivance.
- **Trading ahead of research reports:** No member shall trade a security based on information received from a research report prior to that research report being released publicly.
- **Trading ahead of customer orders:** Members are prohibited from placing their order ahead of a customer's order. Their job is to get their customer the best price, and placing their order ahead of the customer's will likely cause the customer to get a worse price.
- **Not disclosing a financial relationship with the issuer:** It is a violation to not disclose if your firm has a financial relationship with the issuer, where *financial relationship* is defined as being controlled by, having a controlling interest in, or being under common control with the issuer. In the event that there is a financial relationship, it must be disclosed (given to or sent to) the customer prior to the completion of the transaction.
- **Frontrunning:** A violation in which a registered rep executes a trade for themselves, their firm, or a discretionary account based on knowledge of a block trade (10,000 shares or more) before the trade is reported on the ticker tape.
- **Prearranging trades:** A prearranged trade is an illegal agreement between a registered rep and a customer to buy back a security at a fixed price.
- **Paying for referrals:** Members or persons associated with a member (for example, registered reps) are prohibited from paying cash or noncash compensation to any person except those registered with the member firm or other FINRA members. A violation occurs in the event that compensation is paid to a nonmember for locating, introducing, or referring a client.

Some violations include some sort of *market manipulation*. These include

- **Market rumors:** Members are prohibited from spreading false market rumors that may prompt others to either buy or sell a security.
- **Pump and dump:** This is fake news that most often happens with penny stocks. In this case, the promoters send out mass emails or regular mail to paint a glowing report on a particular security, thus pumping it up. Because of the positive reports, many investors purchase the security and drive the price up. At that point, the promoters sell (dump) their shares for a nice profit.
- **Excessive trading:** A violation whereby a trader places both buy and sell orders on the same security around the same time, thus making it look like there's a lot of trading activity on that security.

- **Marking the open/marking the close:** Executing a series of trades within minutes of the open or close to manipulate the price of a security.
- **Matching orders:** Illegally manipulating the price of a security to make the trading volume appear larger than it really is, such as two brokerage firms working in concert by trading the same security back and forth.
- **Painting the tape:** Creating the illusion of trading activity due to misleading reports on the consolidated tape, such as reporting a trade of 10,000 shares of stock as two separate trades for 5,000 shares each.
- **Paying the media:** A violation in which brokerage firms or affiliated persons pay an employee of the media (website, newspaper, magazine, radio, TV show, and so on) to affect the price of a security, such as paying a TV stock expert to recommend a security that the firm has in its inventory.
- **Anti-intimidation/coordination:** Members may not intimidate (threaten, harass, coerce, and so on) other members into changing their price(s) on a security. In addition, a member may not coordinate with another member to adjust the price of a security.

It is also considered a violation for a member firm to distribute cash or noncash compensation to the employees of another member firm regarding the sale and distribution of securities unless all of the following apply:

- The compensation is not conditional on sales by the other firm.
- It has prior approval from the other member firm.
- The total amount of compensation does not exceed the limit of $100 per year.

Noncash compensation could be season tickets for the Jets, sending someone on vacation, gift certificates, and so on. Providing an occasional meal, ticket to a sporting event, and such are considered acceptable business entertainment expenses as long as they're neither too expensive nor too frequent. And certain noncash expenses are considered okay as long as they're business-related — paying for a business dinner, paying for a seminar, providing airline tickets, and so on. In addition, you don't have to keep track of things that provide advertising, such as pens with your name on them, coffee mugs with your picture, and so on.

Also, FINRA wants to make sure that members and their associates are making recommendations based on their belief that they fall in line with their customer's investment strategy and their belief that the product(s) recommended is/are the right one(s). So to curb potential conflict of interest, similar cash and noncash compensation rules are put in place for program sponsors, such as investment companies. FINRA just wants to make sure that recommendations are not based on the fact that members or their associates owe someone.

Following the money: Anti-money-laundering rules

The *Bank Secrecy Act* establishes the U.S. Treasury Department as the regulator for anti-money-laundering (AML) programs. All broker-dealers are required to develop programs to detect possible money-laundering abuses. In addition, all broker-dealers must review the Office of Foreign Asset Control's (OFAC) Specially Designated Nationals (SDN) list to make sure that they're not doing business with individuals or organizations that are on the list. Anti-money-laundering programs are designed to help prevent dirty money that has been cleaned (made to look like it came from a legitimate source) from being used to fund terrorist activities, illegal arms sales, drug trafficking, and so on. Here are three stages of money laundering that you must be aware of for the SIE exam (please, don't try this at home):

1. **Placement**

   In this initial stage of money laundering, the funds, derived from criminal activity, are transferred into the financial system (typically via banks and broker-dealers).

2. **Layering**

   Layering is the money launderer's attempt to disguise the source of the funds, usually by moving the funds from one place to another through a series of transactions.

3. **Integration**

   Integration is the final stage of money laundering, when illegal funds are mixed *(commingled)* with legitimate funds. Launderers usually accomplish this step through businesses that operate using cash, importing and exporting companies, and so on.

REMEMBER

Broker–dealers and other financial institutions must report any cash deposits, withdrawals, or transfers of more than *$10,000* in a single day through a *Currency Transaction Report* (CTR) to *FinCEN* (the U.S. Treasury Financial Crimes Network). An institution must report suspicious activity of *$5,000 or more of any type of transaction* to FinCEN by filing a Suspicious Activity Report (SAR).

Here are some indications of money laundering at the opening of the account:

- » Concern with U.S. government reporting requirements
- » Reluctance to reveal information about business activities
- » Suspect ID such as a license or passport that looks like it was made in someone's basement
- » Irrational transactions that are inconsistent with objectives
- » A fiduciary (the person who can legally make decisions for another investor) who's reluctant to provide information about the customer
- » An individual's lack of general knowledge of their industry

And here are some shady signals to look out for after the account is open:

- » Irregularly making deposits of large amounts of cash or money orders
- » *Structuring* — making cash or cash-equivalent deposits (such as money orders) of just under $10,000 to avoid having them be reported to the U.S. government
- » Making wire transfers to non-cooperative countries (Iran, North Korea, Nigeria, and so on) who do not work with the United States to try to curb money laundering
- » Engaging in sudden and unexplained wire activity
- » Making a deposit and transferring it to another party without any business purpose
- » Buying a long-term investment and liquidating it in the short term
- » Making transfers between multiple accounts for no apparent reason
- » Depositing bearer bonds and requesting the money immediately
- » Displaying a total lack of concern about risks and commissions

TIP

The signs of money laundering tend to make sense, so when answering an SIE exam question about money laundering, think to yourself, "If it looks like a duck and quacks like a duck, it's probably a duck" — or in financial terms, "If it looks and seems like money laundering, it's probably money laundering."

Complying with AML rules

Under the *Bank Secrecy Act*, which is enforced by FinCEN, all financial institutions, including broker–dealers, must develop and carry out anti-money-laundering (AML) programs. These programs must be approved in writing by a firm's senior management. Financial institutions and broker–dealers must do the following:

- Initiate and carry out policies and procedures designed to detect and report suspicious transactions
- Initiate and carry out policies, procedures, and internal controls that are designed to comply with the Bank Secrecy Act's regulations
- Set up annual independent testing to make sure that the firm is complying with the AML rules under the Bank Secrecy Act
- Appoint and indicate to FINRA (by name, title, email address, phone number, and so on) the person (a *designated AML compliance officer*) or people responsible for implementing and overseeing the daily internal controls of its AML program

REMEMBER

AML programs are not necessarily static and are subject to change. Each firm is responsible for making sure that its AML programs remain current.

Working with public info: Following insider trading rules

Insider trading is a violation that occurs when an individual trades a particular publicly traded security based on information that has not been released (or adequately released) to the public (known as *material nonpublic information*). According to the Insider Trading and Securities Fraud Enforcement Act of 1988, both the tipper (the one who shared the nonpublic information) and the tippee (the one who traded based on the tip) are liable.

REMEMBER

There is no violation of insider trading rules *unless a trade takes place* based on that inside information. If a registered rep or anyone working at a firm receives what they believe to be inside information, they should immediately report it to a principal of the firm.

Charges of insider trading have been brought against

- Officers, directors, and employees of a corporation who traded the corporation's securities after learning of important, confidential corporate developments
- Family members, friends, business associates, and other people (tippees) who received tips from the officers, directors, and employees who traded the corporate securities based on confidential information received
- Government employees who traded based on confidential information received because of their employment with the government, which has not (or not yet) been released to the public
- Employees of brokerage, banking, law, and printing firms who executed trades based on confidential information received as part of their job

- Political consultants who have given tips or traded based on material nonpublic information they received from government employees
- Other persons who have taken advantage of or traded on confidential information they received from employers, friends, family, and others

REMEMBER

Putting it in simple terms, material nonpublic (inside) information is information that could affect the market value of a security but the information has not been released (or adequately released) to the public.

Penalties for insider trading

As you can imagine, the penalties for insider trading are pretty severe:

- The maximum criminal fine for an individual is $5 million per violation and $25 million per business per violation.
- The maximum prison sentence is 20 years per violation.
- The maximum civil sanctions are three times the gain or three times the loss avoided plus disgorgement of profits.

Contemporaneous traders

Persons who enter orders at or about the same time as the person trading on inside information on the opposite side of the market are called contemporaneous traders. So, for argument's sake, if the person with inside information sold shares of ABC common stock due to inside information, a contemporaneous trader would be one who bought shares of ABC common stock at or about the same time (and vice versa). In this case, the contemporaneous trader may actually sue the person who violated the insider trading rules. The suits may be initiated up to five years after the occurrence.

The Investor's Bankruptcy Shield: FDIC and SIPC Coverage

The Federal Deposit Insurance Corporation (FDIC) provides deposit insurance, which guarantees a certain level of safety to people who have money on deposit at a bank. FDIC protects accounts from bank failure (bankruptcy). At the present time, each depositor is protected up to $250,000.

The Securities Investor Protection Corporation (SIPC), which was created under the Securities Investor Protection Act of 1970, protects the customer against broker–dealer bankruptcy. Although it's not a government agency, this private, nonprofit organization was created by the government in 1970. The SIPC protects each separate customer's assets (securities and cash) up to $500,000 total, of which no more than $250,000 can be cash.

Although brokerage firms are required to follow *net capital rules* — specifically, SEC Rule 15c3-1 — that are designed to minimize the chances of broker–dealer failure and protect customer assets, broker–dealers occasionally (too often) declare bankruptcy.

All members must advise clients at the opening of the account about SIPC protection and must provide an SIPC brochure and info on contacting SIPC, including the SIPC's web address and telephone number. In addition, clients must receive all that same info in writing at least once a year.

The following question concerns SIPC coverage.

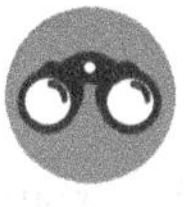
EXAMPLE

Steve Fredericks has a cash account with $150,000 in securities and $300,000 cash and a margin account with $50,000 in equity. Additionally, Steve has a joint cash account with his wife Melissa with $250,000 in securities and $300,000 cash. If Steve's broker–dealer goes bankrupt, what is his coverage under SIPC?

(A) $450,000

(B) $500,000

(C) $850,000

(D) $950,000

The right choice is (D). If one of your customers has a cash and margin account titled under one name, as Steve does, it's treated as though it belongs to one customer. Therefore, Steve's cash and margin account is covered up to $500,000, of which no more than $250,000 can be cash. He's covered for the $200,000 in securities ($150,000 in securities plus the $50,000 equity) and $250,000 of the $300,000 cash for a total of $450,000. Next, the joint account with his wife is treated as though from a separate customer. Therefore, that account is covered for the $250,000 in securities and $250,000 in cash. Add the two together, and you see that Steve is covered for a total of $950,000 ($450,000 plus $500,000).

REMEMBER

If an investor is not fully covered under SIPC, the investor is still owed money by the bankrupt broker–dealer; therefore, the investor becomes a *general creditor* of the firm for the balance owed.

Holding a customer's mail

If one of your customers is not receiving mail at their usual address because they are traveling, moving, or whatever, your firm can hold their mail for a specified time period up to three months (or longer if for safety or security concerns). This typically has to do with confirmations and account statements that the firm would normally mail. The member firm must have a way to contact the customer in a timely manner (by phone, email, and so on), and the firm must provide a way for the customer to receive information regarding their account (typically via email or through the member's website). In addition, the member firm must verify at reasonable intervals that the customer's instructions still apply.

Business continuity plans and emergency contact information

FINRA requires that all member firms must set up and maintain business continuity plans (BCP) to deal with the possibility of a business disruption. The idea is to make sure that customers will still be able to contact the firm and be able to access their securities and funds during an emergency. Although the plan is somewhat flexible depending on the member's business, some of the items the plan should address include the following:

- Hard copy and electronic data backup and recovery
- Alternative communications between customers and members
- Alternative communications between members and their employees

» Alternative physical locations of employees

» Regulatory reporting

» Communication with regulators

» How the member firm will ensure that customers have prompt access to their securities and funds in the event that the member is unable to continue business

TIP

A few other things could be on this list such as "all mission-critical systems" (ways they would be able to handle customers' orders and such), "financial and operational assessments" (how a member's operations would change), and so on. However, the preceding list should be able to get you through SIE exam questions related to what needs to be on a firm's business continuity plan.

Members are required to have a member of senior management (who must be a principal) approve of their business continuity plan. That member is also responsible for conducting an annual review. The member's plan must be disclosed to customers in writing at the opening of their account, posted on the firm's website (if any), and mailed to customers upon request. In addition, besides providing the plan info to FINRA, they must also provide emergency contact information to FINRA. (FINRA must receive the names of two principals and members of senior management to contact in the event of an emergency; if the contact info changes, it must be updated within 30 days.) In the event that any info changes regarding the business continuity plan, the firm is responsible for updating its customers, employees, and FINRA.

Testing Your Knowledge

This chapter was jam-packed full of rules. Unfortunately, there wasn't too much I could do about that except to make them as easy to understand as possible. As you can imagine, because of the size of this chapter, I've given you the most chapter questions . . . oh, joy. Good luck!

Practice questions

1. Which of the following need to be included on a stock order ticket?

I. The customer's signature

II. The time of the order

III. The number of shares

IV. Whether the trade is solicited or unsolicited

(A) I, II, and III

(B) II and III

(C) II, III, and IV

(D) I, II, III, and IV

2. All of the following are self-regulatory organizations **except**

(A) NYSE

(B) SEC

(C) MSRB

(D) FINRA

3. Declan Smith has an account at Ayla Broker–Dealer. Declan has not traded any securities at Ayla Broker–Dealer for over three years. How often is Ayla Broker–Dealer required to send an account statement to Declan?

(A) Monthly

(B) Quarterly

(C) Semiannually

(D) Annually

4. The ex-dividend date is

(A) the same as the record date

(B) one business day before the record date

(C) two business days before the record date

(D) one business day after the record date

5. Which of the following is a violation that includes a form of market manipulation?

(A) Commingling

(B) Frontrunning

(C) Pump and dump

(D) Interpositioning

6. Which of the following are subject to the FINRA 5 percent markup policy?

(A) Principal transactions and riskless transactions

(B) Agency transactions, riskless transactions, and proceeds transactions

(C) Principal transactions, riskless transactions, and proceeds transactions

(D) Principal transactions, agency transactions, riskless transactions, and proceeds transactions

7. Which of the following is an indication of money laundering when a customer opens an account?

(A) Concern with U.S. government reporting requirements

(B) Reluctance to reveal information about business activities

(C) Questionable ID

(D) All of the above

8. A person will be statutorily disqualified from membership from FINRA under which of the following circumstances?

I. If they had a felony conviction within the last 15 years

II. If they have been barred from membership in an SRO

III. If they have made false statements on their application

(A) I and III

(B) II and III

(C) I and II

(D) I, II, and III

9. If you resign from a brokerage firm, how long do you have to register with another firm so that you don't have to take your securities exams again?

(A) 90 days

(B) 6 months

(C) 1 year

(D) 2 years

10. Which of the following are violations?

(A) Commingling of funds

(B) Interpositioning

(C) Signatures of convenience

(D) All of the above

11. Which of the following securities transactions settle in one business day after the trade date?

I. Stock and corporate bond transactions

II. Municipal bond transactions

III. U.S. government bond transactions

IV. Option transactions

(A) I, III, and IV

(B) II and III

(C) I and II

(D) I, II, III, and IV

12. Broker–dealers, investment companies, and investment advisers must have written policies designed to protect customers' records and information. This rule falls under

(A) Regulation S-P

(B) Regulation D

(C) Regulation M

(D) Regulation T

13. All of the following must be included on a trade confirmation **except**

(A) a description of the security

(B) the markup or markdown

(C) the registered rep's ID number

(D) the commission

14. Zimbot Corporation has just announced a 30-cent dividend to shareholders of record. If the record date is Friday, October 8, when is the first day an investor can purchase the stock and not receive the dividend?

(A) Wednesday, October 6

(B) Thursday, October 7

(C) Friday, October 8

(D) Monday, October 11

15. In which of the following procedures for handling complaints is the decision binding and cannot be appealed?

(A) Code of procedure

(B) Mediation

(C) Arbitration

(D) Both (B) and (C)

16. Under FINRA rules, all of the following brokerage firm records must be kept for a minimum of three years **except**

(A) ledgers

(B) trade confirmations

(C) order tickets

(D) U4 forms of former employees

17. Broker–dealers, banks, investment advisers, and so on must report a possible money-laundering transaction to

(A) FINRA

(B) FinCEN

(C) FBI

(D) SEC

18. Which **two** of the following are the maximum penalties for insider trading violations?

I. 20 years in prison per violation

II. 25 years in prison per violation

III. $5 million per individual per violation

IV. $25 million per individual per violation

(A) I and III

(B) I and IV

(C) II and III

(D) II and IV

19. A violation in which a firm attempts to drive up the price of a stock based on false or misleading information so that the firm can later sell their shares at a higher price is known as

(A) churning

(B) trading ahead

(C) frontrunning

(D) pump and dump

20. Mrs. Slick purchased 400 shares of ZIP Corporation common stock and sold it at a profit prior to paying for the purchase. This is a violation known as

(A) freeriding

(B) frontrunning

(C) trading ahead

(D) interpositioning

21. As part of FINRA's business continuity plan, member firms must provide the emergency contact information for ______________ principal(s) of the firm to contact in the event of an emergency.

(A) one

(B) two

(C) three

(D) all

22. Which **two** of the following are **true**?

I. FDIC covers each individual up to $250,000.

II. FDIC covers each individual up to $500,000, of which no more than $250,000 can be cash.

III. SIPC covers each individual up to $250,000.

IV. SIPC covers each individual up to $500,000, of which no more than $250,000 can be cash.

(A) I and III

(B) I and IV

(C) II and III

(D) II and IV

23. Under FINRA rules, which of the following records must be kept by a brokerage firm for a minimum of six years?

(A) Customer account statements, U5 forms, and records of all trades executed

(B) U5 forms, records of all trades executed, and sales literature

(C) Customer account statements and records of all trades

(D) Customer account statements, U5 forms, and sales literature

24. Which of the following records must be kept for the lifetime of a broker–dealer?

(A) Records of closed accounts

(B) General ledgers

(C) Partnership documents

(D) All of the above

Answers and explanations

1. **C.** The items required on an order ticket are the rep's identification number, the customer's account number, a description of the security, the number of shares, whether the account is discretionary, whether the customer is buying or selling, whether it's a market order or GTC order, whether the trade is for cash or on margin, whether it's solicited or unsolicited, the time of the order, and the execution price. Remember that when an order is placed, it's usually for immediate execution, so getting a customer's signature would be nearly impossible.

2. **B.** The SEC is a government agency and is not a self-regulatory organization. SROs include the MSRB, NYSE, CBOE, and FINRA.

3. **B.** For accounts like Declan Smith's, the brokerage firm must send out account statements at least quarterly (every three months); for mutual funds, every six months.

4. **A.** The ex-dividend date is the first day that the purchaser of a stock will not receive a previously declared dividend. Since it takes one business day for the settlement of a stock, the ex-dividend date is the same as the record date. In the event that the record date is not a business day, which you cannot assume, the ex-dividend date is one business day before the record date.

5. **C.** All of the choices listed are violations. However, pump and dump is the only violation listed that is a form of market manipulation. Pump and dump is fake news typically regarding penny stocks that is designed to drive the price of a particular stock up so that the firm can sell their stock at a large profit.

6. **D.** All of the choices listed are subject to the FINRA 5 percent markup policy (5 percent markup policy or 5 percent policy). This means that, under normal circumstances in which you have an average-sized trade and you don't have to jump through hoops to execute the transaction, you shouldn't charge more than 5 percent to execute the trade. Now certainly if the trade is extremely small, you would be able to charge a higher percentage so your firm doesn't lose money. Also, if a trade is extremely large, 5 percent would be considered excessive.

7. **D.** Certainly all of the choices listed would be considered indications of money laundering.

8. **B.** Answers II and III are definitely reasons why a person would be statutorily disqualified. However, answer I doesn't fit because the person would be statutorily disqualified if they had a felony conviction in the last 10 years, not 15.

9. **D.** If a securities licensed individual leaves a brokerage firm, that person has up to two years to get registered with another firm or they will have to take their license exams again.

10. **D.** All of the choices listed are violations. Commingling of funds takes place when a firm combines a customer's fully paid securities with margined securities, or when a firm combines its own securities with a customer's securities. Interpositioning is when two securities broker–dealers act as agents for the same trade, thus requiring the customer to pay more than one commission. Signatures of convenience are ones in which a customer's signature is forged.

11. **D.** Stock, corporate bond, and municipal bond, U.S. government bond, and option transactions settle in one business day after the trade date (T+1). As a reminder, cash trades settle the same business day as the trade date.

12. **A.** Under Regulation S-P, all broker–dealers, investment companies, and investment advisers must have written policies to protect customer's records and private information. This would include things like Social Security numbers, bank account numbers, and so on.

13. **B.** Although a commission must be included on a trade confirmation for an agency trade, a markup or markdown does not need to be included for a principal transaction. Remember, a principal transaction is one in which the dealer is buying for or selling from its own inventory. Therefore, the price the customer pays or receives already includes a markup or markdown.

14. **B.** The first day the stock trades without the dividend is on the ex-dividend date. The ex-dividend date is one business day before the record date — in this case, Thursday, October 7.

15. **C.** Arbitration decisions are binding and non-appealable. Arbitration is certainly less formal and less costly than going through the court system. As a matter of fact, many brokerage firms have customers sign an arbitration clause as part of a new account form stating that the customer agrees to have disputes handled through arbitration.

16. **A.** Ledgers, which are customer account statements, must be kept on file for a minimum of six years, not three. As a reminder, all records must be easily accessible for two years.

17. **B.** Under the USA Patriot Act, if financial institutions are concerned about the possibility of money laundering, they must report the transaction(s) to the U.S. Treasury Financial Crimes Network (FinCEN).

18. **A.** The maximum penalties for insider trading are $5 million per individual per violation ($25 million per business) and up to 20 years in prison per violation. Although not part of this question, the maximum civil sanctions are three times the gain or three times the loss avoided plus disgorgement of profits.

19. **D.** Pump and dump is a violation in which a firm promotes a security that they own using false or misleading information to try to pump up the price of the security. After the price has been driven up, they dump their stock at a profit.

20. **A.** Freeriding is a violation that takes place when a customer places an order to purchase a security and sells it at a profit prior to paying for it. Freeriding is not permitted under Regulation T, and it may require the brokerage firm to freeze the customer's account for 90 days.

21. **B.** Because of the possibility of an emergency, all firms are required to have business continuity plans and provide emergency contact information. In addition, all firms must provide the emergency contact information for two principals to FINRA.

22. **B.** The FDIC covers each depositor up to $250,000. The SIPC covers each investor up to $500,000, of which no more than $250,000 can be cash.

23. **C.** Blotters, which includes records of all trades executed by the brokerage firm; ledgers, which include customer account statements; general ledgers; position records; account records; and information on closed accounts must be kept for a minimum of six years. U5 forms and sales literature must be kept for a minimum of three years.

24. **C.** Corporate or partnership documents of the member firm must be kept for the lifetime of the firm.

5 Putting Your Pencil to Paper: Practice Exams

IN THIS PART . . .

Take two practice exams to see how well you know the material.

Check your scores and read the answer explanations.

Chapter 17

Ready, Set, Go!: Practice Exam 1

This chapter is where you get your chance to shine like a star.

This practice exam has 75 questions in random order, just as they are on the actual SIE exam. Please read carefully — many test-takers make careless mistakes because they miss key words or read too quickly. Focus on the information you do need to know and ignore the information that you don't need. Read the last sentence twice to make sure you know what the question is asking.

Mark your answers on the answer sheet provided or on a separate piece of paper. You may use a basic calculator and scrap paper for notes and figuring. As you're taking the exam, be sure to circle the questions you find difficult. This step can help you determine what you really need to review.

To simulate the real exam, try to finish this practice exam in 1 hour and 45 minutes or less. Resist the urge to look at the answers and explanations as you work through the exam; save the grading for later. After you finish the exam, you can check your answers. (You can find the answers and detailed explanations in Chapter 18, along with an answer key at the end of that chapter.)

Good luck!

Chapter 17
Ready, Set, Go! Practice Exam 1

Good luck!

Practice Exam Answer Sheet

1. Ⓐ Ⓑ Ⓒ Ⓓ
2. Ⓐ Ⓑ Ⓒ Ⓓ
3. Ⓐ Ⓑ Ⓒ Ⓓ
4. Ⓐ Ⓑ Ⓒ Ⓓ
5. Ⓐ Ⓑ Ⓒ Ⓓ
6. Ⓐ Ⓑ Ⓒ Ⓓ
7. Ⓐ Ⓑ Ⓒ Ⓓ
8. Ⓐ Ⓑ Ⓒ Ⓓ
9. Ⓐ Ⓑ Ⓒ Ⓓ
10. Ⓐ Ⓑ Ⓒ Ⓓ
11. Ⓐ Ⓑ Ⓒ Ⓓ
12. Ⓐ Ⓑ Ⓒ Ⓓ
13. Ⓐ Ⓑ Ⓒ Ⓓ
14. Ⓐ Ⓑ Ⓒ Ⓓ
15. Ⓐ Ⓑ Ⓒ Ⓓ
16. Ⓐ Ⓑ Ⓒ Ⓓ
17. Ⓐ Ⓑ Ⓒ Ⓓ
18. Ⓐ Ⓑ Ⓒ Ⓓ
19. Ⓐ Ⓑ Ⓒ Ⓓ
20. Ⓐ Ⓑ Ⓒ Ⓓ
21. Ⓐ Ⓑ Ⓒ Ⓓ
22. Ⓐ Ⓑ Ⓒ Ⓓ
23. Ⓐ Ⓑ Ⓒ Ⓓ
24. Ⓐ Ⓑ Ⓒ Ⓓ
25. Ⓐ Ⓑ Ⓒ Ⓓ
26. Ⓐ Ⓑ Ⓒ Ⓓ
27. Ⓐ Ⓑ Ⓒ Ⓓ
28. Ⓐ Ⓑ Ⓒ Ⓓ
29. Ⓐ Ⓑ Ⓒ Ⓓ
30. Ⓐ Ⓑ Ⓒ Ⓓ
31. Ⓐ Ⓑ Ⓒ Ⓓ
32. Ⓐ Ⓑ Ⓒ Ⓓ
33. Ⓐ Ⓑ Ⓒ Ⓓ
34. Ⓐ Ⓑ Ⓒ Ⓓ
35. Ⓐ Ⓑ Ⓒ Ⓓ
36. Ⓐ Ⓑ Ⓒ Ⓓ
37. Ⓐ Ⓑ Ⓒ Ⓓ
38. Ⓐ Ⓑ Ⓒ Ⓓ
39. Ⓐ Ⓑ Ⓒ Ⓓ
40. Ⓐ Ⓑ Ⓒ Ⓓ
41. Ⓐ Ⓑ Ⓒ Ⓓ
42. Ⓐ Ⓑ Ⓒ Ⓓ
43. Ⓐ Ⓑ Ⓒ Ⓓ
44. Ⓐ Ⓑ Ⓒ Ⓓ
45. Ⓐ Ⓑ Ⓒ Ⓓ
46. Ⓐ Ⓑ Ⓒ Ⓓ
47. Ⓐ Ⓑ Ⓒ Ⓓ
48. Ⓐ Ⓑ Ⓒ Ⓓ
49. Ⓐ Ⓑ Ⓒ Ⓓ
50. Ⓐ Ⓑ Ⓒ Ⓓ
51. Ⓐ Ⓑ Ⓒ Ⓓ
52. Ⓐ Ⓑ Ⓒ Ⓓ
53. Ⓐ Ⓑ Ⓒ Ⓓ
54. Ⓐ Ⓑ Ⓒ Ⓓ
55. Ⓐ Ⓑ Ⓒ Ⓓ
56. Ⓐ Ⓑ Ⓒ Ⓓ
57. Ⓐ Ⓑ Ⓒ Ⓓ
58. Ⓐ Ⓑ Ⓒ Ⓓ
59. Ⓐ Ⓑ Ⓒ Ⓓ
60. Ⓐ Ⓑ Ⓒ Ⓓ
61. Ⓐ Ⓑ Ⓒ Ⓓ
62. Ⓐ Ⓑ Ⓒ Ⓓ
63. Ⓐ Ⓑ Ⓒ Ⓓ
64. Ⓐ Ⓑ Ⓒ Ⓓ
65. Ⓐ Ⓑ Ⓒ Ⓓ
66. Ⓐ Ⓑ Ⓒ Ⓓ
67. Ⓐ Ⓑ Ⓒ Ⓓ
68. Ⓐ Ⓑ Ⓒ Ⓓ
69. Ⓐ Ⓑ Ⓒ Ⓓ
70. Ⓐ Ⓑ Ⓒ Ⓓ
71. Ⓐ Ⓑ Ⓒ Ⓓ
72. Ⓐ Ⓑ Ⓒ Ⓓ
73. Ⓐ Ⓑ Ⓒ Ⓓ
74. Ⓐ Ⓑ Ⓒ Ⓓ
75. Ⓐ Ⓑ Ⓒ Ⓓ

TIME: 1 hour and 45 minutes for 75 questions

DIRECTIONS: Choose the correct answer to each question. Then fill in the circle on your answer sheet that corresponds to the question number and the letter indicating your choice.

1. Regarding Treasury stock, which of the following statements is true?

   (A) It is stock that has been issued by the U.S. government.

   (B) It is stock that has been issued by a corporation that has been repurchased.

   (C) It receives dividends.

   (D) It is authorized stock that has been kept unissued for future use by the issuer.

2. Common stockholders of PXPX Corporation have which of the following rights and privileges?

   (A) The right to receive an audited financial report weekly

   (B) The right to vote for cash dividends to be paid

   (C) A residual claim to assets at dissolution

   (D) The right to vote for stock dividends to be paid

3. Jake Hanson lives in New York and is considering purchasing a bond. He has settled on either a 5-percent municipal bond offered by New York or a 7-percent corporate bond offered by The Greenhorn Corporation, which has headquarters in New York. Jake needs some guidance and would like you to help him determine which bond will provide the greatest return. Which of the following pieces of information do you need to obtain before you can make the appropriate recommendation?

   (A) The business of his employer

   (B) His current tax bracket

   (C) How long he has lived in New York

   (D) His other holdings

4. An investor who is long a call option will realize a profit if exercising the option when the underlying stock price is

   (A) below the strike price minus the premium paid

   (B) above the strike price

   (C) above the strike price plus the premium paid

   (D) below the strike price

5. One of your clients is new to investing and has limited resources. Which of the following investments would you **least** likely recommend to this investor?

   (A) Growth funds

   (B) T-bills

   (C) Blue-chip stock

   (D) Oil and gas developmental program

6. Which of the following is required on the registration statement for a new issue?

   I. The capitalization of the issuer

   II. Complete financial statements

   III. What the money raised will be used for

   IV. The names and addresses of all of the issuer's control persons

   (A) I, II, and III

   (B) I, III, and IV

   (C) I, II, and IV

   (D) I, II, III, and IV

7. Under the Securities Act of 1933, which of the following securities must be registered with the SEC?

   (A) Closed-end funds

   (B) Variable annuities

   (C) Open-end funds

   (D) All of the above

GO ON TO NEXT PAGE

8. A customer's confirmation must include

I. the markdown, if the member acted as a principal in a Nasdaq security

II. the amount of any commission, if the member acted as an agent

III. whether the member acted as an agent or a principal

IV. the markup if the member acted as a principal in a Nasdaq security

(A) I and III

(B) II and IV

(C) I, III, and IV

(D) I, II, III, and IV

9. A letter of intent for a mutual fund purchase is valid for a period of

(A) 90 days

(B) 270 days

(C) 13 months

(D) 18 months

10. Which of the following is **true** regarding qualified retirement plans?

(A) Contributions are made with 100 percent pretax dollars.

(B) Contributions are made with 100 percent after-tax dollars.

(C) Distributions are taxable only prior to age 59 1/2.

(D) Distributions are subject to a 10 percent penalty.

11. Variable annuities must be registered with the

(A) Department of State and the State Banking Commission

(B) Department of State and the State Insurance Commission

(C) Department of State and the Securities and Exchange Commission

(D) State Insurance Commission and the Securities and Exchange Commission

12. All the following items must be included on a trade confirmation **except**

(A) the customer's account number

(B) the customer's signature

(C) the price of the security

(D) the commission, if the trade took place on an agency basis

13. Which of the following is **true** of the Telephone Act of 1991?

I. You cannot make calls before 8 a.m. or after 9 p.m. in the local time zone of the potential customer.

II. You are required to provide your name, company name, company address, and phone number.

III. Individuals who ask not to be called need to be placed on the company's do-not-call list.

IV. You may not send unsolicited ads by fax machine.

(A) I and III

(B) II and IV

(C) I, II, and III

(D) I, II, III, and IV

14. If one of your clients wants to purchase municipal securities that you believe to be unsuitable for their investment objectives, what should you do?

(A) Execute the order as long as you mark the order ticket as "unsolicited."

(B) You must refuse the order unless the client changes their investment objectives.

(C) You must obtain the permission of the firm's compliance officer before executing the order.

(D) You may only execute the order with prior permission of a principal of the firm.

15. All broker-dealers need to maintain customer identification programs and should check the names of all new clients against

(A) a list maintained by the SEC

(B) a do-not-call list maintained by the firm

(C) a list compiled by FINRA

(D) a list of specially designated nationals (SDNs) maintained by OFAC

16. Which of the following statements is **not** true of lifecycle funds?

(A) As lifecycle funds get nearer to their target date, the portfolio holdings will be adjusted to purchase more equity securities and less fixed-income securities.

(B) These funds are usually set up as funds of funds.

(C) The asset allocation of the fund will be rebalanced on a regular basis to make sure that the risk/reward balance is correct given the target date of the fund.

(D) The objective of the fund assumes that most investors cannot tolerate as much risk as they get older.

17. The ex-date is

(A) the date on which the corporation ceases paying a dividend

(B) the date on and after the date the seller is entitled to the dividend

(C) the third business day before the record date

(D) the day the stock price is increased by the amount of the dividend

18. Picture a situation in which the United States would be in an economic recession but inflation would be low. Which of the following actions would the Federal Reserve likely take?

(A) Lower income taxes

(B) Have banks increase their reserve requirements

(C) Purchase Treasury bonds in the open market

(D) Increase the Fed Funds rate

19. Which of the following are factors that affect the marketability of municipal GO bonds?

I. The quality

II. Call features

III. The issuer's name

IV. Credit enhancements

(A) I and II

(B) II and III

(C) I, II, and III

(D) I, II, III, and IV

20. If a customer wants to open a new account but refuses to provide some of the financial information requested by the member firm, which of the following statements is **true**?

(A) The firm may open the account for the customer and make recommendations freely.

(B) The firm may open the account if it can determine from other sources that the customer has the financial means to handle the account.

(C) The firm may open the account and take unsolicited trades only.

(D) The firm may not accept any trades for the account until the information is received from the customer.

21. Which of the following is included in a preliminary prospectus?

I. The purpose for the funds being raised

II. Financial statements

III. A written statement in red citing that the prospectus may be amended and a final prospectus issued

IV. The final offering price

(A) I and II

(B) I, II, and III

(C) II and IV

(D) I, II, III, and IV

22. Which of the following financial situations is true of an individual accredited investor?

(A) They have had an annual income in excess of $200,000 for at least the last three years.

(B) They have had an annual income in excess of $100,000 for at least the last two years.

(C) They have a net worth of at least $1,000,000, excluding any equity they have in their primary residence.

(D) They have a net worth in excess of $200,000.

GO ON TO NEXT PAGE

23. Declan K. holds several securities in his brokerage account at Bucket Securities. There has been no activity in Declan's account for close to two years. How often must Bucket Securities send him an account statement?

(A) Monthly

(B) Quarterly

(C) Semiannually

(D) Annually

24. Which of the following securities is traded on an exchange and is an entity that makes mortgage loans to developers and has a portfolio of properties?

(A) DPPs

(B) ETNs

(C) Hybrid REITs

(D) Mutual funds

25. Which of the following are needed to open a margin account for a corporation?

(A) A corporate charter, a resolution, and a new account form

(B) A corporate charter, a new account form, and a credit agreement

(C) A hypothecation agreement and a credit agreement

(D) A hypothecation agreement, a corporate charter, a resolution, a new account form, and a credit agreement

26. Which of the following partnership documents needs to be filed with the secretary of state in the home state of the partnership?

(A) The certificate of limited partnership

(B) The partnership agreement and the subscription agreement

(C) The certificate of limited partnership and the subscription agreement

(D) The certificate of limited partnership, the partnership agreement, and the subscription agreement

27. Martina Martin is new to investing but has determined that her primary objective is making sure that she is prepared for retirement. Which of the following is the **most** important factor for you to consider when helping her set up her investment portfolio?

(A) Age

(B) Net worth

(C) Education level

(D) Previous investment history

28. An investor buys 100 shares of common stock of T-Prompters, Inc. at $15 per share. Six months later, T-Prompter Inc. is trading at $12.40–$12.65, and the registered representative offers to purchase the 100 shares back from the investor for their own account at $15 per share. This procedure is

(A) permitted by FINRA rules

(B) permitted with the written permission of a manager of the firm

(C) prohibited because it violates the Code of Procedure

(D) prohibited because it is a guarantee against a loss

29. Which of the following is rated by most securities rating services such as Moody's and S&P?

(A) Market risk

(B) Investment risk

(C) Quantity

(D) Quality

30. Which of the following items are required on an order ticket?

I. The time of the order

II. A description of the security (stocks, bonds, symbol, and so on)

III. Whether the registered rep has discretionary authority over the account

IV. The registered rep's identification number

(A) I, III, and IV

(B) I and III only

(C) I, II, and IV

(D) I, II, III, and IV

31. All of the following are important factors when determining the markup or commission on a municipal bond trade **except**

(A) the fact that you and the firm you work for are entitled to make a profit

(B) the difficulty of the trade

(C) The 5% Markup Policy

(D) the market value of the securities at the time of the trade

32. Mrs. Rice owns 150 shares of TUV common stock. The current market price is $30 per share. If TUV conducts a 1-for-3 reverse stock split, what would Mrs. Rice's post-stock position be?

(A) 50 shares at $10 per share

(B) 50 shares at $90 per share

(C) 450 shares at $10 per share

(D) 450 shares at $90 per share

33. Which of the following is **not** a benefit of investing in ADRs?

(A) The dividends are received in U.S. currency.

(B) The transactions are done in U.S. currency.

(C) ADRs are subject to antifraud rules.

(D) Currency risk is minimized.

34. When is call protection most valuable to the holders of callable bonds?

(A) When bond prices are rising

(B) When bond prices are stable

(C) When bond prices are falling

(D) When bond prices are fluctuating

35. John Dow and Jane Dough, who are engaged but unmarried, want to open a new account registered as joint tenants with rights of survivorship. Which of the following should occur?

(A) A principal of the firm should be notified immediately about the account registration so that a report can be filed with FINRA.

(B) The agent must refuse to open the account.

(C) The agent must notify a principal of the firm and a report must first be filed with the SEC.

(D) The agent may open the account but should first discuss the rules of a JTWROS account with the unmarried couple.

36. Which of the following occurs under the provisions of the Uniform Gifts to Minors Act (UGMA) when a minor reaches the age of majority?

(A) The account must be transferred to the donor.

(B) The account is automatically changed to a UTMA account.

(C) The account is closed, and the new adult receives a check in the amount equal to the market value of the account less any commission.

(D) The account must be transferred to the beneficiary after they reach adulthood.

37. GHI convertible bonds are convertible into common stock for $20. If the stock is trading at $24, what is the parity price of the bonds?

(A) $1,120

(B) $1,200

(C) $1,320

(D) $1,000

38. Prior to buying or selling options, a customer must first receive a(n)

(A) ODD

(B) OCC

(C) margin agreement

(D) OPRA

GO ON TO NEXT PAGE

39. The 5% Markup Policy applies to

(A) riskless or simultaneous transactions

(B) markdowns on stock sold from inventory

(C) commissions charged when executing trades for a customer

(D) all of the above

40. Skippy Barrier III has 1,000 shares of DIM common stock in his portfolio. Skippy would like to protect himself in the event that the market price of DIM drops. Which of the following orders would **best** meet Skippy's needs?

(A) A buy stop order

(B) A sell stop order

(C) A buy limit order

(D) A sell limit order

41. Which of the following is **not** an advantage for a customer adding REITs to their portfolio?

(A) Having a professionally managed portfolio of real estate assets

(B) Preferential dividend treatment

(C) Being able to use a REIT as a potential hedge against a negative price movement in other equity securities

(D) Liquidity

42. All the following items would be found on the official statement of a municipal bond issue **except**

(A) the markup

(B) a description of the issuer

(C) the coupon rate

(D) a legal opinion

43. Open-end investment company shares redemption value is based on the

(A) public offering price (POP), which is computed immediately after the order is received

(B) the next net asset value (NAV) computed after the order is received

(C) the offering price computed at the beginning of the day

(D) the current net asset value (NAV)

44. Which of the following investments requires a registered representative to obtain written verification of an investor's net worth?

(A) Aggressive growth funds

(B) Variable annuities

(C) Direct participation programs

(D) Triple-tax-free municipal bonds

45. To be considered a recession, a decline in the gross domestic product (GDP) must last for at least how many consecutive quarters?

(A) One

(B) Two

(C) Three

(D) Four

46. A registered representative may open all the following customer accounts **except**

(A) an account in the name of Mr. Wegner for Mrs. Wegner

(B) a minor's account by a custodian

(C) a corporate account by a designated officer

(D) a partnership account by a designated partner

47. Exchange-listed securities trading over-the-counter takes place in the

(A) first market

(B) second market

(C) third market

(D) fourth market

48. Mutual funds must send financial statements to shareholders at least

(A) monthly

(B) bimonthly

(C) quarterly

(D) semiannually

49. Which of the following GSEs is directly backed by the U.S. government?

(A) FHLMC

(B) GNMA

(C) FNMA

(D) FCS

50. Which of the following establishes the U.S. Treasury Department as the regulator for anti-money-laundering programs?

(A) The Bank Secrecy Act

(B) OFAC

(C) SDN

(D) None of the above

51. Investing in a real estate DPP program includes which of the following advantages?

(A) Depreciation and appreciation

(B) Depletion and cash flow

(C) Depreciation, appreciation, and cash flow

(D) Depreciation, appreciation, depletion, and cash flow

52. The Fed would be inclined to increase the money supply in which of the following conditions?

(A) Declining yields on bonds

(B) Declining gross domestic product (GDP)

(C) Declining interest rates

(D) Rising housing prices

53. Bank savings accounts are guaranteed up to a certain amount by which of the following entities?

(A) FDIC

(B) The Treasury Department

(C) SIPC

(D) The Fed

54. An investor owns the following investments:

The City of New York 5 percent general obligation bonds maturing in 2040 and rated AA

50 Florida State University 6.25 percent revenue bonds maturing in 2041 and rated AA

50 Salt Lake City Utah Airport 5.75 percent revenue bonds maturing in 2040 and rated AA

What type of diversification does this represent?

(A) Maturity

(B) Quality

(C) Quantity

(D) Geographical

55. An investor has shorted XYZ common stock at 55. XYZ common stock has recently dropped to 30, and the investor expects that the price will continue to decrease over the long term. If the investor would like to hedge against a possible increase in the price, the investor should

(A) buy an XYZ call

(B) sell an XYZ call

(C) buy an XYZ put

(D) buy an XYZ combination

56. If an investor buys an equity option contract on issuance which then expires unexercised, what is the investor's tax consequence at expiration?

(A) Short-term capital loss

(B) Long-term capital gain

(C) Long-term capital loss

(D) Short-term capital gain

57. A customer, without giving written authorization, may permit a registered representative to exercise their judgment as to

(A) whether to buy or sell

(B) the security

(C) the price and timing to enter the order

(D) the number of shares

GO ON TO NEXT PAGE

58. Which of the following are nonexempt securities?

I. Municipal unit investment trust shares

II. U.S. government bond fund shares

III. Variable annuity accumulation units

IV. Fixed annuities

(A) I and II

(B) III only

(C) III and IV

(D) I, II, and III

59. If Piper Seagull has a limited amount of funds and wants to invest in the pharmaceutical industry but does not want to limit her investments to only one or two companies, which type of fund would be **most** suitable?

(A) A hedge fund

(B) A sector fund

(C) A balanced fund

(D) A money market fund

60. Interest income from which of the following investments is exempt from state income tax?

(A) Corporate bonds

(B) Treasury bonds

(C) Revenue bonds

(D) General obligation bonds

61. If the U.S. dollar has fallen in comparison with foreign currencies, which of the following statements is **true**?

(A) U.S. exports are likely to fall.

(B) Foreign currencies buy fewer U.S. dollars.

(C) U.S. products cost more for foreign consumers.

(D) U.S. exports increase.

62. You have a new client who is in a high tax bracket and is looking for investments with a tax advantage. Which of the following securities would you **least** likely recommend?

(A) Municipal bonds

(B) GNMAs

(C) Retirement plans

(D) Direct participation programs

63. Adjustable-rate preferred stock has a dividend that adjusts according to

(A) prevailing interest rates

(B) the amount of dividend given to common stockholders

(C) the coupon rate on the issuer's bonds

(D) the rate on CMOs

64. Which of the following items are found on an indenture of a bond?

(A) Callable or convertible features, the coupon rate, the name of the trustee

(B) The maturity date, callable or convertible features, the coupon rate

(C) Callable or convertible features and the coupon rate

(D) The maturity date, callable or convertible features, the coupon rate, the name of the trustee

65. Institutional trading without using the services of a broker-dealer is considered a ___________ market trade.

(A) first

(B) second

(C) third

(D) fourth

66. Which of the following are important to investors evaluating direct participation programs?

I. The economic soundness of the program

II. The expertise of the general partner

III. The basic objectives of the program

IV. The start-up costs

(A) I, II, and III

(B) I, II, and IV

(C) II, III, and IV

(D) All of the above

67. What is the required beginning date (RBD) for traditional IRAs?

(A) The year after the investor reaches the age of 59 1/2

(B) The year the investor turns the age of 73

(C) April 1 of the year after the investor reaches the age of 73

(D) April 15 of the year after the investor reaches the age of 73

68. One of your clients is expecting to receive a lot of money over the next three years. Your client would like to shelter some of that money by investing in a DPP. Which of the following types of DPPs will help your client shelter the most money?

(A) Oil and gas income

(B) Oil and gas developmental

(C) Oil and gas combination

(D) Oil and gas wildcatting

69. Which of the following governmental bodies receives no revenue from ad valorem taxes?

(A) County governments

(B) State governments

(C) School districts

(D) Local municipalities

70. According to MSRB rules, a customer confirmation must include

(A) the markup or markdown

(B) the location of the indenture

(C) the maturity date

(D) whether the trade was done on an agency or dealer basis

71. Which of the following disputes must be resolved using the Code of Arbitration?

I. A dispute between a member of FINRA and a registered rep

II. A dispute between a member of FINRA and a customer

III. A dispute between two members of FINRA

IV. A dispute between a bank and a member of FINRA

(A) IV only

(B) II and IV

(C) I and III

(D) I, III, and IV

72. Two years ago, Duke Wallwalker purchased an LTSBR Corporation convertible bond at 95 on January 20. The bond is convertible at $40, and the investor converts his bond into stock on January 21 of the current year. If the bond is trading at 104 and the common stock is trading at $42, for tax purposes, these transactions will result in

(A) a $10 gain

(B) a $10 loss

(C) a $90 gain

(D) neither a gain nor a loss

73. RANs, BANs, TANs, and CLNs are issued by municipalities seeking

(A) to insure their municipal securities

(B) the approval of the SEC

(C) long-term financing

(D) short-term financing

74. Which of the following statements regarding municipal revenue bonds is **not** true?

(A) Revenue bonds are not subject to a debt ceiling.

(B) Revenue bonds may be issued by interstate authorities.

(C) The maturity date of the issue will usually exceed the useful life of the facility backing the bonds.

(D) Debt service is paid from revenue received from the facility backing the bonds.

75. When the writer of an option covers their position by buying an option, this is called a(n)

(A) opening purchase

(B) opening sale

(C) closing purchase

(D) closing sale

DO NOT TURN THE PAGE UNTIL TOLD TO DO SO **STOP** DO NOT RETURN TO A PREVIOUS TEST

Chapter 18

Answers and Explanations to Practice Exam 1

Congratulations! If you've reached this point, you've completed the first SIE practice exam. (If you haven't, flip back and take the test in Chapter 17. You don't want to spoil all the surprises, do you?) You should stop here and review your answers.

Review, review, review. And if I haven't mentioned this yet, reviewing is definitely a good idea. Look at the questions you had problems with, retake all the questions you got wrong, and make sure you get them right the second (or third) time around. If you're short on time but just can't wait to see how you fared, you can check out the abbreviated answer key (without the explanations) at the end of this chapter. I explain how the SIE is scored in the section "Making the Grade," just before the answer key. But I strongly suggest you come back later and — you guessed it — review.

Wait at least several days to a week before taking the same test again. Retaking the test won't help your cause if you're just memorizing the answers.

1. **B.** (Chapter 6) Treasury stock is authorized stock that has been issued and subsequently repurchased (reacquired) by the issuing corporation.

2. **C.** (Chapter 6) Common stockholders of PXPX Corporation — or, for that matter, any publicly traded corporation — have a residual claim to the assets of the corporation at dissolution. PXPX Corp. common stockholders are entitled to receive a report containing audited financial statements on a yearly, not weekly, basis. Finally, PXPX Corp. stockholders never get to vote on dividends to be paid (whether stock or cash); dividends are decided by the board of directors.

3. **B.** (Chapter 8) In order to determine the best investment for Jake, you must do a tax-equivalent yield (TEY) calculation. To accomplish this, you need to know Jake's tax bracket. Remember, the interest received from municipal bond investments is tax-free, and investors in higher tax brackets save more money by investing in municipal bonds when compared to other investments. The SIE examiners are testing you to make sure you know that the other items listed here are not relevant to the question.

4. **C.** (Chapter 11) For an investor to profit when holding a long call, the investor has to exercise the option when the market price is above the strike (exercise) price plus the premium paid.

5. **D.** (Chapter 10) For this question, you can stop at the point where the investor has limited resources. Typically, DPPs such as oil and gas developmental programs require a large initial investment and a certain liquid net worth. A DPP would definitely not be right for this client.

6. **D.** (Chapter 5) When a company decides to go public, it must file a registration statement with the SEC. The registration statement must include

   - The issuer's name and a description of its business
   - The names and addresses of all of the issuer's control persons (in other words, officers, directors, and investors owning 10 percent or more of the issuer's securities)
   - What the money raised will be used for
   - The capitalization of the issuer
   - Complete financial statements
   - Whether there are any legal proceedings against the issuer

7. **D.** (Chapter 5) The securities listed in this question are all nonexempt, meaning that they all have to register with the SEC. The Securities Act of 1933 requires all new nonexempt issues of securities sold to the public to be registered. In general, exempt issues include municipal securities, U.S. government securities, bank issues, private placements, intrastate offerings, and securities issued by nonprofit organizations.

8. **D.** (Chapter 16) A confirmation sent to a customer must disclose the amount of markup or markdown charged for a principal transaction in a Nasdaq security, whether the member acted in an agency or a principal capacity, and, if the member acted as an agent, the amount of commission.

9. **C.** (Chapter 9) A letter of intent is valuable to mutual fund purchasers who are purchasing funds that provide breakpoints (discounted sales charge) for larger dollar purchases. By signing a letter of intent, the investor can receive the discounted sales charge right away even though not purchasing enough of the fund to get a breakpoint right now. By signing the letter, they have up to 13 months to purchase enough of the fund to get to the breakpoint price. In addition, a letter of intent can be backdated up to 90 days to allow a breakpoint to apply to a previous purchase.

10. **A.** (Chapter 15) Qualified plans under IRS laws allow investors to invest money for retirement with *pretax dollars* (you can write qualified plan contributions off on your taxes). In addition, earnings accumulate on a *tax-deferred* basis (the investor isn't taxed until withdrawal). However, distributions (tax-deferred earnings and contributions) for which the participant receives a tax deduction are 100 percent taxable.

11. **D.** (Chapter 9) Tricky, tricky . . . the examiners want to make sure you know that a variable annuity is derived from two separate products: an insurance contract and securities held in a separate account. Consequently, a variable annuity must be registered with the State Insurance Commission (for the insurance contract) and the Securities and Exchange Commission (for the securities held in the separate account).

12. **B.** (Chapter 16) The customer's signature is not required on a trade confirmation. Logically, you can imagine how unwieldy it would be to have to obtain a customer's signature every time they wanted to trade securities. However, the customer's account number, the registered rep's ID number, the trade date, whether the customer bought or sold, the number of shares or par value of bonds, the yield (if bonds), the CUSIP number, the price of the security, the total amount paid, the commission (if on an agency basis), and the net amount are all required on the confirmation.

13. **D.** (Chapter 12) The Telephone Act of 1991 is designed to set standards for individuals soliciting business. All the choices listed are included in the act.

14. **A.** (Chapter 16) If a registered representative believes that a customer is making an unsuitable trade, the representative may enter the order but must mark the order ticket "unsolicited." In this question, the client is making a trade that you believe is unsuitable for them, but you can still execute the trade as long as you mark the order ticket as "unsolicited," which will protect you and make your client happy.

15. **D.** (Chapter 16) The Bank Secrecy Act establishes the U.S. Treasury Department as the regulator of anti-money-laundering programs. As such, all broker-dealers are required to have programs set up to help detect the possibility of money laundering. Broker-dealers must also review the OFAC's (Office of Foreign Asset Control's) SDN (Specially Designated Nationals) list to determine that they're not doing business with organizations or individuals who are on the list.

16. **A.** (Chapter 9) Lifecycle (target-date) funds are actually funds of funds, which are based on an investor's age. Investors buy a lifecycle fund designed for people their age. Lifecycle funds adjust their holdings every so often so that investors are taking less risk as they get older. Because typically younger investors can afford to take more risk, a larger percentage of their portfolio is in equities and less is in fixed-income securities. As investors get older, they should have an increasing number of fixed-income securities and fewer equity securities. Lifecycle funds automatically take care of that for investors.

17. **B.** (Chapter 16) The *ex-date* or *ex-dividend date* is one business day before the record date and is the date that the buyer would be purchasing the stock without a dividend. On the ex-date, the stock is *reduced* by the amount of the dividend. The corporation is still responsible for paying the dividend and, because the buyer isn't entitled to it, the seller is.

18. **C.** (Chapter 13) In this case, the Fed would like to inject more money into the economy. Out of the choices listed, the only thing that the Fed can control that would actually *do* that is to purchase Treasury bonds in the open market.

19. **D.** (Chapter 8) Factors that affect the marketability (how easy it is to buy and sell) of municipal GO (general obligation) bonds are the quality, maturity date, call features, coupon rate, block size, dollar price, issuer's name, sinking fund, and credit enhancements (in other words, insurance).

20. **B.** (Chapter 12) You will find that this is not an unusual situation. When you're opening an account for a new customer, the customer may not feel comfortable sharing all their financial information with you. However, you can still do trading in the account and make recommendations if you can determine financial information from other sources, such as Dun & Bradstreet (D&B) lead cards. Say, for example, that the D&B card says that the customer is the CEO of a corporation that made $5 billion last year. You can assume the customer has a lot of money. The recommendations you make to a customer should be

suitable to their investment objectives and financial situation. If you can't determine the information from other sources, you can still make trades and recommendations that would be suitable for all investors, such as mutual funds, blue-chip stocks, or U.S. government securities.

21. **B.** (Chapter 5) A preliminary prospectus includes the purpose for the funds and financial statements. Because a preliminary prospectus (*red herring*) is printed before the final price is established, it may include a projected price range that is subject to change.

22. **C.** (Chapter 5) Certain purchases, such as a Regulation D private placement, may require investors to be accredited (although they have a 35 unaccredited investor exclusion). Accredited investors are ones with a net worth of at least $1 million (excluding any equity they may have in their primary residence) or ones with an annual income of at least $200,000 (or $300,000 for joint accounts) for the last two (not three) years that's expected to stay at least the same for the current year. Also, the following have been added to the list of accredited investors: financial institutions; insiders of the private placement; corporations, partnerships, or organizations with a net worth of at least $5 million; registered reps in good standing with SEC, FINRA, and at least one state who have passed the Series 7, Series 65, Series 66, and/or the Series 82 exams; knowledgeable employees of private funds; rural business investment companies; LLCs with more than $5 million in assets; and family offices with at least $5 million in assets under management.

23. **B.** (Chapter 16) Whether the account is active or inactive (such as Declan's), the brokerage firm must send out account statements at least quarterly (once every three months).

24. **C.** (Chapter 10) Hybrid REITs (real estate investment trusts) trade on an exchange, provide mortgage loans to developers, and hold a portfolio of securities. Hybrid REITs are a combination of equity (ownership) REITs and mortgage REITs.

25. **D.** (Chapter 12) When a corporation opens a margin account, the corporation has to provide a corporate charter (which needs to say that the corporation can buy securities on margin) and a corporate resolution (which says who has the trading authority for the account). A new account form is always needed for any type of account. The corporation also needs a hypothecation agreement, which allows the broker–dealer to hold the securities in street name so that they can be used as collateral for a loan. In addition, the corporation needs a credit agreement, which sets the terms for the loan.

26. **A.** (Chapter 10) The certificate of limited partnership is the legal agreement between the general and limited partners and is the only partnership paperwork that needs to be filed with the secretary of state. The certificate of limited partnership includes the primary place of business, the names and addresses of the limited and general partner(s), the objectives of the partnership, the amount contributed by each partner, the roles of the partners, and so on.

27. **A.** (Chapter 12) Certainly, any information you can get about your client will help you set up a portfolio that fits the client's needs. However, because Martina's primary investment objective is making sure that she's prepared for retirement, you need to begin by looking at her age. Someone who is younger can typically take more investment risk than someone who is older.

28. **D.** (Chapter 16) Pursuant to Conduct Rules (not the SEC), registered representatives may never guarantee a customer against losses; therefore, this action is never permitted. If the investor wanted to sell the shares, they would have to sell them at the bid price of $12.40, not $15.

29. **D.** (Chapter 7) The expression "quality over quantity" applies here. Rating services are concerned with quality, defined as the issuer's (or guarantor's) default risk or ability to pay interest and principal on time. The two biggest rating services are Moody's and Standard & Poor's. The highest ratings for these rating services are Aaa and AAA, respectively.

30. **D.** (Chapter 16) All order tickets need to include the items listed in the question plus the customer's account number; the number of shares or bonds being purchased or sold; whether the customer is buying, selling, or selling short; whether the customer is covered or uncovered (option orders); and whether it's a market order, good-till-canceled, and so on.

31. **C.** (Chapter 8) Because municipal securities are exempt from SEC registration, they're not subject to the FINRA 5% Markup Policy.

32. **B.** (Chapter 6) Since this is a reverse stock split, Mrs. Rice will own fewer shares at a higher market price. So, because it's a 1-for-3 reverse-split, you have to divide the number of shares by 3, and you'll come up with 50 shares (150/3). To get the price, you need to multiply the current market price by 3, and you'll come up with a price of \$90 per share (\$30 × 3).

33. **D.** (Chapter 6) The purpose of ADRs (American Depositary Receipts) is to facilitate the trading of foreign securities in U.S. markets. ADRs carry currency risk because distributions on ADRs must be converted from foreign currency to U.S. dollars on the date of distribution. The trading price of the ADR is actually quite affected by currency fluctuation, which can devalue any dividends and/or the value of the stock.

34. **A.** (Chapter 7) Issuers typically have to wait a number of years before being able to call their callable bonds. This is known as call protection. Remember, there is an inverse relationship between bond prices and interest rates. If bond prices are rising, that usually means that interest rates are falling. This is the time that bond issuers would want to call their bonds so that they could issue bonds with a lower coupon rate. This is also the time that holders of these callable bonds would not want their bonds called. Therefore, call protection is most valuable to the holders when bond prices are rising.

35. **D.** (Chapter 12) No rules prohibit opening an account registered as joint tenants with rights of survivorship (JTWROS) for two unmarried persons. The registered representative should, however, take all steps to be sure that the unmarried individuals understand the resulting consequences should one party to the account die. For example, in an account registered JTWROS, if one of the engaged parties to the account (for example, John Dow) dies, the deceased party's ownership interest in the account passes to the surviving tenant (Jane Dough) rather than to the deceased party's (John Dow's) estate.

36. **D.** (Chapter 12) Under the terms of the Uniform Gifts to Minors Act (UGMA), the account must be handed over to the new adult when a minor reaches the age of majority. You don't need to know the age of majority because it varies from state to state, but it's usually between the ages of 18 and 21.

37. **B.** (Chapter 7) Parity price is when a convertible security is convertible into the same dollar amount of the security it's being converted into. So, when you're dealing with questions that are asking for a parity price, you must first determine the conversion ratio, which will sometimes be given. The conversion ratio is the amount of shares the bond is convertible into. You can use the following formula:

$$\text{conversion ratio} = \frac{\text{par value}}{\text{conversion price}} = \frac{\$1,000}{\$20} = 50 \text{ shares}$$

Assume that the par value is $1,000 unless told differently. In this case, after using the equation, you can see that the conversion ratio is 50 shares. To determine the parity price, use the following equation:

parity price of the bond = market price of the stock × conversion ratio

parity price of the bond = $24 × 50 shares = $1,200

So, in this case, if the bond is trading below $1,200, it may make sense for the investor to convert the bond.

38. **A.** (Chapter 11) Because of the additional risk involved when investing in options, such as the ability to lose all money invested or facing unlimited maximum potential loss, all investors must receive an ODD (options risk disclosure document) prior to the first transaction. The ODD is not an advertisement; it contains the pitfalls of investing in options. After the customer receives the ODD, the ROP (registered options principal) has to approve the account. Next, you can do the trade, and after that, the customer has to sign and return an OAA (options account agreement).

39. **D.** (Chapter 16) The 5% Markup Policy is a guideline for broker–dealers to use when executing trades of outstanding securities for public customers. In most cases, for a standard-sized trade of nonexempt securities, broker–dealers should not charge a commission, markup, or markdown that is in excess of 5 percent. The 5% Markup Policy applies to both commission charges on agency transactions and to markups and markdowns on principal transactions, including riskless and simultaneous transactions.

40. **B.** (Chapter 14) Remember that stop orders are used for protection. Because Skippy owns the stock, he would have to enter a sell stop order below the market price of the security. In the event that the price of the stock hits or drops below the stop price, the order would be triggered and the stock would be sold on the next transaction.

41. **B.** (Chapter 10) As with most other investment company products, REITs have a professionally managed portfolio. Many investors use REITs as a potential hedge against a downturn in the market because often there is an inverse relationship between the real estate market and stock prices. In addition, REITs typically have a high degree of liquidity. However, there is no preferential dividend treatment for REITs.

42. **A.** (Chapter 8) The official statement for a municipal bond issue is similar to a prospectus for a corporate issue. The items that you find on an official statement include the offering terms, the underwriting spread, a description of the bonds, a description of the issuer, the offering price, the coupon rate, the feasibility statement, and the legal opinion.

43. **B.** (Chapter 9) As with other securities, mutual funds are purchased at the ask price (POP) and sold (or in this case redeemed) at the bid price (NAV). Mutual funds have forward pricing, so any purchases and redemptions are made at the next computed POP and NAV, which is typically at the end of the day.

44. **C.** (Chapter 10) Because direct participation programs (limited partnerships) may require limited partners to come up with additional cash beyond their initial investment, investors must provide a written verification of net worth. After the general partner signs the subscription agreement, the investor is accepted as a limited partner.

45. **B.** (Chapter 13) Although they have recently changed the definition of a recession to include more than just a decline in the GDP, the GDP must decline for at least two consecutive quarters to have the possibility of a recession.

46. **A.** (Chapter 12) Here's that EXCEPT question type again! You're looking for a false answer here. Although a custodian may open an account with an agent for a minor, a designated officer may open a corporate account with an agent, and a designated partner may open a partnership account with an agent, an agent is not permitted to open an individual account in the name of a third person. This means that choice (A) is the correct false answer that you're looking for.

47. **C.** (Chapter 14) First market involves listed securities trading on an exchange. Second market involves unlisted securities trading OTC (over-the-counter). Third market involves listed securities trading OTC. Fourth market involves institutional trading without using a broker-dealer.

48. **D.** (Chapter 16) Under the Investment Company Act of 1940, mutual funds must provide semiannual reports to shareholders.

49. **B.** (Chapter 7) GNMAs (Government National Mortgage Association — Ginnie Mae) are the only GSEs (Government Sponsored Entities) that are directly backed by the U.S. government. As such, GNMAs are considered the safest of the GSEs.

50. **A.** (Chapter 16) The Bank Secrecy Act establishes the U.S. Treasury Department as the regulator for anti-money-laundering programs. All broker-dealers are required to develop programs to detect possible money-laundering abuses.

51. **C.** (Chapter 10) Real estate DPPs (direct participation programs — limited partnerships) provide advantages for investors such as depreciation deductions, appreciation potential, and cash flow, but not depletion. Depletion only applies to partnerships that deal in natural resources that can be depleted (used up), such as oil or gas.

52. **B.** (Chapter 13) In this question, if the GDP (gross domestic product) is declining, business is slowing down and possibly heading toward a recession; the Fed would therefore want to stimulate the economy by making more money available. Increasing the money supply through lower interest rates usually increases business activity. However, when there are declining yields and interest rates, and rising house prices, there is a danger of increased inflation if the Fed increases (eases) the money supply.

53. **A.** (Chapter 16) The FDIC (Federal Depositor's Insurance Corporation) insures bank savings accounts in the event of bank failure. SIPC (Securities Investor Protection Corporation) protects investors in the event of brokerage firm bankruptcy.

54. **D.** (Chapter 8) Because the investor bought 50 of each bond, they were all rated AA, and they mature around the same time, you can rule out maturity, quality, and quantity as your answers. The investor's funds are an example of geographic diversification because the bonds are from a variety of issuers around the United States.

55. **A.** (Chapter 11) To *hedge* means *to protect*. If the investor would like to hedge their position, they should buy a call on XYZ. Remember that the investor is short the stock and must buy XYZ back at some point to close their short position. Buying an XYZ call gives the investor the right to buy back XYZ at a fixed price, which would allow the investor to protect the position and not face an unlimited maximum loss potential.

56. **A.** (Chapter 15) Options are always taxed as capital gains or capital losses. This investor purchased an option that expired worthless, and, therefore, they lost money. Because the investor held the option for nine months (the typical expiration for an equity option), it's taxed as a short-term capital loss because it was held for one year or less.

57. **C.** (Chapter 16) Without having discretionary authority, registered representatives may not decide on whether to buy or sell, which security to purchase or sell, or the number of shares or dollar amount to purchase for the customer. Registered representatives may, however, without written power of attorney, choose the price or timing of an order.

58. **D.** (Chapter 5) You must distinguish a nonexempt security from an exempt security. A non-exempt security is one that is not exempt from SEC registration; in other words, it must be registered with the SEC. Variable annuities, which carry investment risk, are nonexempt securities under the Securities Act of 1933 and must be registered before public sale. Similarly, unit trusts and mutual funds are nonexempt even though the underlying securities may be exempt, such as municipals and U.S. government securities. However, a fixed annuity is an insurance product exempt from registration with the SEC. It's not considered a security because of the guaranteed payout.

59. **B.** (Chapter 9) A specialized or sector fund invests a minimum of 25 percent of its assets in a particular region or industry and would be the most suitable for Piper.

60. **B.** (Chapter 15) The interest on U.S. government bonds (T-bonds, T-notes, TIPs, and so on) is exempt from state income tax. The interest on municipal bonds is exempt from federal tax.

61. **D.** (Chapter 13) If you look at the answer choices carefully, you'll see that choices (A) and (D) are opposite, which tells you that one of them has to be true. When the U.S. dollar loses value compared to a foreign currency, U.S exports increase because foreign currency strengthens in comparison and now buys more dollars. As a result, U.S. goods are cheaper than normal for foreign consumers.

62. **B.** (Chapter 7) GNMAs (Ginnie Maes) offer no tax advantages to buyers because they are taxed on all levels. However, the interest received on municipal bonds is federally tax-free and sometimes state-tax-free. In addition, retirement plans allow investors to deposit money tax-free (in most cases), and the money grows on a tax-deferred basis. DPPs (direct participation programs) allow for additional write-offs, such as depreciation and depletion, which provide for a cash flow that's greater than the net income.

63. **A.** (Chapter 6) Adjustable (floating rate) preferred stock receives a dividend that adjusts according to prevailing interest rates.

64. **D.** (Chapter 7) The bond indenture (deed of trust) is the legal agreement between the issuer and investors. The bond indenture includes the maturity date, the par value, the coupon rate, any collateral securing the bond, any callable or convertible features, and the name of the trustee.

65. **D.** (Chapter 14) A first-market trade is an exchange-listed security trading on the exchange. A second market trade is an unlisted security trading OTC. A third market trade is an exchange-listed security trading OTC. A fourth market trade is institutional trading without using the services of a broker–dealer.

66. **D.** (Chapter 10) All the choices listed are important to evaluate for investors of direct participation programs.

67. **C.** (Chapter 15) Withdrawals must begin by April 1 of the year after the investor turns age 73. At that point, the investor has to take a required minimum distribution (RMD), which can be determined by looking at the IRS's required minimum distribution worksheet. *Note:* If you're

taking some old tests, the RMD date may be stated as April 1 of the year after the investor turns age 70 1/2, or 72. However, it is now 73.

68. **D.** (Chapter 10) An oil and gas wildcatting (exploratory) program would best suit your client's needs. Oil and gas wildcatting programs drill in unproven areas and create quite a lot of write-offs in the early years. However, if oil is hit, a wildcatting program will bring in a lot of money.

69. **B.** (Chapter 8) Remember that state governments do not collect ad-valorem (property) taxes. Ad valorem taxes are assessed by local governments (for example, towns and counties). Generally, state governments receive the most income from income taxes and sales taxes.

70. **D.** (Chapter 16) The SIE examiners may try to trip you up by throwing in an irrelevant answer choice (like the date of maturity) to find out whether you know your MSRB (Municipal Securities Rulemaking Board) rules. MSRB rules require that confirmations include whether the trade was executed on a principal (dealer) or agency basis. The amount of the dealer's markup or markdown on a principal trade does not have to be disclosed, but the commission on an agency trade does need to be disclosed.

71. **C.** (Chapter 16) As you can see, the one common denominator is that all the answer choices have the acronym "FINRA" in them, which tells you that being a FINRA member must be pretty important. The Code of Arbitration is mandatory in member-against-member disputes including a member firm and one of its registered reps. However, FINRA has no jurisdiction over banks or over disputes between nonmembers such as customers or issuers; in cases such as these, the nonmember decides whether to use arbitration or a Code of Procedure hearing to settle a dispute.

72. **D.** (Chapter 15) There are no tax consequences to Duke for converting a bond into shares of common stock. In order for Duke to have a taxable gain or loss, the shares Duke received as a result of the conversion to common stock must be sold.

73. **D.** (Chapter 8) Municipal short-term notes such as RANs (revenue anticipation notes), BANs (bond anticipation notes), TANs (tax anticipation notes), and CLNs (construction loan notes) are used to provide short-term (interim) financing until a permanent, long-term bond issue is floated, until tax receipts increase, or until revenue flows in.

74. **C.** (Chapter 8) You need to be careful in this case because the examiners are asking you for a false statement. The maturity of revenue bonds may be 25 to 30 years, but the facility being built by the income received from the revenue bond issue is usually expected to last a lifetime. Revenue bonds may be issued by interstate authorities, such as tolls, and the debt service (interest and principal) on the bonds is paid from revenue received from the facility backing the bonds. In addition, revenue bonds are not subject to a debt ceiling; general obligation bonds are.

75. **C.** (Chapter 11) Since they already have an option position, the second transaction isn't an opening transaction, it is a closing transaction. Since they originally sold (wrote) the option, they would have to buy themself out of that position. Therefore, it is a closing purchase.

Making the Grade

Here's how the SIE exam is scored:

- You get 11/3 points for each correct answer.
- You get 0 points for each incorrect answer.

A passing score is 70 percent. To calculate your grade for this exam, multiply the number of correct answers by 1.33 or divide it by 0.75. Whatever grade you get, make sure you round down, not up. For example, a grade of 71.6 is a 71 percent, not a 72.

REMEMBER

The actual test contains ten additional experimental questions that don't count toward your actual score. You can't tell these questions apart from the questions that do count, so you may have to answer a few more questions right to get your 70 percent. Don't sweat it. Simply come prepared, stay focused, and do your best.

Answer Key for Practice Exam 1

1. B
2. C
3. B
4. C
5. D
6. D
7. D
8. D
9. C
10. A
11. D
12. B
13. D
14. A
15. D
16. A
17. B
18. C
19. D
20. B
21. B
22. C
23. B
24. C
25. D
26. A
27. A
28. D
29. D
30. D
31. C
32. B
33. D
34. A
35. D
36. D
37. B
38. A
39. D
40. B
41. B
42. A
43. B
44. C
45. B
46. A
47. C
48. D
49. B
50. A
51. C
52. B
53. A
54. D
55. A
56. A
57. C
58. D
59. B
60. B
61. D
62. B
63. A
64. D
65. D
66. D
67. C
68. D
69. B
70. D
71. C
72. D
73. D
74. C
75. C

Chapter 19
Nothing But Net: Practice Exam 2

If you've just finished the first practice exam and are planning on continuing to this practice exam, please thoroughly review the first exam first. Just like Practice Exam 1 in Chapter 17, this practice exam has 75 questions. For those of you who couldn't wait to take the second exam and bypassed the first one, I review the test basics here.

As in the real SIE exam, the questions in both practice exams are in random order. Please read carefully. You can limit your careless mistakes by focusing on the key words. Zone in on the information you need to know to answer the question and ignore the information that doesn't help you. I suggest reading the last sentence twice to make sure you know what the question's asking. You may use scrap paper and a basic calculator for figuring.

Mark your answers on the answer sheet provided in this chapter or on a separate piece of paper. As you're taking the exam, circle or highlight the questions that you find troublesome. After taking and grading the exam, look over the questions that you got wrong and the questions that you circled or highlighted. Review the test, retake all the questions that you circled or answered wrong, and make sure that you get them right this time.

To simulate the real exam, try to finish this part in one hour and 45 minutes or less. Please resist the urge to look at the answers and explanations until you've finished the exam. You can check your answers and get detailed explanations in Chapter 20. Good luck!

Practice Exam Part 2 Answer Sheet

1. Ⓐ Ⓑ Ⓒ Ⓓ	**16.** Ⓐ Ⓑ Ⓒ Ⓓ	**31.** Ⓐ Ⓑ Ⓒ Ⓓ	**46.** Ⓐ Ⓑ Ⓒ Ⓓ	**61.** Ⓐ Ⓑ Ⓒ Ⓓ
2. Ⓐ Ⓑ Ⓒ Ⓓ	**17.** Ⓐ Ⓑ Ⓒ Ⓓ	**32.** Ⓐ Ⓑ Ⓒ Ⓓ	**47.** Ⓐ Ⓑ Ⓒ Ⓓ	**62.** Ⓐ Ⓑ Ⓒ Ⓓ
3. Ⓐ Ⓑ Ⓒ Ⓓ	**18.** Ⓐ Ⓑ Ⓒ Ⓓ	**33.** Ⓐ Ⓑ Ⓒ Ⓓ	**48.** Ⓐ Ⓑ Ⓒ Ⓓ	**63.** Ⓐ Ⓑ Ⓒ Ⓓ
4. Ⓐ Ⓑ Ⓒ Ⓓ	**19.** Ⓐ Ⓑ Ⓒ Ⓓ	**34.** Ⓐ Ⓑ Ⓒ Ⓓ	**49.** Ⓐ Ⓑ Ⓒ Ⓓ	**64.** Ⓐ Ⓑ Ⓒ Ⓓ
5. Ⓐ Ⓑ Ⓒ Ⓓ	**20.** Ⓐ Ⓑ Ⓒ Ⓓ	**35.** Ⓐ Ⓑ Ⓒ Ⓓ	**50.** Ⓐ Ⓑ Ⓒ Ⓓ	**65.** Ⓐ Ⓑ Ⓒ Ⓓ
6. Ⓐ Ⓑ Ⓒ Ⓓ	**21.** Ⓐ Ⓑ Ⓒ Ⓓ	**36.** Ⓐ Ⓑ Ⓒ Ⓓ	**51.** Ⓐ Ⓑ Ⓒ Ⓓ	**66.** Ⓐ Ⓑ Ⓒ Ⓓ
7. Ⓐ Ⓑ Ⓒ Ⓓ	**22.** Ⓐ Ⓑ Ⓒ Ⓓ	**37.** Ⓐ Ⓑ Ⓒ Ⓓ	**52.** Ⓐ Ⓑ Ⓒ Ⓓ	**67.** Ⓐ Ⓑ Ⓒ Ⓓ
8. Ⓐ Ⓑ Ⓒ Ⓓ	**23.** Ⓐ Ⓑ Ⓒ Ⓓ	**38.** Ⓐ Ⓑ Ⓒ Ⓓ	**53.** Ⓐ Ⓑ Ⓒ Ⓓ	**68.** Ⓐ Ⓑ Ⓒ Ⓓ
9. Ⓐ Ⓑ Ⓒ Ⓓ	**24.** Ⓐ Ⓑ Ⓒ Ⓓ	**39.** Ⓐ Ⓑ Ⓒ Ⓓ	**54.** Ⓐ Ⓑ Ⓒ Ⓓ	**69.** Ⓐ Ⓑ Ⓒ Ⓓ
10. Ⓐ Ⓑ Ⓒ Ⓓ	**25.** Ⓐ Ⓑ Ⓒ Ⓓ	**40.** Ⓐ Ⓑ Ⓒ Ⓓ	**55.** Ⓐ Ⓑ Ⓒ Ⓓ	**70.** Ⓐ Ⓑ Ⓒ Ⓓ
11. Ⓐ Ⓑ Ⓒ Ⓓ	**26.** Ⓐ Ⓑ Ⓒ Ⓓ	**41.** Ⓐ Ⓑ Ⓒ Ⓓ	**56.** Ⓐ Ⓑ Ⓒ Ⓓ	**71.** Ⓐ Ⓑ Ⓒ Ⓓ
12. Ⓐ Ⓑ Ⓒ Ⓓ	**27.** Ⓐ Ⓑ Ⓒ Ⓓ	**42.** Ⓐ Ⓑ Ⓒ Ⓓ	**57.** Ⓐ Ⓑ Ⓒ Ⓓ	**72.** Ⓐ Ⓑ Ⓒ Ⓓ
13. Ⓐ Ⓑ Ⓒ Ⓓ	**28.** Ⓐ Ⓑ Ⓒ Ⓓ	**43.** Ⓐ Ⓑ Ⓒ Ⓓ	**58.** Ⓐ Ⓑ Ⓒ Ⓓ	**73.** Ⓐ Ⓑ Ⓒ Ⓓ
14. Ⓐ Ⓑ Ⓒ Ⓓ	**29.** Ⓐ Ⓑ Ⓒ Ⓓ	**44.** Ⓐ Ⓑ Ⓒ Ⓓ	**59.** Ⓐ Ⓑ Ⓒ Ⓓ	**74.** Ⓐ Ⓑ Ⓒ Ⓓ
15. Ⓐ Ⓑ Ⓒ Ⓓ	**30.** Ⓐ Ⓑ Ⓒ Ⓓ	**45.** Ⓐ Ⓑ Ⓒ Ⓓ	**60.** Ⓐ Ⓑ Ⓒ Ⓓ	**75.** Ⓐ Ⓑ Ⓒ Ⓓ

TIME: 1 hour and 45 minutes for 75 questions

DIRECTIONS: Choose the correct answer to each question. Then fill in the circle on your answer sheet that corresponds to the question number and the letter indicating your choice.

1. Mark Schwimmerr owns 2,500 shares of TP Corporation. Which of the following actions would dilute Mark's equity?

   (A) A primary share offering

   (B) A stock split

   (C) A primary share offering, a stock split, or a secondary share offering

   (D) A primary share offering, a stock split, the payment of a stock dividend, or a secondary share offering

2. Stella Smith is one of your clients. Stella is 55 years old, has a wife, two young adults going to college, and two children living at home. You have helped Stella determine her investment profile and how much risk she should be willing to take. However, Stella is hot on a particularly speculative security that doesn't fit her investment profile. Stella calls you saying she wants to purchase $20,000 worth of this security. What should you do?

   (A) Accept the order and mark it as unsolicited.

   (B) Refuse the order because it doesn't fit her investment profile.

   (C) Do nothing until talking to a principal.

   (D) Limit Stella's exposure by making sure that she doesn't purchase more than $5,000 worth of this speculative security.

3. An investor would like to save money for a child who will be going to college in 15 years without facing reinvestment risk. Which of the following is a suitable investment?

   (A) T-bills

   (B) T-notes

   (C) Treasury receipts

   (D) AAAA aggressive growth fund

4. Which of the following statements is **true** about revenue bonds?

   (A) Their value is measured by the municipal project's capacity for generating revenue.

   (B) They are secured by a mortgage-backed bond.

   (C) They are a type of general obligation bond.

   (D) They are subject to the statutory debt limitations of the issuing jurisdiction.

5. Which of the following is the balance sheet equation?

   (A) Assets = liabilities + shareholder's equity

   (B) Assets + liabilities = shareholder's equity

   (C) Shareholder's equity + assets = liabilities

   (D) None of the above

6. Regarding the taxation of dividends from corporate securities, which of the following is **true**?

   (A) Qualified dividends are taxed at the investor's income tax rate and nonqualified dividends are taxed at the investor's tax rate.

   (B) Qualified dividends are taxed at the investor's income tax rate and nonqualified dividends are taxed at a maximum rate of 20 percent.

   (C) Qualified dividends are taxed at a maximum rate of 20 percent and nonqualified dividends are taxed at the investor's tax rate.

   (D) Qualified dividends are taxed at a maximum rate of 20 percent and nonqualified dividends are taxed at a maximum rate of 20 percent.

GO ON TO NEXT PAGE

7. Where can an investor find the most information about a new municipal issue?

(A) In a prospectus

(B) In an official statement

(C) In a tombstone ad

(D) In a registration statement

8. Which of the following statements made by a registered rep is not prohibited?

(A) "The stock will double in price."

(B) "The earnings of the company will be better than expected."

(C) "I can guarantee that you will not lose money on this stock."

(D) "A research report shows that the company's financial performance may be better than expected."

9. Which **two** of the following are **true** of Roth IRAs?

(A) Contributions are made from after-tax dollars and distributions are tax-free.

(B) Contributions are made from after-tax dollars and distributions are taxed on the amount above the amount of the contribution.

(C) Contributions are made from pretax dollars and distributions are tax-free.

(D) Contributions are made from pretax dollars and distributions are taxed on the amount above the amount of the contribution.

10. Which of the following are **true** of broker-dealer business continuity and disaster recovery plans?

I. They must be in written form.

II. Firms must have backups of data (both hard copies and electronic).

III. Firms must have some sort of alternative communication between the firm and its employees.

IV. They must be approved by a principal.

(A) I, II, and III

(B) II, III, and IV

(C) I, II, and IV

(D) I, II, III, and IV

11. One of your clients wants to start adding some diversity to their portfolio by investing in mutual funds. Which of the following is the most important consideration when choosing a mutual fund?

(A) Whether the fund is load or no-load

(B) Management fees

(C) Investment objectives

(D) 12b-1 fees

12. Common stockholders in a corporation can do which of the following?

(A) Elect the corporation's board of directors

(B) Make decisions about the day-to-day dealings, such as the office supply dealer used by the corporation

(C) Receive interest payments

(D) Expect to be paid par value for their stock if the corporation goes out of business

13. Which of the following investments are suitable for a 21-year-old investor who has limited resources but would like to start investing on a regular basis?

(A) Growth funds

(B) Raw land DPPs and hedge funds

(C) Growth funds, raw land DPPs, and call options

(D) Growth funds, call options, and hedge funds

14. Melissa purchased 1,000 shares of DDD common stock at $42 per share on January 4. On January 4 of the following year, Melissa sold the shares at $46 per share. Which of the following is **true** about the sale?

(A) It will be taxed as a short-term capital gain and taxed at Melissa's tax bracket.

(B) It will be taxed as a short-term capital gain and taxed at a maximum of 20 percent.

(C) It will be taxed as a long-term capital gain and taxed at Melissa's tax bracket.

(D) It will be taxed as a long-term capital gain and taxed at a maximum of 20 percent.

15. Which of the following statements is **true** regarding municipal revenue bond issues?

(A) The bonds are backed by the issuer's unlimited taxing power.

(B) User fees provide revenue for the municipality to make sure they can pay bondholders.

(C) The bonds' feasibility is not dependent on the earnings potential of the facility or project.

(D) Revenue bonds are most suitable for investors with high risk tolerance.

16. Jameson and Johnson Securities sent Art a confirmation of his latest trade of Johnstone Corporation common stock. Which of the following items should be on the confirmation?

I. The trade date and the settlement date

II. Whether Jameson and Johnson acted as an agent or a principal

III. The name of the security and how many shares were traded

IV. The amount of commission paid if Jameson and Johnson acted as an agent

(A) I and III

(B) I, II, and III

(C) I, III, and IV

(D) I, II, III, and IV

17. If a customer, Jessica James, decides to give limited power of attorney to her registered representative, which of the following is **true**?

(A) The registered representative still needs verbal authorization from Jessica for each trade.

(B) Jessica must sign a power-of-attorney document.

(C) The registered representative must sign a power-of-attorney document.

(D) Jessica must initial each order before it is entered.

18. Which of the following is **not** a characteristic of a real estate investment trust (REIT)?

(A) Pass-through treatment of income only

(B) Pass-through treatment of income and losses

(C) At least 75 percent of the assets must be invested in real estate-related projects

(D) Ownership of real property without management responsibility

19. A principal is responsible for approving new accounts opened for

(A) individuals only

(B) individuals and corporations

(C) individuals, corporations, and banks

(D) individuals, corporations, banks, and trusts

20. George Lincoln opens a margin account and signs a loan consent, hypothecation, and credit agreement. Which of the following statements are **true**?

I. George's stock may not be kept in street name.

II. A portion of George's stock may be pledged for a loan.

III. George will be required to pay interest on the money borrowed.

IV. George's stock must be cosigned by the broker-dealer.

(A) I and IV

(B) II and III

(C) I and II

(D) None of the above

21. To protect investors of variable life insurance policies who become disabled, there is a rider called a(n)

(A) disability rider

(B) waiver of premium

(C) early withdrawal rider

(D) none of the above

22. As a client's investment objectives change, a registered rep should keep track of those changes so that they can rebalance the client's portfolio and make proper recommendations. Which of the following changes may affect a customer's investment objectives?

I. Growing older
II. Getting divorced
III. Having triplets
IV. Getting a higher paying job

(A) I and III
(B) I, II, and III
(C) II, III, and IV
(D) I, II, III, and IV

23. JKLM Corporation has declared a $0.40 dividend payable to shareholders of record on Thursday, September 14. What would happen to the opening price of stock on that day?

(A) It would be reduced by the amount of the dividend.
(B) It would remain the same.
(C) It would be increased by the amount of the dividend.
(D) This cannot be determined.

24. Larry Eagle is a resident of Michigan. Mr. Eagle purchased a Michigan municipal bond. What is the tax treatment of the interest that Larry earns on his Michigan bond?

(A) It is exempt from federal taxes.
(B) It is exempt from local and federal taxes.
(C) It is exempt from state and federal taxes.
(D) It is exempt from local, state, and federal taxes.

25. Who is responsible for paying the taxes when securities in a Uniform Gifts to Minors Act (UGMA) account are sold at a profit?

(A) The minor
(B) The donor
(C) The custodian
(D) The parent or guardian

26. An investor wants to invest in a DPP that's relatively safe. Which of the following are you **least** likely to recommend?

(A) A real estate partnership that invests in raw land
(B) An oil and gas developmental program
(C) An oil and gas income program
(D) An equipment leasing program

27. Which of the following is a function of a transfer agent?

(A) Underwriting shares in new corporate stock offerings
(B) Preparing corporate balance sheets
(C) Advising municipalities regarding the debt structure of new issues
(D) Sending out proxies

28. All the following information is required on a preliminary prospectus **except**

(A) the final offering price
(B) the purpose for which the issuer is raising the funds
(C) a statement in red lettering stating that items on the preliminary prospectus are subject to change before the final prospectus is issued
(D) the issuer's history and financial status

29. Which of the following situations requires a broker–dealer to file a currency transaction report?

(A) A customer purchases $20,000 worth of stock with a check from a joint account.
(B) A customer opens an account with $14,000 cash.
(C) A customer opens an account with a wire transfer from their personal account for $25,000.
(D) A customer deposits corporate bonds with a par value of $30,000.

30. A mutual fund has a NAV of $9.30 and a POP of $10. What is the sales charge of this fund?

(A) 5 percent
(B) 6 percent
(C) 7 percent
(D) 8 percent

31. Investments that move in the opposite direction of the economic cycles are known to be counter-cyclical. Historically, investments that are known to be counter-cyclical include

(A) discount retailer stock

(B) utility stock

(C) pharmaceutical stock

(D) food company stock

32. On a competitive bid for a new municipal underwriting, the difference between the syndicate bid and the reoffering price is the

(A) discount price

(B) offering price

(C) spread

(D) bid price

33. If a customer wants to open a cash account at a brokerage firm, the signature(s) of which of the following is/are required?

(A) The guarantor

(B) The registered representative and a principal

(C) The registered representative, the customer, and a principal

(D) The registered representative, the customer, a principal, and the guarantor

34. A sell stop order is entered

(A) below the support level of the stock to limit the loss on a long stock position

(B) below the support level of the stock to limit the loss on a short stock position

(C) above the resistance level of the stock to limit the loss on a long stock position

(D) above the resistance level of the stock to limit the loss on a short stock position

35. The indenture of a corporate bond includes all of the following **except**

(A) the coupon rate

(B) the credit rating

(C) the name of the trustee

(D) the maturity date

36. Which of the following items can be found in the certificate of limited partnership?

I. The goals of the partnership and how long it's expected to last

II. The authority of the general partner to charge a fee for making management decisions for the partnership

III. How the profits are to be distributed

IV. The amount contributed by each partner, plus future expected investments

(A) I, II, and III

(B) II, III, and IV

(C) I, III, and IV

(D) I, II, III, and IV

37. When issued, these securities usually have the longest period until expiration.

(A) Call options

(B) Rights

(C) Warrants

(D) Reverse repurchase agreements

38. Which of the following is/are **true** of a REIT?

I. It must invest at least 75 percent of its assets in real estate-related activities.

II. It must be organized as a trust.

III. It must distribute at least 90 percent of its net investment income.

IV. It must pass along losses to shareholders.

(A) I, II, III, and IV

(B) I, II, and III

(C) I only

(D) II and IV

39. An investor purchases 100 shares of DUD Corp. at $45 per share and purchases 1 DUD Oct 40 put at 6. What is the customer's breakeven point?

(A) 39

(B) 45

(C) 46

(D) 51

40. Under the Securities Act of 1933, which of the following securities are exempt from registration and disclosure provisions?

(A) Railroad equipment trust certificate

(B) Municipal bonds

(C) Commercial paper maturing in 270 days or less

(D) All of the above

41. One of your customers is interested in investing in an oil and gas limited partnership. As their registered rep, which of the following steps are you required to take?

I. Prescreen the customer.

II. Determine the economic soundness of the program.

III. Explain the risks of investing in limited partnerships.

IV. Have your customer fill out a partnership agreement.

(A) I and III

(B) I, II, and III

(C) II, III, and IV

(D) I, II, III, and IV

42. Which of the following funds changes its balance to hold more fixed-income securities and less equity securities as the years pass?

(A) A balanced fund

(B) A hedge fund

(C) A lifecycle fund

(D) A growth fund

43. The first time a company ever issues securities is called a(n)

(A) IPO

(B) first-market trade

(C) rights offering

(D) none of the above

44. Bearish strategies include

(A) selling short and selling covered call options

(B) buying put options and selling covered call options

(C) selling short, buying put options, and selling uncovered call options

(D) selling short, buying put options and selling covered call options

45. One of your customers wants to add some diversity to their portfolio by investing in some defensive stocks. Which of the following stocks would you recommend?

I. CCCold Refrigerator Corporation common stock

II. Smoky Tobacco Inc. common stock

III. Forgetful Vodka Corp. common stock

IV. ImpeeAuto Corporation common stock

(A) I and IV

(B) II and III

(C) I, III, and IV

(D) II, III, and IV

46. Which of the following events, which need to be reported on a U4 Form, would result in statutory disqualification?

(A) A felony conviction for a DUI (driving under the influence) charge

(B) A charge of felony theft

(C) A filing of personal bankruptcy

(D) A complaint written by a customer alleging misappropriation of their assets

47. All the following orders are reduced on the order book for a cash dividend on the ex-date **except**

(A) buy limit

(B) sell stop

(C) sell stop limit

(D) buy stop

48. An investor sells 10 TUV Jan 40 calls for 3. If the options expire unexercised, what would be the tax consequences of this transaction?

(A) Short-term capital loss

(B) Short-term capital gain

(C) Long-term capital loss

(D) Long-term capital gain

49. An investor who purchases a variable life insurance policy faces which of the following risks?

(A) The insurance company may have to increase the premium if the securities held in the separate account underperform the market.

(B) The insurance company may decrease the premium if the securities held in the separate account outperform the market.

(C) The policy may have no cash value if the securities held in the separate account perform poorly.

(D) The death benefit may fall below the minimum in the event that the securities held in the separate account underperform.

50. All of the following are nonfinancial influences that may help determine an investor's investment profile **except**

(A) the investor's age

(B) the amount of marketable securities the investor owns

(C) the number of dependents

(D) investment experience

51. Ginny Goldtrain is a wealthy investor who is in the highest income bracket. Ginny is looking for an investment that would limit her tax liability and put her on equal footing with investors in lower income-tax brackets. Which of the following securities would you **most** likely recommend?

(A) High-yield bonds

(B) CMOs

(C) Municipal bonds

(D) Hedge funds

52. Which of the following bonds most likely has the highest coupon rate?

(A) DEF Corp. mortgage bonds

(B) DEF Corp. collateral trusts

(C) DEF Corp. debentures

(D) DEF Corp. equipment trusts

53. Your client, Dana Griffin, is about to retire and she wants predictable income. Which of the following would **not** be a good investment for Dana?

I. AA rated IDB

II. U.S. Treasury note

III. AA rated debenture

IV. Income bonds

(A) II only

(B) I and III

(C) II and IV

(D) IV only

54. Which of the following is **true** regarding 401(k) plans?

(A) They are qualified and defined benefit plans.

(B) They are qualified and defined contribution plans.

(C) They are nonqualified and defined benefit plans.

(D) They are nonqualified and defined contribution plans.

55. Which of the following is the issuer and guarantor of all listed options?

(A) The OCC

(B) The OAA

(C) The ODD

(D) The CBOE

56. If your customer, William Goate, purchases shares in a municipal bond fund, which of the following statements is **true**?

(A) Dividends are subject to alternative minimum tax.

(B) Dividends are taxable to all investors.

(C) Capital gains distributions are taxable.

(D) Capital gains distributions are not taxable.

GO ON TO NEXT PAGE

57. These municipal notes provide interim financing for a municipality that's waiting for a grant from the U.S. government.

(A) BANs

(B) TRANs

(C) GANs

(D) CLNs

Use the following exhibit to answer Question 58:

Balance Sheet of ABCD Corp.			
Assets	Asset Value	Liabilities	Amount Owed
Cash	$300,000	Accounts payable	$300,000
Accounts receivable	$1,500,000	Taxes payable	$250,000
Inventory	$1,200,000	Bonds maturing this year	$800,000
Land	$5,000,000	Bonds maturing in five years	$2,000,000
Machinery	$1,500,000		
Goodwill	$2,000,000		

58. What is the net worth of ABCD Corporation?

(A) $3,150,000

(B) $1,650,000

(C) $8,150,000

(D) $10,150,000

59. According to industry regulations, an investor purchasing $3,500 worth of common stock as an initial purchase in a margin account would have to deposit

(A) $875.00

(B) $1,750.00

(C) $2,000.00

(D) $3,500.00

60. Which of the following statements regarding municipal bonds with call provisions is **true**?

(A) Bonds are likely to be called when interest rates fall.

(B) Call provisions favor investors.

(C) Bonds are likely to be called when interest rates rise.

(D) Call provisions are not advantageous to issuers.

61. Sam Smith sends an email to his registered rep, John Johnson, complaining about the amount of commission he was charged on his last trade. According to FINRA rules, what should John Johnson do with the complaint?

(A) Ignore it because the complaint needs to be in writing.

(B) Print it out and give it to his principal.

(C) Print it out and send it to FINRA.

(D) Forward it to FINRA's complaint department.

62. All of the following are types of blue-sky registration **except**

(A) registration by cooperation

(B) registration by coordination

(C) registration by qualification

(D) registration by filing

63. A TUV Oct 60 call is trading for 9 when TUV is at $65. What is the time value of this option?

(A) 0

(B) 4

(C) 5

(D) 9

64. Which of the following need approval from a brokerage firm's principal?

I. New accounts

II. Recommendations

III. Handling of complaints

IV. Trades in all accounts

(A) I and II

(B) I, III, and IV

(C) II, III, and IV

(D) I, II, III, and IV

65. Mrs. Smith previously shorted 10 DEF Nov 40 calls at 5 when the market price of DEF was 39.50. Two weeks prior to expiration, DEF is trading at 42 and Mrs. Smith decides to buy 10 DEF Nov 40 calls at 3. The second option order ticket would be marked

(A) opening sale

(B) opening purchase

(C) closing sale

(D) closing purchase

66. All of the following are included on a confirmation for non-callable municipal bonds that were purchased on a yield basis **except**

(A) the purchase price

(B) the par value

(C) the yield-to-maturity

(D) the taxable equivalent yield

67. Members of stock exchanges who are responsible for buying and selling securities for others and for their own inventory are known as

(A) transfer agents

(B) brokers

(C) designated market makers

(D) underwriters

68. Regular way settlement for U.S. Treasury bonds is

(A) on the same day as the trade date

(B) the next business day after the trade date

(C) two business days after the trade date

(D) three business days after the trade date

69. Income derived from an investment in a real estate limited partnership is termed

(A) earned income

(B) passive income

(C) portfolio income

(D) capital gains

70. What is the intrinsic value of a DEF 30 put option which was purchased at 5 when DEF is currently trading at $28.50?

(A) 0

(B) 1.5

(C) 3.5

(D) 6.5

71. An investor purchased 1,000 shares of WXY at $40. If WXY announces a 5-for-4 split, what is the investor's position after the split?

(A) 1,250 WXY at $32

(B) 1,250 WXY at $50

(C) 800 WXY at $32

(D) 800 WXY at $50

72. An investor would like to sell a fixed amount of base (transaction) currency and use it to purchase a counter currency. To determine how much of the counter currency the investor will receive, you need to factor in the

(A) balance of trade between the two countries

(B) the debt of the counter currency's government

(C) the spot exchange rate

(D) all of the above

73. Which of the following is characteristic of commercial paper?

(A) It is quoted as a percent of par.

(B) It is proof of ownership of the corporation.

(C) It is issued to raise capital for a corporation.

(D) It is junior to convertible preferred stock.

74. A mutual fund that invests only in securities within a specific industry is called a

(A) balanced fund

(B) growth fund

(C) hedge fund

(D) sector fund

75. At what time must an individual begin withdrawals from a Roth IRA?

(A) At age 59 1/2

(B) At age 73

(C) On April 1 of the year after turning 73

(D) None of the above

DO NOT TURN THE PAGE UNTIL TOLD TO DO SO **STOP** DO NOT RETURN TO A PREVIOUS TEST

Chapter 20
Answers and Explanations to Practice Exam 2

Congratulations! You've just completed the second exam (unless you're just randomly flipping through the book). After grading both the first and second exams, you should have an idea of where you stand regarding the SIE exam. Kudos if you did really well on both practice exams.

As with the first exam, review all the questions that you got wrong and the ones you struggled with. Test yourself again by answering all the questions you highlighted and the questions you answered incorrectly and make sure you get them right this time! Please give yourself a few days to a week before taking the same test again. Memorizing answers can give you a false sense of security, and you won't get an accurate forecast of how well you'll do on the SIE exam. (You certainly don't want your score to be as unpredictable as the weather.)

I encourage you to take as many SIE practice exams as possible. (More are available online; see the Introduction for directions.) I can only cover so many potential practice test questions in this book. Make sure you have a good handle on *everything* in the book, even if you didn't see it in the practice tests. FINRA's test banks have thousands of questions, and the test will spit them out randomly, so be prepared.

TIP

If you're short on time but just can't wait to see how well you did, you can check out the abbreviated answer key (without the explanations) at the end of this chapter. I explain how the SIE is scored in the section "Knowing the Score," just before the answer key. But I strongly suggest you come back later and do a more thorough review.

1. **A.** (Chapter 5) Another primary issue of shares would dilute Mark's ownership because new shares would be coming to the market. Don't forget that when a corporation issues stock dividends, splits its stock, or makes a secondary offering, the percent of equity does not change.

2. **A.** (Chapter 16) You can accept the trade and mark it as unsolicited. Even if a customer wants to purchase a security that doesn't fit their investment profile, you can still accept it in most cases by marking it as unsolicited. I call this the CYD (cover your derriere) rule. As long as

you mark the ticket as unsolicited, you save yourself some aggravation (and maybe arbitration) if Stella loses money on the deal.

3. **C.** (Chapter 7) T-STRIPS or Treasury receipts are long-term zero-coupon bonds backed by the full faith and credit of the U.S. government. Zero-coupon bonds are ideal investments to plan for future events because investors don't face reinvestment risk. Reinvestment risk is the additional risk taken with interest or dividends received. Since holders of Treasury receipts don't receive interest payments, there is nothing to reinvest. In addition, the purchase price for long-term zero-coupon bonds is comparatively low.

4. **A.** (Chapter 8) The SIE examiners want to see that you can distinguish revenue bonds from general obligation bonds. In this question, Choice (A) is the correct answer. Revenue bonds are backed by a project's earning capacity. Choices (B), (C), and (D) are incorrect because revenue bonds are not secured by a specific pledge of property, are not a type of general obligation bond, and are not subject to debt limitations the way that many general obligation bonds are.

5. **A.** (Chapter 13) When you look at a corporation's balance sheet, the left side lists all the assets and the right side lists all the liabilities plus the shareholders' equity. The left side and the right side balance out (equal the same amount of money).

6. **C.** (Chapter 15) Dividends are profits shared by corporations. Dividends can be taxed as either qualified (up to a maximum rate of 20 percent) or nonqualified (according to the investor's tax bracket). For the dividends to be qualified, the investor must have held onto the stock for at least 61 days. The 61-day holding period starts 60 days prior to the ex-dividend date.

7. **B.** (Chapter 8) An official statement includes all relevant information about a new municipal bond. Municipal bonds don't have a prospectus, but an official statement is along the same lines. An official statement gives information about the municipal issue, such as the reason the bonds are being issued, what revenue is going to be used to pay the bonds, the issuer's payment history, and so forth. A tombstone ad is a brief advertisement that does not go into detail about the security being issued, and a registration statement is used by corporations when they are filing with the SEC.

8. **D.** (Chapter 16) This question is a double negative ("not prohibited"), so it's asking which statement a registered representative *can* make. The answer is pretty much a matter of logic. Choices (A), (B), and (C) are all guarantees. A registered rep who makes guarantees may get into trouble. However, Choice (D) is not a guarantee and may be said to an investor as long as it's true.

9. **A.** (Chapter 15) The main difference between traditional IRAs and Roth IRAs is the tax implications. Contributions to traditional IRAs are made from pretax dollars (you can write them off on your taxes), whereas contributions to Roth IRAs are made from after-tax dollars. (You can't write them off on your taxes.) However, distributions (withdrawals) from traditional IRAs are taxed on the amount withdrawn, whereas withdrawals from Roth IRAs are tax-free. When withdrawing from a Roth IRA, neither the amount invested, which was already taxed, nor the amount the account has gone up in value (appreciation) is taxed, which is a great benefit to Roth IRA holders.

10. **D.** (Chapter 16) All firms must now have business continuity and disaster recovery plans in place in the event of a significant disruption in their business. These plans must be in written form, be approved by a principal, and address the following information:

- The existence of backup data
- A means of alternative communication between a firm and its employees, customers, and regulators
- The creation of an alternative location for all employees
- A means of giving customers fast access to their securities and funds

11. **C.** (Chapter 9) Certainly all the choices listed are important, but the most important one is the investment objectives of the mutual fund. In other words, you need to know whether the investor is looking for a growth fund, an income fund, a municipal bond fund, an international fund, and so on. When comparing funds with the same investment objectives, all the other things, such as comparing management fees, whether the fund is load or no-load, and so on, come into play.

12. **A.** (Chapter 6) Common stockholders may cast votes for candidates to be members of the board of directors; therefore, Choice (A) is the correct answer. Choice (B) is incorrect because while common stockholders may vote on important issues that affect the welfare of the corporation, they do not have voting rights on the day-to-day operations of the corporation, like buying office supplies. Choice (C) is incorrect because a stockholder doesn't receive interest payments; bondholders do. Finally, Choice (D) is incorrect because a common stockholder's initial investment can be lost if a corporation fails; therefore, par value is not guaranteed.

13. **A.** (Chapter 9) The clues in this question are that the investor is 21 years old, has limited resources, and would like to start investing on a regular basis. This investor is screaming out to be put in a mutual fund. Typically, investors of mutual funds are in it for the long haul; they're not in and out like they may be with other investments. Ideally, this investor should probably be set up on a dollar cost averaging plan whereby they invest *x* amount of dollars every so often (for instance, $100 once a month). Because this investor is young, they can take a little more risk, so a growth fund would be ideal. DPPs, buying call options, and hedge funds are too risky, require too much money, and/or require a certain degree of sophistication.

14. **A.** (Chapter 15) Since Melissa sold the stock at a profit, she would be subject to capital gains tax. In order to be a long-term capital gain, she would've had to have held the stock for *over* one year. In this case, she only held the stock for exactly one year so it would be a short-term capital gain, which would be subject to taxes at Melissa's tax bracket.

15. **B.** (Chapter 8) The answer is Choice (B). Choices (A), (C), and (D) are incorrect. Revenue bonds are generally considered low-risk because they're issued by municipalities. The riskiest municipal bonds are IDRs (industrial development revenue bonds), which are backed by a corporation, not the municipality.

16. **D.** (Chapter 16) When a client receives a trade confirmation (receipt of trade), the confirmation must show the trade date, settlement date, the name of the security, how many shares were traded, whether the broker-dealer acted as an agent or principal, and the amount of commission if traded on an agency basis.

17. **B.** (Chapter 12) The correct answer is Choice (B) because when Jessica grants her registered representative a limited power of attorney, Jessica is the one who must sign the document. Although a principal must approve before the registered representative exercises their discretionary authority, the registered representative does not have to sign the document, and Jessica's approval of each order is not required.

18. **B.** (Chapter 10) Real estate investment trusts pass through income earned by the real estate investments, but not losses. Real estate limited partnerships pass through income and losses to investors because DPPs aren't responsible for paying business taxes.

19. **D.** (Chapter 16) I hope this was an easy one for you. Principals must approve all new accounts and must sign all new account forms.

20. **B.** (Chapter 12) Because George is borrowing money through a margin account to purchase securities, he must leave the stock in the broker–dealer's safekeeping, pay interest on the loan, register the stock in street name, and agree to allow the broker–dealer to pledge the securities because he signed a loan consent agreement.

21. **B.** (Chapter 9) Variable life insurance policies often have a rider or statement of condition that allows individuals to keep their policy in force if they become disabled. This waiver of premium forgives policyholders of paying additional premiums if they become totally disabled.

22. **D.** (Chapter 12) Certainly just about anything you can think of could change a client's investment objectives. As people get older, they usually can't take as much risk. Conversely, investors who get higher-paying jobs are likely to want to take additional risk. Someone who is getting (or has gotten) divorced is likely to have less money (due to alimony payments, one person paying for the house instead of two, child support payments, and so on). Obviously, having triplets puts a financial burden on an investor (unless they get a reality show).

23. **A.** (Chapter 6) Remember, the ex-dividend date (the first day the stock trades without the dividend) is on the record date. In this case, the record date is Thursday, September 14, which means that the opening price on the record/ex-dividend date is reduced by the amount of the dividend ($0.40 in this case).

24. **D.** (Chapter 8) When you purchase a municipal bond issued within your home state, the interest you receive is triple-tax-free (exempt from federal, state, and local taxes). In addition, if you purchase a bond issued by a U.S. territory (such as Puerto Rico, U.S. Virgin Islands, Guam, American Samoa, and Washington, D.C.), the interest is triple-tax-free. However, if you purchase a bond issued by another state, the interest is exempt from federal taxes only.

25. **A.** (Chapter 12) The correct answer is Choice (A). All taxes on the account are the responsibility of the minor because the UGMA account was opened for the benefit of the minor and the account is registered with the minor's Social Security number.

26. **A.** (Chapter 10) Of the choices listed, a real estate partnership that invests in raw land is the riskiest. Partnerships that invest in raw land are considered speculative, as are oil and gas wildcatting (exploratory) programs. The risk of investing in raw land is that even though the property is purchased at a low price, developers may not be interested in that area and the partnership may be stuck with relatively worthless property.

27. **D.** (Chapter 6) Hopefully the word "transfer" in "transfer agent" led you to the correct answer. Yes, the transfer agent is responsible for transferring or sending things. Typically, the transfer agent is responsible for sending out proxies (voting by mail), canceling old shares, sending out new shares, distributing dividends, and so on.

28. **A.** (Chapter 5) The final offering price would not be found on the preliminary prospectus (red herring) because the price hasn't been finalized at this point. After the issuer and the syndicate manager come up with a final offering price, they place it on the final prospectus.

29. **B.** (Chapter 16) When determining whether a broker–dealer has to file a currency transaction report (CTR), you need to look at the size of the trade first. Any cash or cash-equivalent (for example, a money order) transaction of $10,000 or more in a single day requires that you file a CTR to FinCEN (the U.S. Treasury Financial Crimes Network) to determine whether it may be money laundering. In Choice (B), the investor is depositing $14,000 in cash, which is over the $10,000 threshold. In addition, an SAR (Suspicious Activity Report) must be filed for any transaction of $5,000 or more for any trade or transfer that just looks suspicious.

30. **C.** (Chapter 9) To determine the sales charge percentage of a fund, use the following equation:

$$\text{Sales charge} = \frac{\text{POP} - \text{NAV}}{\text{POP}} = \frac{\$10.00 - \$9.30}{\$10.00} = \frac{\$0.70}{\$10.00} = 7\%$$

The POP is the public offering price, which is the price that investors pay, including the sales charge. The NAV is the net asset value and is where the fund should be trading, excluding the sales charge.

31. **A.** (Chapter 13) The correct answer is Choice (A). Historically, fast food companies, discount retailers, and precious metals (gold, for example) are counter-cyclical and move opposite of the economic cycles. Choices (B), (C), and (D) are incorrect because utility, pharmaceutical, and food companies are defensive or noncyclical, and their movement isn't tied to the economic cycle.

32. **C.** (Chapter 8) On a competitive bid for a new municipal underwriting, the difference between the bid to the issuer and the dollar price at which the underwriter reoffers the bonds to the public is the spread, which, importantly, is also the underwriter's compensation.

33. **B.** (Chapter 16) Remember, when a customer opens a cash account, the only signatures that are required are those of the registered rep and a principal of the firm. However, if a customer were to open up a margin account, they'd have to sign a margin agreement.

34. **A.** (Chapter 14) Sell stop orders are used for protection. A sell stop order is placed below the support level of the stock and limits the loss on a long position. For argument's sake, say that a stock has a trading range of 30 to 32. An investor may enter a sell stop order at 29.50 to protect themselves if the stock drops to 29.50 or below. If the price of the stock hits 29.50, the sell stop order becomes a market order for immediate execution at the next available price.

35. **B.** (Chapter 7) The *indenture* (trust indenture or deed of trust) of a bond is a legal contract between the issuer and the trustee representing the investors. The bond indenture includes the coupon rate (nominal yield), the maturity date, the name of the trustee, collateral that may be backing the bond, and so on. However, the credit rating isn't found on the indenture because that's something that would change if the financial condition of the issuer changes.

36. **C.** (Chapter 10) The certificate of limited partnership is the legal agreement between the limited and general partners and has to be filed with the secretary of state. The certificate of limited partnership includes the name of the partnership, the partnership's primary place of business, the names and addresses of the limited and general partners, the goals of the partnership and how long it's expected to last, the amount contributed by each partner, how the profits are to be distributed, the roles of the participants, how the partnership can be dissolved, and whether a limited partner can sell or assign their interest in the partnership. The authority that allows the general partner to charge a fee for making management decisions is found in the partnership agreement.

37. **C.** (Chapter 6) Warrants give the holder the right to purchase stock at a fixed price sometime in the future. Warrants are long-term and sometimes perpetual.

38. **B.** (Chapter 10) Choice (B) is the correct answer because three components are true about a REIT. As indicated by its acronym, a REIT is a real estate investment trust. REITs engage in real estate activities and are organized as trusts. In order to qualify for favorable tax treatment, a REIT must pass through at least 90 percent of its net investment income to its shareholders. Statement IV is false because, although a REIT can pass through income to investors, it can't pass through losses.

39. **D.** (Chapter 11) The easiest way to calculate the breakeven point for stock/option problems is to take a look at what's happening. This investor purchased the stock for $45 per share and then purchased the option for $6 per share. The investor paid $51 ($45 + $6) per share out of pocket, so the investor needs the stock to be at $51 per share in order to break even.

40. **D.** (Chapter 5) All the securities listed are exempt from the registration and disclosure provisions under the Securities Act of 1933.

41. **B.** (Chapter 10) Investors of limited partnerships bear additional risks, such as the possibility of money being tied up for a long period of time, little or no liquidity, the making of additional loans to the partnership, and so on. As a registered rep, you need to prescreen your customers to see whether they're a good match for the partnership. You should also look at the partnership and management itself to see whether they have a good track record and whether the partnership makes sense. You need to explain the risks to your customer and have your customer fill out a subscription agreement, not a partnership agreement. The subscription agreement needs to include a check, a signature giving the general partner power of attorney, financial statements, and so on.

42. **C.** (Chapter 9) Lifecycle (target-date) funds are ideal for investors of any age. The idea behind them is that investors buy into lifecycle funds that are targeted for their age. The percentage of equities held by the fund decreases over time, whereas the percentage of fixed-income securities increases, because investors should hold a higher percentage of fixed-income securities as they age. For example, say a 45-year-old investor buys into a lifecycle fund that's targeted for investors who are currently between the ages of 44–47. At this particular point, the fund may have a nearly 50-50 split between equity securities and fixed-income securities. The fund rebalances every so often so that ten years into the future, the fund may have 40 percent invested in equity securities and 60 percent invested in fixed-income securities. Ten years after that, the fund may have a 30-70 split between equity and fixed-income securities. This fund is designed to take the guesswork out of the equation for investors.

43. **A.** (Chapter 14) An *IPO* (initial public offering) is the first time a corporation ever sells securities to the public. A first-market trade is a trade of exchange-listed securities trading on an exchange. A rights offering is when a company offers new shares to existing shareholders at a discount.

44. **C.** (Chapter 13) When someone is bearish on the market or an individual security, they believe that the price is going down. Investors who believe that they can capitalize on their bearish feelings can sell securities short, buy bearish funds (ones that generally increase in value in a declining market), purchase inverse ETFs (exchange-traded funds), sell uncovered (naked) options, buy put options, and so on.

45. **B.** (Chapter 13) Defensive stocks perform consistently no matter how poorly the economy's doing. Stock of corporations that sell goods such as alcohol, tobacco, pharmaceutical supplies, food, and so on issue defensive stocks. However, companies that sell appliances, automobiles, and so on aren't defensive because they sell items that don't sell well in a weak economy.

46. **A.** (Chapter 16) Answers (B) and (D) are about a charge and complaint. In other words, there has been no conviction or findings at this point. Therefore, the individual is considered innocent until proven guilty. A filing of personal bankruptcy is okay in most cases as long as it's been disclosed. However, a felony *conviction* would be grounds for disqualification, even though it's for a DUI, not a financial crime.

47. **D.** (Chapter 14) Here's another question where you must find the false answer. Choices (A), (B), and (C) are wrong because only orders placed below the market price are reduced for cash dividends on the order book. Buy limits and sell stops (BLiSS orders) are entered below the market price. Buy stops are entered above the market price, so Choice (D) is the false — and therefore, correct — answer.

48. **B.** (Chapter 11) As a reminder, all options are capital gains or capital losses. Since options expire in nine months or less (except for LEAPS), it would be a short-term gain or loss. In order to be long-term, it would have to be over one year. In this case, the investor sold options that expired, so it would be a short-term capital gain.

49. **C.** (Chapter 9) Similar to variable annuities, variable life insurance policies have a separate account of securities. All variable life insurance (VLI) policies have a set premium and a minimum death benefit. However, if the securities held in the separate account perform well, the policy will build up cash value, which will increase the death benefit.

50. **B.** (Chapter 12) Certainly, all the choices listed are important when determining a client's investment profile. However, this is an "except" question, which means that you're looking for an investment influence that is financial. The amount of marketable securities an investor owns is part of their financial profile as well as other things like net worth, money available for investing, current income, expenses, home ownership, and so on.

51. **C.** (Chapter 8) The interest received on municipal bonds is federally tax-free. Because Ginny is in the highest income-tax bracket, she can save more tax money by investing in municipal bonds. This strategy will put her on equal footing with other investors because neither high-income nor low-income investors have to pay taxes on the interest received from municipal bonds. Therefore, municipal bonds are more advantageous to investors in high income-tax brackets.

52. **C.** (Chapter 7) Mortgage bonds, collateral trusts, and equipment trusts are all forms of secured bonds. Because these bonds are secured with collateral, the collateral securing the bonds is sold to satisfy the bondholders if the issuer defaults. However, debentures are not backed with collateral and are therefore riskier. Because more risk equals more reward, debenture holders can expect a coupon rate that's higher than that of the secured bonds.

53. **D.** (Chapter 7) Of the answer choices given, Choice (D) is the least preferable and, therefore, the correct answer. AA rated bonds, U.S. Treasury notes, and AA rated debentures can yield predictable income. By contrast, income bonds are issued when a corporation is coming out of bankruptcy and trying to reorganize. Therefore, income bonds only pay interest if the corporation can meet the interest payment and normally trade without accrued interest. Income bonds are not suitable for Dana because she's seeking predictable income.

54. **B.** (Chapter 15) 401(k)s are corporate retirement plans. Employees may contribute a defined percentage of their salary each year. So, they are defined contribution plans, and because they meet IRS standards, they are qualified plans, meaning the contributions are deducted from the employee's gross income.

55. **A.** (Chapter 11) The OCC (Options Clearing Corporation) is the issuer and guarantor of all listed options. The OCC determines which options will be traded and guarantees that option holders can always exercise their options.

56. **C.** (Chapter 9) Dividends that are distributed by municipal bond funds are federally tax-free, but any capital gain distribution is taxable. Choice (C) is the right answer.

57. **C.** (Chapter 8) Hopefully, the "G" in "GANs" was enough to help you get the correct answer. GANs are *grant anticipation notes,* which a municipality issues to provide temporary financing while waiting for a grant from the U.S. government.

58. **C.** (Chapter 13) To determine the net worth of a company, use the following equation:

Net Worth = Assets – Liabilities

Net Worth = $11,500,000 – $3,350,000 = $8,150,000

59. **C.** (Chapter 12) When an investor opens (initial transaction) a margin account by purchasing common stock valued over $2,000, the investor must deposit the Regulation T amount (50%), which is $1,750 ($3,500 × 50%), or $2,000, whichever is greater. If the investor purchases less than $2,000 worth, they must pay in full.

60. **A.** (Chapter 7) The correct answer is Choice (A) because issuers call bonds when interest rates are falling, so they can issue bonds with lower coupon rates. Choice (B) is incorrect because investors would have their bonds with high coupon rates called and, if wanting to keep a similar position, would have to invest in bonds with lower coupon rates. Choice (D) is incorrect because municipal bond call provisions are advantageous to issuers; the call provisions reduce fixed costs by providing issuers with the ability to redeem bonds before maturity.

61. **B.** (Chapter 16) All written complaints need to be handled by a principal and kept on file. Even though the complaint was sent via email, it's still considered a written complaint. The complaint does not need to be forwarded or sent to FINRA.

62. **A.** (Chapter 5) All securities sold in a state must be registered in that state (also known as blue-sky registration). Coordination, qualification, and notification (filing) are all types of state registration; registration by cooperation is not. If an agent wants to sell in a state, the security, the registered rep, and the broker–dealer must be registered in that state.

63. **B.** (Chapter 11) The easiest way to figure out the answer to this question is to use the equation P = I + T, where

- **P** = the Premium of the option
- **I** = the Intrinsic value of the option (how much it is in-the-money)
- **T** = the Time value of the option (how much the investor is paying for the time to use the option)

$$P = I + T$$
$$9 = 5 + T$$
$$T = 4$$

First, put the premium of 9 into the equation. Next, because the option is 5 points in-the-money (call options go in-the-money when the price of the stock goes above the strike price), insert the intrinsic value of 5 in the equation. Because the premium is 9 and the option is 5 points in-the-money, the time value is 4.

64. **B.** (Chapter 16) Principals of a firm must approve all new accounts, advertising used by the firm, handling of complaints, trades in all accounts, and so on. However, as far as the SIE exam goes, principals don't need to approve recommendations made by registered reps. In real life, I would get approval before making recommendations if I were you. You have to remember that principals must sign all order tickets, and if you don't clear a recommendation with them first, they may be reluctant to approve it.

65. **D.** (Chapter 11) When the investor originally sold (shorted) the option, it was an opening sale. Since the investor is purchasing their way out of that position, the second transaction is a closing purchase.

66. **D.** (Chapter 8) Remember that an "except" question is looking for a false answer. The correct answer is Choice (D). Taxable equivalent yields cannot be shown because every investor has a unique tax issue and bracket.

67. **C.** (Chapter 14) Designated market makers (DMMs) are responsible for keeping a fair and orderly market in a particular security or securities. They attempt to keep trading as active as possible by executing orders for others and sometimes buying and selling out of their own inventory.

68. **B.** (Chapter 7) U.S. government securities, such as Treasury bills, Treasury bonds, Treasury notes, and so on, settle in one business day after the trade date.

69. **B.** (Chapter 10) Any income derived from an investment in a limited partnership is termed passive. Passive gains can be written off only against passive losses. Earned income includes money made from salary, bonuses, tips, and so on. Portfolio income includes money made from interest, dividends, and capital gains made from investing in securities.

70. **B.** (Chapter 11) All intrinsic value means is how much the option is in-the-money. Put options go in-the-money when the price of the underlying security drops below the strike (exercise) price. Since the strike price is 30 and the stock price is $28.50 (28.5), the intrinsic value is 1.5 (30 – 28.5).

71. **A.** (Chapter 6) After the split, stockholders are going to have five shares for every four that they had before. If the number of shares is going to increase, the price of the stock is going to decrease to make up for the additional shares. After the split, the investor should have the same overall market value of securities. Use the following equation to determine the number of shares and the stock price after a split:

$$1{,}000 \text{ shares} \times \frac{5}{4} = 1{,}250 \text{ shares}$$

$$\$40 \times \frac{4}{5} = \$32$$

72. **C.** (Chapter 13) When trading currencies, you use the spot exchange rate. The spot exchange rate is the current market price for exchanging one currency for another.

73. **C.** (Chapter 7) Commercial paper is generally issued for the purpose of raising capital for a corporation for the short-term. Choice (A) is incorrect because commercial instruments are not quoted as a percent of par. Choice (B) is incorrect because a commercial instrument is proof of a debt, not ownership. Choice (D) is incorrect because commercial instruments are a debt security; therefore, if a claim is filed against the issuing corporation, the commercial instrument holds a senior position to preferred stock.

74. **D.** (Chapter 9) A specialized or *sector* fund invests within a single industry or geographical area.

75. **D.** (Chapter 15) Withdrawals from a Roth IRA may begin any time after the investor reaches age 59 1/2. However, there's no required beginning date (RBD) or required minimum distribution (RMD) for Roth IRAs like there is for other retirement plans. You need to remember that the money withdrawn from a Roth IRA is tax-free, so the IRS doesn't care when these investors take their money because it isn't getting any of it.

Knowing the Score

Here's how the SIE exam is scored:

- You get 11/3 points for each correct answer.
- You get 0 points for each incorrect answer.

A passing grade is 70 percent. In other words, you need at least 53 correct answers on each practice test to get one step closer to your Nobel Prize in stockbrokerage (okay, economics).

To calculate your score, multiply the number of correct answers by 1.33 or divide it by 0.75. Whatever grade you get, make sure you round down, not up. For example, a grade of 71.6 is a 71 percent, not a 72.

REMEMBER

The actual test contains ten additional experimental questions that don't count toward your actual score. You can't tell these questions apart from the questions that do count, so you may have to answer a few more questions right to get your 70 percent. Don't sweat it. Simply come prepared, stay focused, and do your best.

Answer Key for Practice Exam 2

1. A
2. A
3. C
4. A
5. A
6. C
7. B
8. D
9. A
10. D
11. C
12. A
13. A
14. A
15. B
16. D
17. B
18. B
19. D
20. B
21. B
22. D
23. A
24. D
25. A
26. A
27. D
28. A
29. B
30. C
31. A
32. C
33. B
34. A
35. B
36. C
37. C
38. B
39. D
40. D
41. B
42. C
43. A
44. C
45. B
46. A
47. D
48. B
49. C
50. B
51. C
52. C
53. D
54. B
55. A
56. C
57. C
58. C
59. C
60. A
61. B
62. A
63. B
64. B
65. D
66. D
67. C
68. B
69. B
70. B
71. A
72. C
73. C
74. D
75. D

6 The Part of Tens

IN THIS PART . . .

Discover ways to avoid the ten most common traps on the SIE exam.

Start your career as a financial professional the right way with ten job-related tips.

IN THIS CHAPTER

» Identifying the most common mistakes that SIE exam-takers make

» Uncovering the secrets for avoiding SIE exam traps

Chapter 21 Ten SIE Exam Traps to Avoid

After all the time, effort, and sacrifice you put into studying, elevating the importance of the SIE exam to an unrealistically high level is easy. Step back for a moment. Keep things in perspective. This situation isn't life or death. If you don't pass the test the first time, the worst thing that will happen is that you'll have to retake it.

On the other hand, getting tripped up by some trivial exam traps after you've come this far would be a shame. This chapter lists some common mistakes and gives you some last-minute advice to help you get over the last hurdles that stand between you and the first million dollars you'll earn as a stockbroker.

Easing Up on the Studying

Perhaps you stop studying because you're getting good scores on practice exams and your confidence is high. If you're scoring 80s on exams that you're seeing for the first time, shoot for 85s. If you're getting 85s, shoot for 90s. The point is that you should continue to take exams until the day before your scheduled exam day. I firmly believe that every day away from studying ultimately costs you points on your exam that you can't afford to lose.

By the same token, make sure you don't wait too long before taking the exam. If you have to wait several weeks before you can take the exam, you may lose your sense of urgency, and it's almost impossible to keep up the intense level of preparation needed for many months at a time. If you're directing your own course of study, after you're passing practice exams consistently with 80s or better, take the test as soon as possible.

WARNING

The longer you wait to take the exam, the more likely you are to forget the key points and formulas. If your test date is too far in the future, you also risk falling into the I'll-study-later trap, thinking that you can double your efforts later to make up for any wasted time. Overall, losing your sense of urgency leads to complacency and a lack of motivation, which probably aren't characteristics that broker-dealers are looking for in their employees.

Assuming the Question's Intent

You glance at the question quickly and incorrectly anticipate what the exam question is really asking you. You pick the wrong answer because you were in such a rush that you didn't see the word *except* at the end of the question. What a shame.

You don't want to fail the exam when you really know the material. Read each question carefully and look for tricky words like *except, not,* and *unless.* Then read all the answer choices before making your selection. (For more info on test-taking strategies that apply to certain question types, see Chapter 3.)

Reading into the Question

You're thinking "but what if" before you even look at the answer choices. When reviewing questions with students, I regularly get questions like "Yeah, but what if they're an insider?" and "What if they're of retirement age?" The bottom line is that you shouldn't add anything to the question that isn't there.

TIP

Don't be afraid to take the question at face value and select the right answer, even if it occasionally seems to be too easy. Eliminate answer choices that are too much of a stretch and remember that when two answer choices are opposites, one of them is most likely correct.

Becoming Distracted When Others Finish

Now, this problem won't come into play if you're taking the exam at home (although you have many other sources of distraction at home). You haven't even started looking over the questions you marked for review when the woman next to you leaps from her seat, picks up her results (with a little victory dance), and makes a break for the door.

Don't let people who are taking the exam with you psych you out. If others finish ahead of you, perhaps they're members of Mensa, or maybe this is the fifth time they've taken the exam. (Practice makes perfect.) They may even be taking a different exam. Besides offering the SIE, the testing centers offer other securities exams that have fewer questions. Keep focused and centered on taking your own exam. The only time you need to be concerned about is your own.

Not Dressing for Comfort

You're trying to calculate the taxable equivalent yield on Mr. Dimwitty's GO bond, but the pencil keeps slipping out of your sweaty hand. At home, you can certainly set the temperature to your comfort level, but at the test center, the temperature may not be ideal. You'd swear that the test center has the heat cranked up to 80 degrees. Hmm. Maybe wearing your warmest wool sweater wasn't the best idea.

Whether you're taking the test at a testing center or at home, dress comfortably. Don't wear a tie so tight that it cuts off the circulation to your brain. You're under enough stress just taking the exam. If you're taking the exam at a test center, dress in layers. A T-shirt, a sweatshirt, and a jacket are great insulators against the cold. Another advantage is that you can shed layers of clothing (without ending up sitting in your underwear) if the exam room is too warm.

Forgetting to Breathe

You sit down to take the exam, brimming with confidence. All of a sudden, the exam begins, and some of the words look like they're in a foreign language. Your heart starts pounding, and you feel like you're going to pass out.

If stress becomes overwhelming, your breathing can become shallow and ineffective, which only adds to your stress level. Focus before the exam by closing your eyes and taking a few deep breaths. This same process of closing your eyes and breathing deeply is a great way to calm yourself if you become stressed or anxious at any time during the exam.

Trying to Work Out Equations in Your Head Instead of Writing Them Down

While you're taking the exam, your memory starts to cloud, and somehow, the fact that 2 plus 2 equals 5 begins to make sense to you, and the only formula you can remember is that there are 12 inches in a foot.

You won't need a whole lot of equations for the SIE exam — not as many as for the Series 7 exam. But don't throw away easy questions; memorize your equations while you're studying for your SIE exam so that you know them cold before you sit down to take the exam.

If your nerves are getting the best of you and clouding your memory, jotting down the equations you want to remember as soon as your exam begins may be helpful. (This process is known as making a *brain dump.*) When you're working out the math problems, you have scrap paper and a basic calculator to work with. Use them. Some formulas, such as determining the value of a right (cum rights), require you to find sums and differences before you can divide. Even simple calculations, such as finding averages, can involve quite a few numbers. In problems with multiple parts, it's easy to skip steps, plug in the wrong numbers from the question, or forget values that you calculated along the way. Writing things down helps you keep things in place without cluttering your short-term memory.

Spending Too Much Time on One Question

When taking the SIE exam, you don't want to get bogged down on one question. If you spend too much time on one question, you may lose points for many questions you didn't have time to even look at because you wasted so much time on the one that gave you trouble. If you find yourself taking too long to answer a question, take your best guess, mark it for review, and return to it later.

Changing Your Answers for the Wrong Reasons

You change an answer because you already selected the same letter for the preceding three or four questions in a row. Just a touch of paranoia, right?

You've probably been told from the time you started primary school not to change your answers. Trust your instincts and go with your original reaction. You have only two good reasons to change your answer:

- You find that you forgot or didn't see the words *not* or *except,* and you initially chose the wrong answer because you didn't see the tricky word.
- You find that the answer choice you originally selected isn't the best answer after all.

Calculating Your Final Score Prematurely

You waste valuable time concentrating on the number of questions you think you got wrong instead of focusing on the SIE exam questions you still have to answer.

Just read each question carefully, scrutinize the answer choices, and select the best answer. You'll find out whether you passed right after you complete the exam; you don't need to figure out your possible grade in advance to avoid sleepless nights until you receive your score. If you have additional time, use it to check your answers to the questions you marked for review.

IN THIS CHAPTER

» Understanding how to survive and prosper as a stockbroker

» Socking away (or investing) money

Chapter 22
Ten Ways to Start Your Career Off Right

Passing the SIE and one of the corequisite exams can be one of the high points in your life. You've dedicated yourself to attaining your goal, put your life (and partying) on hold while you studied, and fulfilled your commitment to long hours of studying and hard work. Now you're ready to reap the rewards. As you begin your new profession, you'll encounter many new hurdles. I give you this chapter to help prepare you for what to expect and (I hope) to maximize your chances of a long, successful career.

Win at the Numbers Game

A majority of you will start out as cold-callers. Like any other sales job, selling securities to investors is a numbers game. Some people actually track the number of calls it takes to open a new account, but I'm not among them. There are no specific economic benchmarks, but you may have to make 500 cold calls to get to talk to 150 people. From these 150 people, you may generate ten leads. From every ten leads, you may open one account.

The point is that you have to pick up that phone day in and day out and make the calls. If you're making 200 to 300 phone calls per day, you're likely to open an account every few days. But if you're making 50 phone calls a day, you'll probably open an account every couple of weeks, and unless you hook a *whale* (a huge investor who likes to trade), you'll have trouble paying for gas for your new car.

REMEMBER

You're participating in a numbers game. Every "no" brings you one call closer to a "yes."

Be an Apprentice

There's no better way to hit the ground running than to have a top producer as a role model. Find the person in your firm who has sales techniques that are most comfortable for you and invest as much time as possible watching how this particular mentor conducts themselves on a daily basis. Top producers earn the most income because they've found a way to stand out in a competitive market.

Maybe this person can take you under their wing and show you the ropes in return for leads you develop while under their supervision. You can even have a contract between you and your mentor that sets forth the agreed-upon terms for each of you for a fixed period of time.

Do Your Homework

Take time to find out as much as possible about your job and the securities you're trying to sell. When you know what you're talking about, you inspire confidence among potential customers. Spend some of your free time watching investing programs and reading the *Wall Street Journal* and any other trade magazines or newspapers you can get your hands on. The more you learn, the more comfortable you'll be on the phone, and the more sales you'll make.

Treat the Minnow Like a Whale

More often than not, new customers don't disclose all their financial background to you. Whether a customer has $10,000 or $10 million to invest, however, the money is important to them. So treat every customer as though they're the most valuable person in the world. Who knows? You may be speaking to someone who has a lot of money to invest now or will have a lot of money to invest in the future, or your customer may be a friend or relative of someone who has substantial resources. A strong referral is a most influential lead.

Smile When You Dial

Be positive. You're going to have good days and bad days. You have to accept that fact as part of the business, but don't let it get you down. If you need to, take a five-minute break to gather your thoughts. If you aren't in a positive state of mind, you'll reflect that mood in the way you talk to existing or potential customers.

When a Security Falls, Don't Be a Stranger

You can't guarantee success, and that's okay. Savvy investors know that not every investment can end up a winner, no matter how good the situation looks in the beginning. If you recommend a security that gets beaten down, call your customer. The customer is just waiting to hear from you. This call may be right up there with the most uncomfortable tasks you'll ever have to perform. Remember, however, that a savvy customer is most likely aware of what's going on, and your news won't be a surprise. Customers just want to be comforted and reassured that you'll be there with them — in good times and bad. Ideally, the other seven or eight securities that you recommended will be doing well.

Put In the Hours

You have to educate yourself about selling your products and cold-calling, so in the beginning, be prepared to put in approximately ten hours each day. As you grow more experienced, you'll receive more leads and open more accounts in a shorter period of time, but in the beginning, you have to play the numbers game to earn money while you develop a confident sales pitch.

Broaden Your Horizons

Consider obtaining other licenses to increase your skills and your ability to compete in the securities and financial industry. The Series 65 and 66 (investment adviser exams) allow you to receive a fee for giving investment advice; Series 24 (the principal's license exam) allows you to manage other registered reps; and a Life, Accident, and Health Insurance license allows you to sell insurance policies and variable annuities to customers. If you take prep courses to obtain these licenses, you may also be exposed to a network of professionals who can become sources of future referrals.

Pay Yourself First

The stock market (and you with it) will have many peaks and valleys, but your financial security doesn't have to be quite so uneven. In the peak times, put away half your earnings when you receive your big paychecks. Tell yourself that you aren't going to make a big purchase until you have a certain amount socked away. (See the upcoming section "Set Some Goals: The Brass Ring.") I've seen too many new brokers go out and buy a new car, a new boat, or whatever with their first big paycheck, expecting to make that much every month. The first time they have a bad month, they're wondering how they're going to make the payments (and possibly pay the rent).

KEEP HUNGER IN YOUR EFFORTS, NOT YOUR STOMACH

When I began my career as a stockbroker, the sales manager at the securities firm where I worked began the staff meetings by introducing himself and stating that he'd earned $100,000 his first year in the business and spent $150,000 of it — and he considered that to be a good thing! Somehow, that doesn't make sense either mathematically or logically (no matter how much your spending stimulates the economy). Some of the other trainees at the meeting were very impressed by the sales manager's suggestion, especially when he told us that he stayed hungry by spending so much more than he earned.

I remember looking at the sales manager and the other trainees who were attending this meeting and thinking, "What an idiot!" You'll get a lot of foolish suggestions along the way. If you want to stay hungry in your efforts, work hard, sock away (or invest) half your earnings, and pretend that the money isn't there. Otherwise, you may be hungry for another reason: You can't afford to buy food!

REMEMBER

Stockbrokers are supposed to be good with money. Burying yourself in debt looks kind of bad.

Set Some Goals: The Brass Ring

Focus on your goals. Successful people have realistic short-term and long-term goals and a plan to achieve them. Whether your short-term goal is to put $5,000 away per month or to open ten new accounts, identifying what you want to do is the first step in creating a plan for your future.

What's the first thing every broker wants to do with the first big paycheck? You guessed it: Buy a new car. Although that glistening Porsche can be an awesome incentive, set yourself smaller milestones to reach before making a big purchase. You can break down long-term goals — such as paying for a wedding, buying a new car, or purchasing your first house — into monthly income goals after you figure out the costs involved. Take a picture of your dream car or house and put it in a frame on your desk to remind you of the reward that awaits you.

Whatever your plan is, setting your mind on what you want, defining the steps you have to take to get there, and focusing your efforts on accomplishing each goal are the essential elements of a lucrative, rewarding career. You control your destiny.

Glossary

401(k) plan: Qualified corporate retirement plan in which employee and employer contributions are voluntary.

403(b): Salary reduction retirement plans for public school (elementary school, secondary school, college, and so on) employees, tax-exempt organizations, and religious organizations. These plans are also known as tax-sheltered *annuities*.

5% Markup Policy: The FINRA 5% Markup Policy is more of a guideline than a rule. For most trades, registered reps should not charge more than 5 percent commission, or it is deemed excessive.

ABLE (Achieving a Better Life Experience) account: These accounts are designed for individuals with provable disabilities and their families. These accounts allow individuals to invest after-tax dollars into an ABLE account, and distributions are tax-free provided they are used to pay for qualified disability expenses for the beneficiary.

Account statements: Account statements are sent out by a firm and provide the customer a list of holdings as well as the market value of the securities held at the time the statement was issued.

Accredited investor: According to the Securities Act of 1933, an accredited investor is a large investor or an experienced investor who is eligible to buy a private placement.

Accrued interest: Accrued interest comes into play when a trade of debt securities takes place in between coupon dates. So, when purchasing a debt security, the purchaser must pay the seller the portion of the following coupon that the seller has earned.

Acquisitions: When a larger corporation takes control of a smaller one or a portion of another corporation.

Adjustable (variable- or floating-rate) preferred: Preferred stock in which the dividend adjusts according to prevailing interest rates.

Agreement among underwriters (underwriting agreement): An agreement between the issuer and the managing underwriter.

Agreement of limited partnership: Document that discloses the rights and responsibilities of general partners and limited partners.

American Depositary Receipts (ADRs): Issued by U.S. banks as receipts for foreign stock traded in U.S. markets; priced in U.S. dollars; and pays dividends in U.S. dollars.

Annuities: Retirement plans issued by insurance companies that provide lump-sum payments at retirement or monthly payments for life.

Annuity units: Pay-out units of variable annuities that determine amount of money withdrawn by investors.

AON (all-or-none):

1. For newly issued securities, AON is an underwriting agreement between the issuer and underwriters in which a securities offering must be completely sold by a deadline in order not to be canceled.
2. For outstanding securities, AON is a customer order in which the order for a security must be executed in its entirety at the same price and at the same time.

Ask (offer) price: The price at which an investor or market maker is willing to sell a security that originates from sell limit orders.

At the close order: An order that must be executed at the closing price at the close of the market or the order is canceled.

At the open order: An order that must be executed at the opening price at the open of the market or the order is canceled.

Authorized shares: Amount of shares a company has registered with the SEC on the corporate charter; amount of shares a company is allowed to issue publicly.

Backing away: An illegal activity representing the failure of a market maker to honor a quote displayed.

Balance of payments: Comparison of money coming into a country and going out of a country based on exports and imports.

Balance sheet (statement of financial condition): Used to indicate business, organization, or investor assets, liabilities, and net worth to determine ability to cover debt.

Balanced fund: Invests in bonds and stocks to provide income and appreciation potential.

Bank Secrecy Act: Federal law that requires currency transactions of more than $10,000 within the same business day to be reported to FINCEN.

Banker's Acceptance (BA): Short-term loans issued as time drafts (postdated checks) to importers and exporters for protection against currency fluctuation.

Basis point: Basis points are used in the bond market. A point on a bond is 1 percent; a basis point is 1/100th of a percent.

Bearish: If the market is bearish, the prices of securities are generally declining. If an investor is bearish, they invest in a way that they would profit if the market (or individual security) declines.

Best efforts underwriting: A type of securities underwriting in which the underwriter(s) make their best effort to sell the securities as compared to a firm commitment underwriting in which they are purchasing all of the securities. The two types are all or none (AON) and mini-max. In a best efforts underwriting, if a certain amount of the securities aren't sold, the offering is canceled.

Bid wanted: This is an order indication or notice that an investor or broker–dealer wants to sell a security at a specific price. This is typically used when no current buyers of a security are available.

Blue-sky laws: Cover the state registration of persons and securities.

Bonds (debt securities): Securities that represent loans to companies or governments.

Book entry: Security with computerized certificates such as U.S. Treasury securities.

Breakpoints: Reduced sales charges for large dollar purchases in an individual mutual fund or a family of funds that is only offered in class A shares.

Breakpoint sale: Illegally inducing a sale just below a breakpoint level without disclosure of how to receive the reduced sales charge.

Broker: Person that trades investments for others. Orders are sent elsewhere for execution (an exchange, another brokerage firm, or a customer). A broker may be referred to as an agent according to federal law. Brokers charge commissions for executing trades.

Broker–dealer (BD): A person who trades investments for others as brokers and for themselves as dealers.

Brokered (negotiable) CD: Low-risk investments that originate from a bank and are outsourced to broker–dealers to sell to investors. Unlike typical CDs, which are purchased directly from a bank, brokered CDs can be traded in the market. Negotiable CDs that require a minimum investment of $100,000 are often called *jumbo CDs*.

Bullish: If a person is bullish on the market or a security, they are expecting the market or price of the security to go up. If the market is bullish, it is generally increasing in value.

Business risk: The risk that a corporation does not perform to expectations.

Buy limit order: An order to buy a security at a specific price or lower.

Buy order: An order to buy a security at the current market price.

Buy stop limit: An order that is a buy stop order when entered and becomes a buy limit order after activation.

Buy stop order: An order used to protect short positions or to prepare for a breakout in the price of a security above resistance.

Callable bond: A bond in which the issuer may pay off debt earlier than the maturity date.

Callable preferred stock: A preferred stock that may be taken away by the company at the call price on the certificate.

Call option: Allows a person buying the option to buy investments — usually 100 shares of stock — at a fixed price from the seller of the option.

Capital gains: Money made when selling investments for higher than cost basis (overall amount spent on investments).

Capital losses: Money lost when selling investments for lower than cost basis (overall amount spent on investments).

Capital risk: The risk of losing all money invested.

Cash account: A brokerage account in which all trades executed by customers must be paid for in full.

Cash dividends: A way of corporations to share profits with their common and preferred stockholders.

Cash trade (cash settlement): Trades of securities in which settlement occurs on the same day as the trade date since payment in cash for the trade is in the purchaser's account prior to trade execution.

Certificate of limited partnership: Document that establishes the limited partnership business and includes objectives, names of partners, amount of money contributed by each partner, and so on.

Chicago Board Options Exchange (CBOE): An exchange that makes and enforces option exchange rules.

Churning: Excessive trading of a customer's account illegally for the sole purpose of generating commissions.

Class A shares: Mutual fund shares in which sales charges are paid on purchases. Class A shares offer breakpoints for investments of large dollar amounts into one fund or a fund family. Class A shares are front-end load shares.

Class B shares: Mutual fund shares in which sales charges are paid on redemptions that are CDSCs (contingent deferred sales charges). Class B shares are back-end load shares.

Class C shares: Mutual fund shares in which sales charges are paid annually. Class C shares may be referred to as level load.

Closed-end fund: An investment company that raises money only when securities issued by the fund are traded between investors after being issued publicly.

Closing purchase: In options trading, a closing purchase is when an investor purchases an option that they originally sold to close their existing short option position.

Closing sale: In options trading, a closing sale is when an investor sells an option that they own.

Code of arbitration: The code of arbitration is an informal hearing (heard by two or three arbiters) that's primarily conducted for disputes between members of the FINRA. Members include not only broker-dealers but also individuals working for member firms. A dispute between a member firm and a customer may also be decided through arbitration if the customer signed an arbitration agreement or the customer wishes it to be settled through arbitration.

Code of procedure: The code of procedure is FINRA's formal procedure for handling securities-related complaints between public customers and members of the securities industry (broker–dealers, registered reps, clearing corporations, and so on).

Coincident (coincidental) indicators: Economic statistics that indicate how the economy is performing as of now.

Collateral trust: Secured bonds backed by stocks and bonds owned by the company.

Combined (split) offering: A combined primary and secondary offering in which the company and shareholders (usually insiders) raise money.

Commercial paper: Unsecured debt securities issued by a corporation to finance its short- term cash flow needs. Maturities are 270 days or less to be exempt from SEC registration.

Commingling:

- Illegally combining assets of customers with assets of the broker–dealer or investment adviser and using them together to obtain loans.
- Illegally combining assets of customer cash accounts with customer margin accounts and using both accounts to obtain loans.
- Legally combining assets of margin accounts of different customers to obtain a loan for the broker–dealer.

Commission: Charge of a broker executing trades expressed at a total dollar value.

Common stock: Stock that has voting rights; may or may not pay dividends; provides growth or capital appreciation potential.

Competitive offering: Typically used by municipalities, a competitive offering is when the municipality allows bids from different underwriters instead of choosing an underwriter directly regarding the offering of securities.

Confirmation: Receipt provided by a broker–dealer that displays details of execution of a trade.

Contraction: Stage of an economic cycle in which the economy is slowing down.

Convertible bond: A corporate bond that is convertible into common stock of the same company.

Convertible preferred stock: A preferred stock that is convertible into common stock of the same company.

Cooling-off period: Time needed for the SEC to review a registration application for a security; usually lasts about 20 calendar days.

Coordination: This method involves registering with the SEC and states at the same time. The SEC helps companies meet the blue-sky laws by notifying all states in which the securities are to be sold. This type of registration is typically used for initial public offerings (IPOs).

Corporate account: A securities account opened by a corporation. When opening a corporate account, you'll need a copy of the corporate resolution, which will tell you who has trading authority over the account.

Corporation: A business in which the debt of the business is separate from the debt of the stockholders. The business and investors are not responsible for each other's debts.

Correspondence: Targeted promotions to 25 or fewer retail persons within 30 days or less.

Coupon (interest) rate: The rate of annual interest paid to bondholders expressed as a percentage of par value; remains fixed for the life of the bond unless otherwise stated; also referred to as the nominal yield.

Credit agreement: Margin agreement that must be signed by customers in which interest charges will be applied to debit balances daily.

Credit rating: Moody's, Standard & Poors, Fitch, and so on rate issuers debt securities based on their likelihood of default.

Credit risk: The risk that the principal and interest is not paid on time.

Cumulative preferred stock: A preferred stock that promises to pay previous dividends that were not paid before common stockholders of the same company receive dividends.

Cumulative voting: A voting method for common stockholders in which votes may be divided in any way; beneficial for smaller investors.

Currency (exchange rate) risk: Risk of foreign currency value decline.

Current assets: Most liquid assets of a business, organization, or investor that are convertible into cash within one year or less. Current assets are cash, securities, accounts receivable, prepaid expenses, and inventory.

Current liabilities: Debt owed by a company that needs to be paid in one year or less. Current liabilities are reflected in accounts payable.

Current yield: Annual income on a security compared to the security's current market price. The formula is annual dividends or interest divided by the current market price of the security.

Cyclical: A company whose performance is based on the economy. Examples of cyclical companies are companies involved in selling household appliances, autos, travel, tourism, construction, and manufacturing.

Date of sale: The date when the bids are submitted to the issuer for competitive offerings.

Day order: Order that must be executed by the end of the trading day when entered, or the order is canceled.

Dealer (principal or market maker): Person who trades with customers directly using inventory. Dealers charge markups to customers buying and markdowns to customers selling.

Debentures: Unsecured bonds backed by the full faith and credit of the issuing company. Debenture holders are the last creditors to be paid in the event of bankruptcy.

Declaration date: The day that the corporation announces that a dividend will be paid to investors.

Defensive: Corporations whose sales remain relatively stable no matter how the economy performs. Defensive industries include utilities, food, clothing, alcohol, tobacco, and cosmetics.

Department of the Treasury: The U.S. Department of the Treasury (USDT) was established to manage U.S. government revenue. As such, the USDT oversees the printing of all paper currency and minting of all coins. In addition, they are responsible for collecting taxes through the IRS.

Depository Trust and Clearing Corporation (DTCC): The DTCC provides safeguards to the world's financial markets. Its role is to provide clearing, settlement, institutional matching, asset servicing, collateral management, and so on.

Direct participation program (DPP): A business that does not pay business taxes and passes income and write-offs through to investors. Examples of DPPs are limited partnerships, general partnerships, LLCs, and Subchapter S corporations.

Discount bond: Bond priced below par value.

Discount rate: The interest rate that the Fed charges to member banks for loans.

Discretionary account: A brokerage or advisory account in which the account owner or owners allow another person to execute trades without verbal approval. Discretionary authority is required if an account owner allows another person to determine what to do in trading the account (what security to trade, whether to buy or sell the security, or the quantity of the order).

Discretionary order: When a client gives the registered rep the discretion as to when to place an order. For this to happen, the client must provide the name of the security, the amount of the security, and whether to buy or sell.

Diversification: Spreading investments to different companies in different fields. Diversification helps to minimize business or sector risk.

Dividends: Bonuses that may be paid by companies to stockholders; common stockholders may receive cash, stock, or product dividends; preferred stockholders are promised fixed cash dividends based on a percentage of par value.

DMM (designated market maker, formerly specialist): A NYSE broker–dealer that is responsible for maintaining a fair and orderly market for the security that the DMM is assigned to.

Do not reduce (DNR): An order qualifier placed by a customer on stop or limit orders in which they're telling the broker–dealer to not reduce the price of their order based on a dividend.

Double-barreled bonds: A combination of a municipal revenue bond and general obligation (GO) bond. If the revenues from the revenue producing facility are insufficient to pay the principal and/or interest on the bonds, it will be paid by the taxing power of the municipality.

Dow Jones Composite: Index that includes 65 large-cap, exchange-listed common stocks. The index includes the Industrial, Transportation, and Utility indexes.

Dow Jones Industrial Average (DJIA): Broad-based index that includes 30 listed common stocks and is the most commonly used indicator of a bullish or bearish market.

Dow Jones Transportation: Narrow-based index that includes 20 listed common stocks.

Dow Jones Utilities: Narrow-based index that includes 15 listed common stocks.

Dow theory: Economic trends are indicated by the Industrial and Transportation indexes, but not the Utilities index.

DPP (Direct Participation Program): A business that does not pay business taxes and passes income and write-offs through to investors. Examples of DPPs are limited partnerships, general partnerships, LLCs, and Subchapter S corporations.

Due-diligence meeting: A meeting toward the end of the cooling-off period between the managing underwriter and the issuer during which they finalize all matters before the release of securities to the public.

Earned (active) income: Work-related income including wages, self-employed income, tips, bonuses, and royalties.

Equipment trust bond: Bond secured by transportation assets and mainly issued by transportation companies (autos, airlines, railroad, package and delivery, and so on).

Equity REIT: A real estate investment trust that buys properties and receives rental income.

Equity securities: Represent ownership interest in the issuing corporation. These include common and preferred stock.

Estate taxes: Taxes paid by a deceased person's estate.

ETF (exchange-traded fund): Fund that tracks an index that is usually an open-end fund, but issues new shares only to broker–dealers. ETFs trade between investors once publicly available. ETF shares can be purchased on margin and sold short. ETF shares are not redeemable.

ETN (exchange-traded note): Loan issued by a bank in which the amount received at maturity is unknown and based on the performance of an index chosen by the issuing bank. An ETN is a liquid structured product with no coupon rate and no collateral.

Ex-dividend date: The first day that the stock trades without dividends. The price of a stock or mutual fund share is reduced by the dividend at the market open to reflect that the dividend is no longer available to a person who does not own the stock or mutual fund.

Exchange: Auction market that automatically determines highest bid and lowest ask and automatically executes market orders that need to be executed immediately.

Exchange offers: When a corporation decides to exchange some of its securities for other ones.

Exchange-Traded Products (ETPs): ETPs include exchange-traded funds (ETFs) and exchange-traded notes (ETNs). They provide diversification (like mutual funds), but unlike mutual funds, they may trade on an exchange.

Exempt security:

- According to the U.S. government, an exempt security is a security that is not required to register with state administrators.
- According to the Securities Act of 1933, an exempt security is a security that is not required to register with the SEC.

Exempt transaction:

- According to the U.S. government, an exempt transaction represents a trade allowing the security to be issued or traded without state registration.
- According to the Securities Act of 1933, an exempt transaction represents a trade allowing the security to be issued or traded without SEC registration.

Expansion: Growth phase of an economy.

Face Amount Certificate Company (FACC): An investment company that borrows money from investors to invest in bonds.

FDIC (Federal Deposit Insurance Corporation): The FDIC provides a certain degree of safety for people holding money in a bank. In the event of bank failure, each depositor is protected up to $250,000.

Federal Farm Credit Consolidation System (FFCS): Responsible for giving low-cost loans to farmers. The system includes the following U.S. government agencies: FLB (Federal Land Bank), FICB (Federal Intermediate Credit Banks), and COOP (Bank for Cooperatives).

Federal funds rate: The interest rate that banks, broker-dealers, and financial institutions charge each other for overnight loans.

Federal Reserve Board (FRB, Fed): The central bank of the U.S. government that may lend money to institutions and trade bonds with institutions. The FRB controls monetary policy.

FHLMC (Freddie Mac or Federal Home Loan Mortgage Corporations): FHLMC is a government-chartered corporation that buys mortgages from banks, packages the loans into bonds, and sells the bonds to the public.

Fill or kill (FOK): An order for a security in which the entire order must be executed at the same time and at the same price immediately, or the order is cancelled.

Final prospectus: A document that discloses all information about an issuer of a public securities offering that may be delivered after the effective date. The delivery of a final prospectus is an offer of securities.

FINRA (Financial Industry Regulatory Authority): An SRO funded by broker-dealers to regulate broker-dealers and their registered representatives. SROs have regulatory and enforcement power to create rules and punish persons for violations of rules.

Firm commitment underwriting: A type of securities underwriting in which the underwriter(s) purchase(s) all of the securities being sold.

Fixed annuities: Retirement plans issued by insurance companies that provide guaranteed lump-sum payments or fixed payments for a person's lifetime.

Fixed assets: Tangible and intangible assets of a business, organization, or investor that are not liquid.

Floor broker: Individuals who act as agents on the floor of an exchange when executing buy or sell orders on behalf of the firm's customers.

FNMA (Fannie Mae or Federal National Mortgage Association): FNMA is a congressionally chartered corporation that buys mortgages from banks, pools the loans, and sells them as mortgage-backed securities to investors.

Fourth market: Institutional trading without using the services of a broker-dealer.

Frontrunning: Illegally executing a trade based on knowledge of a block trade of 10,000 shares or more before the trade is reported on a ticker tape.

Fundamental analysis: Determining what to buy and sell based on financial and management status of companies and their industries (bottom up) and economic conditions (top down).

GDP (Gross Domestic Product): Sum of all goods and services produced by the U.S. economy that includes all business located in the United States whether U.S. companies or foreign companies. GDP is a major indicator of growth or contraction of the economy.

General obligation (GO) bonds: Municipal bonds backed by the full faith and credit (taxing power) of the municipality; issued to fund non-revenue producing facilities such as public schools, libraries, police and fire stations, and so on.

General partners: Managers of partnerships who have unlimited liability.

GNMA (Ginnie Mae or Government National Mortgage Association): A government-owned agency that buys mortgages from lending institutions and packages them to sell them as bonds to investors. Payments to investors are guaranteed by the full faith and credit of the U.S. government. Interest and principal is paid monthly.

Good-'Til-Canceled (GTC): Customer's stop or limit orders that are price specific and kept until executed or canceled by the customer. GTC orders must be renewed every so often.

GNP (Gross National Product): Sum of all goods and services produced by U.S. businesses located inside and outside of the United States.

Growth companies: Companies that are usually relatively new and have a higher potential for growth. Growth companies are typically riskier than non-growth companies.

Growth fund: An investment company that looks for long-term capital appreciation potential.

Guaranteed bond: A corporate bond backed by the issuer and another company.

Hedge fund: A fund that raises money privately and is unrestricted as to types of investments purchased, methods of trading investments, and investment strategies. A hedge fund is usually established as a DPP that distributes income and write-offs to investors.

Hedging: This is when investors try to reduce the risk of losing money with securities they are holding by purchasing or selling other securities.

Hypothecation agreement: An agreement that must be signed by customers who open margin accounts that allow purchased securities to be used as collateral to borrow money from the BD and for the BD to borrow money from a bank.

IDR (Industrial Development Revenue) bond: A municipal bond issued to raise money to fund a facility to be used by a business (private user). Rental or lease payments made to the municipality cover the debt. IDRs are the riskiest municipal bonds since the municipality has no responsibility to pay off the debt.

Immediate annuity: An investor purchases the annuity with a large sum, and the payouts begin right away or within a couple months.

Immediate or cancel (IOC): These are limit orders that may be partially or fully filled. This must take place immediately, or the order has to be canceled.

Income (adjustment) bond: The riskiest of all bonds; income bonds are issued by companies in Chapter 11 (reorganization) bankruptcy that are attempting to remain in business. These bonds do not pay interest until the company is profitable.

Income fund: An investment company that provides current investment income. An income fund invests in bonds paying interest and stocks paying consistent cash dividends.

Income statements: Indicates revenues and expenses of businesses, organizations, and investors to disclose what was earned and spent in the past.

Indenture (deed of trust, resolution): An indenture is a legal agreement printed on the face of a bond — a list of promises that bond issuers make to bondholders in which agreements are enforced by trustees hired by issuers to take care of investors; includes maturity, coupon rate, par value, if there are callable or convertible features, and if there is collateral securing the debt.

Index fund: An investment company that tracks the performance of an index with low portfolio turnover and low management fees.

Index option: Options that cover an index of securities such as the S&P 500, S&P 100, energy sector securities (IXE), and so on. Index options are always settled in cash.

Inflation: Rate of annual increase in prices of consumer goods as measured by the CPI (Consumer Price Index).

Initial Public Offering (IPO): A company's first sale of stock to the public.

Inside information: Non-public information related to an issuer.

Insider trading: Illegal trading of securities based on inside information.

Institutional account: Accounts held by institutions such as banks, mutual funds, insurance companies, pension funds, and investment advisers.

Institutional communications: Promotions targeted to institutions only.

Institutional investor: Companies having a large amount of funds invested in the market. Institutional investors include insurance companies, banks, pension funds, mutual funds, and so on.

Intangible assets: Fixed assets that are non-physical such as trademarks, patents, and goodwill.

Integration: Third and final stage of money laundering in which illegal money is commingled with legal money.

Interest payments: Payments that bondholders receive from the issuer for lending money to the issuer. Interest payments are expressed as a percentage of par value based on the coupon rate or nominal yield. Interest on bonds is usually paid semiannually.

International fund: Investment company that invests in foreign companies.

Interest rate risk: Risk of interest rate increases that cause prices of securities to decline.

Intrastate offering (Rule 147): An offering of securities that are offered and sold to investors within the same state where the issuer is incorporated only. Intrastate offerings are exempt from SEC registration, not state registration.

Intrinsic value: Amount that an option is in-the-money.

Inverse ETF: An exchange-traded fund that moves in the opposite direction of an index.

Investment adviser (IA): A person who offers advice about securities for fees directly or through the mail.

Investment Advisers Act of 1940: A Federal law that regulates SEC registered IAs.

Investment banking firm: A brokerage firm that advises an issuer on how to raise money; usually acts as an underwriter for an issuer.

Investment company: A company that raises money from investors to invest in a diversified pool of investments.

Investment Company Act of 1940: A Federal law that regulates publicly available investment companies. The law identifies the three categories of investment companies as management companies (open-end and closed-end funds), unit investment trusts (UITs), and face amount certificate companies (FACCs).

Investment grade: Top four bond credit rating in which debt should be paid on time.

IRA (Individual Retirement Account or traditional IRA): Tax-qualified retirement accounts, so deposits in the account are made from pretax dollars. (They're tax-deductible.) IRAs are completely funded by contributions that the *holder of the account* makes.

Issued shares: The amount of authorized shares sold publicly.

Joint account: A brokerage or advisory account registered in the name of more than one adult that can be opened as joint tenants with rights of survivorship, joint with tenants in common, community property (married couples only), and tenants by the entirety (married couples only).

Joint and last survivor annuity: When one investor dies, the surviving owner owns the annuity until their death.

Joint tenants with rights of survivorship (JTWROS): If one account owner dies, their portion of the account is transferred to the surviving account owners.

Joint with tenants in common (JTIC): If one account owner dies, their portion of the account reverts to their estate.

Keynesian: The theory that states that the government should stay active through spending and intervention to ensure economic growth.

Lagging indicators: Economic statistics that indicate what happened in the past.

Layering: Second stage of money laundering in which persons make continuous deposits with institutions that are not detecting the illegal activities.

Leading indicators: Economic statistics that indicate what may happen in the future.

Legal opinion: Is prepared by a municipal bond attorney and printed on the face of municipal bond certificates. It states that this issue is legally binding on the issuer and conforms to current tax laws. In addition, the legal opinion may state that the interest received from the issue is tax-exempt.

Letter of Intent (LOI): Allows a mutual fund investor to receive a breakpoint immediately with the initial purchase with less money than is normally required. The LOI is valid for 13 months and may be backdated for up to 90 days.

LGIPs (Local Government Investment Pools): LGIPs are established by states to provide other government entities (cities, counties, school districts, and so on) a short-term investment vehicle for investing their funds.

Life with period certain annuity: Annuity withdrawal plan in which investors choose a minimum time frame for withdrawals. If the investor dies before period certain, the beneficiary or beneficiaries receive payments for the remainder of the period certain. If the investors lives past the period certain, there are no beneficiaries.

Limited partners: Investors owning limited partnerships with limited liability.

Limited partnership: Business that includes at least one general partner who manages the business and at least one limited partner who invests in the business.

Limited tax general obligation bonds (LTGO): General obligation bonds issued by a municipality in which the taxes backing the bond are limited to a certain amount.

Liquidity (marketability) risk: The risk that a security is not easily traded.

Listed REIT: A real estate investment trust that is listed on one or more national exchanges. Listed REITs provide a high degree of liquidity.

Listed securities: Securities that are listed on an exchange and may trade on the exchange or in the OTC market.

Loan consent form: A portion of a margin account agreement that is not required to be signed by customers to allow the BD to loan customer securities to a short seller.

Long-term capital gains: Capital gains realized more than a year after purchase that are taxed at 0 percent, 15 percent, or 20 percent, usually 15 percent.

Long-term liabilities: Balance sheet item that reflects debt owed in more than one year, including bonds with long-term maturities and money owed to employees in defined benefit plans.

Management company: An investment company with a portfolio managed by an investment adviser (open-end or closed-end fund).

Managing (lead) underwriter: A brokerage firm that manages a syndicate and negotiates with the issuer of securities.

Margin: Customers borrowing money from broker-dealers to buy securities or customers borrowing securities for short sales.

Margin account: A brokerage account in which trades may be executed on margin or trades may be paid for in full.

Margin call: Amount that a customer must pay for securities traded in a margin account.

Market maker (principal): A broker-dealer that displays bid prices and ask prices for securities publicly and trades for the broker-dealer's trading account.

Market order: Order that must be executed immediately at the best available price for an exchange listed security or at a fair and reasonable price for an OTC unlisted security.

Market risk: The risk that a security will decline due to negative market conditions.

Matching orders: Illegal manipulation of the price of a security. This occurs when two persons trade the same security back and forth in the same accounts in large amounts to artificially move the price of a security.

Maturity date: The date that the bondholders get paid back for loans and receive par value; all bonds are issued with a stated maturity date.

Mediation: An informal way of handling complaints between an investor and broker–dealer. Unlike arbitration, decisions reached through mediation are non-binding.

Merger: Two existing corporations may decide to merge their two companies, often to gain market share, expand one corporation's reach, or possibly to expand into new segments. Mergers typically have a positive impact on investors.

Mini -max: A type of securities underwriting in which a minimum number of securities must be sold, or the offering is canceled.

Monetary policy: Policy that determines the direction of interest rates and the money supply.

Money laundering: The process of obtaining money illegally and placing the money in legal circulation.

Money market fund: This mutual fund invests in short-term debt securities, computes dividends daily, and pays dividends to investors monthly.

Money market instruments: Short-term debt securities that mature in one year or less. Examples of money market instruments are T-bills, commercial paper, banker's acceptances, jumbo CDs, Eurodollars, and Eurodollar bonds.

Moral obligation bonds: Bonds issued by a municipality but backed by a pledge from the state government to pay off the debt if the municipality can't. Given the additional backing, they're considered to be safe. Moral obligation bonds need legislative approval to be issued.

Mortgage bonds: Secured bonds backed by property owned by the issuing corporation.

Mortgage REIT: REIT that invests in real estate mortgage and construction loans to produce interest income passed through to investors.

Municipal adviser: Firms or professionals who provide advice on bond sales and other financial advice to state and local governments.

Municipal bonds: Local government bonds issued by states, cities, counties, towns, and so on. The interest received on municipal bonds is usually federally tax-free.

Municipal fund securities: Accounts established by states that allow investors to invest in open-end and closed-end funds for certain purposes:

- 529 college savings plans.
- ABLE (Achieve a Better Life) accounts for persons with disabilities.
- LGIPs (Local Government Investment Pools) are pools established by states for local governments within their states to provide safety of principal.

Municipal notes: Short-term municipal bonds. Municipal notes include BANs, RANs, TRANs, GANs, TANs, CLNs, tax-exempt commercial paper, and variable-rate demand notes.

Municipal Securities Rulemaking Board (MSRB): An SRO that regulates the trading and issuance of municipal bonds. Even though dealing with securities that are exempt from SEC registration, the SEC supervises the MSRB. The MSRB does not enforce the MSRB rules. The MSRB is responsible for the creation of rules related to municipal securities.

Mutual fund: An open-end investment company that is a continuous offering of new shares. Shares are purchased from the issuer and sold back to the issuer for redemption.

NASAA (North American Securities Administrator Association): Group of state administrators.

NAV (net asset value per share): The value of an investment company portfolio for each share outstanding or net worth per share [(Total assets: Total liabilities) / Number of outstanding shares]. NAV is usually calculated once per day at the close of the market. The NAV is the bid price or redemption price for mutual funds.

Negotiated offering: In this type of offering, the issuer chooses the underwriter(s) (a group of underwriters is called a syndicate) directly, with no competition from other underwriters.

New account form: Forms filled out by new broker–dealer customers. It would include items such as the customer's name, contact numbers, address, Social Security numbers, bank references, marital status, date of birth, investment objectives, and so on.

New York Stock Exchange (NYSE): The largest securities exchange in the United States. The NYSE is an auction market where buyers and sellers get together to bid on or offer securities. Companies listed on the NYSE must meet certain standards related to the number of outstanding shares, market price, net worth, and so on. NYSE securities are "covered" securities that are exempt from state registration.

No load funds: Investors don't pay a sales charge but may be charged some sort of transaction fee. Unlike load mutual funds, no-load funds may not charge a 12b-1 fee greater than 25 basis points.

Nominal yield: The coupon rate on a bond expressed as a percentage of par value.

Noncumulative (straight) preferred stock: In the event that the issuer fails to pay a dividend, holders of noncumulative stock are not required to receive those dividends at a later date.

Nonqualified retirement plans: Plans in which contributions are from after-tax (non- deductible) dollars. Withdrawals are usually partially taxed; the amount of money withdrawn above contributions is taxable. If established by employers, the employers are not required to include all employees in the plans.

Nonsystematic (unsystematic, unique, or diversifiable) risk: Risk that can be eliminated by portfolio diversification.

Not held order (NH): A person has authority to determine when to execute an order for a customer. The recipient of the order only determines the time and price of the order and does not require power of attorney.

Notification (registration by filing): The simplest and quickest form of state registration for securities. Notification can be used for only established companies that have issued securities publicly.

Numbered (street-name) account: A person's account that is held in the name of the broker–dealer for the benefit of the customer.

OAA (Options Account Agreement): Agreement signed by a customer agreeing to abide by OCC rules that must be signed and returned to a brokerage firm within 15 days after approval of the opening of the options account.

OCC (Options Clearing Corporation): The issuer and guarantor of all listed options. The OCC creates options that may be traded on exchanges and sets the conditions of the contracts (strike prices, expiration dates, and contract sizes, for example).

ODD (Options Risk Disclosure Document): Booklet or brochure that explains the risk of options trading that is provided to new options customers at or prior to the approval of the opening of the options account.

Official statement: Unlike corporations that offer securities through a prospectus, municipal bonds don't have a prospectus; instead, municipalities usually provide an official statement. Like prospectuses, official statements come in preliminary and final versions.

Open-end fund: A fund that raises money from the public continuously. An open-end fund is also known as a mutual fund.

Open Market Operations: The tool most commonly used by the Fed to control the money supply. Open Market Operations involve the Fed trading bonds with banks. The policy is controlled by the FOMC (Federal Open Market Committee).

Opening purchase: When an investor opens an option position by buying a call or put option.

Opening sale: When an investor opens an option position by selling a call or put option.

Options: Contracts between buyers and sellers in which the buyers who pay for the options have the right to trade investments (usually stock) at fixed prices with the sellers of the options.

Order ticket: Document used by BDs and IAs to enter an order with instructions on how the order should be executed.

Outstanding shares: The number of shares of a company that are publicly available.

Over-the-counter (OTC) market: A negotiated market where trades of securities are executed without the use of exchanges. In most cases, brokerage firms negotiate trades with each other for themselves and/or for their customers.

Participating preferred stock: Preferred stock that receives preferred dividends and common dividends.

Partnership: A business that flows through its income and write-offs to its investors; investors and the business are responsible for each other's debts.

Partnership account: Two or more individual owners of a business that's not set up as a corporation may set up a partnership account.

Partnership agreement: Relating to direct participation programs (DPPs), the partnership agreement is a document that includes the rights and responsibilities of the limited and general partners.

Par value for bonds: The amount repaid to an investor when the bond matures; usually $1,000 per bond.

Par value for common stock: An arbitrary value per share used by the corporation for bookkeeping purposes based on the net worth of a company included in stockholders' equity.

Passive income: Income earned from limited partnerships and rental properties.

Passive losses: Business expenses (write-offs) passed through to limited partners that may only offset passive income.

Payment date:

- The day that the buyer of the securities must pay for the trade.
- The day that a company delivers dividends to stockholders who are on record as owners of its stock on the record date.

Peak: Stage of the economic cycle in which the economy is at its best performance in the cycle.

Periodic payment deferred annuity: Payment plan for an annuity in which investors deposit money periodically (monthly, quarterly, or annually) and begin withdrawals several years later.

Placement: The first and most important stage of money laundering in which money obtained illegally is first deposited.

Political (geopolitical) risk: Risk caused by unstable government, usually a foreign government.

Portfolio income: Money earned from investments that includes capital gains and ordinary income, whether investments are securities or not.

Portfolio rebalancing: Keeping the percentage of equity securities, debt securities, cash equivalents, and so on at a certain percentage. Whatever the percentage chosen, a person would occasionally rebalance their portfolio to keep the percentages the same.

Position limit on options: A number placed on the amount of option contracts that a person can hold or write on the same side of the market (bullish or bearish) on the same security.

Preferred stock: May or may not be issued by companies that promises fixed cash dividends to investors annually based on a percentage of par value; preferred stock does not come with voting rights and is senior in priority to common stock with dividends and bankruptcy repayment.

Preliminary prospectus (red herring): A document that discloses information about an issuer of a public securities offering that may be distributed to potential investors about an offering of securities. The delivery of a red herring is not an offer since the securities are not registered yet.

Premium:

- The amount that the market price of a bond is above par.
- The amount the buyer of an option pays to the seller of an option.
- For a closed-end fund, the amount that the POP is above NAV.
- The amount paid by a person for an insurance product such as an annuity or a life insurance policy.

Prepayment risk: The risk that CMO tranches will be called earlier than expected due to refinancing by customers when interest rates decrease.

Primary offering: An offering from a publicly traded company of authorized but previously unissued securities.

Prime broker: Prime brokers are used mainly by institutional accounts or large retail clients. Prime brokerage accounts are ones set up for individuals or entities with more complex financial needs. Besides helping the client combine information from all firms they are using into one statement, they also provide services such as lending, leveraged trade execution, and cash management. Often, hedge funds use a prime brokerage account.

Prior (senior) preferred: In the event of corporate bankruptcy, owners of senior preferred stock would receive compensation before all other preferred stockholders.

Private securities transactions (selling away): Associated persons (i.e., registered representatives) are not allowed to engage in private securities transactions without the consent of the employing broker-dealer if earning compensation.

Proceeds transactions: When a person sells a security and uses the proceeds to immediately buy another security. When this happens, the firm must treat it as one transaction and not charge commission on both the sale and purchase.

Progressive taxes: Taxes with different tax rates that increase as taxable income increases (income, gift, and estate taxes).

Prospectus: A document that discloses all relevant information about an issuer of a public securities offering.

Proxies: Votes by mail available to common stockholders.

Public communications: Communications from BDs and IAs to the general public, including retail communications, institutional communications, and correspondence.

Public housing authority bonds (PHAs): These bonds, also called new housing authority (NHA) bonds, are issued by local housing authorities to build and improve low-income housing. These bonds are backed by U.S. government subsidies, and if the issuer can't pay off the debt, the U.S. government makes up any shortfalls.

Public offering price (POP):

- Purchase price of newly issued securities.
- Purchase price (ask price) of open-end funds and closed-end funds.

Purchasing power (inflation or inflationary) risk: Looks at how the return on the investment compares with the inflation rate.

Put option: Allows the buyer of the option to sell an investment (usually 100 shares of stock) at a fixed price to the seller of the option.

Puttable bond (put bond): Bond that allows investors to require issuers to pay debt earlier than maturity.

Qualification: The hardest form of state registration for securities that register with states, but not the SEC, such as intrastate offerings.

Qualified retirement plans: Retirement plans that allow contributions from pre-tax (tax deductible) dollars in which withdrawals are fully taxed. If the plans are established by employers, all employees who meet work requirements must have opportunities to establish the plans for themselves.

Record date: The day when the corporation inspects its records to see who gets the dividend.

Registered representative (RR): According to federal law (Securities Exchange Act of 1934), registered reps are employees of broker-dealers involved in offering or selling securities.

Registrar: An independent financial institution that works along with a company's transfer agent to maintain a record of stock and bond owners. The main function of a registrar is to make sure that the outstanding shares don't exceed the amount of stock the issuer authorizes under its corporate charter or bylaws (rules the company lives by).

Registration statement: Unless the securities are exempt from registration, all issuers must file a registration statement with the Securities and Exchange Commission (SEC). The registration statement includes information about the company and what they need to raise the money for.

Regressive taxes: Taxes with one flat tax rate no matter what amount is taxable (sales and excise taxes including gas, alcohol, and tobacco).

Regulation A offering: An offering of securities worth $20 million or less (Tier 1) or $75,000,000 or less (Tier 2) within a 12-month period. A Reg A offering is an exempt transaction according to federal law, but not state law.

Regulation D offering: Also known as a *private placement* (private securities offering), this offering is to no more than 35 unaccredited (nonaccredited) investors per year. Companies that issue securities through private placement are allowed to raise an unlimited amount of money but are limited in terms of the number of unaccredited investors. Sales of Reg D securities are subject to the sales limitations set forth under Rule 144. All unaccredited investors must meet specific suitability requirements.

Regulation SHO: Regulation SHO provides rules related to short selling. Under Regulation SHO, all order tickets must be marked as *short sale* rather than long sale, which is when a customer is selling securities they own. Additionally, all brokerage firms must establish rules to locate, borrow, and deliver securities that are to be sold short.

Regulation SP (Safeguarding of Privacy): Federal law that regulates institutions in protecting customer identity. The law was enacted as part of the Graham-Leach-Bliley Act.

Regulation T: Regulation of the Fed that applies to broker–dealers for cash accounts and margin accounts in which trades of nonexempt securities are executed according to federal law.

Regulatory (legislative) risk: The risk that changes in government agency interpretations of law may affect the return on investments.

Reinvestment risk: The additional investment risk taken with interest and dividends received from investments. Reinvestment risk occurs when prices increase since fixed income received will not be able to buy as many securities. In addition, if a bond is called or reaches maturity, reinvesting in a securities with similar rates of return becomes more costly.

REIT (Real Estate Investment Trust): Investment that must earn at least 75 percent of gross income from real estate investments such as properties, mortgage loans, and construction loans. Although REITs are not investment companies, they must pass through at least 90 percent of annual net income to investors annually. REITs are not redeemable and do not pass through losses or write-offs to investors since REITs pay business taxes on money retained.

Repurchase agreements: Contract between a buyer and a seller. The seller of the securities (usually, T-bills) agrees to buy them back at a previously determined price and time. Repos are short-term loans.

Reserve requirements: The percentage of a bank's money that may not be loaned to customers (controlled by the federal government).

Retail communications: Public communications distributed by BDs and IAs to more than 25 retail persons in 30 days or less. Retail communications are advertisements and sales literature.

Retail investors: Nonprofessional investors who trade for their own account.

Retained earnings (earned surplus): Undistributed profits kept by a business, organization, or investor after paying all expenses, loan interest, taxes, and cash dividend. On the balance sheet, retained earnings represents the amount of money kept by the business since its start date or inception. On the income statement, retained earnings reflects the amount of money retained for the year, which is added to (or subtracted from if negative) the balance sheet retained earnings.

Revenue bonds: Issued by municipalities to fund revenue producing facilities (tolls, turnpikes, public hospitals, mass transit, and so on), revenue bonds are paid off with revenues from the facilities.

Rights (subscription or pre-emptive rights): Allows existing common stockholders to buy additional shares of common stock of their companies at a discount price to maintain percentage ownership. They have short-term expirations and may be traded with other investors.

Riskless (simultaneous) transactions: A firm buys a security for its own inventory for immediate resale to the customer (riskless to the firm).

Roth IRA: IRA in which contributions are always nonqualified (after-tax). Withdrawals are qualified to be tax-free if the account has been open for at least five years and the withdrawals are made after age 59 1/2. Roth IRAs have income restrictions in which high income persons cannot contribute.

Rule 144: An SEC rule that regulates investors who buy securities issued privately (restricted stock) in which investors must wait at least six months to sell the securities publicly.

Rule 144A (portal market): Provides an exemption for QIBs (qualified institutional buyers) that buy securities issued through private placements. QIBs can sell restricted stock to other QIBs immediately after purchase.

Second market: Trading of unlisted securities OTC.

Secondary market (non-issuer transactions): The trading of outstanding securities (exchange or OTC). An investor receives money from the sale of securities, not the issuer of the securities. The secondary market includes the first market, second market, the third market, and the fourth market.

Secondary offering: An offering of securities by shareholders (usually insiders) that were previously issued; shareholders raise money instead of the issuer.

Section 529 savings plan: Section 529 savings plans are specialized educational savings accounts available to investors. These plans are also known as *qualified tuition plans* (QTPs) because they're designed to allow money to be saved for qualified expenses for higher education (colleges, postsecondary trade and vocational schools, postgraduate programs, and so on).

Secured bonds: Corporate bonds secured with collateral.

Securities Act of 1933: The federal law that covers the registration of new issues. All issuers of nonexempt securities offered in nonexempt transactions must file registration statements including prospectuses with the SEC.

Securities and Exchange Commission (SEC): The federal agency that administers the U.S. securities laws. The SEC was created under the Securities Exchange Act of 1934.

Securities Exchange Act of 1934: The Federal law that regulates trading of outstanding securities and:

- Created the SEC.
- Regulates exchange and OTC trading.
- Regulates the extension of credit (margin).
- Requires registration of broker-dealers and registered representatives.
- Prohibits price manipulation of securities.

Selling group: A group of brokerage firms that help the syndicate sell new issues to the public without purchasing the securities.

Sell limit order: An order placed by a customer to sell a security at a specific price or better.

Sell order: An order to sell a security at the market price.

Sell stop order: An order used to protect a long position or to prepare for a security price to breakout below support.

SEP IRA: IRAs established by businesses for employees in which only businesses may make qualified contributions to employees. Employees are not allowed to contribute. All contributions are fully vested immediately.

Serial bond: Bond issue in which an equal amount of debt matures yearly.

Settlement date: Date that security certificates are received by the buyer's brokerage firm; date that issuer of securities adds buyer's name to list of security owners.

Short margin account: An account for investors who sell securities short.

Short sale: Securities are not owned, but borrowed. This is a bearish strategy in which investors hope to buy back securities at lower prices to pay back lenders of securities. Unlimited loss potential exists since securities may increase in price infinitely.

Short-term capital gains: Capital gains realized in one year or less after purchase that are taxed at regular tax rates.

Short-term capital losses: Capital losses realized in one year or less. Can be used to offset capital gains for tax purposes.

Single account: An account registered in the name of one person only.

Single payment deferred annuity: Payment plan for an annuity in which an investor deposits a lump sum and begins withdrawals at a predetermined date.

Single payment immediate: Payment plan for an annuity in which an investor deposits a lump sum and begins withdrawals several years later.

Sinking fund: If the issuer has put money aside to pay the bonds off at or prior to maturity in the open market, the bonds are more marketable because the default risk is lower.

SIPC (Securities Investor Protection Corporation): SIPC protects customers from broker-dealer bankruptcy for up to $500,000 of which no more than $250,000 can be cash.

SLMA (Sallie Mae; Student Loan Marketing Association): U.S. government agency that issues bonds to fund student loans.

Solicited order: An order that was recommended by an agent, BD, IA, or IAR.

Special assessment (special district) bond: Municipal bonds issued to fund special projects such as sewers, sidewalks, streets, and so on. The homeowners who benefit from these projects will be taxed at a higher rate to fund the project(s).

Special tax bond: Municipal bonds secured by sales taxes on fuel, tobacco, alcohol, business licenses, and so on.

Specialized (sector) fund: Invests in a single industry or geographic area.

SRO (Self-Regulatory Organization): A federal regulator of broker-dealers funded by broker-dealers to regulate BDs and their registered representatives. Examples of SROs include FINRA, the MSRB, and all exchanges.

State administrator: A regulator and enforcer of state securities laws.

Statutory (regular) voting: Voting method for common stockholders in which investors may not use more votes for any board of director candidate than the number of shares owned; votes must be divided evenly if all votes are used.

Stock: An equity security representing ownership of a company. The two types of stocks are common and preferred.

Stock dividend: This dividend provides more shares for stockholders at lower prices; it does not require voter approval unless the dividend is 25 percent or more.

Stock split: A change in shares of common stock and price to make the stock price more attractive, a stock split must be voted on by common stockholders. A regular (forward) split leads to more shares at lower prices; a reverse-split leads to less shares at higher prices.

Stop order:

- An order entered by a customer that names an activation, trigger, or election price that is used for protection or to take advantage of a price breakout. A stop order becomes a market order when activated.
- An order from the SEC or state administrator that denies the registration of a security due to missing information on a registration statement (deficiency letter).

Straight life annuity: An annuity contract in which once the investor dies, nobody else receives the payouts.

Strike (exercise) price: The fixed price on an option contract that an owner of an option can trade a security for with the seller of the option.

Subscription agreement: Application for investors who wish to become limited partners.

Syndicate: A group of underwriters that buy new securities from issuers and sell to the public at higher prices.

Systematic (systemic) risk: Risk that cannot be eliminated through diversification. The systematic risks are market risk, interest risk, reinvestment risk, and purchasing power risk.

Taxable equivalent yield (TEY): The yield needed on a taxable investment for the after-tax return to equal the tax-free return on a municipal bond. The formula is the municipal yield divided by (100% – Tax Bracket %).

Technical analysis: Determining when to buy and sell securities (timing of trades) based on market conditions, price patterns, and momentum indicators.

Telephone Consumer Protection Act of 1991 (Telephone Act of 1991): Provides rules for when registered reps can call potential customers as well as what information needs to be provided to that person. If customers do not want to be called, they must be placed on a "do not call" list.

Tender offers: Occurs when a corporation, person, or group attempts to gain control (make a *takeover bid*) of a corporation (the *target corporation*).

Term bond: Bond with all debt maturing at the same time; all debt has the same coupon rate and the same price.

Third market: Exchange listed securities trading OTC.

Timing risk: The risk of an investor buying or selling a security at the wrong time, thus failing to maximize profits.

Tombstone advertisement: An ad promoting a securities offering during the cooling-off period and after offering trades publicly until all securities offered are sold. The publishing of a tombstone ad is not an offer.

Total return: Evaluates percentage earned on investments in a one-year holding period that reflects increases and decreases in prices of securities as well as interest and dividends received.

Trade date: The day that the securities transaction is executed.

Transfer agent: A bank hired by a company or an investment company to maintain a list of shareholders and to deliver items to shareholders such as distributions and proxies.

Treasury Bill (T-bill): A debt security issued by the U.S. government and backed by its full faith and credit. T-bills can have initial maturities of 4, 6, 8, 13, 17, 26, and 52 weeks.

Treasury Bond (T-Bond): A debt security issued by the U.S. government and backed by its full faith and credit. T-bonds are issued with maturities of 20 years and 30 years.

Treasury Inflation Protected Security (TIPS): A debt security issued by the U.S. government and backed by its full faith and credit. TIPS are issued with 6 months to 30-year maturities. Coupon rate remains fixed, but par value adjusts according to inflation.

Treasury Note (T-note): A debt security issued by the U.S. government and backed by its full faith and credit. T-notes are issued with initial maturities of 2, 3, 5, 7, and 10 years.

Treasury stock: Number of shares issued and repurchased by a company; no votes or dividends.

Treasury STRIPS: Bonds issued by the U.S Treasury with 5-, 10-, and 30-year maturities and no coupon rates; issued at deep discounts.

Triple tax-free municipal bonds: These are bonds issued by U.S. territories such as Puerto Rico, Guam, U.S. Virgin Islands, American Samoa, and Washington D.C. The interest received from these bonds are free from federal, state, and local taxes.

Trough: Stage of an economic cycle in which the economy is at its worst.

Trust account: An account established by a grantor with an attorney through a trust agreement, a trust account includes at least one grantor who contributes the assets, at least one beneficiary who benefits from the investments made, and at least one trustee who manages the account.

Trust Indenture Act: This act, formerly called the Trust Indenture Act of 1939, prohibits bond issues valued at more than $50 million from being offered to investors without an indenture. The trust *indenture* is a written agreement that protects investors by disclosing the particulars of the issue (the coupon rate, the maturity date, any collateral backing the bond, and so on). As part of the Trust Indenture Act, all companies must hire a trustee who's responsible for protecting the rights of bondholders.

Two-dollar broker (independent brokers): These brokers assist other exchange floor brokers in getting orders executed on busy days.

U4 form: A FINRA form required to be submitted for financial professionals, such as registered reps.

UGMA (Uniform Gift to Minors Act) account: An account managed by a custodian (adult) for the benefit of a minor in which the minor assumes full control of assets when becoming an adult.

Unaccredited investor: According to the Securities Act of 1933, an unaccredited investor is a small and inexperienced investor who may or may not be able to invest in securities issued through private placements.

Underlying stock: The stock that the owner of the option has the right to buy or sell at a fixed price.

Underwriter (investment banker): A brokerage firm that buys newly issued securities from issuers and sells them to the public at higher prices.

Unit Investment Trust (UIT): Investment company with a fixed portfolio of securities with no investment adviser and no board of directors. Units are purchased from the issuer and redeemed with the issuer.

Unsolicited order: An order entered by a customer, which was not recommended by an agent, BD, IA, or IAR.

U.S. government securities: These debt securities are issued by the U.S. government and include Treasury Bills, Treasury Notes, Treasury Bonds, Treasury Inflation Protected Securities, and so on.

Variable annuities: Retirement plans issued by insurance companies in which the amount received at retirement as a lump sum or the amount of monthly withdrawals for life are not guaranteed.

Variable life: Life insurance with fixed premiums, minimum guaranteed death benefits that may fluctuate, but cash value that is not guaranteed.

Variable universal life (VUL): Life insurance with flexible premium payments, fluctuating death benefits with no minimums, and fluctuating cash value with no minimums.

Warrants: Allow investors to buy stock at a fixed price from the issuing company. Warrants are issued as sweeteners to new stock or bond offerings to make the new securities more attractive. They have long-term expirations (or may be perpetual without expiration) since they are out-of-the-money when first issued.

Wash sale:

- Sale of securities at a capital loss and repurchase of the same securities or securities that are convertible into securities sold within 30 days or less prior to or after the sale. The capital losses on the securities sold are disallowed based on the number of securities purchased. The disallowed loss is added to the cost basis of securities purchased.
- Illegal manipulation of the price of a security in which two persons trade a security back and forth with each other to artificially move the price of a security up or down.

Yield to call: Annual overall rate of return based on coupon rate, market price, and amount of time until the first call date of a bond.

Yield-to-maturity (basis): Annual overall rate of return based on coupon rate, market price, and amount of time until maturity. YTM is the most accurate way to compare the rates of return on bonds and to indicate the price volatility or duration of bonds.

Yield to worst: Relating to bonds, the yield to worst is the lower of the yield-to-maturity and the yield to call (including if the bond was called at any of the call dates).

Zero-coupon bond: A long-term bond with no coupon rate, a zero-coupon bond is issued at a deep discount. This bond has a high duration (price volatility) and may be used to plan for a future event such as college tuition.

Index

Numerics

A

B

C

D

E

F

G

H

I

J

K

L

M

N

O

P

Q

R

S

T

U

V

W

Y

About the Author

After earning a high score on the Series 7 exam in the mid '90s, **Steven M. Rice** began his career as a stockbroker for a broker dealership with offices in Nassau County, Long Island, and in New York City. In addition to his duties as a registered representative, he also gained invaluable experience about securities registration rules and regulations when he worked in the firm's compliance office. But only after Steve began tutoring others in the firm to help them pass the Series 7 did he find his true calling as an instructor. Shortly thereafter, Steve became a founding partner and educator in Empire Stockbroker Training Institute (`www.empirestockbroker.com`).

In addition to writing *Securities Industry Essentials Exam For Dummies with Online Practice* and multiple editions of *Series 7 Exam For Dummies*, Steve developed and designed the Empire Stockbroker Training Institute online (Series 7, Series 6, Series 63, Series 65, Series 66, Series 24, and more) exams. Steve has also co-authored a complete library of securities training manuals for classroom use and for home study, including the Series 4, Series 6, Series 7, Series 11, Series 24, Series 63, Series 65, and Series 66. Steve's popular and highly acclaimed classes, online courses, and training manuals have helped tens of thousands of people achieve their goals and begin their lucrative new careers in the securities industry.

Dedication

I dedicate this book to my beautiful wife, Melissa. Melissa was the love of my life, my inspiration, and my best friend. Sadly, my soulmate lost her eight-year battle with cancer in 2017. Throughout our relationship, and no matter what was going on in her life, she always made me her top priority. I was blessed to spend every day of the last 33 years with the most loving and selfless person I've ever met. Her fearless battle with cancer was something to admire. She faced every chemo treatment and every surgery saying to me, "I'll do whatever I have to do so that no one else gets you." I spent every day trying to become the man deserving of her love. Her undying love and support helped me through the toughest times. I am eternally grateful, and I will love her forever.

Although he passed only a few short months after my wife, I would also like to thank my dad and role model, Tom Rice, his wife Maggie, my sisters Sharlene and Sharlet, and my amazing grandchildren for always making me laugh and smile. I feel truly blessed to have such a wonderful family.

Author's Acknowledgments

A fantastic team over at Wiley Publishing made this book possible. I'd like to start by thanking acquisition editor Lindsay Berg for planning the project and setting up a great team. I would also like to sincerely thank project/copy editor Kezia Endsley for reviewing, editing, and making constructive suggestions regarding this book. Thank you also to managing editor Kristie Pyles and to the production team at Wiley. The entire team was extremely helpful and helped make a book that we can all be proud of. The whole team's attention to detail was phenomenal.

Publisher's Acknowledgments

Acquisitions Editor: Lindsay Berg
Project/Copy Editor: Kezia Endsley
Senior Managing Editor: Kristie Pyles
Production Editor: Umeshkumar Rajasekhar
Cover Image: © metamorworks/Getty Images